COLOSSIANS AND PHILEMON

Paul's letter to the Colossian church addresses the challenges encountered by a Christian community living in the Hellenistic world. Shaped by folk religion, Hellenistic mystery religions, Roman imperial cults, and other trends, the community lived in fear of turmoil and oppression if they did not placate the right gods and practice the correct rituals. Colossians is Paul's salvo into this context. More than a forceful response to a single church, it was a missive that addressed Hellenistic spiritual tendencies and how Christ confronts them. Gary M. Burge's study of this letter explores the Roman context for Colossians and demonstrates how Paul's gospel would overturn the religious beliefs that affected their lives. He also interrogates Paul's overlooked letter to Philemon, which accompanied Colossians and in which Paul intervenes on behalf of a Christian runaway slave named Onesimus. His novel interpretation offers new insights into this situation and how it enables us to understand slavery today.

Gary M. Burge is Emeritus Professor of New Testament at Wheaton College and Adjunct Professor of New Testament at Calvin Theological Seminary. The author of over twenty books, he has won numerous teaching awards and is a frequent speaker at conferences and churches, where he brings cultural insights from the ancient world to bear on the New Testament.

NEW CAMBRIDGE BIBLE COMMENTARY

GENERAL EDITOR: Ben Witherington III

HEBREW BIBLE/OLD TESTAMENT EDITOR: Bill T. Arnold

The New Cambridge Bible Commentary (NCBC) aims to elucidate the Hebrew and Christian Scriptures for a wide range of intellectually curious individuals. While building on the work and reputation of the Cambridge Bible Commentary popular in the 1960s and 1970s, the NCBC takes advantage of many of the rewards provided by scholarly research over the last four decades. Volumes utilize recent gains in rhetorical criticism, social scientific study of the Scriptures, narrative criticism, and other developing disciplines to exploit the growing advances in biblical studies. Accessible jargon-free commentary, an annotated "Suggested Readings" list, and the entire *New Revised Standard Version, Updated Edition* (NRSVue) text under discussion are the hallmarks of all volumes in the series.

PUBLISHED VOLUMES IN THE SERIES
2 Peter, A. Chadwick Thornhill
Isaiah 40–66, Katie Heffelfinger
The Pastoral Epistles, Scot McKnight
1–2 Samuel, Marvin A. Sweeney
The Letters of John, Duane F. Watson
The Book of Lamentations, Joshua Berman
Hosea, Joel, and Amos, Graham Hamborg
1 Peter, Ruth Anne Reese
Ephesians, David A. deSilva
Philippians, Michael F. Bird and Nijay K. Gupta
Acts, Craig S. Keener
The Gospel of Luke, Amy-Jill Levine and Ben Witherington III
Galatians, Craig S. Keener
Mark, Darrell Bock
Psalms, Walter Brueggemann and William H. Bellinger, Jr.
Matthew, Craig A. Evans
Genesis, Bill T. Arnold
The Gospel of John, Jerome H. Neyrey
1–2 Corinthians, Craig S. Keener
Exodus, Carol Meyers
James and Jude, William F. Brosend II
Judges and Ruth, Victor H. Matthews
Revelation, Ben Witherington III

Colossians and Philemon

Gary M. Burge
Calvin Theological Seminary, Michigan

CAMBRIDGE
UNIVERSITY PRESS

Shaftesbury Road, Cambridge CB2 8EA, United Kingdom

One Liberty Plaza, 20th Floor, New York, NY 10006, USA

477 Williamstown Road, Port Melbourne, VIC 3207, Australia

314–321, 3rd Floor, Plot 3, Splendor Forum, Jasola District Centre, New Delhi – 110025, India

Cambridge University Press is part of Cambridge University Press & Assessment, a department of the University of Cambridge.

We share the University's mission to contribute to society through the pursuit of education, learning and research at the highest international levels of excellence.

www.cambridge.org
Information on this title: www.cambridge.org/9781108492508

DOI: 10.1017/9781108592048

First published 2026

A catalogue record for this publication is available from the British Library

A Cataloging-in-Publication data record for this book is available from the Library of Congress

ISBN 978-1-108-49250-8 Hardback
ISBN 978-1-108-71685-7 Paperback

For EU product safety concerns, contact us at Calle de José Abascal, 56, 1°, 28003 Madrid, Spain, or email eugpsr@cambridge.org

To Carol
Without whom . . .

Contents

Preface

Many authors begin writing a commentary burdened by the worry that there is no room for yet another treatment of a familiar text. Commentaries abound on every book of the Bible. Each new volume entering this field, however, needs to be serviceable to its intended audience while it reflects the themes and discoveries that are new in current research. The New Cambridge Bible Commentary series does this well.

The original Cambridge Bible Commentary series established a legacy for this series and served readers from the 1960s until the end of the twentieth century. It was a shorter series that fairly and honestly interpreted the text of the New and the Old Testaments, but it also recognized that theological reflection and service to the church should not be awkwardly hidden away. Their dark blue covers (for the New Testament) were often a solace for preachers needing guidance for the upcoming Sunday. George H. P. Thompson's useful (though brief) commentary in this series was published in 1967 and covered Ephesians, Colossians, and Philemon – all in about 200 pages. It is delightful to read if for no other reason than to learn how far such commentaries have come in sixty years. Thompson ended his remarks on Colossians with these pastoral sentences:

The Letter to the Colossians with its dogmatic assertion of the uniqueness of Jesus Christ challenges the assumption that all religions are the same, with something equally valuable to offer. Rather it claims that the Christian faith gives the answer for which all religions are looking.

The present volume covers Colossians and Philemon more exhaustively and reflects new ways that we have conceptualized the social context from which letters such as these were originally read. We are confident that we can identify the geographical location of the letters – western Anatolia's Lycus Valley – but the social location of the letters has proven more challenging to discern. Today we can imagine more accurately the cultural context of this setting in newer and hopefully better ways.

Roman imperial presence in remote regions such as western Anatolia now has become clearer. And although Colossae was relatively remote (1,200 miles from Rome), these outlying provinces have proven to have been strongly influenced by Roman politics and propaganda. In addition, we have been able to reconstruct the religious currents – both imperial piety and innumerable religious cults – that circulated in this period. Together these newer discoveries have helped us understand the Colossian context more confidently.

Earlier commentaries focused on the theological heresy being con-fronted by Paul, and the successes of this research clarified helpfully the inroads Hellenistic dualism and popular Judaism had made in the church – so far, so good. While debate continues as to whether Paul's opponents were decidedly Hellenistic or Jewish – or a hybrid of these – recent authors now rightly see that Paul is framing his theological outlook in dialogue with the Old Testament, and this too is coded in ways that the modern reader might miss. Occasionally these references are explicit, but usually they are implicit, hidden away from the modern reader.

The Roman context of Colossae, the religious currents alive in western Anatolian cities, and the theological formulations of Paul, rooted in the Old Testament, now shape the agenda of the study of the letter. But likewise, as we know, Philemon belongs to this same setting. These two letters went "out the door" at the same time and speak to concerns in the Lycus Valley that we can explore today. Philemon (which follows the story of a converted slave) invites us to examine slavery in Rome generally and Paul's treatment of one specific case. This can then lead to further modern reflections on slavery, race, and the present moment.

This commentary is based on the *New Revised Standard Version* (updated in 2022: NRSVue). This new edition made about 10,000 substan-tial changes and about 20,000 minor changes to the NRSV (1989). The new edition promises to offer both a contemporary and an accurate representa-tion of the original text. Where I recommend readings that depart from the NRSVue, I will make appropriate notes. But throughout, when referring in the text to the NRSV, it is the updated edition I am referencing.

Thanks are due to Ben Witherington III and Beatrice Rehl for their invitation to join this Cambridge University Press series. And thanks are due to my editors, John Marr and Thenbavani Prabhu, as well as Bharathan Shankar, who each improved the manuscript significantly. My prayer is that the discoveries I have enjoyed making in this book will also inspire those studying it to serve the church, or those reading it without a scholarly focus to understand these letters as literature.

Abbreviations

AB   *Anchor Bible Dictionary*, Friedman, D. N., ed., 6 vols. (New York: Doubleday, 1992)

ANRW   *Augsteig und Niedergang der römischen Welt*, Temporini, H. and Haase, W., eds. (Berlin: Walter de Gruyter, 1972–present)

BAR   *Biblical Archaeology Review*

BBR   *Bulletin for Biblical Research*

BD   *A Greek Grammar of the New Testament and Other Early Christian Literature*, Blass, F. and DeBrunner, A., eds., English translation 9th edition, Funk, R. W. (Chicago: University of Chicago Press, 1961)

BDAG   *A Greek–English Lexicon of the NT and Other Early Christian Literature*, revised and edited by F. W. Danker, 3rd edition (Chicago: University of Chicago, 2000)

BECNT   *Baker Exegetical Commentary on the New Testament*

BSac   *Bibliotheca Sacra*

BZ   *Biblische Zeitschrift*

CBC   *Cambridge Bible Commentary*

CBQ   *Catholic Biblical Quarterly*

CBR   *Currents in Biblical Research*

DNTB   *Dictionary of New Testament Background*, Evans, C. and Porter, S., eds. (Downers Grove: InterVarsity Press, 2000)

DPL   *Dictionary of Paul and His Letters*, Hawthorne, G., Martin, R., and Reid, D., eds. (Downers Grove: InterVarsity Press, 1993)

EDNT   *Exegetical Dictionary of the New Testament*, Balz, H. and Schneider, G., eds., 3 vols. (Grand Rapids: Eerdmans, 1990)

EkkPhar	*Ekklesiastikos Pharos*
ESV	*English Standard Version*
ExpT	*Expository Times*
HTR	*Harvard Theological Review*
ICC	*International Critical Commentary*
Int	*Interpretation*
JBL	*Journal of Biblical Literature*
JETS	*Journal of the Evangelical Theological Society*
JGRChJ	*Journal of Greco-Roman Christianity and Judaism*
JRS	*Journal of Roman Studies*
JSNT	*Journal for the Study of the New Testament*
JSNTSup	*Journal for the Study of the New Testament, Supplemental Series* (now LNTS)
JSPL	*Journal for the Study of Paul and His Letters*
JTS	*Journal of Theological Studies*
LCL	*Loeb Classical Library*
LNTS	*Library of New Testament Studies* (formerly JSNTSup)
LouwNida	*Greek–English Lexicon of the New Testament Based on Semantic Domains*, Louw, J. and Nida, E., eds. (New York: United Bible Society, 1996)
LXX	*Septuagint*
MT	*Masoretic Text*
NASB	*New American Standard Bible*
NCB	*New Century Bible*
NCBC	*New Cambridge Bible Commentary*
NICNT	*New International Commentary on the New Testament*
NIGTC	*New International Greek Testament Commentaries*
NIV	*New International Version*
NLT	*New Living Translation*
NovTSup	*Novum Testamentum Supplements*
NRSV	*New Revised Standard Version* (1989)
NRSVue	*New Revised Standard Version, Updated Edition* (2022)
NT	*New Testament*
NTOA	*Novum Testamentum et Orbis Antiquus*
NTS	*New Testament Studies*
OCD	*The Oxford Classical Dictionary*, 3rd edition, Hornblower, S. and Spawforth, A., eds. (Oxford: Oxford University Press, 1996)

OT	Old Testament
PRSt	*Perspectives in Religious Studies*
RB	*Revue Biblique*
REB	*Revised English Bible*
ResQ	*Restoration Quarterly*
RSV	*Revised Standard Version*
SBT	*Studies in Biblical Theology*
SNTSMS	*Society of New Testament Studies Monograph Series*
TDNT	*Theological Dictionary of the New Testament*
TNTC	*Tyndale New Testament Commentaries*
TynB	*Tyndale Bulletin*
TZ	*Theologische Zeitschrift*
VE	*Vox Evangelica*
WBC	*Word Biblical Commentary*
WUNT	*Wissenschaftliche Untersuchungen zum Neuen Testament*
ZECNT	*Zondervan Exegetical Commentary on the New Testament*
ZNW	*Zeitschrift für die neutestamentliche Wissenschaft und die Kunde der älteren Kirche*

I Introduction to Colossians

BACKGROUND AND SETTING

The Wider Contextual Setting

The city of Colossae (*Kolossai*) belonged to the region of ancient Phrygia and could be found in the Lycus Valley. Located in western Anatolia (modern Türkiye/Turkey), Phrygia was an old and distinct territory with its own culture, language, and religion centuries before the arrival of Rome. Phrygia's home was originally along the Sakara (*Saggarios*; Latin *Saggarius*) River in northwest Anatolia, and its civilization peaked in the eighth century BCE, extending far south beyond Colossae. Major empires conquered it, from the Persians to Alexander the Great to even the Celtic tribal warlords who had migrated from the north.[1] Each conqueror desired to control the trade routes running east to west. Centuries before Paul, the Persian Xerxes the Great camped near Colossae on his way to Greece, as did the Persian Cyrus. Herodotus says that Xerxes arrived at Colossae and described it as a "considerable city of Phrygia" (*Herodotus* 7:30).[2] Both saw the Lycus Valley as a strategic gateway to the west (see Map 1).

Eventually the prosperity of Laodicea and Hierapolis dominated the valley, and soon the city of Colossae began to decline. Ptolemy, Alexander's successor in the fourth century BCE, refers to many cities in the region but fails to mention Colossae.[3] The region fell to Rome in the second century BCE, and by 25 BCE Rome had devised a plan to subdivide

---

[1] S. Mitchell, "Ethnography and Settlement of the Anatolian Celts," in *Anatolia: Land, Men, and Gods in Asia Minor*, vol. 1 (Oxford: Clarendon Press, 1993), 42–58.
[2] See Lightfoot, *Colossians*, 14–16, for classical references.
[3] Ibid., 16.

Map 1 Map of the Mediterranean.

the area into provinces, with Phrygia split among the imperial provinces of Asia, Bithynia, and Galatia. A generation before Paul, Strabo could write that Colossae was a "small town (*polisma*)."[4] While Ptolemy also lists many towns of importance, he fails to even mention Colossae (see Map 2).

Nevertheless, Phrygian culture persisted in the Roman period and is represented today in over seventy tombstones showing "Old Phrygian" in their writing (something a Roman or Greek tombstone would rarely do).[5] In the widely shared culture of Greco-Roman Hellenism, Phrygia was like Wales or Scotland in the United Kingdom: sharing in the whole but distinctly apart in its deeper interests; preserving its own language as well as it could while resisting absorption by the larger empire.

Thus, Colossae was in Roman provincial "Asia" but had a background of Phrygian regional culture. It was located about 120 miles east of the great

[4]   Strabo, *Geography*, 12.8.13. Lightfoot remarks, "Without doubt Colossae was the least
       important church to which any epistle of St. Paul is addressed . . ." (16).
[5]   S. Mitchell, *Anatolia: Land, Men, and Gods in Asia Minor*, vol. 1 (Oxford: Clarendon
       Press, 1993), 174.

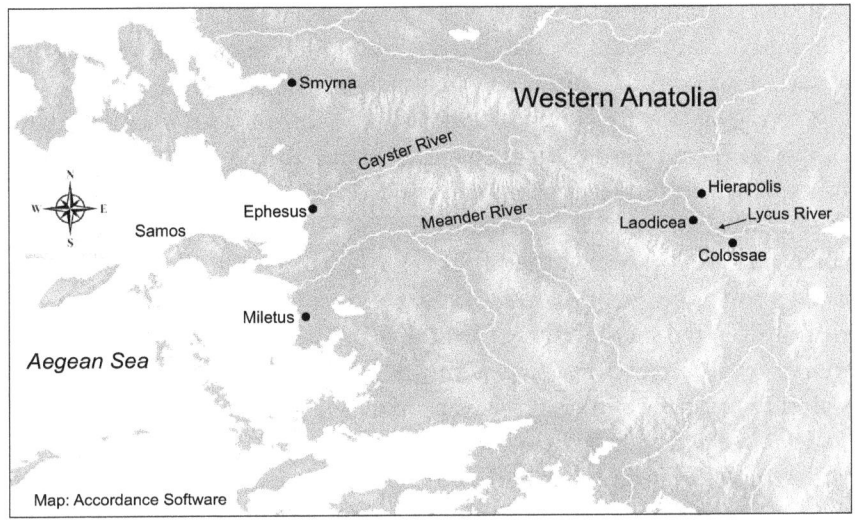

Map 2 Map of the Aegean Sea and western Anatolia focusing on Ephesus to Colossae (the Lycus Valley).

coastal city of Ephesus, and its "mound" was identified in 1835. Today it can be found in the verdant Lycus Valley, whose Lycus River flows into the larger Meander River running west to Miletus.[6] Three cities, about twelve miles apart, were located in this valley – Hierapolis, Laodicea, and Colossae – but they were a part of a larger network of cities that were important centers of Roman trade and government (Apamea, Pisidian Antioch, Tralles, etc.). We should imagine abundant trade passing through the Lycus Valley, interacting with its citizens, and following a route west (joining the Meander Valley) and northwest to Ephesus.[7] Roman efficiency had built an impressive network of roads across this region that moved troops and goods safely and rapidly. By the early first century CE, Colossae was a small though significant Roman city still overshadowed by its

[6] E. Yamauchi, *The Archaeology of the New Testament Cities in Western Asia Minor* (Grand Rapids: Baker, 1980), 155.

[7] The Meander (or Maeander) River (today: the Menderes; Greek *Maiandros*) is 240 miles long and winds considerably as it descends west. Its patron deity was Miandros, one of the water gods in the Greek pantheon. The river gave us the English word "meander," which is to ramble through the countryside.

neighbors, as referred to in Col 4:13. Laodicea was the financial and administrative center in the region, and Hierapolis' mineral springs attracted many visitors from afar in search of medicinal cures.[8]

The region was tremendously fertile and known for its wool and dyed cloth.[9] The geographer Strabo remarks about the region: "The country round Laodicea produces sheep that are excellent, not only for the softness of their wool, in which they surpass even the Milesian wool, but also for its raven-black color, so that the Laodiceans derive splendid revenue from it, as do also the neighboring Colosseni from the color which bears the same name."[10] To the south of the valley, the high Cadmos Mountains were the source of the Lycus River and gave the region a never-ending supply of water. In antiquity and even today, people have viewed the water from the Cadmos as healing and therapeutic.

The success of Colossae came to an end sometime in the mid-first century (late in Paul's life) when an earthquake damaged it severely (along with Hierapolis and Laodicea). Tacitus says that the earthquake was so terrific that twelve cities in Asia were ruined in one night (he gives their names).[11] Rome immediately rushed to their aid, offering money, tax relief, and construction help. Unfortunately, the city of Colossae was not rebuilt, nor has it been excavated even to this day.[12] All that remains are surface debris and a partially visible, unexcavated theater that could host about 5,000.[13]

---

[8]   See W. M. Ramsay, *The Cities and Bishoprics of Phrygia*, 2 vols. (Oxford: Clarendon Press, 1897), 1–121.

[9]   Strabo, *Geography*, 12.8.16; Pliny, *Natural History*, 11.51; Herodotus, 7.30. Describing Hierapolis, Strabo comments: "[I]t was the fertility of its territory and the prosperity of certain of its citizens that made it great."

[10] Strabo, *Geography*, 12.8.16.1–2, translation: The Loeb Classical Library, *Strabo*, 8 vols., 5:511.

[11] Tacitus, *Annals*, 2.47; Pliny refers to it as well, calling this earthquake under the reign of Tiberius "the greatest within the memory of humanity" (*Natural History*, 2.86).

[12] Many have tried to gain permission to excavate, but the Turkish authorities have denied them. This was true mid-century (see H. W. Mare, "Archaeological Prospects at Colossae," *Near East Archaeological Society Bulletin* 7 (1976) 39–59) and continues to be so today: M. Trainor, "Colossae? Colossal in Name Only?" *BAR* 45.2 (2019) 44–50; M. Sauter, "Where Is Biblical Colossae? The Unexcavated Site of Colossae Awaits to Be Excavated," *BAR* (online) June 14, 2023. The most recent archaeological report (over 800 pages) is A. H. Cadwallader, *Colossae, Colossians, Philemon: The Interface*. Novum Testamentum et Orbis Antiquus/Studien zur Umwelt des Neuen Testaments, Band 127 (Göttingen: Vandenhoeck & Ruprecht, 2023); see the review by P. Foster, "Understanding Colossae through Material Culture," *ExpT* 135.1 (2023) 18–20.

[13] See A. H. Cadwallader and M. Trainor, eds., *Colossae in Space and Time: Linking to an Ancient City*. NTOA 94 (Göttingen: Vandenhoeck & Ruprecht, 2011); M. Trainor, "Colossae: The State of Forthcoming Excavations," *JSPL* 1 (2011) 133–135.

Estimates are that the city held a population of about 25,000, making it far smaller than its two neighbors in the valley that today display extensive remains of temples, baths, theaters, aqueducts, gymnasia, and monumental ruins.

Rome

The Roman imperial presence in remote regions such as western Anatolia has now become clearer. Today epigraphic and ancient architectural remains – including many still passable Roman roads – attest to the widespread presence of Roman culture. But it is important to recall the inner workings of Roman politics to see how turmoil in Rome was putting pressure on cities like Colossae and its Christian community.

The late first century BCE was a time of turbulence in Rome. Julius Caesar's assassination in 44 BCE was followed by his successors falling into war – which ended at the Battle of Actium in 31 BCE, leaving Octavian (or Augustus) as emperor. Despair and concern gripped many Roman elites, who felt that the republic had been lost. To a degree, their fears were not unfounded: The Roman republic, for which they felt enormous pride, had been lost, only to be replaced by an empire (Imperial Rome) with strictly centralized governance under the charismatic Augustus and his successors.

Augustus brought a revival to Rome that was nothing short of eschatological. Turmoil could be replaced by tranquility and insecurity by peace if only Rome and its provinces entered into a new social contract. Augustus built a renewed professional military that secured "the roads" and the barbarian borders, cleared the Mediterranean of pirates, and began a massive revitalization of infrastructure that inspired Romans to believe in the power of Rome again. Commitment to this vision could be seen in the new temples built rapidly in every province. The elite did as they had always done: sponsoring civic projects on a grand scale, whose remains are with us to this day.

It was this "Augustan" program of cultural renewal – revival, really – complete with a mythology blending nationalism with religious piety that no province could avoid. Roman imagery was everywhere, and we can imagine that even in remote valleys like the Lycus one could not escape the pressures to conform to the new imperial world of Roman religion and life. Paul Zanker's fascinating *The Power of Images in the Age of Augustus* provides abundant pictures of how everything from family altars to coins bore homage to Augustus and the new Roman vision.[14] Coins depicted Augustus' defeat of the Parthians and his distribution of olive branches to compliant subjects. Jewelry depicted kneeling Parthians and Augustus as victor. Mirrors, lamps, hairpins, tables, and wall art employed the same images. In some cases, statues of Augustus imitated ancient Greek images of Hercules. That this was going on in the Lycus Valley can be seen with a brief trip to the modern archaeological museum at Ephesus.

But this was not simply propaganda; this was mythology – an eschatology – that swept up the imagination of the empire. Moral and cultural renewal led to new festivals, buildings, games, temples, and arts, all heralding a new age. A golden age was dawning. Images of fertility and victory decorated buildings as the sculptor's chisel reflected the sentiment on the street. Rome was back. Power had returned. Augustus would march into Anatolia like Alexander the Great and reestablish Roman hegemony.

Perhaps the best representation of this is the statue of Augustus found at the Villa of Livia at Prima Porta, north of Rome.[15] Originally cast in bronze, it was copied frequently in marble and presented Augustus as warrior-savior, relaxed and with a jaunty stance, his right arm uplifted and pointing to the future, spear held firmly. Defeated Parthians pay homage on his breastplate (or cuirass). He is the image of a Greek athlete, young and virile, echoing the golden age of Greece – which the Romans admired.[16] But this type of image became the standard. Even after Augustus' death (14 CE) the renewal continued, and depictions of Tiberius and Caligula used the same imperial style.

This mythology also integrated religion directly. Augustus proclaimed divine authority for the "Julian family" (descending from Julius Caesar), and this began with the posthumous deification (or apotheosis) of Caesar himself. In 17 CE the first coin of a deified Caesar appeared, and soon after

---

[14]   Zanker, *The Power of Images*.
[15]   This was the villa owned by Augustus' third wife, Livia Drusilla. The statue was discovered in 1863, and it is 6 feet 10 inches tall (2.08 meters) and weighs 2,200 pounds (1,000 kilograms). Today it can be seen in the Vatican Museum in Rome. Scholars believe it is a marble replica of an original bronze statue.
[16]   See Zanker, *The Power of Images*, 190. Images of *Primaporta Augustus* abound on the web. See also H. O. Maier, "A Sly Civility: Colossians and Empire," *JSNT* 27.3 (2005) 323–349; H. O. Maier, *Picturing Paul in Empire: Imperial Image, Text, and Persuasion in Colossians, Ephesians, and the Pastoral Epistles* (London: Bloomsbury, 2013).

Augustus was labeled *divi filius* or "divine son" on currency. Images portrayed Caesar ascending to heaven in a chariot, and his heavenly rising star appeared on coins. Augustus intended for his two grandsons, Gaius and Lucius, to succeed him, and quickly this divine identity was attached to them. Their untimely deaths made Augustus reluctantly choose a military commander named Tiberius to follow him (who was the adopted son of his third wife, Livia). This kept the Julian flame alive.[17]

Imperial propaganda represented the two options set before every region: One could be defeated like the Parthians – which was the warning – or one could enjoy the *pax* (or peace) of Rome and flourish. Overall, this so-called *Pax Romana* was contagious, causing some provinces to join the new order with zeal, but others (such as Judea) continued to look at it warily. This was a world order demanding compliance in exchange for peace. And this unmasked its reality: This *pax* was also a fiction. Some regions would not comply, and this led to war. As Tacitus later remarked, "Peace there was, without question, but a bloody one" (*Annals*, 1.9.5; 10.4).[18]

This detour has been necessary because it draws us into the world that every Colossian knew intimately. This was the air they breathed. It was impossible to live in Colossae and not be profoundly aware of imperial expectations and imperial promises. Temple participation was akin to political loyalty; *pietas* (piety) for the gods was the norm; home decor announced one's embrace of imperial symbols and mythologies. This may be analogous to the British royal cypher "ER" (*Elizabeth Regina*) and its stylized crown that appear on British passports and mailboxes (pillar boxes) in the UK. I also think of the portraits of Queen Elizabeth (the "queen mum") often found on kitchen walls throughout the UK in the late twentieth century.

A church planted in such a setting would have to deal with these realities and ask what costs its members would incur if they rejected this mythology and instead embraced a different narrative of salvation. What if they followed a different *divine son*? Paul will discuss this in Colossians, but

---

[17]   Tiberius' father was the distinguished patrician Tiberius Claudius Nero. His mother, Livia Drusilla, divorced her husband and went on to marry Augustus, becoming the emperor's third wife. Tiberius became the second emperor of the imperial period in 14 CE, ruling until 37 CE.

[18]   Cited in Zanker, *The Power of Images*, 187.

he will have to navigate this intense environment of religious–political conformity with care, and any criticism of it will have to be coded carefully.

We also have to remember that most of the Colossians would not have been able to read this letter (illiteracy was widespread), and so when Paul sent it, the letter came with a courier who would read it and interpret its meaning. This public reading served as an announcement – a "forthright social, economic and political announcement that King Jesus rules the cosmos."[19] Colossians offers, then, a worldview, a reframing of salvation and an implied upending of Rome. Jesus was the supplier of true salvation and the *telos* toward which history had been moving.

Roman Imperial Religion

It is impossible to imagine life in antiquity without religion. The "irreligious" or secular life is a modern invention that the ancient world did not know. Human destiny involved an interplay with "the gods," whose secrets were ferried to humanity through priests, oracles, and mysteries of innumerable varieties. The gods' anger or generosity shaped common life. Blessing or placating them was a human duty. In this sense, Colossae, like every Roman city, was steeped in religion, with many forms of syncretism where ancient faiths merged with new Roman beliefs. Jews lived alongside these cults – and soon, Christians joined them. But in each case, it was inevitable that common Roman religious instincts would infiltrate these monotheistic faiths. The same is true today. Most churches in the world have to some degree absorbed the civil religions or political eschatologies that forever present themselves as more exciting or convincing than the gospel itself.[20] The Colossians were no different.

The Hellenistic world was a time of cultural syncretism. There were few beliefs about one universal god (except among philosophers, and then only in the later Roman era), but instead religious practice was usually local and linked to one's region or culture. Often these gods merged, and what was once Greek took on a Roman name (Zeus was eventually identified with

---

[19] McKnight, *Colossians*, 2. See also P. Achtemeier, "Omne Verbum Sonat: The New Testament and the Oral Environment of Late Western Antiquity," *JBL* 109 (1990) 3–27.
[20] Writing this in the USA during the period between 2015 and 2025, I can't help but think about how civil religion and its political entailments have captured the imaginations of countless conservative Christians.

Jupiter, Artemis with Diana, Poseidon with Neptune). If you were Roman, it was expected that you observed Roman forms of devotion. If a city was a Roman colony, one could expect to see multiple temples devoted to Roman deities and, after the fall of the republic, to the emperor. Someday archaeologists will likely find the remains of a Roman temple at Colossae just as we have at Ephesus, Laodicea, and Hierapolis.

In the Roman period, one of the first features of religious piety was a commitment to the *pax deorum* (peace with the gods). This was a harmonious relationship with the gods that could prevent war, public disasters, plague, and famine, and could lead to both national and personal prosperity. In times of crisis, placating these gods was critical: Temple sacrifice, prayer, and elaborate liturgies each aimed to rectify the situation. But also, watchfulness for impiety was critical. In the Roman imperial period, divine blessing for the emperor became a common public duty.

The Romans had their own pantheon, headed by Jupiter Optimus Maximus (Jupiter, the Best and Greatest), and he was a part of *dii consentes* (the twelve united gods) that oversaw Rome's fate. Temples to these were abundant. But many more divinities also existed. These were often nameless, and they were viewed as divine actors who could hamper life or bless it. Many of these were continuations of old regional gods that were vastly popular among ordinary people.[21] To orchestrate the *pax deorum* there were numerous orders of priests, each tasked with bringing this peace. Public divination was vital to their work when they needed to diagnose the source of calamities. Among them were *augures*, priests who interpreted the meaning in the movement of birds (who lived close to the heavens). *Haruspices* were priests who interpreted the entrails of sacrificed animals.

Under imperial Rome, devoted residents of Colossae would have participated in each of these practices. In the first century, most religious activity would have focused on the emperor, thanksgiving for his life, and prayers for his prosperity (and thus the prosperity of Rome), and, in this sense, religion joined with patriotism, demonstrating one's fidelity to the empire. A family might also have a small altar in their home, paying homage to deceased relatives or to the gods whose will directed their lives.

---

[21] Centuries later, Augustine listed the countless gods as if to ridicule common Roman religion, *City of God*, 4.11.

Mystery Religions

But imperial religious devotion was not the only religious option in Colossae. In addition to all of these formal activities, there were also *mystery religions*, whose popularity was sweeping the Hellenistic world by the first century BCE. The Greek term *mystēs* meant "initiate," and a *mystērion* was a ritual of initiation. Marvin Meyer summarizes their purposes:

The mysteries advocated salvation for individual followers who chose to seek initiation into the mysteries and thus to draw close to the divine and to each other. . . . They celebrated the death and new life that may be experienced not only in nature but also in the world of humankind.[22]

Followers of the mysteries believed that their rituals and liturgies as well as their experiences were so sacred that they devoted themselves to secrecy, and even today we know little about them. Most of their practices were private and did not include the public display of faith found in temples. But we do know that they had sacred symbols, purification rituals, meals, and initiation rites. They employed the imagery of death and life liberally as a metaphor for the initiation–transformation. In a fragment attributed to Plutarch, we read about a cult initiation as a death:

At first there is wandering, and wearisome roaming, and fearful traveling through darkness with no end to be found. Then, just before the consummation, there is every sort of terror, shuddering and trembling and sweating and being alarmed. But after this a marvelous light appears, and open places and meadows await, with voices and dances and the solemnities of sacred utterances and holy visions. In that place one walks about at will, now perfect and initiated and free, and wearing a crown, one celebrates religious rituals and joins with pure and pious people.[23]

Some sources describe public parades that invited onlookers to join. The *Metamorphoses of Apuleius* describes a colorful cult parade carrying an

---

[22]   M. Meyer, "Mysteries," in *DNTB*, 720. See also M. Meyer, ed., *The Ancient Mysteries: A Sourcebook of Sacred Texts* (Philadelphia: University of Pennsylvania Press, 1999); J. Z. Smith, *Drudgery Divine: On the Comparison of Early Christianities and the Religions of Late Antiquity* (Chicago: University of Chicago Press, 1990); and D. Ulansey, *The Origins of the Mithraic Mysteries: Cosmology and Salvation in the Ancient World* (Oxford: Oxford University Press, 1989).

[23]   Cited in Meyer, "Mysteries," 721.

image of the Egyptian goddess Isis who was preceded by singers, dancers, music, and criers. Many people dressed as Egyptian gods and followed the parade. The key is that in these cults members believed they would find *sōtēria* (salvation) both in this life and the next through their rituals.

It is likely that when some Romans encountered a Christian gathering in a city like Colossae, they may have considered it a mystery religion since it employed the religious vocabulary familiar to mystery cults. For some scholars, the opponents Paul meets in Colossae may well have promoted features known in some of the mysteries. This is the thesis of the important work of Clinton Arnold, *The Colossian Syncretism: The Interface between Christianity and Folk Belief in Colossae.*[24] Rather than finding the source of the philosophy (2:8) of the opponents in Colossians in Jewish mysticism, he points to the mystery religions and their ascetic practices as mixing with Jewish belief in a highly pluralistic setting. The scholars who disagree with Arnold do not point to a more purely Hellenistic set of beliefs as the origin of the problem but instead lean more heavily into Judaism and see a fluid relationship between Jewish and Christian communities.[25] For some, the clearest evidence of these opponents is in 2:8–23, and it can be explained entirely within first-century Jewish views.

Judaism

For the most part, Judaism was outside this mainstream's wildly diverse religious setting. As a monotheistic faith, showing obedience to the God of Israel and devotion to the temple in Jerusalem made achieving harmony with the Roman cults difficult though not impossible. While small migrations of Jews may have come to the area as early as the sixth century BCE, Josephus says that Antiochus III moved about 2,000 Jewish families from Babylon to Phrygia to increase his hold on the region. As military settlers, they were given homes and were exempt from paying taxes for ten years.[26] They continued to live in the region undisturbed. In 62 BCE, Lucius

---

[24] C. E. Arnold, *The Colossian Syncretism: The Interface between Christianity and Folk Belief at Colossae* (Grand Rapids: Baker, 1996).

[25] See Dunn, *Colossians*, 23–35.

[26] Josephus, *Antiq.*, 12.125. Antiochus wrote to his father, Zeuxis,

> King Antiochus to Zeuxis, his father, greeting. If you are in good health, it is well. I also am in sound health. Learning that the people in Lydia and Phrygia are revolting, I have come to consider this as requiring very serious attention on my part, and, on taking counsel with my

Valarius Flaccus (governor of Asia) impounded the annual half-shekel tax that all Jewish men were sending to the Jerusalem temple. This number can give us an estimate of the Jewish male population (over twenty years of age). At Apamea they took 45,000 half-shekels; at Laodicea they took 9,000. As Bruce suggests, these probably represent the Jewish population of the region surrounding these cities, not the cities themselves.[27]

Rome's awareness of these Jewish communities surfaces again in the reign of Augustus, who declared in 14 BCE that the half-shekel tribute to Jerusalem would be protected for the Jews of Asia.[28] Ramsay believed that Jews in this region of the diaspora also showed reciprocal favor to Rome. An inscription of a Jew named Julia Severa honors her leadership at the synagogue (as *archisynagōgos*), but she also appears on coins honoring her work (along with her husband, Servenius Capito) in municipal office – a role one could hardly play without some participation in the imperial cult.[29] But Jewish stories also merged into popular local Roman life. In the Phrygian city of Apamea a local flood legend combined with the Noah story. Coins from the third century CE show an inscription with Noah's name along with a raven and a dove holding an olive branch. The later *Sibylline Oracles* (1:261–265) even placed Mount Ararat in Phrygia.

Josephus cites a letter written in about 45 BCE from the officials of the leaders of Laodicea to an unnamed Roman official saying that he should not impede the local Jewish residents and the practice of their religious duties.[30] In 3 CE Augustus made a formal declaration of Jewish rights, and this undoubtedly affected the region.[31] And later, after the First Jewish War

friends as to what should be done, I determined to transport two thousand Jewish families with their effects from Mesopotamia and Babylonia to the fortresses and most important places. For I am convinced that they will be loyal guardians of our interests because of their piety to God, and I know that they have had the testimony of my forefathers to their good faith and eagerness to do as they are asked.

[27]   F. F. Bruce, "Colossian Problems Part 1: Jews and Christians in the Lycus Valley," *BibSac* 141 (1984) 3.

[28]   Josephus, *Antiq.*, 16.27–65.

[29]   Bruce, "Colossian Problems Part 1," 7; See Ramsay, *Cities and Bishoprics of Phrygia*, 2:650.

[30]   See Bruce, "Colossian Problems Part 1," 6. Josephus, *Antiq.*, 14.241–243. The decree defends the loyalty of Jews: "[I]t shall be lawful for them to observe their Sabbaths and perform their other rites in accordance with their native laws, and that no one shall give orders to them, because they are our friends and allies, and that no one shall do them an injury in our province . . ."

[31]   See Bruce, "Colossian Problems Part 1," 6. See Josephus, *Antiq.*, 16:162–165. A complaint had been filed in Rome by Jews in Asia who had suffered acute discrimination. Augustus' decree is given by Josephus:

(66–70 CE), more epigraphic evidence on tombs illustrates further signs of a Jewish community that lived throughout Phrygia.[32] There is no question of a thriving Jewish community in Phrygia. Even in Acts 2, in the list of nations found at Jerusalem's Pentecost gathering, we read about Jews who had come from Anatolia: "Cappadocia, Pontus, Asia, *Phrygia* and Pamphylia" (2:9–10).

The Narrow Contextual Setting

On his first tour, Paul left Perga in southern Anatolia and traveled north, where he entered Antioch of Pisidia, which was viewed as in the easternmost reaches of Phrygia. On his second tour, Luke writes, "They went through the region of Phrygia and Galatia" (Acts 16:6). Of course, we cannot know if they entered the Lycus Valley. However, on his third tour, we have a provocative hint. Luke says, "While Apollos was in Corinth, Paul passed through *the interior regions* and came to Ephesus, where he found some disciples" (Acts 19:1). This phrase *the interior regions* (*anōterikos*) means anyplace away from the shore – "the uplands" or "the interior." Luke may mean that as Paul traveled west toward Ephesus, he took the Lycus Valley route and entered Ephesus from the upper plateau east of the valley. We also know that Paul remained at Ephesus for over two years, so that Luke can summarize, "All the residents of Asia heard the word of the Lord, both Jews and Greeks."

If Paul was located at Ephesus and traveled to nearby locations, he most certainly knew the cities of the Lycus. But, apparently, he did not go to Colossae nearby. Col 2:1 tells us that the Colossians and the nearby Laodiceans had not "seen his face" and thus did not know him personally. A colleague of Paul's named Epaphras was the first to bring the gospel to

Caesar Augustus, Pontifex Maximus with Augustus' decree in favor of the Jews of Asia. Tribunician power, decrees as follows. Since the Jewish nation has been found well-disposed to the Roman people not only at the present time but also in time past, and especially in the time of my father the emperor Caesar, as has their high priest Hyrcanus, it has been decided by me and my council under oath, with the consent of the Roman people, that the Jews may follow their own customs in accordance with the law of their fathers . . .

The decree goes on to support and protect monies sent from Jews to the Jerusalem treasury. See also E. M. Smallwood, *The Jews Under Roman Rule* (Leiden: Brill, 1975), 120–143.

[32] See Ramsay, *Cities and Bishoprics of Phrygia* and Frey, P. J.-P., *Corpus of Jewish Inscriptions. Jewish Inscriptions from the Third Century B.C. to the Seventh Century A. D.* Volume 1: Europe (New York: KTAV, 1975).

the Lycus Valley (Col 1:7), and Paul heaps praise on him to support his work and to gain the endorsement of their friendship. To Paul, Epaphras was a "beloved fellow servant" and a "faithful minister of Christ" (1:7). Apparently when Paul is later imprisoned in Rome, Epaphras was with him ("my fellow prisoner"; Phlm 23). This is expansive praise and shows that Epaphras, who founded the Colossian church, was one of Paul's most valued personal colleagues.

The letter to the Colossians was carried by the courier Tychicus, who was accompanied by Onesimus (4:7–9), the former slave and resident of Colossae. We can imagine that Christian communities had been established in all three of the Lycus Valley cities thanks to the work of Epaphras. The Christians in these small churches likely knew each other by name. Paul knows, for instance, that a woman named Nympha hosts the Laodicean church (4:15).[33] Thus Paul can tell them to have this letter read in Laodicea and likewise to have the Laodicean letter read in Colossae (4:16). What was this other letter? Many have supposed that this is Ephesians, a circular essay also carried by Tychicus (Eph 6:21; cf. 2Tim 4:12). This means that, as a courier, Tychicus was carrying three letters: Colossians, Philemon, and Ephesians. Tychicus would tell everyone about Paul's circumstances and circulate the more general Ephesian letter.

A final reference to the Lycus Valley appears in Rev 3:14–22, where we find an exhortation for the church of Laodicea near Colossae. The letter to Laodicea is filled with cultural allusions that give us insights into life in the valley during this time. The prosperity and commercial successes of Laodicea was likely shared by all three cities in the valley.[34]

AUTHORSHIP

I have been presupposing thus far that Paul is the author of Colossians and that descriptions of his travels through Phrygia might bear some relevance

---

[33] We will see in the commentary that debate surrounds the gender of this name. The common reading today sees this name as feminine, along with the pronoun that follows. Manuscripts differ as scribes chose one view or another.

[34] For a careful cultural analysis of this letter (and each of the letters in Rev 1–3), see J. Weima, *The Sermons to the Seven Churches of Revelation: A Commentary and Guide* (Grand Rapids: Baker Academic, 2021).

to this letter. The letter itself makes this claim (1:1, 23), but today the subject of its authorship has seen wide disagreement.

The letter presents itself as highly personal, often using the first person ("I am now rejoicing in my sufferings for your sake ..." 1:24). It also ends with a highly personal conclusion ("I, Paul, write this greeting with my own hand. Remember my chains. Grace be with you." 4:18). This is similar to Gal 6:11, a generally accepted letter. These may be the hallmarks of authenticity.[35]

The letter also includes personal links to an itinerary and personalities that all fit the Pauline setting (4:7–17). For instance, the author says that he is in prison (4:3, 18; possibly 1:24), and we know of this from Paul's own history. Acts implies that he may have been imprisoned in Ephesus near Colossae. But the letter's affinity with Philemon and the more likely setting of a runaway slave finding refuge and hiding in Rome suggest Rome may be the best locale for the letter's origin and Paul's imprisonment.

Overall, Paul refers to seven persons with surprising personal details. Timothy is "his brother," and Archippus is sufficiently well known that Paul can give him an assignment (4:17). Aristarchus and Justus are apparently with Paul in prison (4:10), and he alerts the Colossians that "Mark the cousin of Barnabas" may come to see them. These, Paul says, are the only persons from "the circumcision," likely referring to Jewish-Christians, but here using a phrase repeated in Galatians. These details are important because they offer more about Paul's visibility to us and his circumstances than we might expect. John Barclay concludes, "If Colossians is by a later Paulinist, it is unparalleled in its sophisticated adaptation of incidental details to camouflage its inauthenticity."[36]

However, this question of authorship is vexing not only for Colossians but also for a number of Paul's letters.[37] Scholars wonder if an imitator of Paul (or a well-intended disciple) could have included so many personal

---

[35] For some scholars, these are signs of a carefully calculated pseudepigraphy, veiling the later writer by employing personal identifiers.

[36] Barclay, *Colossians*, 24, cited in Moo, *Colossians*, 29.

[37] The most comprehensive discussion of authorship to date is Moo, *Colossians*, 28–41; see also Beale, *Colossians*, 1–8. Moo, *Colossians*, 29n5, provides lists of scholars who support and deny Pauline authorship. Roughly 60 percent of scholars do not hold to some form of Pauline authorship.

features and even imitated the apostle's style in some cases. The debate centers on easily identifiable problems.

Vocabulary and Style

One of the primary arguments against Pauline authorship has been the number of words in the letter that occur only once or do not appear in the other so-called accepted Pauline letters.[38] There are thirty-four *hapax legomena* (once-used words) in the letter.[39] These are terms that appear nowhere else in the NT. Based on comparisons with the "accepted" seven Pauline letters, Colossians has eighty-seven non-Pauline words. Scholars also point to favorite Pauline terms such as the word group for "righteousness" (*dikaios*). It is absent in Colossians but occurs sixty times in the authentic Pauline letters (forty-one times in Romans alone). However, 1 Corinthians only uses it once (1:30), and it is absent from 1 Thessalonians, and this does not disqualify these letters. 2 Corinthians does not use "law" (*nomos*), and it uses "believe" (*pisteuein*) only once in 4:13 – both common Pauline terms. Philippians has seventy-nine words that do not appear in the other six accepted letters of Paul, and this poses the same challenge.[40] The problem with arguments from statistics is methodology. Variation is common, and only the degree of variation may disqualify a letter.

The truth is, vocabulary in any letter can shift due to the letter's subject, its context, its possible use by a scribe, and even the year when it was penned. An author's style may change with time. Thus, it is impossible to use this criterion confidently, and it is fair to suggest that Colossians falls within the range of how Paul might write.

While scholars are increasingly reluctant to launch an argument on vocabulary, many find stylistic arguments more compelling. Here we find variations from the critical Pauline canon that deviate significantly. It is well known that Colossians employs genitives frequently (e.g., "the word of

---

[38]   Since the nineteenth century, the assured letters of Paul have been Galatians, Romans, 1 Corinthians, and 2 Corinthians. In recent years this list has included three more: Philippians, 1 Thessalonians, and Philemon. Many scholars often then refer to the "seven" authentic letters.

[39]   For a list, see Lohse, *Colossians*, 85–86.

[40]   For a full list of word statistics, see Abbott, *Colossians*, lii–liv.

the truth of the gospel," 1:5). It is also argued that Colossians uses a liturgical or lyric style and departs from Paul's usual rhetorical or debating tone. But this too is not entirely persuasive. After reviewing data for vocabulary and style, Lohse can conclude that while Colossians exhibits several peculiarities, it also shares so many features with Paul, such that, after 100 years, an argument against Paul's hand cannot be sustained.[41]

Scribes in Antiquity

In every case where there are vocabulary or stylistic issues, we cannot forget how common it was in the ancient world for writers to employ the services of a scribe (called an *amanuensis*). For example, Paul uses Tertius (Rom 16:22) as a scribe. In Colossians, did Paul similarly use Timothy (1:1b)? Paul's addition of a "signature" in 4:16 certainly suggests that a scribe is working alongside the author. Cicero (*To Atticus*, Letter 333 [13.25]) describes two types of dictation for a scribe: "Tiro, takes down whole sections together," but "Spintharus" writes down "syllable by syllable."[42] Here Cicero is describing a variety of roles for a scribe: One might strictly hold to the exact language of the author, another might have freedom to improve the language, grammar, or logic of longer sections. Cicero assures Atticus that he is using Spintharus because of his precision in the details. This underscores something we now know well: *Trusted scribes had a broad range of involvement in these efforts.* And in Paul's case, he often used trusted colleagues. Anyone who has published a book knows precisely this range of editorial involvement Cicero is describing.

McKnight offers a lengthy argument based on this use of scribes. He is critical of the entire enterprise of locating differences in Pauline letters and the presumption of knowing what the authentic or pure Paul sounded like.[43] He is actually flipping the entire debate on its head. His complaint centers on the assumption that we can possess a "known Paul" in, say, Galatians or Romans, and then we move toward an "unknown" document like Colossians *that then does not match the known Paul.*

---

[41] Lohse, *Colossians*, 91.
[42] See Beale, *Colossians*, 2, who credits G. Fee with this reference (2n5).
[43] See McKnight, *Colossians*, 5–12.

The problem is not with Colossians (or other presumed non-Pauline letters); the problem is with the supposed "canon" of Paul against which everything is measured. We assume we know more than we do, and this distorts our judgments. We move from the known to the unknown when our methods using the known-Paul are infected by historically precarious presuppositions. McKnight writes, "The historical error at work here is repeated over and over . . .. That solely the man, the apostle, the Jew Paul is responsible for Galatians and that therefore in Galatians or Romans or 1 and 2 Corinthians we have a pure sample of Paul, the authentic voice of Paul."[44]

Part of the difficulty is because we know so much more about how authorship was viewed in antiquity. Paul himself says that he is not skilled at writing (Gal 6:11), which means he used scribes generously in his letters (Rom 16:22). And if this is the case, if these scribes contributed substantially to the form and content of the letters, then we cannot even say that Galatians represents "the pure Paul." Nor does Romans. If these conclusions are correct, then arguments based on vocabulary and style collapse. This is not to deny that there is variation in style and vocabulary in Colossians when compared with the so-called authentic letters of Paul, but that these differences do not bear the importance we once thought they did.

In sum, it is defensible today to open the door to the Pauline authorship for this letter. And scholars are increasingly willing to reexamine assumptions we have held in the academy since the nineteenth century. This is not inspired by canonical or confessional commitments. But it reflects a generous reconstruction of history that other historians of classical antiquity generally give to their documents. The confidence with which we dismiss certain documents as non-Pauline surprises many of them.

THE LETTER OF COLOSSIANS IS SENT

If Colossians is linked to the circumstances of Paul's own life, particularly in the prison letters, we can assume that this letter too came from an imprisonment. From Acts we know of three imprisonments for Paul (16:23–40; 21:32–23:30; 28:30): Philippi, Caesarea, and Rome. Most

---

44 Ibid., 7.

scholars point to Rome (Philippians seems to provide direct evidence, 1:13; 4:22), where Paul was imprisoned for two years (Acts 28:30).[45] In his final greeting in Col 4:18 he urges the Colossians to "remember my chains" (or imprisonment, *desmos*). In 4:3 he repeats this reminder. The close associations with Ephesians (see later), Philemon, and Philippians all point to the same setting (Eph 6:20; Phlm 1, 23; Phil 1:19, 2:3).

We know that Paul had free custody in Rome, which means that he could be surrounded by many friends and coworkers and be able to send correspondence as well as receive visitors. Paul lived in a world without public postal services, and, like anyone else, he relied on couriers to deliver his letters to their recipients. In some cases, letter writers might hire travelers headed in the direction of their recipients. Others enlisted friends. But letter writing as we have it here in the NT was common. Today we have recovered many such letters from places like Egypt, where we have found approximately 6,761 papyrus letters. Today we have 800 letters belonging to Cicero, 124 from Seneca, and 247 from Pliny the Younger.[46]

The early Christians used trusted followers who could not only deliver the letter reliably but also interpret Paul's meanings. On occasion we have the names of Paul's couriers. For Colossians and Ephesians, Paul employed Tychicus (Col 4:7; Eph 6:21). Philemon is also a prison letter, and since the opening verses of Philemon and Colossians mirror each other we think that they were written together. This brings the letters into the same basic orbit. Philemon, however, is a personal letter addressed to the former owner of the slave Onesimus (Phlm 10). We can imagine then that Tychicus left Rome accompanied by Onesimus carrying at least three of these four prison letters. Philippians refers to Paul's plan to send Epaphroditus back to Philippi (2:25), and if this is the same mission, Epaphroditus may have traveled with Tychicus.

It is hard for us to imagine the dedication that was required for couriers such as these. Tychicus and Onesimus could have either taken a ship from the port of Rome (Ostia) or traveled south on the Appian Way (125 miles) to the great shipping harbor of Puteoli, a port once used by Paul (Acts

---

[45] Some have suggested other locations for Paul's imprisonment (Ephesus in particular), but today the traditional location of Rome is widely supported.

[46] P. Head, "Who Carried the Epistles?" https://tyndalehouse.com/explore/articles/who-carried-the-epistles/ (accessed January 20, 2026). See also J. Weima, *Paul the Ancient Letter Writer: An Introduction to Epistolary Analysis* (Grand Rapids: Baker Academic, 2016).

28:13).[47] They would have joined an eastbound ship and then transferred to another vessel in southern Achaia (Greece) at either of the Greek islands of Crete or Delos, eventually making their way to the Aegean ports of Anatolia.

Or they could have traveled overland, following the Appian Way from Rome south to Brundisium, where a ship across the Adriatic Sea would bring them to the Egnatian Way, a major highway that crossed northern Macedonia (from the Macedonian coast to Byzantium).[48] But once they came to eastern Macedonia, they could set sail from Thessalonica or Neapolis (near Philippi) to cross over to Anatolia at either Smyrna, Ephesus, or Miletus. From there it was a relatively short trek to the Lycus Valley. We suspect that these Christian couriers met with Christian communities as they traveled (much as Paul did). Hospitality such as this was a mainstay of Mediterranean culture. For example, when Paul came into Puteoli on his imprisonment journey he met a church there, remained for seven days, and many accompanied him north to Rome. Tychicus could have followed Paul's itinerary in reverse.

RELATIONSHIP TO EPHESIANS

Colossians and Ephesians share many common features. In some cases, entire sections are the same. For example, the greetings at the end of each letter are the same (Eph 6:21–22; Col 4:7–8). Turns of phrase appearing in one seem to be duplicated in the other (Eph 1:4 and Col 1:22; Eph 1:7 and Col 1:14; Eph 2:5 and Col 2:13; Eph 4:2 and Col 3:12, 14). Both letters offer what is called a "household code" giving directions on the duties of household members from slaves to children (Eph 5:21–6:9 and Col 3:18–4:6). Both letters bear a high Christology showing Christ as resplendent in his glory and status.

The chief solution to these parallels is literary dependence. And the majority of scholars see Ephesians as dependent on Colossians due to the way that Ephesians further amplifies themes in Colossians. This

---

[47] Puteoli was famous among the great ports of Rome and possibly the most important. The largest naval fleet in the world was stationed nearby, and it had sophisticated anchorage for Egyptian grain vessels. These many commercial ships would have provided cheap passage for a couple of passengers heading east.

[48] These ships could have put in at either Appolonia or Dyrrhachium.

observation impacts considerably views on the authorship of Ephesians and has led many to believe that Ephesians was penned by a disciple of Paul after the apostle's death, imitating themes from Colossians.[49]

Literary borrowing was not unknown in antiquity. The synoptic gospels provide one example, as does the literary relationship between 2 Peter and Jude. In this case, some scholars infer that one of these letters must be pseudepigraphical, while others suggest that the letters' similarities stem from them originating at the same time. Theoretically at least Paul could have written Colossians and Ephesians together and sent both out to different destinations. He could have used Colossians as the template around which he wrote the more expansive essay (known to us as Ephesians) that would have a wider circulation.

USE OF THE OLD TESTAMENT

One of the striking features of Colossians is the absence of formal quotations from the Old Testament.[50] However this does not mean there are no allusions – there are many. But some commentators see these echoes or allusions as sufficiently subtle that arguments for them seem unpersuasive. Therefore, this discussion centers on probability, and this is always difficult. Is it possible that Paul's deeply rooted understanding of the OT led to him assuming a shared understanding with his audience?

A good example of this dilemma is found in Paul's opening words in 1:6, 10, where Paul describes the gospel bearing fruit in all the world. Is this an echo of Gen 1:28, where God speaks to humanity's role in creation (". . . be fruitful and multiply and fill the earth and subdue it and have dominion")? Parallels to the LXX are absent, but interpreters believe that Paul may be

---

[49] D. Hagner, *The New Testament: A Historical and Theological Introduction* (Grand Rapids: Baker, 2012), 566. For a full examination of this, see A. T. Lincoln, *Ephesians.* WBC 42 (Dallas: Word, 1990), xlvii–lxxiii and P. T. O'Brien, *The Letter to the Ephesians* (Grand Rapids: Eerdmans, 1999), 8–21.

[50] See G. K. Beale, "Colossians," in G. K. Beale and D. A. Carson, eds., *Commentary on the New Testament Use of the Old Testament* (Grand Rapids: Baker Academic, 2007), 841–870; C. Beetham, *The Scriptures of Israel in the Letter of Paul to the Colossians.* PhD dissertation (Wheaton: Wheaton College Graduate School, 2005); G. Fee, "Old Testament Intertextuality in Colossians: Reflections on Pauline Christology and Gentile Inclusion in God's Story," in S.-W. Son, ed., *History and Exegesis: New Testament Essays in Honor of Dr. E. Earle Ellis for His 80th Birthday* (New York: T&T Clark, 2006), 2001–2021.

looking at the MT (which is not Paul's usual pattern). Nevertheless, the foundational ideas of Gen 1:28 – the call for humanity to bear God's image as his vice-regents to all the world – are exactly what Paul has in mind in Colossians, as he understands that the gospel is our reclaiming of the call to inaugurate a new era fulfilling this mandate. Being "fruitful and multiplying" now refers to the growth of the kingdom, not to the populations descending from the first human pair. Paul then is employing a vital idea embedded in the redemptive story of Israel: the reclamation of *all the Earth* for God. He takes the structure of an OT argument and then reapplies it to a new setting: Fruitfulness no longer refers to progeny, but to new converts throughout the world.

Similar echoes are at Col 1:9, 12–14, 15, 19, 26–27; 2:2–3; 3:1, 9–10; 4:5. We will look at these in turn within the commentary, but the same methodological issues will rise: *When do we know that Paul is leaning into assumed concepts understood by his readers?* The absence of a citation hardly means that Paul is unaware of the great theological backdrop that has shaped him and his Jewish world. We who write *as Christians* to a well-informed *Christian audience* do this very thing regularly.

PAUL AND THE DIFFICULTIES AT COLOSSAE

It goes without saying that Colossians is a theologically rich letter with important emphases on Christology, the church, and the Christian life. However, many of these themes are linked to difficulties that are also mentioned in the letter. No doubt 2:8–23 is the key passage in the letter that gives us some insight into these problems being stirred up by teachers in the church.

This raises one persistent problem with outlining a Pauline theology. Paul's writing is frequently engaged in a polemical debate with opponents. In many of his letters (see Gal 1:8; 4:17; 5:12; 6:12–13; 2Cor 11:4–5, 13–15, 20–23; 12:11; Phil 3:2, 18–19; 1Tim 1:3–7; 4:1–3; 6:3–5) Paul refers to false teachers and criticizes them directly. But Colossians is not quite like this. In Colossians, "false teachers" may even be the wrong label altogether because the nature of Paul's debate is vague. Paul does not point out particular teachers as he does in 2 Corinthians but instead speaks generally about someone (2:4) who might teach incorrectly. Generally, we think that these teachers are inside the church, but even that is not absolutely clear.

Needless to say, what has emerged is a view of the letter that points to the "Colossian heresy" or "the Colossian error," which represents some mix of Jewish or proto-Gnostic influences. Today there is a bewildering number of suggestions for who these opponents might be.[51]

But the problem becomes worse when we try to reconstruct what these teachers were saying. We speculate about them only using Paul's rebuttals, particularly in Colossians 1 and 2. The danger here (called "mirror reading") comes when we read strong rejoinders by Paul and then conclude that Paul's words are mirroring the problem of false teaching. It is like overhearing a telephone conversation and thinking you know what is being said on the other end. Of course, what are missing are the voices of these teachers. And without them, our reconstructions must remain speculative.

Some have wondered if there ever was a Colossian heresy. Or perhaps, with Dunn, we can first ask how we can use such a term, since "heresy" implies an established orthodoxy that someone at Colossae has violated.[52] Dunn is not denying that there was a system of belief that found a degree of consensus in the early church. He is simply warning that such a volatile term as "heresy" distorts how we see what is going on. But were there teachers in Colossae who were contradicting this early system of faith and who were gaining a following in the Colossian church? Some say that even this goes too far. Morna Hooker was the first to ask whether the idea of "opponents" has been overplayed. Only one verse (2:19) refers to a system of thought ("philosophy," see commentary) that Paul opposes.[53] Perhaps instead Paul is fully aware of the religious environment in its setting and is writing to immunize the Christian readers "against the possibility of being misled."[54] In this view, Paul is sounding a warning, not engaging in a polemic.

---

[51] I. Smith, *Heavenly Perspective. A Study of the Apostle Paul's Response to a Jewish Mystical Movement at Colossae*. LNTS 326 (London: T&T Clark, 2006), 19, refers to the summary of Gunther (*St. Paul's Opponents and Their Background*. NovTSup 35 (Leiden: Brill, 1973), 3–4), who outlined forty-four different views on these opponents.

[52] Dunn, *Colossians*, 24. "Such a view [referring to a Colossian heresy] can no longer be sustained, at least in simple form."

[53] M. Hooker, "Were There False Teachers in Colossae?", in B. Lindars and S. Smalley, eds., *Christ and Spirit in the New Testament: Studies in Honor of C.F.D. Moule* (Cambridge: Cambridge University Press, 1973), 315–331; followed by Wright, *Colossians*, 27; and Dunn, *Colossians*, 26.

[54] Dunn, *Colossians*, 26n19, citing W. Schenk, "Der Kolosserbrief in der neueren Forschung (1945–1985)," *ANRW* 2.25.4 (1987) 3327–3364.

Many scholars, however, come away from Colossians 2:8–23 convinced that something more concrete is on Paul's mind. When Paul warns against "*someone* who will deceive you" (2:4), or someone who "will take you captive" (2:8), or someone who may "judge you" (2:16, 18), he likely has specific identifiable opponents in mind. Paul describes these views as a "philosophy" (2:8) and its practitioners as putting pressure on members of the church (2:16, 18). That specific regulations are being imposed (2:20–22) suggests a movement within the church that wants to promote spiritual rigor and presents itself as elitist: Their teaching stems from visions that promise to elevate the average believer. In 2:23 Paul provides a brief list of the benefits that have been promised: self-abasement, devotion, and, above all, severity to the body. This is an austere form of faith that Paul knows is a departure from anything Epaphras taught this church, and he is writing to correct it.

The first explanation of this "philosophy" Paul opposes has always been Hellenism. In this view, either Gnosticism or an early form of it (proto-Gnosticism) is to blame. The number of scholars intrigued by this option is enormous (G. Bornkamm, H. Conzelmann, etc.). The origin of this view may come from F. C. Baur in the nineteenth century, who suggested that the Colossian error points to an early gnostic philosophy that concentrated on mediating religious figures ("elements of the universe," 2:8, 20) who could supply wisdom (*sophia*, 1:9, 28; 2:3, 23; 3:16; 4:5), insight (*synesis*, 1:9; 2:2), and knowledge (*epignōsis*, 1:6, 9–10; 2:2–3; 3:10). It is only by placating these cosmic powers (2:10, 15) that one can enter into the fullness (2:9) of life.[55] Further, 2:18 refers to "initiatory visions," which suggests a cult initiation (*embateuō*, to initiate). Christ, therefore, must be fitted into this schema, and, of course, Paul will object to this idea strenuously.

On the other hand, a growing number of scholars believe that the principal features of these teachings stem from some form of Judaism. This view began in 1879 with J. B. Lightfoot, who saw this as a *form of Judaism* that had been shaped by Hellenistic influences.[56] The references to

---

[55]   In Gunther's overview of interpretative options, a strong majority point to gnostic influences.

[56]   J. B. Lightfoot, "The Colossian Heresy," in *Colossians*, 73–113; also available at F. O. Watson and W. A. Meeks, eds., *Conflict at Colossae: A Problem in the Interpretation of Early Christianity Illustrated by Selected Modern Studies* (Missoula: Scholars Press, 1975), 13–59.

sabbath and circumcision (2:11, 16) suggest this, but other references to fullness (2:9), angel worship, and visions (2:18) imply a second background. As Lightfoot wrote, "We discern an element of theosophic speculation which is alien to the spirit of Judaism proper."[57] He referred to it as a "Judeo-Gnostic heresy."

Some have tried to narrow the Jewish context further. Some have pointed to Qumran and suggested distinct parallels.[58] Others have suggested a Jewish mysticism that was tainted by Hellenistic popular religion.[59] This latter idea today has considerable support and has led to deeper explorations into how popular religion in the Roman Empire likely influenced Jews living there.

We can at least affirm the following things about these teachers in Colossae:[60] First, it is clear that the fundamental ideas associated with this teaching stemmed from Jewish faith and practice as well as the OT. This is clear from 2:16 and 2:21–23. Therefore, this means that we are not dealing here with a syncretistic Hellenistic philosophy with only a few marginal Jewish beliefs. Even talk of "Gnostic Judaism" should be dismissed.[61] Jewish belief is central. Dunn writes:

In other words, the number of distinctively and definitively Jewish features are such that it is scarcely possible to envisage the Colossian "philosophy" as a non-Jewish core that has attracted Jewish elements; at most we have to speak of an apocalyptic or mystical Judaism transposed into the diaspora that has been able to make itself attractive to those sympathetic to Judaism by playing on familiar fears and making more impressive claims.[62]

Dividing the world into "circumcised" and "uncircumcised" (2:11–13) and rules regarding the sabbath (2:16) are characteristically Jewish. This is

---

[57] Lightfoot, "The Colossian Heresy," 73. Also, G. Bornkamm, "The Heresy of Colossians," in Watson and Meeks, *Conflict at Colossae*, 123–145.

[58] Lightfoot suggested that the Essenes ("Essene mysticism,"), 82, were illustrative of this synthesis. See further E. M. Yamauchi, "Sectarian Parallels: Qumran and Colossae," *BSac* 121 (1964) 141–152.

[59] Arnold, *The Colossian Syncretism* and Smith, *Heavenly Perspective*, followed by Moo, *Colossians*.

[60] Here I am following Ian Smith's thorough treatment, *Heavenly Perspective*, McKnight, *Colossians*, 29–34; Dunn, *Colossians*, 27–35, and Beale, *Colossians*, 12–16, who each give thorough summaries.

[61] Dunn, *Ephesians*, 33–34.

[62] Ibid., 34.

also true of language about the religious calendar, food law, and purity. But more, Paul is able to presuppose the wide structures of Jewish faith as he presents a counter to their teaching: Exodus, inheritance, wisdom and Torah. Why is Paul intent on defending the Colossian identity with reference to these traits? One possibility is that these teachings are pouring into the church from Jews living nearby and/or these ideas have made inroads among the Jewish-Christians within the church.[63]

Second, we should not imagine a uniform Judaism in the diaspora any more than we imagine such uniformity in first-century Judea. There were a variety of practices, and in the Hellenistic world some of these no doubt were shaped by their context. Jewish cultural identity could be held intact while embracing, for example, a dualism foreign to historic Jewish belief (compare Qumran). One key may be to reconstruct the opponents' beliefs based on what they fear: the powers of darkness (1:13), a notion that was widely prevalent in the ancient world. In some manner, religious practice involved the management of these powers and the possibility of escaping their threat. This could have led to promoting ascetic practices that were required to maintain safety and prosperity. Therefore, we can imagine people in the Colossian community claiming to have superior access to power ("fullness," 1:19; 2:9) through spiritually rigorous practices and visions. And from Judaism they have embraced commitments to dietary rules and sacred calendars. Above all they were anxious about angels and spiritual beings that could sorely impact their well-being.

We know not to draw a bright line between Judaism and Hellenism as if the two communities did not mix and share their identities and beliefs. If the Book of Acts provides a pattern, we need to imagine small communities of Christians in which both Jews and Gentiles lived together *and in that shared life* also shared many of the common religious sentiments of their familial communities. If the problematic teaching in Colossae emerged from the synagogue, it also arrived bearing Hellenistic influences.

A growing number of scholars have defined the Colossian problem as coming from the world of Jewish mysticism and asceticism. Some have pointed to "Merkabah" mysticism (Smith), Halakik mysticism (McKnight),

---

[63] A. R. Bevere, *Sharing in the Inheritance: Identity and Moral Life in Colossians*. JSNTSup 226 (Sheffield: Sheffield Academic Press, 2003), as noted in McKnight, *Colossians*, 30.

or Jewish folk religion (Arnold). While many still contend that these teachers may simply be rival Jews from a nearby synagogue who reject the teaching of this new church (Dunn, Garland, Wright), nevertheless these teachers have appropriated some views about salvation and enlightenment that they gathered from their religious surroundings – which makes Arnold's thesis so compelling. These antagonistic voices originated from nearby Jewish spaces but also were intimately known to those inside the church. And their views not only contradicted the growing theological agreements about Jesus in the Pauline churches, but also they added elements from Hellenistic folk religion that were aimed at undermining Christian belief. They sought out enlightenment through abstinence from eating and drinking and through these hoped-for visionary experiences that provided "heavenly ascents" to arenas where angels lived. This was then attached to much Jewish religious tradition (laws, calendars, dietary rules) as a reflection of the new spirituality they had attained. This sort of mash-up of traditional theology and folk religion should not surprise us. Christians today regularly do the same thing: They challenge and disqualify fellow Christians on peculiar issues (Christian Zionism, prosperity gospel, views of the Holy Spirit, political positions) that they believe are central to the faith but which are not – and in many cases are utterly misguided.

The number of views resolving the "philosophy" of these opponents is utterly endless, but we will argue for some synthesis of Judaism and Hellenism, with one providing the organizing center. For our efforts we will simplify their profile to some basic certainties: These are teachers who come from the synagogues and who are making claims against Gentile converts, arguing that their position is not secure. This explains – as we will see – many of the echoes to other Pauline polemical writing such as Galatians, where Paul's opponents are similar. But here in Colossae this presents itself with slight differences. The ascetism found here may well be Jewish, *but it has been living in Hellenistic settings* for a very long time. We should expect to hear echoes of the OT alongside echoes of Hellenistic mysticism and folk belief.

One example may suffice. Asia Minor exhibited remarkable interest in angels as intermediate heavenly beings. Along with this, mystics promoted the notion of the *accessibility* of these heavenly regions to those who knew their secrets. And, remarkably, this was a Jewish practice as well as

Hellenistic.[64] The *Merkabah* (Hebrew, "chariot") mysticism promoted entry to these regions, and its practice is attested widely in Jewish writings from the period.[65] Even Paul, for example, in 2Cor 12:1–10 describes his own interest in and experience with such visions and revelations. In this letter, Paul must explain that Christian faith concerns itself not with our *ascent* into the heavens but with Christ's *descent*. Our focus remains on him and his activities, not the refinement of our religious or mystical skills. This shows Paul's chief theological interest in the letter. The centrality of Christology will return again and again, and practices that strive to supplement our identity in Christ will incur sharp criticism as both inadequate and unnecessary.

PAUL'S THEOLOGICAL INTERESTS

It is hard for us to imagine the world of these Colossian believers. The celestial and the terrestrial existed in tension, and any sense of control over one's life in this world was hard-won. Divine entities (or spiritual powers) guided the fate of the average person, and the one question held by everyone was how to achieve the means to control their fate. For the most part, life seemed incomprehensible and uncertain, which inspired numerous religious systems that brought assurance and security. Some offered access to this spiritual world, which was gained by associating with intermediary powers, joining mystery cults, or pursuing visions. Personal disciplines were enforced as a way to keep from disqualifying oneself for divine benefits. Everyone (Jews included) would have been affected by this worldview.

Christology

This context helps us understand why Christology is the central focus of Colossians. Any reading of 1:15–20 or the similar texts found in 2:2–3, 2:9–10, or 2:13–15 makes this clear. To be sure, Paul has taken the Christological categories we read in his other letters and advanced them

---

[64] Smith, *Heavenly Perspective*, 47.
[65] Ibid., 48–64.

to new levels.[66] But the framework here is different. Paul portrays Christ as supreme not simply over all human life or as the fulfillment of Israel's Messianic hopes, but in connection to the cosmos itself.[67] It is Christ's supremacy that rings through every chapter of this letter. Christ is not an intermediary who may be relied on to simply aid us in all things; Christ is the Lord who rules all things. Christ's relationship with God is unlike any other (the "fullness" of God resides in him, 1:19). Therefore, Christ's power can make ultimate claims on everything, both in heaven and on Earth. There is no realm of creation that is not subject to his authority (1:15–17) because the "whole fullness of deity dwells in him bodily" (2:9). Therefore, those who are affiliated with Christ – who belong to Christ – belong to a person who has mastery over the powers that they once feared. If Christ enjoys the fullness (*plērōma*) of God, so, too, believers are "filled" in him (*plēroō*) in 2:10.

This set of affirmations works in two directions. On the one hand, the authority of Christ is absolute. He is supreme in the cosmos and is not a peer among the powers that influence the world. In fact, they are subject to him (1:16), as the creation is subject to its creator. Throughout Colossians the relationship between Jesus Christ and the Father is reinforced again and again. God is Christ's father (1:3), but also Christ is his son (1:13). Christ is now seated at God's right hand (3:1). Christ bears the visible image of the invisible God and is the "first-born" of all creation (1:15, a verse we will examine closely). The cumulative effect of these ideas is singular: Jesus Christ shares *ontologically* in the very personhood of God. Or, in different language, Jesus Christ is divine. Colossians could be seen as the capstone of an idea that sweeps through the gospels and ends here: Christ did not enter history *to represent God*; Christ entered history *to present God*. While today we may take this idea for granted, it is remarkable by any standard. In Christ, God himself has descended, *and this does not compromise a commitment to monotheism.* The gospel has rearranged the nature of creation and humanity's place in it. The gospel claims that God himself has taken charge of the

---

[66] Dunn, *Colossians*, 36, who writes,

The Christology expressed in 1:15–20 and 2:9–10 and 15 looks to be further along the trajectory ... than that of the undisputed Paulines; closest would be Rom 10:6–13; 1Cor 8:4–6; and Phil 2:6–11, but even so the thought of 1:19–20 and 2:9 is a step beyond those passages.

Also, McKnight, *Colossians*, 13.

[67] Moo, *Colossians*, 61.

presumed chaos of the world; he has penetrated this world and come himself to make a renewed claim on his creation. There is no hint here in Colossians or anywhere in Paul that this high Christology in any manner compromises monotheism. This thinking will lay the groundwork that will shape the fourth-century councils and creeds.

Christian Life

The second outworking of this idea concerns those who live in this world and who have feared the principalities and powers that rule it. If Christ is supreme, Christ is also sufficient. There is no need to *ascend* into the divine world to discover security or solace in life because God himself has *descended*. There is no need to pursue spiritual practices that will guarantee some sense of control over outcomes in life: We have been raised in Christ (3:1) and have taken on his protections and life. There is no need to fear the powers of the cosmos; believers are dead to these things (2:20). Thus everything to be had in every religious pursuit can be found in Jesus Christ, who is "the head" (2:19) of the entire body, giving it life. In a word, we are sheltered in Christ – in God – and therefore all fears should recede.[68]

Anyone who offers wisdom or secrets, rituals or mysteries does not realize that in Christ we are recipients of all wisdom (2:3), and as new persons re-created in Christ we orient not toward religious machinations in this world but to realities "above," where Christ is seated (3:1). We thus belong to another reality. "[Christ] has rescued us from the power of darkness and transferred us into the kingdom of his beloved Son" (1:13). This transfer means we belong someplace – to someone – and are not adrift in a chaotic world with various religious claimants.

I do not imagine that Paul saw this attachment to Jesus and his kingdom as simply an intellectual exercise of belief or an association with a new community (the church). For Paul, this is a Spirit-empowered rebirth, a connection with true Power that employed the categories common in the

---

[68] This brings me back immediately to students I once taught in Ndola, Zambia, where I was a visiting faculty member. One student had married a young woman whose father was a *shaman* (or witch doctor) in his village. The *shaman* was troubled by the young man because when he was present the *shaman's* "power seemed to disappear." My student concluded: "This proved that the power of Jesus was stronger than the power of the witch doctor. This is why I believe."

Colossian (or Hellenistic) context. In a world of deviant and threatening powers, Christians now are attached to the one true Power that makes the others powerless. If the mark of Christ's circumcision is on us (2:11), if we have been buried with him and raised with him (2:11), we have entered a reality that is both familiar to the religious vocabulary of antiquity but also fundamentally different. Christ-in-power now has come to reign, and we are subsumed into his rule.

While Paul will argue against those who wish to impose rules on personal conduct as a means to achieving deeper religious success (2:20–23), he does not abandon the importance of Christian conduct. The "commandments" still matter (1Cor 7:19). He can argue against "the law" in Galatians but still argue for "the law of Christ" (Gal 6:2). There is for Paul indeed saving faith, but there is also "the obedience of faith" (Rom 1:5). In Colossians we find Paul doing the same. In chapters 3 and 4 Paul outlines guidelines for conduct that will attend the lives of those who belong to the kingdom of Christ. Their basis will not be in religious traditions found in the surrounding culture. They must be rooted in this new reality found in Christ. As Moo says, "Rules must never take the place of Christ as the source of spiritual nourishment and growth; and any rules that we propose to follow must be clearly rooted in and lead back to Christ."[69] Paul's ethics in Colossians are anchored to *transformation* (3:7). We have put on a new nature (3:10) in which the peace of Christ reigns (3:15) and Christ's word dwells (3:16).

Salvation and the Church

It goes without saying that in Colossians we find then not simply a theological rearrangement that will set right the thinking of the Christians in this city. Paul's intent is not simply to locate Jesus Christ rightly in the Colossian imagination (Christology). Paul wants to make clear the choices that are before every member of the church. *This is not simply a casual affiliation*, as if membership here would be an alliance against other rival communities.

The work of Christ is cosmic, just as his Christological identity is cosmic. Christ has been at work bringing about the reconciliation and

---

[69]   Moo, *Colossians*, 70.

redemption of creation to its creator. He has provided an opening for forgiveness and the defeat of malevolent powers through his work on the cross (1:20). *Joining with this work is the decisive question that is now set before every reader of this letter.* It is not just a matter of consent to good ideas; it is a transformational experience that includes the power of God. It is not an association of good people with shared interests doing good things; it is an enclave of people who possess a vision and a life – both fueled by the Spirit – to renew this world.

If the identity and work of God is cosmic, then it follows that those who join with this work are also located in a community where the reconciliation and redemption of creation are the first order of business. If we have died and been raised with Christ (2:12) and been given new life (2:13), then the church *participates* in the ongoing life-giving, reconciling work of Christ. In Ephesians Paul describes an ecclesiology that lives at the juncture of the reconciliation of Jew and Gentile (Eph 2:11–22). This idea alone Paul finds to be astonishing, and it should lead to the church understanding race and culture in new ways. In Colossians the reconciling work of the church discovers a larger, cosmic platform, and the inclusion of Gentiles is but one example of this larger work. The church joins the reconciling work of Christ only when it sees itself as a part of this creational restoration and re-creation in all of its forms: Wherever creation is disordered – socially in human conflict and division, economically in disparities of wealth leading to poverty and suffering, racially where one claims privilege and excludes another, spiritually where malevolent powers oppress, or creationally where the world itself has been damaged through sin – in these and myriad ways the church becomes the church when it joins Christ in asserting God's rule over creation and setting things right.

COLOSSIANS AND EMPIRE

If this cosmic Christology and cosmic ecclesiology are as they seem, then it is a short step to wonder how these views would have settled in a Roman Empire that also made cosmic claims. How would these divine claims for Jesus Christ live alongside the divine claims of Caesar and his divinely endorsed rule? Colossians has become a source of fascination, and many scholars have wondered if Paul's Christology is probing imperial claims and challenging them.

What I am describing, of course, is the currently popular interest in imperial studies in Paul, which today has enthusiastic supporters and strong dissenters. Henry Maier has charted much of this territory[70] and points to Paul's description of the gospel affecting the "whole world" (1:6) and Christ's victory (2:15) as a Roman triumph as the most obvious signals of Paul's awareness of an imperial gospel opposed to his own.[71] But there is more. Hints abound that allude to imperial propaganda (universal reconciliation and "making peace," 1:20), setting Christ against a political gospel. Maier concludes:

A first-century Christian audience hearing the letter read aloud would immediately have recognized imperial-sounding themes, greeted as it was daily by ubiquitous imperial images – in market squares, theatres, baths, law courts, temples, households, on coins, on triumphal arches and public buildings, not to mention the many sacred precincts dedicated to the worship of the emperor and his family – celebrating the Roman order as a divinely ordained order representing a pacification of erstwhile hostile and ethnically dispersed peoples, brought by military might into a global *pax by* a divinely appointed emperor heading a moral, natural and spiritual renewal.[72]

Maier and others have pointed out that the principle focus of Colossian study has examined Christology alone, and this now should be viewed as too limiting, even parochial. Colossians is (for him) an "imperially charged text" bearing "potent resonances" that happily mimic and twist the language of Rome. However, the great paradox – the destabilizing idea – that Paul offers is that this victory of Christ has been achieved by defeat. "It is from the cross – a symbol of Roman pacification of enemies – in the body of Jesus' death, that a new Imperium issues forth (1.20; 2.15)."[73] The peace

---

[70] H. Maier, *Barbarians, Scythians, and Imperial Iconography in the Epistle to the Colossians.* WUNT 2.193 (Tübingen: Mohr Siebeck, 2005); H. Maier, "Reading Colossians in the Ruins: Roman Imperial Iconography, Moral Transformation, and the Construction of Christian Identity in the Lycus Valley," in Cadwallader and Trainer, *Colossae in Space and Time*, 212–231; Maier, "A Sly Civility," 323–349. For a dissenting view, see S. McKnight and J. B. Modica, *Jesus Is Lord, Caesar Is Not: Evaluating Empire in New Testament Studies* (Downers Grove: InterVarsity Press, 2013).

[71] Maier, "A Sly Civility," 326.

[72] Ibid.

[73] Ibid., 348.

has been achieved not by the suppression of Rome's enemies; peace comes from the death not of the ruled but of the ruler, and opponents are converted and invited to join a kingdom grounded in love and care for one another, a kingdom ruled by Christ himself. As Maier says, "This is an imperial *pax* by other means."[74]

Critics have pointed out that this subversive view of Rome's ideology could have easily emerged from Paul's own identity as a Jew. And this is correct. In the Roman period Israel engaged in a tricky dance with this empire that rarely tolerated dissidents. And yet Jews enjoyed remarkable freedom, all while rejecting the many gods of Rome, refusing its idols, and promoting the one true God who was the God of Abraham. This implied, of course, that Rome's gods (and the emperor?) were false claimants to divine authority. And this likely contributed to a theoretical framework for Israel's catastrophic war with Rome in the first century. But before this, at least in Paul's time, Judaism had discovered a delicate détente in relations with its imperial occupier.

LITERARY STRUCTURE

Commentators debate how to organize Colossians, but at least we can see some widely agreed-upon divisions. The letter begins with common features of greetings, a prayer, and encouragement for the readers. But the chief divider comes in 2:6, where Paul provides an array of problems concerning false teaching in the church. This "core" of the letter moves from 2:6 to 4:6. The letter closes with lists of introductions and greetings to people living in the Lycus Valley. This type of closing was also common in ancient letters. Curiously, note how Paul writes the final line in his own hand. This tells us two things: First, Paul is likely using a scribe who was professionally skilled to serve him; and second, Paul wants to add a personal mark to the letter using his imperfect writing. We see something similar in Gal 6:11, 1Cor 16:21, and particularly 2Thess 3:17, where he writes, "I, Paul, write this greeting with my own hand. This is the mark in every letter of mine; it is the way I write." This practice was common in the ancient world and is similar to our pattern

---

[74]   Ibid.

of signing letters that have been formally printed. The signature signals the letter's authenticity.

- Opening Greeting, 1:1–2
- A Prayer of Thanksgiving, 1:3–23
- A Summary of Paul's Own Ministry, 1:24–2:5
- The Concerns of the Letter, 2:6–4:6
- Final Greetings, 4:7–18
- Paul's Closing Signature, 4:18

II Commentary on Colossians

OPENING GREETING, 1:1–2

1:1   Paul, an apostle of Christ Jesus by the will of God, and Timothy our brother,

1:2   To the saints and faithful brothers and sisters in Christ in Colossae: Grace to you and peace from God our Father.

To modern readers this opening may sound abrupt, but it was a formula in ancient Roman letter writing. Acts 23:26 begins another letter that traveled with Paul from Jerusalem to Caesarea following his arrest: "Claudius Lysias to his Excellency the governor Felix, greetings." This is simply efficient: It identifies the author and, in some cases, includes the destination. Keep in mind that this letter did not travel with a modern envelope. It was likely rolled and then sealed for privacy. Only the courier knew its destination. 1 Thess 1:1 shows a similar introduction: "Paul, Silvanus, and Timothy. To the church of the Thessalonians in God the Father and the Lord Jesus Christ: Grace to you and peace." By comparison 1 John has no greeting, and this suggests it is an essay; 2 John and 3 John are classic short letters written as custom expected.

The greeting also provided writers with an opportunity to express their self-identification. The writer identifies himself as Paul (*Paulos*, **1:1**). Since Paul lived in a multilingual world, he moved regularly between Aramaic–Hebrew contexts and Roman Greek-speaking contexts. When he was in the former, he likely used the name Saul (Acts 7:58; 9:4), but when he was in Greek-speaking settings, he used Paul.[1] This was common for Jews who

---

[1]   This explanation excludes the mistaken notion that Paul's name changed from Saul to Paul as a result of his conversion (much as Abram became Abraham). For comparison, Peter's original name was the Hebrew Simeon (Acts 15:14; 2 Pet 1:1), but like many Jews

possessed Roman citizenship or had come from Hellenistic settings as Paul did. In the Book of Acts, the first time Luke refers to him as "Paul" is when he leaves Syrian Antioch and enters Cyprus (Acts 13:9). In these chapters when Paul recounts his conversion, he remembers Jesus calling him "Saul, Saul" (Acts 21:7; 26:14), which would be his personal name used at home.

Of course, finding Paul's name at the beginning of the letter opens the question of the letter's authorship, which is discussed in detail in Chapter I. But here we can say at least that the letter is claiming Paul's authority. The closing greeting of 4:18 uses it in a highly personal manner, which implies that something of Paul at least stood behind the letter. Skeptics should at least be able to imagine that the limitations of Paul's imprisonment may have led him to rely on the writing of trusted colleagues (Timothy?), which he endorsed with his own signature because it reflected his own teaching. More likely Paul's own voice (with a scribe's hand) explains the origin of the letter, with a final verse (4:18) signaling to the recipients that Paul was authorizing everything they were reading.

When Paul introduces himself as an "apostle" this refers less to a role or status he held and more to the mission that belonged to him. This term (*apostolos*) was not Paul's claim to belong to the Twelve original followers of Jesus; it was not about membership. He recognized that he did not belong to this circle (1Cor 15:5–6). However, *apostolos* carried a broader use. An apostle was an emissary, an agent, or a representative authorized by one person to deliver a message, a gift, or money to another. Such emissaries were common in the ancient world and represented one of the chief means of long-distance communication. In Jewish circles this was the *shaliach* or "agent," who had the power to do whatever his sender could do.[2]

The agent's authority was entirely based on who had sent him. Thus, an imperial courier carried imperial protection and authority. He could demand the right to be heard. Here Paul wants to be absolutely clear:

---

he began using the Greek Simon (seventy-five times in the NT) because of its similar sound. In John 1:42 Jesus assigns him the new name of Cephas (Aramaic: rock), and this too has a Greek form: *petros* or Peter (see Matt 16:18). In Gal 2:7–9 Paul can refer to him as both Cephas and Peter.

[2]   This understanding in reflected in m.Ber. 5:5, "[This is on the principle that] a man's agent is like [the man] himself." J. Neusner, *The Mishnah: A New Translation* (New Haven: Yale University Press, 1991).

He is an emissary of Christ Jesus.[3] When Paul was in prison in Rome, Epaphroditus was sent by the Philippians "as an apostle" to convey the church's commitment to Paul and serve his needs (Phil 2:25). Still others represented Christ, and so, like Barnabas, they could be called apostles (Acts 24:4, 14). In Gal 1:19 Paul suggests that James (the Lord's brother) had this title even though he was not one of the Twelve.

Still, Paul understood his apostleship as bearing a significance beyond that of, say, a church's courier. This theme is firmly asserted in Galatians 1:1 ("Paul an apostle – sent neither by human commission nor from human authorities but through Jesus Christ and God the Father") because Paul's entire effort is linked to his personal commissioning by Jesus. He does not represent a church in Jerusalem nor a decree given by a council. He has been *personally* authorized. This is important because he is making a claim that runs parallel to those original twelve apostles whose teachings were sometimes leveraged against him. Paul was authorized as they had been authorized. Paul had been sent out with a personal endorsement and commission from Jesus – and this rings through not only in his three conversion accounts in Acts, but in his own narratives about himself (Gal 1:15–16, "I did not confer with any human . . ."). In 1Cor 15:8–9 he both acknowledges the primary revelation of the resurrected Jesus to the Twelve and to as many as 500 people, but then he can describe Jesus' revelation to him, thus making him an *apostolos* as well. Still, because of his early persecution of the church, he viewed himself as an apostle with a checkered past. "For I am the least of the apostles, unfit to be called an apostle, because I persecuted the church of God" (1Cor 15:9).

When we see Paul referring to Christ Jesus without further explanation, we can see that already the title of "Christ" had become a part of the native vocabulary among the Gentile Christians. This phrase of course is Jewish: "Christ" means "messiah" or "anointed one" in Greek (*christos*), but by the time of this letter the title was fixed, and we can only wonder how thoroughly the Colossians understood that their faith was linked to a Jewish confession that Jesus was indeed the Jewish messiah. But it may

---

[3]   Paul uses both "Christ Jesus" and "Jesus Christ" in his writing. Among the so-called seven authentic Paulines, Christ Jesus appears forty-five times and Jesus Christ appears fifty-eight times. However, numerous text variants in these uses make any word count uncertain. In Colossians both terms appear: Col 1:1, 4; 2:6 (Christ Jesus) and 1:3 (Jesus Christ). There is no apparent difference.

well have meant more (without losing touch with its original Jewish context). In a Roman world where centralized authority belonged to Caesar and his empire, this title echoed a definitive rulership or possibly hinted at "King Jesus"[4] among those who had embraced Jesus at the expense of showing loyalty to Rome. Jesus was a king bringing a kingdom, "and this would have aroused deep suspicion."[5]

When Paul can refer to Christ Jesus like this, we can assume that there is a world of theological meaning behind this use. Paul is not simply a messenger from Jesus: He is a messenger bearing the body of teaching connected to this Jesus. For the earliest Christians, attachment to Christ was sufficient code to signal that they belonged to a wide religious movement with a founder (Jesus) and custodians (Paul) who protected the faith.

This effort enjoys further legitimizing[6] inasmuch as it is unfolding according to "the will of God." This addition is common in Paul's letters (Rom 1:1, 7–8; Gal 1:1; Phil 1:3–4; 1Thess 1:1–3) and underscores that this movement and this messiah belonged to efforts that stemmed from God himself. Christian mission was not merely an effort *from below* – that is, from human interest. This was a divine work *from above*. We can note how we see in Paul's mind a succession of authoritative commissions: God had given this authority to Jesus, and now Jesus had given this authority to Paul. A web of theological affirmations was already at work for how Jesus was viewed and how Paul would work.

Timothy was one of Paul's closest friends, and his name appears frequently in many of Paul's letters (2Cor 1:1; but also, Rom 16:21; Phil 1:1; 1Thess 1:1; 2Thess 1:1; Phlm 1). He served as Paul's representative frequently in difficult situations (1Cor 4:17; 16:10; Phil 2:19; 1Thess 3:2, 6). We also possess two letters sent by Paul to him. This suggests that Timothy was Paul's closest colleague, who was recognized widely among Paul's churches and who may have contributed to the writing of Colossians itself (note in 4:18 where Paul admits that he did not "write" the letter). This does not mean that Timothy wrote Colossians and that Paul signed it off, but that Paul used a scribe who, if he were Timothy, could have enjoyed remarkable freedom in this effort. It is not surprising that Paul calls him

---

4   McKnight, *Colossians*, 79–80.
5   Ibid., 80.
6   Dunn, *Colossians*, 46.

"our brother" – which is a symbolic kinship, indicating intimacy and trust. Both Jews and Greeks used this term frequently for personal familiar relationships.[7] In 1Cor 4:17 Paul can write to the Corinthians, "For this reason I sent you Timothy, who is my beloved and trustworthy child in the Lord, to remind you of my ways in Christ Jesus." In Phil 2:19–23 Paul refers to him "as a son with a father who has served with me in the gospel" (22).

The letter is addressed to "the saints and faithful brothers [and sisters][8] in Christ in Colossae" (1:2). There is one definite article covering this phrase, and so the notion is singular: These are brothers and sisters who are both holy and faithful. The NRSV "saints" translates *hagios*, which in its Jewish form refers to sacred separation from things that are profane. It means those who are dedicated (to God) or consecrated with a singularity of purpose. Paul frequently opens his letters with this greeting (Rom 1:7; 1Cor 1:2; 2Cor 1:1; Phil 1:1; Eph 1:1), and for Jewish readers it was a common descriptor of God's people (Ps. 16:3; 34:9; Dan 7:18; Tob 8:15). It is all the more striking here that Paul would write to a Gentile church and apply to them an adjective well-known in the Hebrew Bible. This is in accord with Paul's interests throughout his letters. He expects the full inclusion of Gentile Christians into the family of Israel who have been adopted through faith in Jesus Christ. They too are children of Abraham (Rom 4:16).

Paul rarely addresses his readers as "faithful" (only elsewhere Eph 1:1). Some have tried to make this a backhanded compliment and to suggest that Paul means the opposite of what he says. That is, because of the philosophy now infiltrating the church (2:8), the Colossians have been less than faithful. This suggestion of a hidden nuance or a cynical purpose is entirely unnecessary. Paul is not shy about exhorting his churches when their faith or loyalty to Christ are failing. In Eph 1:1 Paul uses the term with no such intent. Thus, here, Paul is recognizing their faithfulness, *and this is the ground of his thanksgiving* that begins in 1:3. Despite what they

---

[7]   BDAG, 18–19, which illustrates widespread figurative usage of *adelphos* by Jesus (Matt 12:50; Mark 3:35) and Christians in their relation to each other (Rom 16:23; 1Cor 1:1, etc.), as well as other writers such as Josephus, Qumran, Clement, Barnabas, and Ignatius.

[8]   Paul here uses the plural *adelphoi* (*adelphos*, brother), which would be understood to include all members of the church, men and women.

have experienced and the deviations to faith they have seen, still they are holding fast to Christ (2:19).

Note that Paul can understand that these believers live both "in Colossae" and "in Christ." The Greek form of these phrases is identical and suggests the dual identity that Christians held. They belonged to their city – something every Roman held seriously; but they also belonged to Christ in a parallel manner. This is the first of three uses of "in Christ" in Colossians (1:2, 4, 28; but see 2:5). If life in Colossae was known as a location, life "in Christ" was equally comprehensive. They have been incorporated into him, they died in him, and they have been made alive in him (2:12). Therefore, Christ was making a claim on them and shifting their identity potentially but also significantly away from identities assigned by Rome.

The greeting that follows ("grace to you and peace") is one of the most common features of every Pauline letter and likely reflects the apostle's habitual form (see Phlm 3). 1 Thessalonians differs but is written quite early. The use of grace in a greeting was not unique to Christians but was a standard known widely among Greek writers. A form of it (*chairein*) was simply how you said "hi" to a friend. Paul here has adapted it with a noun (*charis*, grace) and joined it to peace, which was the ancient form of Jewish greeting (Hebrew *shalom*). Jews would often employ peace with mercy as their twin greetings (Isa 54:10; Sir 50:23), which is what Paul does in 1 Timothy and 2 Timothy: "Grace, mercy, and peace from God the Father and Christ Jesus our Lord."[9] But it is not surprising that, for Paul, grace was the critical word – not because it was a familiar congenial saying, but because it reflected the theological idea so central to his message. But more, where Paul was addressing churches like Colossae, where conflict and division were active, these greetings would have special importance.

But the source of this grace and peace did not belong to Paul. He was an apostle, a courier of something commissioned by his sender. And in this case, he was bearing a gift of grace and peace that came from *God our Father*. This, then, is a casual greeting that is bearing a significant theological message. To call God "father" was familiar to Romans who

---

9   The Greek text of Col 1:2 in its shorter form (shown here) is likely original. Scribes extended it to reflect a longer greeting: "Grace to you and peace from God our father *and our Lord Jesus Christ.*"

frequently called their own many gods with this title. Paul does not need to explain that this reference is entirely Jewish: *The God of Israel was known as the Father of Israel* (Dt 32:6; Jer 31:9). And, most remarkably, here Paul is addressing Gentiles and incorporating them in this relationship. *This is "our" Father.* Here we find a hint of a theme that appears throughout Paul's letters and will surface strongly in Colossians. The identity of these Gentile Christians now lives in the same relationship with the God of the Old Testament as did any Jew who claimed this privilege due to their link to Abraham. The Gentiles of Colossae who held faith in Jesus were sons and daughters of Yahweh alongside any other believing Jew.

This opening reminds me of Barth's remarkable comments on Romans 1:1 penned in 1918 (and revised five times).[10] There Barth remarks on Paul's word that his gospel is a gospel *of God*. "Yes, precisely – *of God*. The Gospel is not a religious message to inform mankind of their divinity or to tell them how they may become divine. The Gospel proclaims a God utterly distinct from men." For Barth, this gospel was to be compared with the many forms of religious nationalism active in Germany in the early twentieth century. Paul's declaration here strikes the same note: This is a gospel from *God our Father*. It is not a message that competes with imperial decrees; it is a message that makes them obsolete because its authority supersedes any other claimant to divine authority.

A PRAYER OF THANKSGIVING, 1:3–23

1:3–8 A Prayer of Thanksgiving: For the Church

1:3 In our prayers for you we always thank God, the Father of our Lord Jesus Christ,

1:4 for we have heard of your faith in Christ Jesus and of the love that you have for all the saints,

1:5 because of the hope laid up for you in heaven. You have heard of this hope before in the word of the truth, the gospel

1:6 that has come to you. Just as it is bearing fruit and growing in the whole world, so it has been bearing fruit among yourselves from the day you heard it and truly comprehended the grace of God.

---

[10] K. Barth, *The Epistle to the Romans*, 3rd edition (London: ET Hoskyns, E.C., 1950), 28.

1:7 This you learned from Epaphras, our beloved fellow servant. He is a faithful minister of Christ on our behalf,

1:8 and he has made known to us your love in the Spirit.

Both Jews and Romans had a legacy of opening a letter with prayers for their recipients (Lev 7:12–13, 15; 22:29; 2Chron 5:13; 33:16; Neh 12:8; Ps 42:4; 50:14, 23; Isa 51:3; Jer 30:19, etc.). Prayers begin most of Paul's letters, and the one we find in Philemon – written at the same time – is particularly interesting in comparison (Phlm 4–7). We could also view a prayer like this as Paul's introduction of himself and his desire to build goodwill with the Colossians. He has not been to the church (1:4), and so what he writes shapes his image in his readers' minds. It therefore has a rhetorical strategy of persuasion and anticipates the argument he will make in later paragraphs. The prayer itself has two movements: a prayer of thanksgiving for the church (1:3–8) and a prayer for the fellow believers in Colossae (1:9–14). Together these prayers provide an outline of the apostle's commitments – priorities that have been emulated by Christians for centuries.

Paul's first prayer rises to a note of celebration. He is grateful that the gospel that God has brought into the world through Jesus has arrived in Colossae. His celebration is not simply that there is a Colossian church, but that God's efforts are increasingly successful in the world, *and now the Colossians are an outpost of this divine incursion.* The Colossians need to be clear about what they belong to. Their identification as "followers of Jesus" is nothing short of a commitment to the "genuine truth which is the gospel" (1:5). This truth centers on the grace of God and has now been made visible (1:6). This nod to the truth so early sets a tone that we (and they) must anticipate. If the gospel reflects what is true about creation, we must imagine that there are others who are contending for the truth as well, and their claims are wrong. However, this realization of what is true is not the only feature of their identity. The Colossians are exhibiting lives shaped by the Spirit (1:8), which makes them stand out in the world. They love other believers (the saints, 1:4, 8), and their lives are bearing fruit (1:6) – all of which signaling that they belong to a grand unfolding of God's plan in the world. Two signposts thus stand as markers of God's-people-in-Christ: They understand and defend the truth and they live exemplary lives inspired by the Spirit.

Immediately Paul has announced the alien character of this discipleship. The Colossians' new Christian identity is not a casual involvement that aims simply to improve their prospects in life or their religious loyalty to Rome (something many religions offered). *In fact, Christ and Rome are at odds* – and this will become the unsettling revelation. Jesus' gospel is demanding an alternative imagination for the world[11] and will contest the nature of fruitfulness and the nature of truth itself.[12] It is *comprehensive* in the fullest sense of the word, and every alternative voice that claims they possess the truth without the gospel is now null and void. This is a gospel that does not live in cooperation with the ideologies of the world; it contends with them and forces them to reckon with something more powerful than they had imagined.

Paul and Timothy ("*our* prayers") direct their petitions (**1:3**) to God, who is defined *not* as a solitary figure but in relationship to Jesus Christ. That is, Paul cannot imagine God the Father without imagining likewise how he is linked to Jesus Christ. Paul's reflex is always to think Christologically. As a Jew might closely define God as the "God of Abraham" (Gen 26:24) – that is, the God who was known to Abraham and began his redemptive work through him (and Israel) – so now Paul *as a Jew* is offering his own close redefinition: This is the God of the Lord Jesus who is also the Messiah.

However, there is more. This is "*the Lord* Jesus Christ," and this attribution (*kyrios*, lord) tells us more (see also Rom 10:13; 1Cor 8:5–6; Phil 2:9–11). Some have tried to see in this title a rivalry with Caesar, who was also *kyrios*. This might be true, but the most obvious meaning penned by a Jew is to find our antecedent in the OT. In the LXX *kyrios* was the usual translation of "Yahweh." Therefore, Paul wishes to be clear. With Dunn: "[T]he high Christology to be enunciated shortly is kept within the constraints of Jewish monotheism."[13] Prayer, then, is to be offered to God, but given through the Lord Jesus (Col 3:17), or, as in Rom 1:8, thanksgiving is offered to God, but also through Jesus Christ. Jesus is the sole mediator for access to and understanding of the one true God.

---

[11]   B. Walsh and S. Keesmaat, *Colossians Remixed. Subverting Empire* (Downers Grove: InterVarsity Press), 64.
[12]   Ibid., 65, 96.
[13]   Dunn, *Colossians*, 56.

When Paul says that he prays *always* (*pantote*), he does not mean that he prays all day. We think that Paul was practicing the standard regimen of Jewish prayer. This meant prayer twice per day ("when you lie down and when you get up," Ez 9:5; Dan 9:21), and this was mirrored by temple services at the same time: just after sunrise and just before sunset (Josephus, *Antiq.* 4.212).[14] To this some Jews added a mid-afternoon prayer of thanksgiving, which Jesus may refer to in Mt 6:5–6. This triple discipline is likely to have been with Paul his entire life, and, as a Christian, he simply continued with it.

Paul's knowledge of these Colossians is secondhand (1:4), and he indicates that he had heard reports of their lives ("for we have heard"). But what did he hear? What follows in **1:4–5** is the famous triad of Christian identity and life noted throughout the NT: faith, love, and hope.[15] Its most famous formulation is in 1Cor 13:13: "And now faith, hope, and love remain, these three, and the greatest of these is love" (see the similar but abridged list in Phlm 5).

The triad consistently begins with faith, but this is not an ambiguous sentiment of wishing for something; this is faith in Jesus, which is the anchoring concept, and it is accompanied by both love and hope.[16] Faith is our investment in the saving activity of Jesus Christ throughout Paul (Rom 10:9, 14; 13:11; 1Cor 1:21; 2:5; 15:2, 11; Gal 2:16). This is obedient acceptance of God's grace shown at the cross, and so faith is often associated with grace in Paul (Col 1:2, 6; Rom 4:4f, 16).[17] Therefore faith is not merely an intellectual assent to doctrines. "It is a vibrant force that expresses itself in how we live."[18] It is heart-knowledge wed to heartfelt investment in the life of another. Paul will soon enough acknowledge that the Colossian faith needs strengthening (2:5), but for now it is enough.

---

[14] E. P. Sanders, *Jewish Law from Jesus to the Mishna* (London: SCM, 1990), 74–75; B. Hunter, "Prayer," *DPL* 725–734; Wright, *Colossians*, 50.

[15] In Paul: 1Thess 1:3; Gal 5:5–6; Rom 5:1–5; 1Cor 13:13; Eph 4:2–5; elsewhere: Heb 6:10–12; 10:22–24; 1Pet 1:3–8, 21–22.

[16] Generally, Paul refers to faith in Christ using *eis Christou Iēsou* rather than *en Christō* as we have here in 1:4. The so-called post-Pauline letters reflect *en* with the dative; the so-called authentic Pauline letters use *eis* followed by the genitive (Gal 2:16; Rom 10:14). However, there is no significant difference in meaning between the phrases. Dunn, *Colossians*, 57.

[17] G. Barth, "*pistis*," *EDNT*, 3:97.

[18] Garland, *Colossians*, 46.

A foothold has been found; these men and women are attached to Christ, and this has begun to change them.

Accompanying this faith is love. This too isn't merely an abstract affection. They love "the saints" – that is, the believers in Christ who can be found anywhere. This term (*hagios*, saints) refers to holiness (*hagiazō*) or, better, those who are consecrated or dedicated to God's purposes. Thus, Jesus is "the holy one of God" (Mark 1:24; John 6:69). Paul can refer to the church as a holy temple (Eph 2:21; 1Cor 6:19), and so Christians are made holy by Christ (1Cor 1:2), including Gentiles (Eph 2:19). This is not an inherent status but a gift, given through grace, through Jesus' purifying death on the cross (Rom 1:6; 1Cor 1:24; Phil 1:1).

Loving the saints means loving the church. We might find it unremarkable that Paul would underscore love as the second attribute for Christian identity. But it was unusual in his period. Christians used a peculiar term, *agapē*, and this was rarely used in the non-biblical Greek of the period. But for Paul it is the key noun that expresses the fullest nature of Christ's work (Rom 5:6–8) – an expression of love – and the nature of Christian life within the community of believers. The work of Christ into which we invest faith is an exhibit of the love of God, and such love inspires ongoing love among God's people. Note that love heads the list of "fruit of the Spirit" described by Paul in Gal 5:22.

It is fascinating that in **1:5** Paul does not say what we might expect: that faith in Christ brings with it hope. He reverses this: Faith is grounded in hope (*because* of this hope). Hope is not simply a disposition of expectation but refers to something specifically hoped for. And here we see that Paul has in mind the glorious future God has prepared for us in heaven (John 14:1–4; Rom 8:24; Titus 2:13). This is a sentiment that belongs to antiquity as much as it belongs to us. Our discipleship may begin when we escape a worldview of despair that seems so prevalent in the modern world. When our hope in Christ is seen with clarity, faith emerges with new strength.

We might think of this hope taking two forms: There is the eschatological hope that a heavenly place for God's people is secure (**1:5a**), but also we know of this hope because it lives within that larger truth found in the gospel (**1:5b**). This recognition that truth can be had and that certainty about the world may be possessed is an enormous gift to people living in a world with many contenders for truth. Ultimately, they may abandon confidence in truth altogether, but here Paul says that truth is located in what God has done, and it begins with the revelation of Jesus Christ.

Together, this triad – faith, love, and hope – is the fruit that is the first evidence of the Spirit's work in the world (**1:6**). In 1:8 Paul will say that love inspired by the Spirit is already at work in the church. Notice that the catalyst for this hope is what came before: our initial (or earlier) hearing of "the word of truth, namely, the gospel." The biblical idea of hearing (Hebrew *shema*) appears throughout the OT and describes the posture of God's people before God's word. There are three foci: We listen carefully and attentively, we absorb this word into our hearts and embrace it, and we act with obedience. This is why the word "hear" sometimes means "obey." It describes a process in which we do not listen casually but we engage ourselves completely and obediently.[19] The Colossians thus have "heard" the word through Epaphras (**1:7**), and no doubt this hearing-as-obedience has resulted in the transformation of their hearts and minds. And now this hearing is producing the fruit of changed lives that unlearn skepticism and relearn how to believe, how to love, and how to hope.

The revelation embraced by them is *the gospel*. This word was not common in religious circles but became crucial for Paul's explanation for what he preached (sixty of seventy-six uses of it in the NT belong to Paul). Of course the term simply means "good news," but we are easily mistaken here. This is not simply the good news of our salvation or the moment we are saved. The gospel is where we *comprehend* the grace of God (**1:6b**), and here Paul uses a peculiar term for this knowing (*epiginōskō* rather than the usual *ginwōskō*). The prefix likely intensifies the verb, and so translations attempt to reflect this: They understood, comprehended, even experienced the truth of the gospel. He even adds an intensifier (truly) that underscores this further. This points to an authentic encounter with grace (not intellectual knowledge), which is a different sort of knowing, and one that shapes us. But knowing the gospel is also knowing the substance of what fills the gospel with grace. The gospel is the fullest message about Jesus. As Paul says in 1 Tim 2:8, "Remember Jesus Christ, raised from the dead, a descendant of David – *that is my gospel*." The gospel is a comprehensive (creedal perhaps) message about Jesus' fullest identity – messiah, Son of

---

[19] McKnight, *Colossians*, 96.

David, Lord, Son of God – and his saving work – death, resurrection, ascension. It is good news that bares the substance of Christian belief.

Moreover, Paul tells us that this gospel is *true* (**1:5b**). This is the prophetic message of Paul's declaration. Paul believes that we have a tenuous commitment to the truth. He writes in Rom 1:18: "For the wrath of God is revealed from heaven against all ungodliness and injustice of those who by their injustice suppress the truth" (also Rom 1:25). People reject the truth (Rom 2:8). The important Johannine story of the blind man in John 9 ends with Jesus' judgment of the Pharisees: They claim to see this truth, but in fact they are the blind ones because they cannot truly see it (9:39–41). Therefore, by implication, this declaration of truth revealed in Christ makes other contenders for truth *untrue*. This would include some religious teachers at Colossae as well as political claimants – including Rome. The truth must begin with Jesus and not any rival way of thinking.

Paul provides praise for Epaphras[20] (**1:7**), who was likely the founder of the church at Colossae. We know nothing substantial about him but that he belongs to the ranks of those unrecognized leaders of the church (both then and now) who rarely enjoyed any acclaim. He possibly met Paul in the older church at Ephesus, which Paul knew so well (it was only 120 miles away). Recall that Paul first came to Ephesus at the close of his second tour (Acts 18:19–20) and midway through his third tour when he remained in the church for two years (Acts 19:1–41, 10). Paul returned for the last time at the end of this final tour when he called together and addressed the Ephesian elders with tears (Acts 20:17–28). We can imagine Epaphras within this audience. But Epaphras' hometown was Colossae (Col 4:12), and we can also imagine him bringing the gospel to the entire upper Lycus Valley as Paul's representative. But now Epaphras was with Paul supporting him in Rome, serving him dutifully during this imprisonment (Col 4:13; Phlm 23).

This is perhaps why Paul can refer to Epaphras so personally and give him a double endorsement (1:7–8; 4:12–13). But this is more than an endorsement: It is an *apostolic* endorsement that certainly carried significant weight and gave the Colossians confidence in the gospel they now

---

[20] This is likely a shortened form of the Greek Epaphroditos (BDAG 360) but probably not the same person as we have in Phil 2:25; 4:18. Abbott, *Colossians*, 199.

embraced.[21] He is both a beloved fellow servant (*syn* + *doulos*) and a faithful minister (*diakonos*). Epaphras understood that he was working *on behalf* on Paul (**1:7b**).[22] He belonged to a network of missionaries and ministers, headed by Paul, who represented the gospel *as explained* by Paul. But if Paul was a slave of Christ – and Epaphras is working alongside him or under him – this means that Epaphras' work is also being done in coordination with God's work. Wright comments: "As Epaphras works, God works; as he preaches, God opens the understanding of the hearers; as he lays before them the facts about Jesus, they recognize those facts to be true. Like a man who suddenly learns that he has inherited a fortune, the Colossians are possessed of new knowledge which cannot but revolutionize their lives."[23]

These affirmations for Epaphras are inspiring. *Beloved* is one of Paul's most frequent words given to his coworkers (Rom 16:9; 1Cor 4:17; Col 4:7, 9; Phlm 1) as well as ordinary believers (Rom 16:8). It echoes the intimate nature of the earliest church, when family metaphors ("brother," "sister") were commonly used (Col 1:2). *Fellow slave* (*syndoulos*) is striking. Epaphras was joined with Paul in the apostle's most grave self-designation. Paul commonly referred to himself as a slave in his letters (Rom 1:1; Gal 1:10; Phil 1:1, etc.). To Greek and Roman ears, such a reference would be viewed as odd since slavery meant the loss of freedom – a treasured status. But it also had a wide variety of religious uses. Israel could refer to itself as a slave of God (Dt 32:36; Josh 24:29; Ps 89:3; 105:26; Mal 4:4), and members of Roman cults could use slavery titles for themselves to reflect their utter devotion to their god. Lastly, Epaphras was *faithful* or, perhaps, trustworthy as someone serving Paul (*pistos*). But here as a servant, Paul says, Epaphras could be trusted, affirming once again the reliability of his teaching when he was at Colossae.

---

[21] Ibid., 199.
[22] Some manuscripts and translations reflect a variant in 1:7b. On "our" behalf is reflected in the RSV, NIV, NASB, NET, and REB. On "your" behalf appears in the ESV, NRSV, NLT, and NAB. The new NRSVue has now changed this to "our." If we read "your," then the verse point to Epaphras' faithfulness as a minister to Colossae. If we see this as "our," then it points to Epaphras' reliability, which is precisely what Paul wants to underscore. Lightfoot (*Colossians*, 136) supports *our behalf* and suggests that the change to *your behalf* came through a scribal confusion with 1:3 and especially 1:9.
[23] Wright, *Colossians*, 55.

But the Colossians have admirable traits as well. They love the church broadly (1:4), but now Paul tells them that he is aware of one hallmark in their lives (1:8). Epaphras has not only reported to Paul about their faith, but more, he has reported about their remarkable love. This is more evidence of the growing fruit (of the Spirit) that is sweeping the world (1:5). This may even mean more than is evident in the text. Paul may be alluding with subtlety to the Colossian love for him, which, in prison, would give him enormous encouragement.

1:9–14 A Prayer of Thanksgiving: For the Colossians

1:9 For this reason, since the day we heard it, we have not ceased praying for you and asking that you may be filled with the knowledge of God's will in all spiritual wisdom and understanding,

1:10 so that you may walk worthy of the Lord, fully pleasing to him, as you bear fruit in every good work and as you grow in the knowledge of God.

1:11 May you be made strong with all the strength that comes from his glorious power, so that you may have all endurance and patience, joyfully

1:12 giving thanks to the Father, who has enabled you to share in the inheritance of the saints in the light.

1:13 He has rescued us from the power of darkness and transferred us into the kingdom of his beloved Son,

1:14 in whom we have redemption, the forgiveness of sins.

It is not unusual for Paul to move in prayer from thanksgiving to the personal needs of a church. In his first section (1:3–8) Paul gives praise for what he has heard about the Colossians, no doubt through the report of his friend Epaphras. Much of this is by way of affirmation. But indirectly, by describing his reasons for celebration in 1:9–14, he is signaling to the church what things he values most: their love for the church (and him), their faith, and their comprehension of the gospel and all that it entails. It is these good things already at work in them that he will now build on as the letter progresses.

Because of these realities ("For this reason," 1:9), Paul now tells the Colossians what he prays for them. This is a form of encouragement, to be sure, but it also migrates into something else. Paul tells them that he desires that they fully know God's will, and this is broken down in detail with a series of explanatory phrases. As the Colossians read this, a subtle exhortation emerges, much as if someone told us, "I am praying for your growth in wisdom." At once we might wonder if *we need to grow in wisdom*. But this is all by way of preparation because, in the next section, Paul will convey the very substantial things they need to know – and underlying this next section will be the assumption that things are not well at the church. These petitions, then, give us a fuller profile of what Colossian life was like and what it needs.

The section is a very long Greek sentence suspended by a series of participles and conjunctions. But it begins with Paul's opening affirmation: He has not stopped praying for them *so that* they might be filled with the knowledge of God's will in all spiritual wisdom and understanding. The content of that will and its implications are then explained, one modifying the other. But as Garland points out, Paul's desire is not that they gain knowledge for its own sake. This knowledge will have "ethical implications" because it requires them (and us) to live lives aligned with what God desires: lives that are "fully pleasing" to the Lord – lives that are "worthy of the Lord." And this, Garland suggests, is why so many will not explore God's will like this. *It will make a claim on us* and force us to suspend many of our other commitments. We will be forced to see life from God's perspective. "God gives us knowledge to lead us to a deeper faith, greater virtue, and more devout service."[24] We may prefer collecting knowledge that does not impinge on how we live and believe.

The prayer could be divided into three parts. Paul describes that he is asking that the Colossians will know God's will – and that this knowledge will result in lives lived that are pleasing to the Lord. He then lists what such a life might look like and uses four participles to explain it (bearing fruit, growing, being empowered, giving thanks). Finally, Paul reminds them that this embrace of God's will has led to their rescue: both from sin but also from the power of darkness.

Again and again, Paul will use the language of knowledge in a variety of ways. And this likely springs from his awareness of how *knowledge* is being bandied about in the community, particularly among the false teachers in

---

[24]   Garland, *Colossians*, 65.

the church. The knowledge of God's will implies that there is something to be known, something to be revealed, such as a "corpus of divine truth."[25] Paul will not fall into the trap of debating the merits of differing bodies of truth either from Jewish legalists or Hellenistic philosophy. For him, "God's will is embodied in a person,"[26] and apart from a right understanding of what God has done in Jesus, it is not possible to understand the most important truths about this world.

Paul's prayers have been inspired by news of the Colossian love for him, the church, and its mission (**1:9**). And this has led him to pray consistently and regularly for them (see 1:3 on Paul's prayer disciplines). Paul often refers to praying for his churches regularly (Rom 1:9–10; Eph 1:17; Phil 1:9; 1Thess 1:2–3; Phlm 6), and here he continues to employ the plural, drawing Timothy into this effort (*we have not stopped praying*). Here Paul unfolds the content of those prayers. He has not stopped (1) praying and (2) asking God for one gift on behalf of this church: *that they may be filled with the knowledge of God's will* – and that this knowledge would be shaped by wisdom and spiritual understanding. As in 1:6 Paul uses a specialized term for knowing (*epiginōskō* rather than the usual *ginwōskō*), and it may refer to a deeper comprehension.[27] For many of us today, we see this reference to God's will and privatize it. *We want to know God's will for us.* But this is not Paul's meaning. We might paraphrase to get at Paul's intent: *knowing God's purposes.* This then hints at what is to come. Knowing God's will is a common refrain in the OT, where knowledge, wisdom, and understanding – the three terms appearing in 1:9 – appear as virtues, often accompanied by the Spirit (Ex 31:3). Here Paul modifies each: It is knowledge *of God's* will; *all* wisdom; and understanding *in the Spirit.* "The Spirit" can just as easily modify both wisdom and understanding as it appears in many translations.

The aim of this prayer must be seen in light of the polemic that will emerge with force in 1:15. If the church is having to contend with Hellenistic or Jewish mystics who were presenting an alternative

---

[25] Caird, *Colossians*, 170.
[26] Ibid.
[27] Here Paul uses *epignōsis* for knowledge (rather than *gnosis*). It is unclear whether these are to be distinguished here, but at best the prefix *epi* is an intensifier: *thorough knowledge.* See their parallel uses in 2:2, 3. See Lightfoot, *Colossians*, 138, who cites patristic remarks. See also on 1:6.

explanation of the world and particularly claiming access to knowledge from the heavens (from where they learn what they know), Paul's prayer here is anticipating the problem. Paul is addressing the larger question about how we know God's purposes for his world. Or we might say: Paul yearns that they would comprehend God's relation to and purposes for his creation. Such knowledge will demand discernment (**1:9b**). But if gained rightly, it will be like a good compass in a storm in which, despite the chaos of the weather, true north is within reach. When Paul says he desires that they be "filled" (*plēroō*), this is evocative as well. This *filling* was a popular Hellenistic term for the utterly comprehensive or ecstatic experience of revelation in various cult settings. And Paul will use its nominal form to express how the fullness of God (1:19) and the fullness of deity (2:9) rest on Christ. Paul prays that the Colossian depth of knowledge would fit into this world of ideas.

This reflex to discern God's will and obey it is a deeply Jewish idea (Ps 143:10) that was echoed by Jesus ("May your will be done; on earth as it is in heaven," Mt 6:10) and the early Christians ("So do not be foolish, but understand what the will of the Lord is," Eph 5:17). For Jews, this knowledge could be obtained through the law (or God's word), and while Paul implies no contrast, he is thinking along the same lines: *Knowing God's will can change us and lead to new obedience.* But this requires spiritual wisdom and spiritual understanding.[28] These two terms, wisdom (*sophia*) and understanding (*synesis*), would have been recognized immediately by any who knew Greek philosophy. For Aristotle these were among the three great virtues (including *phronesis*, moral insight) deeply related to the qualities of a person's soul. And from these could spring the great virtues of a well-lived life.[29] Like Judaism, this deep discernment of God's will comes from God's Spirit (Ex 35:31) and is not an intellectually won ability. In Is 11:2 this is the attribute that will belong to the anointed messiah and all those who fear the Lord (Prov 1:7; 2:2).

The object of this Spirit-inspired knowledge (**1:10**) is not simply the acquisition of knowledge for its own sake. Its purpose is ethical and

---

[28] The adjective "spiritual" (*pneumatikos*) appears the end of the phrase but grammatically can be used as a modifier for both terms.

[29] TDNT 9:220–235.

moral.[30] An awakening in our thinking should lead to a transformation in how we live. This is knowledge that changes us. "Walking" is not a usual Greek term for moral conduct but is typically Jewish (Exod 18:20; Deut 13:4–5; also, Col 2:6; 3:7; 4:5) describing the conduct or rhythms of a life.[31] The Hebrew context imagines life as a path one walks, and the destination as well as the conduct along that path determine who we are. Proverbs 2:12–20 describes this well.[32]

The language of **1:9–10** describes a full-orbed view of the Christian life. We grow in knowledge and, thanks to the Spirit, deepen in wisdom and understanding. This leads to a life that is fruit-bearing (in good works) and a life that is deepening in divine knowledge.[33] Of course, this does not mean that Paul expects the Colossians to be perfect – this still awaits us in the future (Phil 3:12). Nevertheless, those who pursue this sort of discipleship do please God (Rom 12:1–2). And they are characterized by "good works," something Paul stresses in many of his letters (Rom 13:3; 2Cor 9:8; Phil 1:6; Gal 6:10; 2Thess 2:17; Titus 1:16).

What follows (**1:11**) is a continuation of the attributes of this desired life pleasing to God. Such a life is strong. Another participle fills out the profile of this life now defined through the power of God similar to Paul's reference to the Spirit in 1:9. This life is (literally) *empowered in all power* (which is a Hebrew idiom), and without doubt this directs us again to the Spirit. But here Paul sees this power as sourced in the glory of God. This too is a Hebrew concept referring to the OT *kabod* or glory of God, which radiates from his presence (Exod 16:10; 24:16–17; 33:17–23; Isa 66:18–19) and resided at the Temple. Its radiance brought power, and this inspired fear among the Israelites (Exod 19:19–24; Num 16:19–35). This idea of divine radiance as power was as familiar to Paul, as it was common in the Judaism of his time (Rom 1:20; 9:17; 1Cor 1:18; 2Cor 13:4). But it was also something that was significant in Hellenistic religion and may be intentionally prominent here.[34] Here Paul prays that they will be empowered "in

---

[30] Paul here introduces the purpose clause with an infinitive, *so that you may walk*, and this is followed by participles describing this walking. Some argue that this infinitive introduces result, but this changes the meaning of the verse little.

[31] TDNT 5:941.

[32] Moo, *Colossians*, 95.

[33] Both *bearing fruit* and *knowing* are participles standing together to show the twin outcomes of this life pleasing to God.

[34] See C. E. Arnold, *The Colossian Syncretism: The Interface between Christianity and Folk Belief at Colossae* (Grand Rapids: Baker, 1996), 158–194.

all things," which simply refers to something that is complete or unlimited. Moo translates effectively: "strengthened by God with the greatest strength possible."[35] Or more fully: "empowered fully and completely by the strength of God's glory which will result in all endurance and forbearance."

We know from Col 2:8, 20 that the threat of spiritual powers leveraging their influence in Colossae was a major concern. As we will see in chapter 2, the threat is either from powers governing the physical elements such as the sun and moon or personal heavenly powers such as demons who may have descended upon them. The powers could even angels. Here in 1:11 Paul is providing reassurance (as he will in chapter 2) that, despite the spiritual forces arrayed against or around them – spiritual forces that fascinated both Jews and pagans in this period – the Colossians have access to power, strength, and endurance that exceed anything someone else may point to. Modern Western Christians think of the promise of God's power as his presence strengthening our moral resolve. The ancient world understood this, but it was secondary to an imagined reality populated by spiritual powers that could harm them. Controlling and interpreting such powers was the work of mystics and magicians. Paul's simple words to the Colossians: *They are protected.* The strength of the glory of God is upon them. My own experiences teaching in Central Africa and the Middle East awakened me to worldviews that we in the West may have lost, where power is central to religious life (not reason or feeling).

This (**1:12**) is now the fourth of four participles (begun in 1:10) that expand the definition of a life that is flourishing and pleasing to God: *bearing* fruit in good works, *growing* in the knowledge of God, *being empowered* with strength in endurance, and *giving* thanks. Recall that the NT did not have verse divisions in its original form. Paul's reference to joy at the end of 1:11 easily applies to the following phrase (*giving thanks*) in 1:12. Thus: giving thanks joyfully. Paul often writes to his churches that joy should be an attribute of our life with God (Phil 4:4–6; 1Thess 5:16–18) despite the hardships of this world. Discipleship is not a matter of "grim endurance,"[36] but joy can be sustained when we realize how God is participating on our behalf. Joy accompanies the thanksgiving Paul prays

---

[35] Moo, *Colossians*, 97.
[36] Dunn, *Colossians*, 75.

for these Colossians because they have been endowed with the good things just listed.

The basis of this joyous thanksgiving is that the Colossians now share in "the inheritance of the saints in the light." That God has enabled (*ikanoō*) or made us able to inherit speaks to his grace and generosity. Gentiles who were not able to share in Israel's legacy now are invited into it as full members. This notion of inheritance would resonate with readers from a Jewish background. The inheritance of the saints (**1:12b**) is Jewish language for all of the blessings that flow from Israel's covenants. Inheritance in particular refers to land – holy land – linked to the Abrahamic promises. For Paul, who connects Gentile believers directly to Abraham (Gal 3:6–9), this is an incidental application of what he works out in detail in Romans 4.

But are these saints human or angelic? The former is often Paul's meaning (1Thess 3:13; 2Thess 1:10), but Paul may also have in mind angelic beings ("in the light"), since "saints" can bear this meaning as well (Job 5:1; Tob 11:14; Mark 8:38).[37] In this case, the concern in 2:18 referring to the worship of angels becomes immediately relevant. Paul is saying that rather than being subservient to these heavenly beings, the Colossians have in Christ inherited a placed shared by these angels.

This joy-in-thanksgiving now takes on another dimension (**1:13**) because not only are we heirs with those in the light, but we have been rescued from the powers of darkness. This now is the second dimension of the Father's work: *He qualifies us and rescues* (rhoumai) *us.* This language follows a vital OT motif of Exodus–rescue from Egypt. God is a redeemer who enters the enemy territory that holds his people captive and rescues them, bringing them to safety. The LXX language of redemption mirrors this: "I am the LORD, and I will free you from the burdens [or power] of the Egyptians and deliver (*rhoumai*) you from slavery to them. I will redeem you with an outstretched arm and with great acts of judgment" (Exod 6:6; cf. 14:30). But here Paul does not have Egypt in mind; the rescue is from cosmic forces, about which we will hear more in 2:15. These ideas link to the dualistic world the Colossians knew so well: light versus darkness, captivity versus freedom, Satan

---

[37] BDAG 10–11.

versus God (1Cor 4:5; Rom 2:19). And, in particular, it reflects the fear of demonic powers that was common in antiquity. The "power of darkness" evokes the same realm as the principalities and powers. *This is the captivity of the world in the sphere of evil.*[38] The phrase (power of darkness) only occurs elsewhere in Luke 22:53 when Jesus explains the forces behind his arrest. Paul similarly elsewhere prays that his audience may turn "from darkness to light" (Ac 26:18). This rescue might be viewed as a second exodus in which God's powerful redeeming work defeats the powers of darkness.[39]

Box 2.1 Bridging the Horizons: Rescued from the Power of Darkness

When Paul refers to being rescued from "the power of darkness" (1:13), many of us pause and wonder if this is a pronouncement from a now-antiquated worldview filled with superstition. To some degree there is a cultural elitism I can feel, and, without overtly admitting to it, I believe that my own views, graced by the Enlightenment, are superior to Paul's views of reality. Has not science discredited ancient beliefs that many people once held closely?

I believed the primacy of my own worldview up until I made my first trip to Africa and taught NT to a room full of pastors. They soon expressed disappointment with my exegesis of numerous passages of scripture in which I avoided admitting their views of spiritual power into the text. As one student remarked, "My faith is true not because it is reasonable or moral, but because it has power, power greater than the most powerful shaman."

Of course, I could have chosen to dismiss this comment as coming from a person who has yet to be "enlightened." But, after a time, I began to question who was actually unenlightened here. He told me a story: His father-in-law was a shaman, and he prohibited his daughter from marrying this young man because of his Christian faith. But then this shaman perceived that genuine power, spiritual power, was present in this young man. "It was only because the power of Jesus was greater than his powers as a shaman that he let me marry his daughter." For all of my students, battling "the power of darkness" was as much a pastoral skill as preaching in the pulpit.

---

[38] See Arnold, *Colossian Syncretism*, 288.
[39] G. Shogren, "Presently Entering the Kingdom of Christ: The Background and Purpose of Col 1:12–14," *JETS* 31 (1988) 176–177. As a second Exodus, McKnight (*Colossians*, 132) points out that this is one more hint from Paul that Gentiles who have been rescued now join the community of God's people *as Israel* had been redeemed. This is Paul's hint at what he says fully in Rom 11:17: The Gentiles have now been grafted in.

It was then that I came across an essay by Valentine Chukwujekwu Mbachi, professor of theology at Nnamdi Azikiwe University in Awka, Nigeria.[40] Mbachi argues that the context of Paul's letter mirrors many of the cultural assumptions of many African societies. And, in this respect, most African churches can better understand the fears of Paul's audience than many of us in the West. In his summary, he says, "It stands to reason that unless Christ is proclaimed as the One who has defeated all the evil powers of darkness and is able to liberate people from fear, like Colossian and African syncretists, many people may turn to other answers such as magic, charms, amulets, rituals and other occult practices for protection against the enslaving and binding spirits."

This place of safety is a new realm, a new location, a safe harbor where these dark powers cannot reach. *It is the kingdom belonging to Jesus, the Son loved by the Father.* "Kingdom" is, of course, the common phrase used by Jesus throughout the gospels. But here and elsewhere Paul thinks of the kingdom in its present reality.[41] This is not merely a sphere of divinely inspired goodness; it is a place that is as real as any place in the world: the church.[42] This is the arena where we find gathered disciples who have experienced the redemptive work of Christ and the power of the Spirit. It is a safe place where the powers of darkness cannot extend their dominion.

One more subordinate clause takes us deeper into the nature of this divine rescue (**1:14**). This kingdom belongs to the Son – and he is the agent of our rescue. Exod 6:6 (see earlier) refers to both rescue *and redemption*, meaning that God not only defeated the Egyptians, but also a payment was made to free Israel. Redemption (*apolytrōsis, lytroō*) refers to buying something back or making a payment that releases someone or something. The people of Israel, of course, had been slaves, and the payment had been the Passover lamb that prefigured the death of Christ (Col 1:20). And while theologians have often debated the nature of this redemption, still, the simple idea is what is central: Christ died, our liberation had been won, and because we (and Israel) had been redeemed through payment, we moved (as slaves) to new owners. Redeemed slaves belong to their redeemer, and

---

[40] V. C. Mbachi, "Paul's Teachings on All-Sufficiency of Jesus Christ for Salvation in Colossians 2:8–3:5 in Relation to Christianity in Africa," *Journal of Religion and Human Relations* 13.1 (2021) 331–349.

[41] This is the realized eschatology that sets Jesus apart from Judaism in the gospels.

[42] So McKnight, *Colossians*, 127.

here Paul notes in 1:13 how we have been transferred to the Son's kingdom. In Romans Paul can write that those who have been set free become *slaves of God* (6:16–22) while formerly we had been slaves of sin (6:17). This redemption brings freedom *and a new captivity-in-freedom* inasmuch as we belong to the Son. But this redemption also brings forgiveness (Col 1:14b), and, through the power of God's grace, we become "slaves of righteousness" (Rom 6:18).

The Son's capacity to accomplish these great works of salvation now will take center stage. For Paul, the salvific work of Jesus is utterly linked to Christology. This connection will lead Paul to write some of the most important Christological verses of his career.

1:15–20 A Hymn of Praise for Christ

1:15　He is the image of the invisible God, the firstborn of all creation,

1:16　for in him all things in heaven and on earth were created, things visible and invisible, whether thrones or dominions or rulers or powers – all things have been created through him and for him.

1:17　He himself is before all things, and in him all things hold together.

1:18　He is the head of the body, the church; he is the beginning, the firstborn from the dead, so that he might come to have first place in everything.

1:19　For in him all the fullness of God was pleased to dwell,

1:20　and through him God was pleased to reconcile to himself all things, whether on earth or in heaven, by making peace through the blood of his cross.

There seems to be an abrupt transition at 1:15 as Paul opens a densely theological description of Christ. But it is closely linked with the previous paragraph because there Paul ended by giving acclaim to the Son, who is the source of our redemption and the king of this new kingdom. Paul now provides a tour into a deeper understanding of who Jesus Christ actually is, what he has done, and what he can do. This is a celebrated series of verses that are no doubt the most studied in all Colossians.

Scholars have debated whether this section is a portion of a hymn that the Colossians would have recognized. There is clearly a hymnic or poetic quality to these sentences, and they remind us that the early Christians had their own familiar liturgical forms that Paul may have been partially citing.

We see hints of this hymnic allusion elsewhere in the NT (Phil 2:5–8; 1 Tim 3:16; 1 Pet 2:21–24). In our verses we find two relative pronouns (*who is*) in 1:15 and 1:18b, which introduce two themes further defining Jesus, and we wonder if these phrases opened separate stanzas. This is followed by a conjunction (*hoti en auto, for in him ...*) in 1:16 and 1:19 that explains the earlier affirmation.[43] The first theme (1:15–18a) explains how Jesus Christ is supreme over the cosmos and all of its powers, and the second (1:18b–20) explains how he is Lord over the new creation, the church, which is the community of reconciliation in the world. Of course it is impossible to prove that Paul is using a preexisting hymn – or if he has edited it here and there – and so any theories have to be held loosely.

Others have objected to this altogether, arguing that Paul is not using a hymn and that here the apostle is expressing himself with poetic language worthy of his subject. Perhaps Paul was aware how these words would be read aloud in the Colossian church and so felt free to wax eloquent for liturgical purposes.

But as there might be earlier, older sources behind this section, scholars for almost a century have pursued the origin of these in order to gain some understanding of Paul's theological background. For instance, Lightfoot's great commentary from 1879 shows how Col 1:15–20 is filled with words found in the language of various Hellenistic writers.[44] This evidence led some mid-twentieth-century scholars to point to the language of Gnosticism or Hellenistic redeemer myths.[45] Today this view is rarely defended since our understanding of Gnosticism and its origin has changed dramatically.[46]

A second view runs in the opposite direction and points to Jewish thinking in the period. In a classic article in 1926, C. F. Burney suggested that the language of 1:15 ("first-born of all creation") is a veiled allusion to

---

[43]   Abbott, *Colossians*, 209; see further J. F. Blanchin, "Colossians 1:15–20: An Early Christian Hymn? The Arguments from Style," *VE* 15 (1985) 65–93; N. T. Wright, "Poetry and Theology in Colossians 1:15–20," in *The Climax of the Covenant: Christ and the Law in Pauline Theology* (Minneapolis: Fortress, 1992), 99–119.

[44]   Lightfoot, *Colossians*, 144–160.

[45]   See the summary of Martin, *Colossians*, 40–43 who refers to E. Käsemann's article, "A Primitive Christian Baptismal Liturgy," in *Essays on New Testament Themes* (English translation) (Naperville: Allenson, 1964), 149–168.

[46]   We have no evidence, for example, of a pre-Christian Gnostic redeemer myth that Paul might have used.

Gen 1:1 and, above all, Prov 8:22: "The LORD created me at the beginning of his work, the first of his acts of long ago."[47] The Hebrew term for "create" in Prov 8:22 (*rêshîth*) was carried over to interpret Gen 1:1 (Hebrew *bᵉrêshîth*, to create), which begins the Hebrew Bible. Here rabbis viewed creation in Gen 1:1 as having taken place *by Wisdom*. Paul understands these methods.[48] Pauline scholars today recognize that Paul was dependent on and skilled in the exegetical tendencies of Second Temple Judaism, and here we have one more example. The inspiration for Paul stemmed from his reflection on Jewish Wisdom and how it had been personified and elevated in Jewish thought. Thus, if Wisdom was lifted up as the preexistent agent ordering and directing creation (Sir 1:4; Wis 9:9), Paul has found a ready-made analogy for Christ, who mirrors Wisdom's nature and exceeds it.

By giving Christ preeminence over all creation and, in particular, the "powers," Paul is addressing an aspect of the universal fear we discussed at 1:13. The forces of the world have now been subjugated to the One who has the power to control them, and therefore any who would come from these threatening spheres – or those who make claims to manipulate them – now must reckon with this new reality.

But this also shows us that early Christians such as Paul were willing to engage in categories of wider philosophical thought in order to explain the significance of what God had done in Christ. Dunn correctly says, "The hymn is itself a sharp reminder that there were front-rank thinkers among the first Christians eager to engage with their contemporaries in the attempt to explain reality."[49] As such, we find emerging in these verses a cosmic Christology that views Christ not "from below" – that is, from his accomplishments in the incarnation – but "from above," from his role before the incarnation and in relation to the entire cosmos. This turn should astound us, for it now makes a claim that will become central to Christian theological expression for the next two millennia.

---

[47] C. F. Burney, "Christ as the ARCHE of Creation," *JTS* 27 (1926) 160–177.
[48] W. D. Davies, *Paul and Rabbinic Judaism* (London: SPCK, 1970), 150–152, who outlines Burney's argument. A current discussion and summary can be found in McKnight, *Colossians*, 138–145, who gives many pages of examples from the Wisdom tradition.
[49] Dunn, *Colossians*, 86.

The subject now changes (**1:15**) from God and his work to Christ's identity and power for six verses.[50] In what has been one of the most controversial verses in Colossians, today we see it as central to Paul's thought.[51] Four key terms advance Paul's argument in 1:15–16: First, Christ is the image of God (*eikōn*). At first this seems to be a contradiction. How can something invisible (God) be shown by something visible? But dualistic writers such as Plato or the Jewish Philo were not troubled by this.[52] Without some divine representation in the world, knowledge of God would be impossible. An *eikōn* can reveal and represent its subject fully by having substantial participation in its reality. The *eikōn* was not a "weak and feeble" copy of something but was able to represent the "inner core or essence" of it.[53] Within Hellenistic Judaism, divine Wisdom served in this role. Wisdom could be the *image of God* (Wis 7:26), or even the *Word (logos) of God* could be his image. In some cases, Torah devotion was elevated to become God's eternal (and preexistent) self-expression. Moreover, both Wisdom and Word were personified to give them a self-authenticating existence. Ps 36:6 LXX is typical: "By the word of Yahweh the heavens were made." Similarly, Ps 107:20 LXX: "He sent forth his word and healed them." In Wis 7:26 we learn that Wisdom is an image (*eikōn*) of God's goodness. God himself may act within his creation, and these are his tools. Wisdom and Word are not creations of God but instead features of God's own divine life. Thus, we might say, "Wisdom bridged the invisible God and visible creation."[54]

This possibility made God knowable while at the same time protected his transcendence and separation.[55] The key, however, is that such an *eikōn* is not an intermediary holding a space between God and the world. This was a presentation (or reaching) of God himself into his creation while maintaining his difference and holiness. Therefore, Paul (and the NT

---

[50]   The NRSVue begins 1:15 with a new sentence and a pronoun ("He is ..."). This makes for good clarity. But the Greek begins with a relative pronoun ("who is ..."). The antecedent can be found in 1:13b and 14, where Paul describes the Son as the agent of God's activity. These clauses will give sharp definition to Christ (or the Son) who has just been discussed.

[51]   The verse has been disputed as Pauline and sometimes given as proof that Paul could not have penned Colossians. Davies (*Paul and Rabbinic Judaism*, 150–176) surveys this view that was prevalent in his era and demonstrates how the thinking of 1:15 fits well within the writing of Rabbinic Judaism's Wisdom literature.

[52]   See many references in Lightfoot, *Colossians*, 144–145; also TDNT 2:388–389.

[53]   TDNT 2:389.

[54]   McKnight, *Colossians*, 147.

[55]   J. D. G. Dunn, *Christology in the Making* (Philadelphia: Westminster, 1980), 168–176.

generally) has appropriated a theological category within Judaism (Wisdom) and employed it for Christ.[56] The acting and speaking of Christ is all one with the acting and speaking of God.

Second, of course, such an *eikōn* was necessary because God is *invisible* (*aoratos*). This was an axiom of OT thought that the NT uses frequently (Rom 1:20; Col 1:15–16; 1 Tim 1:17; Heb 11:27). God cannot be seen and so may not be represented in idols (Exod 20:4–6) but instead is known through agents (such as the angel of the Lord, Exod 3:2–6). This same affirmation is in John 1:18: "No one has ever seen God," but then we quickly are told us that this privilege belongs to the Son alone, who in Johannine Christology is the supreme agent of God. In the Hellenistic world, this notion of invisibility fit with Platonic systems that divorced God from creation. Here Paul is echoing this theme with a difference, acknowledging the uniqueness inherent in who God is – but also upending it by announcing that this God, this invisible God, has made himself visible though a gesture of his own design. Christ is God's divine gesture in history. In this sense, this *eikōn* refers to representation or manifestation and means that Christ is a credible and faithful presentation of God. He is a representation of what is invisible, a divine revelation, enjoying a genuine participation in the one revealed: God himself.

Third, Paul's use of "firstborn" (*prōtotokos*) can either refer to first (*protos*) in number (first in a list, oldest child in a family) or rank (first above all, as in Ps 89:27, where the king is described in proximity to God). To refer to a firstborn son may be an explanation of birth order, but its nuance is wider and refers to the authority of this son over all that the father owns. This type of language is also used for Wisdom in Prov 8:22 (Wisdom as the firstborn of God's creations). In later centuries, Arius would use *prōtotokos* in Col 1:15 to prove an adoptionist Christology. Athanasius' response was to point to 1:16, where this view is proven wrong.[57] Even today a mistaken Arian reading of Col 1:15 persists.[58]

---

[56] Caird, *Colossians*, 177, points out how the Talmudic rabbis debated which realities (such as Wisdom) were said to preexist and which were created.

[57] "But if all the creatures were created in him, he is other than the creatures, and he is not a creature but the creator of the creatures," Athanasius, *Orations against the Arians*, 2:62, cited by Martin, *Colossians*, 45 and T. E. Pollard, *Johannine Christology and the Early Church* (Cambridge: Cambridge University Press, 1970), 213.

[58] Col 1:15 appears in many Jehovah's Witness publications of proof that the Son (Jesus Christ) was a created being never equal to the Father. A similar adoptionist view is held

And fourth, Paul's reference to creation (*ktisis*) makes our understanding of "firstborn" clear. It expresses not that Christ was the first created, but that he ranks above all creation. And this is clarified in **1:16** – he is the *source* of all creation (and thus cannot be a part of creation itself). He has created *all things* (*ta panta*), which means that his sovereignty is comprehensive, and there is no realm that lives apart from his rule. Thus, Christ is the agent of God's creative effort, not as if an assignment were given to a subordinate, but that God himself creates through the life and being of his Son ("... for *in him* all things ..."). But this is precisely what we find in Judaism regarding Wisdom. Thus Ps 103:24 LXX (104:24): "O Lord, you have made all things (*panta*) by Wisdom" (also Prov 3:19; Wis 8:5).

This dramatic connection between Wisdom and Christ was a profound theological idea. It meant not simply that Jesus Christ in his incarnation was God's self-revelation on earth, but that Christ possessed a life and mission *before the incarnation* in full cooperation with God – in fact, a life that shared God's life fully. Thus, Christ had a preexistence. In 1:16 note that the verb is passive ("was created") rather than active ("Christ created"). Here we have the delicate interplay between divine agency and the role of Christ ("... for in him ..."). Did the Father create through or within Christ or was Christ the creator of all things? The text is unclear, but it is likely that the passive refers to Christ as being the One within whose powers creation occurred. This would fit with Paul's use of the Wisdom motif. And above all, this (as with Jewish Wisdom) did not compromise his commitment to monotheism.

Here we find some of the earliest beginnings of the theological thought that will come to its full form in the fourth century at Nicaea. But Paul is not alone in this understanding. John expresses the same idea in his poetic prologue (1:1–3): "In the beginning was the Word, and the Word was with God, and the Word was God. He was in the beginning with God. All things came into being through him, and without him not one thing came into being." Here we see the implication of an ontological connection between the Father and the Son.

by Muslims, who believe that this ontological connection between the Father and the Son contradicts monotheism.

Box 2.2 A Closer Look: Christology

It is difficult to imagine the Christological decisions of either Nicaea (325) or Chalcedon (451) without the contributions of Colossians. The first affirmed the eternal unity of the Father and the Son; the second affirmed the complete humanity of the Son without compromising his divinity. These creeds commonly used the term "same essence" (*homoousion*), which not only denied an Arian view that taught a creationist Christology (that Christ was "made" or created), but for all time confirmed that the Son shared an eternal and divine life with the Father – he was "begotten not made" – and so bore God's divine life into the world. The relationship of the Father and the Son is thus sacrosanct in Christian theology and forms the foundation for all trinitarian belief. Christ did not represent the Father to the world. Christ presented the Father to the world.

We can see this Christology worked out dramatically in Col 1:15–20. Christ not only brings the very image of God into the world (1:15), but he has the capacitates of the Father as creator, revealer, and reconciler. "In him the fullness of God was pleased to dwell" (1:19) likely echoes OT language of the temple known exclusively as the dwelling place of God (Ps 68.16 [LXX 67:17]; Hag 2:7).

The Fourth Gospel stands alongside Colossians as offering these same Christological features. The Johannine prologue opens with this same ontological affirmation about the Son (1:1–5), and throughout its narrative we are given numerous signals that characters encounter not simply a messiah of creaturely origin, but God himself. Philip's question in 14:8–9 is met with this answer: "Whoever has seen me has seen the Father." And the gospel ends with Thomas' recognition: "My Lord and my God" (20:28). These climactic scenes join other narrative hints (the I AM sayings; Jesus' work on Sabbath) that indeed Jesus was more that anyone in the gospel expected – that, in some manner, God was being encountered. It was left to the creeds to give this notion detail.

Nevertheless, there are no texts that compare with Col 1:15–19 for the sheer concentration of Christological affirmations. This corresponds to Paul's use of Lord as a title for Jesus in this letter (Col 1:3, 10; 2:6; 3:13, 18, 20; 4:1, 7, 17). More than a title of respect (as might be true of any use of *kyrios*), this is a title of Christological importance that makes a claim no different than the ancient creeds.

This comprehensive work of the Son is also given rich clarity in what follows (**1:16b**). This work of creating "all things" includes everything that is visible and invisible whether in heaven or on earth. Paul uses four terms (thrones, dominions, rulers, and powers), and these may well refer to the powers that threaten the Colossians in their present crisis. Some have viewed these as pairs: thrones and dominions as heavenly powers; rulers and powers (*exousiai*, authorities) as their earthly agents. The second pair (*archai* and *exousiai*) are commonly linked together in Paul (1Cor 15:24; Eph 1:21), and they will appear together later in Col 2:10, 15. However these two – along with the first pair – often appear in contexts of spiritual beings that contest God's rule and live in rebellion. Arnold has made a convincing case for this and provided evidence from Jewish writers of this period that all four terms can represent heavenly powers.[59] If this is correct, Paul is claiming that the rule of Christ has power over those beings that threaten, that are in league with the powers of darkness, and are now at work in the Colossian church. Christ is supreme, and, in a world where threats from spiritual forces may be extreme, Christ's power exceeds any powers that they may fear.

But does this exclude the possibility that Paul is also thinking about how these powers are alive within the visible structures of Colossian life? Many modern commentators are eager to find in these words secular powers at odds with truth or goodness, powers that should be confronted in the name of Christ within the church.[60] In a Roman world saturated by political-religious imagery, a claim for Christ's comprehensive authority over *all things* would be nothing less than treasonous.[61] The modern separation between spiritual powers and earthly powers is a modern convention. While Paul may not be making an explicit claim against Roman rule, still, the implications of Paul's Christology put Christ at odds with powers *in heaven and on earth* that do not acknowledge God's rule or his Son.

Together these four terms found in 1:15–16 are a summary of Paul's link between Christ and God modeled by the Jewish concept of personified of Wisdom. Christ is fully connected to God and yet also is present in creation, forming a genuine tension between transcendence and immanence. Bauckham summarizes: "[W]hat the passage does is to include Jesus Christ in God's unique relationship to the whole of created reality and thereby to include Jesus in the unique identity of God as Jewish

---

[59]   Arnold, *Colossian Syncretism*, 252–255. Other scholars dispute Arnold on this and think that Paul is pointing to earthly authorities, possibly in Rome. Scholars who demythologize these verses see Paul as claiming Christ's righteous rule over political powers that oppress.

[60]   See McKnight, *Colossians*, 252–253.

[61]   Walsh and Keesmaat, *Colossians Remixed*, 83–95.

monotheism understood it."[62] This high Christology is central to the glory of the Christian gospel,[63] which says that the gospel announces that God's glory is seen in the face of Jesus (2Cor 4:6). Similarly, when Philip asks in the upper room for Jesus to show him the Father, Jesus responds, "Whoever has seen me has seen the Father" (John 14:9). When we read Col 1:15–16 we are reading one of the earliest theological efforts to tease out the divine reality present in Jesus Christ and to assert that his divine rule – begun at creation and continuing into the present – has genuine implications for the reality we live in today.

The idea that God's Wisdom not only preceded creation but was its sustaining power was common among Jews of the Hellenistic period (Sir 1:4; Wis 7:26–27; 10:1–2).[64] Paul now applies this to Christ as well (**1:17**). Wisdom holds all things together, orders the world, creates the world, and is superior to "scepters and thrones" (Wis 7:28). In praise of Wisdom we read: "For she is a breath of the power of God, and a pure emanation of the glory of the Almighty; therefore, nothing defiled gains entrance into her" (Wis 7:25 RSV). Indeed, the Wisdom of Solomon is a window into the role Wisdom is seen to have had in guiding history. Sometimes Wisdom is synonymous with the Spirit or the Word, or even Torah (see Wis 1:6–7).

In 1:17 Paul describes Christ with "poetic imagination"[65] and applies to him roles that will form a Christian cosmology. Christ is not only the creator of the cosmos; he is also the bearer of divine presence in creation, and he is the One who sustains creation. Christ brings order to an otherwise uncertain world that is pulled by the power of darkness (1:13), and since he bears the power of God, he can defeat any powers that may rival him. As H. C. G. Moule once put it: "He keeps the cosmos from becoming chaos."[66]

The language of **1:18a** ("He is the head of the body ...") is really a continuation of the cosmic Christology found in 1:17. It asserts once again

---

[62] R. Bauckham, "Where Is Wisdom to Be Found? Colossians 1:15–20," in D. F. Ford and G. Stanton, eds., *Reading Texts, Seeking Wisdom: Scripture and Theology* (Grand Rapids: Eerdmans, 2003), 129–138; cited in Moo, *Colossians*, 111.

[63] Martin, *Colossians*, 45.

[64] For a full list of Hellenist references to Wisdom sustaining the world, see Beale, *Colossians*, 122n127.

[65] Dunn, *Colossians*, 93.

[66] H. C. G. Moule, *Colossian Studies* (London: Doran, 1898), 78, cited in Garland, *Colossians*, 89.

the Lordship of Christ over the world but uses language common in the Hellenistic era. Romans and Greeks believed that all things were derived from and held together by what they called *logos* (word; reason or similar). Jews added the idea that Wisdom held creation intact. For both, the cosmos was compared with "a body" that was controlled by a head (in some cases, the god Zeus), or, as in Philo, the cosmos was a body with a "reasonable soul" and reason (Logos) as its head.[67] Paul employs this language to locate Christ within this ordering of things. *Where Hellenists expected to find reason or logos and Jews located Wisdom, so now Paul finds Christ.* The Greek word "head" (*kephalē*) can certainly mean having authority over – but it also may bear the nuance of origin or source.[68] This would then match the idea that Christ is the origin of creation and so its sovereign (or firstborn).

The next two words (the church) come as a surprise (**1:18b**). The body over which Christ rules is suddenly the church, which opens the way to seeing it as a model of the cosmos itself: the church playing a role that is larger than anyone would expect. This application does not limit Christ's rulership to just the church; it expands the significance of the church's place in creation. The lord of the cosmos is, in particular, the lord of the church, which now shares his interests and program. And this suggests that "the destinies of creation and the church are bound together."[69] The church is bound up in Christ's work to redeem creation (1:14) and not merely to sustain its own life.

When Paul uses the word "church" (*ekklēsia*)[70] he may well have in mind the civic gatherings of Greco-Roman cities; but it is more likely that Paul has been influenced by the LXX, where the word refers to the congregation of Israel. *Ekklēsia* occurs about 100 times in the LXX (usually translating Hebrew *Qāhāl* or congregation, Deut 9:10; 1Kgs 8:65). The addition "of the Lord" in the LXX (*ekklēsia kyriou*, a gathering of the Lord) points directly to the assembly of Israel (Deut 23:2). Paul picks this up

---

[67] TDNT 7:1025–1032.
[68] This second interpretation of the word "head" is widely disputed due to its use in Eph 5. See C. E. Arnold, "Jesus Christ: 'Head of the Church,'" in J. B. Green and M. Turner, eds., *Jesus of Nazareth: Lord and Christ* (Grand Rapids: Eerdmans, 1994), 346–366.
[69] Garland, *Colossians*, 91.
[70] Many scholars believe that the original hymn, "He is the head of the body," was edited by Paul to include the words "the church," which strikes many as an insertion by Paul.

from the LXX, using *ekklēsia* 60 times for the Christian church. In this case, "the church is the Israel of God in the new-covenant age,"[71] and it plays not simply a local role in Judea, but an expanded role in the rule of Christ himself. Both are juxtaposed by Paul: Christ is lord over "all things" and Christ is head over "the church," namely the people of God who have continuously been God's people from the beginning of Genesis. Now the argument can come full circle. As "head" Christ is the lord of the original creation, the cosmos, and he is lord of the new creation, found in the church.

Paul now lists a series of accolades, giving further basis for Christ's place as the head of all things. In **1:18c** he is "the beginning, the firstborn from the dead." This is another echo from Gen 1:1 showing that Christ is the origin of all. And as we saw in 1:15, *firstborn* refers not to primacy due to birth order but to supremacy by virtue of position. But here we are pointed to the resurrection (*firstborn from the dead*, also Rev 1:5), signaling that Christ has opened a new beginning for creation. He is the archetype of all who follow. In his resurrection a new era has turned, and he has preceded all those who will be raised after him, making him the "first fruits" (1 Cor 15:23) of this new kingdom.

Thus, the NT understands that this resurrection was not simply Christ's vindication, but more: It inaugurated his new-creation reign with the Father. Elsewhere Paul writes, "He was declared to be Son of God with power according to the spirit of holiness by resurrection from the dead, Jesus Christ our Lord" (Rom 1:4). We can see the double emphasis of creation and firstborn in 1:15 and 1:18: Christ created and he also has re-created; and in this second effort, he has won our salvation and established his kingdom. Therefore, we can say that the supremacy of Christ is anchored in the beginning of all things (creation) but now is permanently established by this new-creation eruption of power, making him unrivaled over all things. *This was the point of the resurrection* (the 1:18c purpose clause employs *hina*): in order to make Christ first (*prōteuō*, related to firstborn), supreme, preeminent.

This establishes Christ as a person who is unparalleled in all creation. We are not just talking about him being a more important person than

---

[71] Beale, *Colossians*, 125; also G. K. Beale, "The Background of *Ekklēsia* Revisited," *JSNT* 38 (2015) 151–168.

others. "We are talking authority, honor, and power all rolled into one."[72] And we can be forgiven for thinking that some of Paul's readers would see a comparison here with Rome and its imperial founder, Augustus, the "firstborn" of the "Augustan Age," who exceeded everyone in *auctoritas*, or power and prestige combined.[73] He was given titles such as *Pontifex Maximus* (high priest) of the empire. He was called *Imperator Caesar divi filius*, emperor and son of a god. He (too) was preeminent within his imperial realms. And even though Augustus was not living at this time (Paul was living under Tiberius), even in death these emperors had divine powers that continued. Augustus had joined the gods when he died in 14 CE; now we learn that Christ in his death and resurrection is ruler even over Augustus.

Further explanation for what was said in 1:18 is now given in **1:19**. Christ is first over all creation *because* (*hoti*) the fullness (of God) was delighted (*eudokeō*, or pleased) to dwell in him.[74] There is an intentional parallel in Greek between this line and 1:16 ("*for in him*, all things . . . were created"), which once again juxtaposes the twin points of Christ's work: creation and resurrection. But here we gain the impression that the resurrection was a theological inevitability since God himself was present and at work within the tomb. *The tomb could not hold him any more than the tomb could not hold back God.* The reason for this is no longer Christ's relationship to or role in history or creation, but it springs from the essential (or ontological) nature of who he is.

In the Greek of this verse, it is unclear what fullness we are referring to. A literal translation says that "all fullness" was pleased to dwell in him. All fullness is the obvious subject. But the content of this fullness is unclear, and many speculate that this is God's fullness. Comparisons with other parallel uses in Paul give us confidence to expand this translation. In Col 2:9 Paul refers to "the fullness of deity (*theotēs*, not God, *theos*)," which points clearly to God as its subject. In Eph 3:19 Paul refers to believers as "filled with the fullness of God." In Eph 4:13 we read about the "fullness of Christ." Moo suggests that Paul has Ps 67:17 LXX in mind, where God is the subject and the verb "pleased" and the infinitive "to dwell" appear

---

[72]   Bird, *Colossians*, 56.
[73]   Ibid. Bird supplies a helpful summary of the powers of Augustus, 56.
[74]   In Greek, *for in him all fullness was pleased to dwell.*

together.[75] Together these suggest that using God as the subject in 1:19 ("the fullness of God," NRSV) is correct.

Box 2.3 A Closer Look: Fullness

Fullness (*plērōma*) was a densely theological or philosophical term in this period, and it refers to "divine powers and attributes."[76] The word *plērēs* means "full," such as a ship that is fully manned or a person that is "fully" satisfied after a meal. In the LXX, we read about "the earth and its fullness" (Ps 23:1). It is only with great difficulty that scholars have tried to pin down the source of this term, and some have wondered if the original hymn was actually a Hellenistic philosophical ode to divinity.[77] This is doubtful, even though later Christian Gnostics used *plērōma* to describe features of their cosmos. The best parallel where God dwells fully is to be found in the OT, where God "dwells" within his temple (Ps 68.16 [LXX 67:17]; Hag 2:7).[78] We also read that God fills the whole world (Ps 72:19; 139:7; Isa 6:3; Jer 23:24; compare Eph 1:23). In Second Temple Jewish thought, Wisdom was described in the same manner (Wis 1:6–7). Therefore, having this "fullness" echoes the idea of the OT *shekina*: It is the power and glory of God that fills a space, making it his own. This is particularly true in the LXX. Ezekiel can say, "And I looked, and the glory of the LORD filled the temple of the LORD, and I fell upon my face" (44:4; cf. Isa 6:1; Hag 2:7).

Paul uses fullness in a variety of contexts (Rom 11:12, 25; 13:10; 15:29; 1Cor 10:26; Gal 4:4), but this is the only place in his writing that employs it with a direct theological application. Paul's use of *plērōma* in 1:19 then answers the anxieties of the Colossians, who felt defeated by the powers that surrounded them. O'Brien concludes rightly: "The Colossian Christians need not fear those supernatural powers under whose control men were supposed to live . . . .. God in all his divine essence and power had taken up residence in Christ."[79]

---

[75] Moo, *Colossians*, 131.

[76] Lightfoot, *Colossians*, 159. See his extended note on the history of the term, 257–273. Delling (TDNT 6:304) writes, "The *plērōma* statements in Colossians present the full unity of the work of God and Christ in such a way that the distinctness of person is preserved and yet monotheism is not imperiled. God works through Christ in His whole fullness (1:19), in His full deity (2:9)."

[77] The suggestion that this is a gnostic peon to divine fullness is rarely defended today. Dunn reminds us that Hellenistic thought understood that God, his Spirit, or reason "filled or permeated the world." *Colossians*, 99.

[78] See further Beale, *Colossians*, 126–128; also G. Beale, *The Temple and the Church's Mission: A Biblical Theology of the Dwelling Place of God* (Leicester: Apollos, 2004), 267–268.

[79] O'Brien, *Colossians*, 53.

In 2:9 Paul repeats these reassurances: "For in him, the whole fullness of deity dwells bodily." But this time he is using it in a setting where he wants to strengthen the resolve of his readers. Christ is full or complete (*all the fullness*, 1:19); he is overflowing with the presence of the one true God, and therefore there is nothing to fear. In Ephesians Paul expresses the same. Christ is filled with the presence of God (1:23), and the promise of discipleship is that this same filling can be ours (3:19; 4:23).

In the end, Col 1:19 becomes a pivotal verse in Paul's argument for the essential natures of God and Christ. God was in Christ in a manner unlike anyone in creation, and this was clear not simply within Jesus' incarnate life but was demonstrated powerfully in the resurrection. For the Colossians, this important idea may be linked to their experiences within the controversy facing the church. In 2:8 the false teachers were likely urging the church to see that true "fullness" of spiritual experience could be found if they followed this newly promoted philosophy or set of rules. Paul's answer is that this fullness (or spiritual completeness) can be found only in Christ (2:9), who is endowed with "all" the fullness of God (1:19). This language is not a far cry from what we read in the prelude-hymn that opens the Fourth Gospel (1:1–18) as well as the indwelling language of John 10:38 and 14:10.[80] We have here in Paul and in John the beginning of an understanding of Christ that will evolve into the theology of the early Fathers and eventually the councils of Nicaea and Chalcedon. Rather than seeing artificial development in the fourth and fifth centuries, we should see faithful continuity that drew on ideas carefully embedded in the NT.

Box 2.4 Bridging the Horizons: The Primacy of Christ

Most of us already know the carefully reasoned results of the early councils of Nicaea and Chalcedon. We understand how to frame an orthodox Christology and why (with Athanasius) if you deconstruct major ideas such as incarnation and resurrection, the edifice of the Christian faith collapses. We understand this clearly. As the creed of Nicaea reminds us, Christ was "begotten from the Father before all ages; God from God, Light from Light, true God from true God, begotten, not made; of the same essence as the Father."

---

[80]   McKnight, *Colossians*, 161.

In these verses of Colossians (1:15–20), Paul makes clear the definitive nature of Christ and the world. *Christ was not a creature "from below" but a person "from above."* In the incarnation, an unparalleled event transpired. In Christ "the fullness of God" came to dwell (1:19), making Christ our Lord (1:3; 2:6). In him divine life and human existence met "without confusion" or compromise. In him, the invisibility of God became visible (1:15).

Nevertheless, it is this ancient understanding of Christ that we are tempted to dismiss when we try to reach out to people who do not share our faith or, worse, have no religious faith at all. It is always the first item to go because by its very nature it is non-negotiable and, thus, divisive. I remember being in an interfaith gathering in Tripoli, Libya, with Muslim scholars. "Our aim is to build unity among people of faith," one of them said. "And if you'd only let yourself accept that Jesus was merely a prophet – as the Qur'an teaches – then together we could unite in faith and work together for the good of the world." But this was the hill I could not climb. I could no more abandon my view of Christ than my Muslim friends could abandon their view of monotheism.

Paul understands this temptation. It is as modern as it was ancient. When the church in Colossae gained a clearer understanding of who Christ is, their fears and quandaries could begin to dissipate. They would have a more coherent faith, but simultaneously their faith, *rightly anchored*, would separate them more completely from their opponents.

The argument of 1:19 continues in **1:20** both logically and syntactically. "Because *in him* all the fullness of God was pleased to dwell . . . and *through him* [that same God was pleased] to reconcile all things . . ." The subject remains God-in-his-fullness, now expressing two actions: indwelling Christ and, through Christ, reconciling the world. In 1:14 we heard about the redemptive work of the Son; now we learn that, in cooperation with God, the reconciling work of Christ joins with the cosmic features of Paul's Christology. It is interesting that this indwelling and reconciling are intrinsically related. The indwelt Christ who lives in full concert with the life of God proceeds in his work precisely as God does: He is reclaiming and restoring his creation ("all things"), things visible and invisible (1:16), whether in heaven or on earth.

The root idea in reconciliation (*apokatallassō*[81]) is *allassō*, which means to change something so that it will be restored to harmony (Acts 6:14; Gal 4:20;

---

[81] This term appears only here, in Col 1:22, and in Eph 2:16. There is virtually no difference in meaning between *apokatallassō* and its usual form, *katallassō*.

1Cor 15:51–52). It assumes estrangement or conflict. Sometimes it refers to an exchange of two things that now become interchangeable. In marriages, *katallassō* could refer to the reconciliation of estranged spouses (1Cor 7:11). In the NT it chiefly refers to the restoration of the relationship between God and his creation (2Cor 5:18–20; Rom 5:10). The assumption is that *something* has changed to make this restoration possible. And here as well as in 1:22 it is the crucifixion of Christ ("the blood of the cross") that no doubt echoes 1:14 and points to a sacrifice that forgives sin.

This verse requires that we return to the larger context of Colossians. The God who in Christ created "the heavens and the earth" (1:16) now, through Christ, will reconcile "heaven and earth." This final affirmation is thus about God's reclamation of his creation, and the removal and defeat of any who have disordered it. Reconciliation presumes struggle or disarray, and the powers standing in opposition to God both in heaven and on earth now will be reclaimed, reordered, and brought into submission by Christ's divine power. Christ brings peace by the defeat of these disordered powers of the cosmos. Making peace (*eirēnopoieō*) is an odd word that occurs only here in the NT (and Prov 10:10 LXX). But the Hebrew idea of *shalom* is likely behind it (Isa 11:6–9). The term had also been coopted by Rome, and "peace" (Latin *pax*) was the first promise of Rome (hence, *Pax Romana*). Augustus did not bring peace by cajoling his enemies; he brought peace by defeating those opposed to his divine rule. Christ's resurrection was thus also a triumph over his foes (see Col 2:15) that removed their power and pacified them.

Paul certainly sees the church as playing a role in this effort. In 1:6 it is the church that will carry this gospel into the whole world. In 1:18 it is the church that holds a unique relationship with Christ (he is its head, while also the firstborn of all creation). Thus, whatever the church does *in the world*, the gospel and its orthodoxies are not ends in themselves: The church is an instrument of Christ's peacemaking work. It is a fellow saboteur with Christ, defeating *all things* that work on behalf of the darkness. Only when the church remains faithful to its Lord can it successfully complete what Christ has promised to do. In this sense, the church may not be secular. It enjoys a spiritual governance that demands faithfulness to the Son, and it works to imitate his achievements.

Apokatallassō does not occur before the NT, leading some to wonder if this is an invention of the apostle.

Box 2.5 Bridging the Horizons: The Church and Its Work

I once had a faculty colleague who kept an arresting poster on his door. The picture showed two men embracing and the poster read: "Modest Proposal: Let the Christians of the world agree they will not kill each other." The poster was from South Africa: One man was black, the other was white. And they were embracing with tears. The poster has bothered me for twenty-five years. *Is this really a true depiction of who we are?* Rather than being encouraged to love and forgive, we now must be encouraged not to kill.

It is indeed a modest proposal. In Col 1:20 Paul understands that reconciliation is central to the work of Christ. *All things* are to be reconciled both in heaven *and on earth*. I can only assume this means that our shared life *in this world* – among those who claim to belong to Christ – should exhibit tangible evidence of reconciliation and "peacemaking." But instead, we can find example after example of Christians who demonstrate every manner of intolerance and hostility not only toward those outside the church, but even toward those who are brothers and sisters.

Perhaps it is a matter of where we "set our minds" (3:2) – maybe it is just that simple. When Paul makes his list of things to be discarded from our lives (3:5–10), he assumes that these behaviors, such as anger, dishonesty, slander, and abusive language, are present in the church, and that these things must be expelled from us as a feature of belonging to Christ. If this is so, then the Colossian Christians had learned to adapt to such behavior. They had acclimated to it and let it live alongside their newfound identity as believers in Christ.

And that may be the root of the problem. God does not acclimate to things like this ("the wrath of God is coming," 3:6). Perhaps we misunderstand what God is asking of us. We are to be the reconcilers and peacemakers of the world. Our work is a continuation of Christ's work: to bring unity where there are divisions (3:11) and to become exemplars of Christ's peacemaking in the world.

1:21–23 A Call to Respond

1:21 And you who were once estranged and hostile in mind, doing evil deeds,

1:22 he has now reconciled in his fleshly body through death, so as to present you holy and blameless and irreproachable before him,

1:23 provided that you continue securely established and steadfast in the faith, without shifting from the hope promised by the gospel that you heard, which has been proclaimed to every creature under heaven. I, Paul, became a minister of this gospel.

The prayer of Paul for the Colossians began in 1:9, but in 1:15–20 it incorporated a hymn or poem to Christ that we learned might well have been an earlier liturgy that Paul edited. Reference to the Son in 1:14 led Paul to digress, giving us one of the most dramatic portrayals of Jesus Christ that we possess. However, 1:14 also refers to the Son's work of redemption and the forgiveness of sin – and now this line of thought is picked up in 1:21 ("You who were once estranged ... he has now reconciled ..."). Therefore, we might imagine this section as a beautiful Christological hymn bookended by prayerful pastoral concerns Paul has for the Colossians. Reading 1:9–14 and then moving directly to 1:21–23 make these thematic connections stand out.

The emphasis of 1:21–23 centers on three great themes: First, Paul describes the reconciling work of God-in-Christ, which God does not achieve by simply dismissing sin but through the physical death of Christ on the cross. Second, Paul explains that the aim of this reconciliation is not for the benefit of those who are saved but for God himself, so that this community of the kingdom might be "holy and blameless and irreproachable," offered up to God as a gift from the Son to the Father. Finally, Paul exhorts them that this new identity in Christ requires their fidelity and steadfastness so that, despite their precarious circumstances and despite the spiritually dubious world they live in, they will choose faithfulness to the gospel over the shifting promises of the world. Essentially the truths about Christ outlined in 1:15–20 are given to show who Christ is and what he has done *so that* a community of the transformed might emerge into the world. As in 1:9–14, this is a community that will know God's will, endure with strength, and live lives pleasing to God. In Paul's mind, *this gospel* (1:22b), this hope for us as creatures, is the essence of his message and why he became its servant. It is for hope (1:5, 23, 27) so that the whole world (1:6) might be different than it is, reconciled to God and finally at peace. This is new creation language setting in history promises for a creation that has been ruined and made captive by darkness.

The language of **1:21** illustrates the shift from the abstract to the personal. Paul uses direct address ("you") in its most emphatic form (*hymas*) to remind them that he is talking to *them*, to these Colossians, who illustrate the successful work of reconciliation (1:20). Paul has not referred to the Colossians beyond complementing their faithfulness (1:4). But now he provides a retrospective that points to the far side of their conversion. *They once had a history with God and it had not been commendable.* They had been participants or perhaps promoters of the very darkness that is being defeated by Christ. But like refugees from this world, they were lifted out of their captivity to darkness. God rescued them and now, as is true universally, standing within their redemption, looking back, their previous life seems more hideous than ever. They had moved from the kingdom of darkness (1:13) to the kingdom of light (1:12), and this transition brought with it entailments, both benefits and duties, which now they possessed in Colossae. The sentence has no active verb until 1:22, and so we might translate, "And you – once estranged and hostile in your thinking due to your evil deeds, (22) [Christ] has now reconciled through his body of flesh . . ."

Paul describes their former life as both estranged and hostile. Being estranged (*apallotrioō*) occurs only here and in Eph 2:12 and 4:18 in the NT, and in its passive form it suggests the idea of someone who has been given over to another (*allos*) who is alien or unsuitable, even strange (*allotrios*).[82] The word's meaning evolved to explain someone so "other" that they were an enemy (1Macc 1:38; 2:7; *Diod. Sic.* 11.27). Such a separation from God led the Colossians to a position fully corrupting their thinking and their behavior. Literally they had become enemies (*exthroi*) both *in mind* and *in works* (that were evil). They belonged to the "other camp," and this resulted in open hostility to God. This is similar to Paul's language in Rom 5:10, where Paul also describes humans without God as enemies of God whose only hope emerged after the death of God's son. Paul also uses the language of fallen thinking in his profile of fallen humanity in Rom 1:21. But here in Colossians he uses the strongest possible terms: Such behavior that springs from a darkened mind is not simply mistaken or bad; it can be evil (*ponēros*, see also Rom 12:9), which in Greek is remarkably forceful – such activity is vile, malevolent, and wicked. This recalls the climax of Paul's description of fallen humanity provided in Rom 1:29–32. Paul sees the influence of sin as systemic: Alienation from God breaks our reason, our behavior, and our interests as we promote this hatred of God (Rom 1:30) among others.

---

[82] BDAG 47–48. *Allotrios*, belonging to another (*allos*), is the opposite of *idios*, one's own.

The great reversal of spiritual and personal fortune is often expressed by
Paul with "but now" (*nyni de*). As in Rom 3:21, "*But now*, apart from the
law, the righteousness of God has been disclosed . . ." Or in Rom 6:21, "*But
now* that you have been freed from sin . . ." This is the grammatical hinge
Paul uses to introduce the turning of a person to their redeemed state. *But
now you have been reconciled* (**1:22**). The Colossians had moved from
enemy to ally because God had reconciled them to himself.

In 1:20 Paul referred to the blood of the cross; now he underscores this
again. This reconciliation was achieved by the cross of Christ or, more
precisely, "in the body of his flesh." What can this mean? Looking at Paul's
similar uses can help us. In Rom 7:4 Paul can say, "you have died to the law
through the body of Christ," and in 8:3 he says God accomplished our
salvation "by sending his own Son in the likeness of sinful flesh and to deal
with sin, he condemned sin in the flesh." Body and flesh are similar but not
synonymous, and it is their nuances that are important.[83] The body (*sōma*)
can be the embodiment or reality of a person or object that makes it visible
in the world, while flesh (*sarx*) is the material that composes this object.
Thus, in 1Cor 15:44 Paul can distinguish different types of bodies (natural,
spiritual) as determined by their setting (heaven or earth). And this
explains why "flesh and blood" cannot inherit the kingdom of God
(1Cor 15:50). In his incarnation Christ was bodily present in human flesh.

But such emphasis on the physicality of Christ's "fleshly body" advanced
a key point for Paul's readers.[84] In the Hellenistic world of Colossae, the
physical, material body was considered limiting, and therefore deeper
spirituality was found in harnessing or denying this material existence,
this world of "flesh." They even had a pun for this: *sōma sēma* ("the body
as tomb"). Philosophers like Plato did not hate the body (consider
Hellenistic sculpture that adores the body), but they wanted us to exceed
what the body provided – to see that a fuller, deeper reality lay beyond
what we experience in our physicality.

Some teachers may have echoed Plato's searching question: *Do the
boundaries of your body share the boundaries of your spirit?* Of course
not. We are more than our bodies. To exercise this stretch beyond the

---

[83]   This summarizes the incisive explanation of Dunn, *Colossians*, 107–109.
[84]   See Meye, *Colossians*, 43, citing R. Hays, *The Moral Vision of the New Testament* (San
        Francisco: Harper, 1996), 48–49.

body, some teachers in Colossae were advocating "practices of self-denial, and deprecation of the body as a means to a deeper knowledge of God (Col 2:20–23)."[85] Paul's description of Christ denies this. In appropriating human flesh, Christ demonstrated God's comprehensive interest in who we are. In contrast, salvation was wholistic, incorporating all that we are – and addressing our sin on the cross fully – and in his bodily resurrection modeling the transformed life promised to his followers.

But bearing our flesh *to the cross* had another potent meaning. For Paul, *sarx* could also hold the idea of humanity's sinful capacity (Rom 7:7–8:3), and while Christ had no sin, still, he bore that human capacity and our human guilt to the cross, becoming the reconciling sacrifice.

Paul's thought now becomes clearer: Reconciliation was achieved by God because Christ identified fully with God (Col 1:19) and humanity (having a body of flesh but without sin). He experienced everything that we do in our ordinary lives in this world. But in his identification with our sinful lives, he had the capacity to absorb the consequences of sin in his body and deal with them on the cross, thereby setting free those who were once embedded in sin and darkness. With Wright, "The cross was simply the outworking of this explosive meeting between the holy God and human sin."[86] Paul's thoughts in Col 1:21–22 can almost be summed up by Rom 5:10: "For if while we were enemies we were reconciled to God through the death of his Son, much more surely, having been reconciled, will we be saved by his life."

The result of this reconciliation, this peacemaking between God and humanity (Rom 5:1), is the restoration of our lives in him as holy and without blemish – all of our lives, our bodies included. This language hints at temple sacrifice (holy, present, blameless), suggesting a sacrificial offering. Even the term "blameless" (*amōmos*) is likely better translated "without blemish" as it is elsewhere in the NT (Eph 1:4; 5:27; Heb 9:14; 1Pet 1:19; Rev 14:5) because animals brought to the altar could have no blemish.[87] Caird expands,

When a man offered an animal in sacrifice, he laid his hand on it in order to identify himself with his offering and to express his aspirations to be himself holy

---

[85] Ibid.
[86] Wright, *Colossians*, 82.
[87] Caird, *Colossians*, 182.

and unblemished. Paul's thought then is that Christ has offered himself to God as the perfect sacrifice and that Christians must in their turn identify themselves with his sacrificial self-giving.[88]

We thus become one with Christ, one with his body. And as we read in 1:18, the church is *the body of Christ*, the living presence of Christ in the world. The church is thus caught up in the redemptive activity of Christ-in-the-world.

Therefore, there is a necessary participation on the part of the Colossians (**1:23**). This mirrors the expected participation of any Israelite offering a sacrifice. God's saving provision outlined here now must be matched with human participation in what God has done. This sort of exhortation to persist in the faith is not uncommon in Paul's letters (Rom 8:13, 17; 11:22; 1Cor 9:27). In this case, his exhortation is twofold: that they hold to an unflinching commitment to the faith and that they hold firmly to the gospel they originally heard in the beginning, no doubt when Epaphras first explained it. Col 1:23a does not express doubt about them. He does not say, "only if you *actually will* continue securely . . ." This language is simply explanatory and is what we call a *real condition*.[89] Their new status as holy and without blemish comes with a natural entailment that along with salvation comes a secure and steadfast faith. The established character of their faith is an outward expression of what God has already done inside of them.

But, of course, 1:23a still remains a conditional clause, and therefore Paul is reminding the Colossians that grace is not simply given without expectation. This verse has thus stepped into the long-argued discussion concerning freely given grace and obligation and whether this duty to respond is a condition of our security in Christ. But for Paul there always is a conditional aspect to grace: It is not simply transactional; it is relational. And here is perhaps where Barclay's work on "gift" has been most promising.[90] Barclay maintains that the tension here is misplaced. Paul's understanding (as in all antiquity) is that gift/grace are generous but not free. The one who receives a gift is summoned to respond with gratitude

---

[88]   Ibid.
[89]   The Greek *ei ge* begins the sentence confidently (it is a real condition using *ei* with the indicative but without uncertainty), as it does in Eph 3:2: "This is the reason that I, Paul, am a prisoner for Christ Jesus for the sake of you gentiles, 2 *for surely* you have already heard of the commission of God's grace that was given me for you . . ." See BD §371(1).
[90]   J. Barclay, *Paul and the Gift* (Grand Rapids: Eerdmans, 2015).

and obedience, even loyalty to the giver. McKnight writes, "What Barclay has done here is to move the discussion away from the standard theological problematic, namely, the relationship of grace to obedience, into a broader topic, namely to the various manifestations of grace."[91] Or we might add: Barclay has helped us see the cultural context of grace and gift and how it impinges on the recipient.

The descriptive language of Paul's exhortation is striking. He wants them to remain or stand firm in the faith with full conviction and be found to be "well established" (*themelioō*), which derives from the noun for a foundation (*themelios*). This term only appears elsewhere in Paul in Eph 3:17 but is not uncommon. In Matt 7:25 it serves the climax of the Parable of the Builder who lost all because when the rains came his works were found to be without a foundation (*themelioō*); see also Heb 1:10 and 1Pet 5:10. But this is the language Paul prefers. His own work is that of a craftsman laying foundations (Rom 15:20; 1Cor 3:10–12). Again and again he refers to Christ as the foundation of the church (1Cor 3:11).[92] The image here is of a faith known for its solidity, its immovability, thanks to the deep structures that hold it in place. "Steadfast" (*hedraios*) refers to someone who is "seated or settled" (*hedra* is a seat or bench, *hedos* can be the base of a statue) and could metaphorically describe a tradesman confirmed or established in his trade. In 1Cor 7:37 this is the person who is filled with resolve and whose desires are under control. He is unwavering. In the Greek OT this term was used for God, seated on his throne (Ps 33:14; 92:2 LXX).[93] The third image ("without shifting," *metakineō*) is a rare word that means to move or alter something, such as in Deut 19:14 where a landmark is moved (cf. Isa 54:10).[94] Paul's use here in 1:23 is figurative and, in the passive voice, refers to being pushed around. This, then, is the profile of Paul's followers: that they have a secure faith, that they are strongly established in that faith, and that they are not pushed away from it by anyone who would lead them from the hope of the gospel that Epaphras preached.

---

[91] McKnight, *Colossians*, 177–178.
[92] Dunn, *Colossians*, 111.
[93] TDNT 2:362.
[94] Some scholars wonder if in his use of "shifting" Paul has an earthquake in mind. The Lycus Valley knew these quakes well. One hit Colossae in 60–61 CE. So Martin, *Colossians*, 59.

Two clauses now define this gospel that needs to be protected. It is a gospel that has been proclaimed widely (to every creature under heaven) and a gospel that made Paul who he is: namely, a minister of its message. The final line of this section concludes Paul's opening remarks that began in 1:1 and is both lavish and inspiring. From Paul's vantage, now with many years of missionary effort behind him and with a long list of cities where he faithfully proclaimed the gospel, Paul looks at his world and reflects, with obvious hyperbole, that his world has heard this gospel (see also 1:6). But this is not simply exaggeration. Paul understands that this gospel is not simply a local or limited message belonging to Judea and its people. In Paul's world this is also a gospel that has now been presented to the Roman Empire, which is the dominant reality of Paul's life. Antioch, Ephesus, Philippi, Athens, Corinth, and now Rome – these are among the cities that now have heard and are now accountable. Rome has been notified that a new Son is bringing his kingdom to bear on an empire whose peace has proven to be empty. But there is more. Col 1:15–20 announced that this gospel is about a Christ whose identity and work sweep across all of the cosmos, far beyond Rome. "Every creature" in 1:23b includes the "all things" mentioned in 1:16. Therefore the audience of this gospel is not simply Rome; it is the creation that has now met the One who will set all things right, who will subdue the powers and defeat the darkness. This is a cosmic gospel that announces a cosmic Christ.

The story of Paul's conversion was probably well-known among most of his churches. He had been called by Jesus himself to become his follower and to be a courier of the gospel to the Gentile nations (Acts 9:15; also Rom 11:13). His apostolic authority was not being challenged in Colossae as it had been in Galatia. Here in 1:23 he simply reinforces his calling and validates that this gospel they own is the same one he preaches. However, this same gospel has him under its command. He is no longer a free man but a man under orders. He had been called and set apart for this task (*egō* or "I" as an emphatic pronoun; cf. Gal 5:2): "I [myself] had become a minister." This title for Paul (*diakonos*, also in 1:25) was shared by Epaphras (1:7) and the courier Tychicus (4:7) and is modest by any measure.[95] We often translate *diakonos*

---

[95]   Some Greek manuscript editors wanted to expand Paul's titles. Sinaiticus deletes "minister" and adds two titles for Paul: "I Paul became *a preacher and an apostle.*" The Codex Alexandrinus includes all three titles. See Abbott, *Colossians*, 228.

as deacon, but essentially it means a server or one who serves. It could refer to someone who waits on tables (Luke 17:8) or tends to the needy or ill. Paul has a range of titles he could use to describe himself. For example, in the opening of Romans Paul writes, "I Paul a servant/slave (*doulos*) of Jesus Christ, called to be an apostle." Here Paul is juxtaposing two very different titles, one low, one high: a slave and a formal emissary. In Col 1:23 he has chosen something decidedly low, and here he imitates what had become a common Christian reflex. While Greeks and Romans saw service as undignified, Jesus had made service the hallmark of his ministry (Luke 22:27), most famously at Mark 10:45: "For the Son of Man came not to be served but to serve and to give his life as a ransom for many." This title quickly became a feature of the self-understanding of the earliest Christian communities. They were people who served. In the NT Erastus, Timothy, Onesimus, and Onesiphorus are typical of people who bear this title along with Paul (Acts 19:22; Phlm 13; 2Tim 1:18).

Paul's closing reference to himself in 1:23 also serves as a bridge. He now will turn to the heart of his message to the Colossians. He knows that they are under duress and being pressed by teachers to abandon the faith first explained by Epaphras. But he wants them to know as well what it means to belong to the gospel of Christ. His commitment has been total – he is an emissary of this gospel (1:1) as well as someone who serves its interests. But this has been costly as well. He has suffered (1:24) for the gospel. He hopes to encourage the Christians of Colossae (2:2) through all of these words so that if they do suffer for standing firm, they are in good company with him.

A SUMMARY OF PAUL'S OWN MINISTRY, 1:24–2:5

1:24–29 Paul's Ministry in the Gospel

1:24 I am now rejoicing in my sufferings for your sake, and in my flesh, I am completing what is lacking in Christ's afflictions for the sake of his body, that is, the church.

1:25 I became its minister according to God's commission that was given to me for you, to make the word of God fully known,

1:26 the mystery that has been hidden throughout the ages and generations but has now been revealed to his saints.

1:27 To them God chose to make known how great among the gentiles are the riches of the glory of this mystery, which is Christ in you, the hope of glory.

1:28 It is he whom we proclaim, warning everyone and teaching everyone in all wisdom, so that we may present everyone mature in Christ.

1:29 For this I toil and strive with all the energy that he powerfully inspires within me.

These verses represent a continuation of Paul's introduction of himself, which he began at the start of the letter. Here, however, he takes a surprising turn in referring to his suffering as a feature of his apostolic mission to preach the gospel with courage.

Paul commonly refers to his own labors as a missionary in his letters (notably Rom 1:11–15; Gal 1:10–2:21; 1Thess 2:17–3:11). And he frequently refers to his sufferings as if these credentialed him in his work (1Cor 4:9–13; 2Cor 11:23–27). At the end of Galatians, he can say, "From now on, let no one make trouble for me, for I carry the marks (*stigmata*) of Jesus branded on my body" (6:17). In 2 Corinthians he lists some of these experiences:

countless floggings, and often near death. Five times I have received from the Jews the forty lashes minus one. Three times I was beaten with rods. Once I received a stoning. Three times I was shipwrecked; for a night and a day I was adrift at sea; on frequent journeys, in danger from rivers, danger from bandits, danger from my own people, danger from gentiles, danger in the city, danger in the wilderness, danger at sea, danger from false brothers and sisters; in toil and hardship, through many a sleepless night, hungry and thirsty, often without food, cold and naked (11:24–27).

The narrative sections of the NT describe more: He experienced verbal attacks, false charges, ejection from cities, imprisonment, beatings, threats to his life, and betrayal. It is an exhausting and sobering list. In 2Tim 3:12 Paul sums this up for even the average Christian: "Indeed, all who want to live a godly life in Christ Jesus will be persecuted."

In Col 1:24–29, Paul wants to explain in the fullest terms what it means to have complete attachment to Christ. His understanding of Christ crucified and his union with him *in his death* provided a dramatic framework for interpreting his own life. And this is as true for him as it is for the Colossians, who have to decide how they will embrace this life of difficulty.

They are facing opposition that is no different than what he faced throughout his career.

This suffering, however, is purely for Christ and the message of the gospel (1:23). This gospel unfolds a mystery that applies to the entire world – Christ in you, the hope of glory – and through it he both proclaims and warns his audiences about the significance of its truth. No wonder, then, that his words might immediately divide his audiences. Some will embrace this truth; others (who are warned) will reject it to their peril.

Box 2.6 Bridging the Horizons: Suffering in the West and the Developing World

I live with the assumption that Christ's project in the world is to alleviate pain, vanquish suffering, and, well, make my life easier. When I flourish, I will be grateful. When I am happy, my worship will be that much richer. *I see little redemptive value in loss or suffering.* I do not want to descend; I want to ascend. This is Christ's job.

When Paul refers to rejoicing in suffering (1:24), he presumes that suffering can have some redemptive feature: Paul can suffer or experience loss, and through this something good can be found. Still, his words in Philippians have always been troublesome: "I want to know Christ and the power of his resurrection and the sharing of his sufferings by becoming like him in his death" (Phil 3:10).

When I speak with Christians from Nepal, China, Nigeria, Egypt, or India, I hear a different view than my own. These Christians have woven suffering into their very existence *because they have had to.* They often live without surplus, safety, convenience, or insulation from disease. Loss has become sufficiently common that entire theologies of loss have grown up around them. They strive to learn how to redeem suffering not by eliminating it but by discovering how they can be shaped by it and how God can work within it. The popular expression "cruciformity" comes to mind. Christ-on-the-cross now is a metaphor for their life-on-the-cross, or, as a Palestinian priest living under occupation once told me, it is our life under the cross.

God may do his most powerful work within us when we experience descent, risk, and loss. But I usually find this incomprehensible. I once admitted this to a pastor/ student from Nepal. "You cannot understand this?" he said. "Finding God in loss is one the secrets of a profound spirituality. You only know what God can do when you can't do anything for yourself."

When Paul talks about his suffering (**1:24**), he often refers to rejoicing. In Rom 5:3–4 he writes that "we also boast in our afflictions, knowing that affliction produces endurance, and endurance produces character, and character produces hope …" He can describe such suffering casually because he compares it with the glory that awaits us (Rom 8:18). In 2Cor 4:10 Paul refers to himself as "always carrying around in the body the death of Jesus, so that the life of Jesus may also be made visible in our bodies." In 4:12 he can say that this is "death working in him," but that it is a fruitful suffering because it will bring life to others. Most Romans (with the exception of some Stoic writers) would see this theology of suffering as peculiar, since it was widely believed that suffering was to be avoided as it always led to diminishment.[96]

For Paul, however, his own suffering was a feature of his union with the suffering of Christ. Paul was uniting himself to Christ's suffering, and this was the source of his own suffering's virtue (Rom 8:17; 2Cor 1:5; 4:10–11). "I want to know Christ and the power of his resurrection and the sharing of his sufferings by becoming like him in his death" (Phil 3:10). Rom 6:5 is particularly telling in its use of the perfect tense: "For if we have been united (*symphytos gegonamen*, perf.) with him in a death like his, we will certainly be united with him in a resurrection like his." Dunn remarks, "The force of the perfect is to indicate a past event establishing a state which continues to persist in the present."[97] The idea is that the Christian is "fused" to or entwined with (*symphytos*)[98] the death of Christ and that this remains unchanged. The same idea appears in Paul's use of the perfect in Gal 2:19: "I *have been crucified* in Christ," or in 6:14: "the world *has been crucified* to me."

This notion of suffering as a feature of Jesus' Messianic identity may well have been influenced by Jewish apocalyptic ideas of Messianic woes that would precede the Messianic era.[99] That is, Judaism understood that the world had two ages: the present age we occupy today and the age to come. And the threshold of the new age would consist of God's people suffering

---

[96] Stoic writers viewed personal deprivation and loss as beneficial. The Romans did make exceptions for beneficial suffering. Soldiers, for instance, might suffer, but this was a demonstration of courage and a service to those whom they protected.

[97] J. D. G. Dunn, *The Theology of Paul the Apostle* (Grand Rapids: Eerdmans, 1998), 484; Dunn illustrates (484n99) how a perfect tense such as "I stand" means "I took my stand and am still standing." BDF §340 refers to it as "the continuance of completed action."

[98] Literally to "grow together" (*phuton*, a plant) and metaphorically something united intrinsically, innately – two things that share the same life and growth.

[99] See Dan 7:21–27; 12:1–3; Hab 3:15; Zeph 1:15; Jub 23:22–31; IQH 3:28–36; TMoses 5–10; N. T. Wright, *The New Testament and the People of God* (Minneapolis: Fortress, 1992), 277–279; N. T. Wright, *Jesus and the Victory of God* (Minneapolis: Fortress, 1996), 577–579.

profoundly as collective punishment for national sin. These sufferings were the birth pangs of the Messianic age.[100] Paul may have taken up this Jewish idea, modified it significantly, and here understood Christ as inaugurating it. These sufferings were the fulfillment of the eschatological sufferings native to this shift in the ages, and Paul (as well as the Colossians) was sharing in it.

But Paul goes further. He says that his suffering in some manner "completes" what is lacking in Christ's afflictions, and this idea has baffled countless commentators.[101] He cannot mean that something is missing in Christ's suffering on the cross and that Paul is filling up this lack. Paul believed Christ's death was complete, "once for all" (Rom 6:10). In 1:24 it is no doubt important that Paul changes his language from his suffering (*pathēma*) to Christ's "afflictions" (*thlipsis*), and this latter term is never used in the NT for the redemptive sufferings of Christ.[102] With Lightfoot, we see here that Christ's sufferings may be considered from two points of view: its sacrificial efficacy on the cross (which needs no supplement) and its pastoral use or its spiritual edification (Latin *aedificatoriae*) that may lead to the improvement of mind or character.

There have also been questions regarding the meaning of the word "complete" where Paul says he "completes" what is lacking (in some translations, "fulfill"). The Greek verb is a double compound: *anti + ana + plēroō: antanaplēroō*). And if these prefixes bore meaning during this Hellenistic era (and here we are unsure), their use may be significant. To fill (*plēroō*) up (*ana*) is simple enough (1Cor 16:17; Gal 6:2), but the larger compound is rare (only here in the NT). *Anti* may refer to "filling up" in place of another, or rather "filling up" for another, in which case Paul may be suggesting that his suffering occurs in place of the church's suffering – he suffers in its stead.[103] In this sense, his suffering is a part of his service to the Colossians.[104] Moreover, if Christ's body had suffered on the cross, even more the church *as his body* will continue to be afflicted in

---

[100] TDNT 9:672.

[101] See the excursus in McKnight, *Colossians*, 187–192.

[102] Moo, *Colossians*, 151.

[103] Ibid., 150–151, provides grammatical options; also Caird, *Colossians*, 184.

[104] Lightfoot argues that *anti* refers to a reciprocal "other," in the sense that the verb describes a need satisfied simply from a source *opposite* (*anti*) to that of the deficiency. Thus, Paul is filling up *from himself* what Christ has left for him to do. Paul suffers in his turn after Christ had suffered, both for the sake of the church. He points to 2Cor 1:5,

the world, and this will only end when the final victory over evil is complete.[105]

In sum, many theories have been offered to explain this interest in suffering in Paul and its relation to Christ, but the best returns to the Jewish eschatological view of Messianic woes.[106] Jesus' own suffering on the cross triggered the onset of the Messianic era in which the church lives. Participation in suffering as disciples demonstrates that we belong to this Messianic era in history, and, for Paul, this vocation to suffer is a part of his forming his life around the cross. The suffering of the church is thus a *continuation* of the cross, an extension of the cross, suffering of a different kind – *not* as if the work of salvation required a supplement, but that the time of *Messianic woe* has longer to go before the coming of the new age. But this is also missional. Paul understands that this suffering is in fact *for the sake of the church* (Christ's body), and inasmuch as his suffering serves the church, his suffering mirrors what Christ has done. This is about continuity: the flesh of Christ from the cross and the flesh of Paul that suffers for the body of Christ.[107]

All of this (1:24) is truly astonishing and should make any reader pause. While the church rightly announces that our union is also to the resurrection (Rom 6:5) and to the victory of Christ, still, life in this age includes suffering that (as with Paul) may have liberating effects for others. Christ's sacrificial suffering was complete, and his body – the church – continues this suffering in the world. While the Western medieval church took this call to suffer to extreme lengths (using flagellation and other forms of self-inflicted pain), the modern Western church barely knows what to do with this, since, in our world, such suffering is foreign and unwelcome. The churches of the developing world have a deeper relationship to suffering, which is why this one theme lives so close to their self-understanding.[108]

---

where Paul refers to the sufferings of Christ "overflowing" upon the apostle. *Colossians*, 165.

[105] Caird, *Paul's Letters from Prison*, 184; Lightfoot, *Colossians*, 166.
[106] See McKnight, *Colossians*, 188n499, for the many scholars who support this view.
[107] Dunn, *Colossians*, 117.
[108] I have often noted in the Middle East how the Orthodox and Catholic churches – the most ancient churches from Iraq to Egypt – openly exhibit the suffering of their saints in graphic detail on their walls and icons. The protestant churches do not.

Paul's vocation is that of a minister (**1:25a**), and as we saw in 1:23, this term (*diakonos*) evokes images of service of the most basic kind (such as table service). He understands that he is an apostle (1:1), but now all talk of suffering and deprivation remind him that a humble title such as this is fitting. His service, however, is for the "commission" (*oikonomia*) of God. The term *oikonomia* referred to the administration of a household (so *oikos*, house; *oikeō*, to dwell) or to the task itself of administration. It could refer to an office (RSV), but generally it is flexible and could refer to a role of custodianship or stewardship. Similarly, an *oikonomos* was a household steward (Luke 16:2–4; 1Cor 9:17). In the NT, ministers of the church are called *oikonomoi* (1Cor 4:1, 7; Tit 1:7), meaning that they bear responsibility for the well-being of the church.

In Rome, such stewards (*oikonomoi*) were generally slaves who oversaw their master's household duties. Paul, who has just referred to himself as a *diakonos* or minister, now takes on a term of parallel lowliness. He is a man who belongs to a household, who bears responsibilities, and who is fulfilling his master's orders.[109] He has become a servant of the church, and, in particular, God has given to him the administrative duty to care for the Colossians ("for you"; cf. Eph 3:2). Paul is likely pointing to his wider apostolic ministry here that began with his conversion that directed him to work with Gentiles (Acts 9:15; 22:21). He is indicating that care for the Colossians is central to his tasks.

This assignment is now explained and given its purpose (**1:25b**). It is quite literally "to fulfill the word of God." This is an unusual use of fulfill (*plēroō*) and likely means to bring to completion the full teaching of the gospel with which Paul has been entrusted (1:23). Paul uses the same verb in Rom 15:19 describing his ministry "from Jerusalem to Illyricum" as fulfilling (the preaching of) the gospel of Christ.[110] But note that Paul's commission is not simply to teach or admonish these churches. He is bringing to completion (another use of *plēroō*) what that word teaches. And in 1:26 he will hint at this. There is a mystery that has been hidden in the scriptures that has now is being unveiled through his ministry in the church.

---

[109] Dunn, *Colossians*, 118.
[110] BDAG 828, *plēroō*, §3.

This word – this unveiling – is for Paul a mystery (*mystērion*, **1:26**). An alert Roman reader would note this word immediately. We have already seen that a vast array of Roman cults coexisted in Roman cities like Colossae. These groups were called "mystery religions" because they held secret, arcane rites and knowledge that could not be openly divulged. When Paul refers to wisdom, knowledge, or now mystery, he could be drawing on a vocabulary well-known to these groups.

Box 2.7 A Closer Look: Mysteries

The term *mystērion* had wide currency in Jewish settings (Qumran, Jewish apocalyptic), and this is likely the best context for Paul. This era of Judaism held an understanding that indeed the age in which we live would pass to a future age, and yet many thought that God held a plan – an as-yet undisclosed (*mystērion*) plan – that would show how these things were to unfold. This plan, of course, is what every thoughtful person yearned to know. In this context, the dramatic message of Paul and his colleagues (called saints, see 1:2; apostles and prophets, Eph 3:5) was that they knew the plan that had been ordained by God from the beginning of history.

The chapters of human history were *unfolding* in a pattern set by God's will. Thus, it is no accident that Paul understands that the word at the center of his ministry is a *mystērion*. It is not a puzzle or a secret; it is a new revelation about Christ-in-history and the Gentiles in the covenant that now he and his fellow leaders were serving. Paul refers to this perspective more than once (Rom 16:25–27; 1Cor 2:6–10; Eph 3:4–11), which shows how central it was to his thinking.

He claims that the deep secrets of God have been revealed and can be found in Christ. The divine plan that had been set for creation was now open for all to see (Eph 1:3–10). Thus, Paul is not saying that the plan of redemption is mysterious as we might use the word today; he means that it was a plan that had not yet been shared. It had been kept in abeyance until now (*nyn*, 1:22, 26). In this case, the great mystery stems from Genesis, where Paul can at last explain that the great promises of Abraham for land and children included a blessing on the nations (Gen 18:18). Gen 26:24 holds all three: "I will make your offspring as numerous as the stars of heaven and will give to your *offspring* all these *lands*, and all the *nations* of the earth shall gain blessing for themselves through your offspring." Paul knows these three promises, and, in his conversion, he suddenly saw that in Christ the third of these promises was being realized. The arrival of

Christ and the inclusion of Gentiles would bless the nations of the world
and redefine everything about God's saving purposes. Gentiles could be
folded into the family of Abraham (Rom 4:9–25). In Gal 3:8 Paul cites the
Genesis promise to the nations and sees it fulfilled as Gentiles embrace
Christ.[111] Paul ends Romans by declaring this succinctly: "Now to God
who is able to strengthen you . . . according to the revelation of the mystery
that was kept secret for long ages but is now . . . made known to all the
gentiles, according to the command of the eternal God, to bring about the
obedience of faith." This great revelation might be described as God now
making a comprehensive claim on his creation. It is not about the redemption of one nation (Israel); it is about the redemption and obedience of
the world.

In Ephesians, where we have close parallels with Colossians, we see the
outworking of this revelation in the incorporation of Gentiles into the
family of God and the reconciliation of Jews and Gentiles. Jews and
Gentiles are now "joint heirs" to the Messianic promises now unfolding
(Eph 3:6). Those who are far have come near, making one new person (Eph
2:13–15). But in Colossians (**1:27a**) this blessing takes a different turn.
Here Paul underscores God's intention: "To them, God chose (or resolved)
to make known what are the riches of the glory of this mystery." This
movement is anchored, then, to God's own desire and does not spring
from Paul's personal interests or a movement in the Hellenistic churches.
This movement in history, this theological shift that is utterly inclusive of
all nations, is a divine plan.

The "riches of the glory" is common in Paul (Rom 9:23; Phil 4:19; Eph
1:18; 3:16) and gives the overwhelming sense Paul had of the power of this
revelation he was bearing. For Paul, "riches" is a frequent modifier (fifteen
times) and can refer to the riches of God's kindness (Rom 2:4), of his glory
(Rom 9:23), of the wisdom and knowledge of God (Rom 11:33), of his
generosity (2Cor 8:2), of his grace (Eph 1:7), and of the inheritance

---

[111] Even if Paul is contending with false teachers claiming to hold religious mysteries that
will benefit the Colossians (a view less in vogue today), here he is undermining that view
by showing the sufficiency of what has been given in Christ already (so Caird, *Paul's
Letters from Prison*, 185). *The deepest mysteries are held in the gospel.* Moreover, these
mysteries have been hidden "from ages and from generations." The first term (*aiōn*) is
viewed by some as a reference to the powers that rule the ages. In Eph 2:2 Paul refers to
"the *aiōn* of this world." But combined with the term generations (*genea*), it likely
should be seen as the common reference to the duration of time.

reserved for the Gentiles (Eph 1:18). "Riches" expresses the extravagance of God, who, in his generosity and gift-giving desire, blesses his people. In Ephesians it is used repeatedly for the way God is showering on the Gentiles his goodness and promises, and that is the force of 1:27. But here the riches describe God's *glory*, a term with its cognates Paul uses about eighty times. Glory is the essential radiance of God, located in particular at the Temple. God had also shown this glory to Israel (Rom 9:4), but now the glory revealed in Christ has eclipsed that of the old covenant (2Cor 3:7–11).[112] God's glory became visible in Christ's incarnation (John 1:14; 2Cor 4:6) and particularly in his resurrection (Rom 6:4). This is the hope embedded in this mystery that Paul holds: Inasmuch as Christ bears the glory of God, those who are one with Christ share his glory (Rom 5:2) and begin to be transformed. This is the "hope of glory" (**1:27b**) that is promised. This sharing of God's glory and its hope of transformation, then, is no longer restricted to the Jews but is offered to all.[113] There is no holding back. God's generosity to Israel is matched by his generosity to the Gentiles. And this is easily explained: because both (if they are in Christ) belong to the same family of God.

Box 2.8 A Closer Look: Gentiles and the Family of God

A common reflex in the church is determining who belongs and who does not. We can easily disqualify the outsider by their errant theology, their social class, or their ethnicity. We wonder who is elect and who is not because we know that some among us are not "in." In my own Reformed world, a doctrine such as election can fail to give assurance, and instead it provokes suspicion: We cannot be sure who belongs to the family of God, and so we look for signs of election. We look for these signs in ourselves as well as in others. It may be one of the sad legacies of European Protestantism. When Dutch theologies of election took hold in South Africa, the results were alarming. Black African Christians who shared the faith nevertheless were not invited into the full life of their country.

When Paul writes that gentiles now share in the glory of God (1:27) we often miss his own context. He has abandoned a view that said one ethnicity or one nation enjoyed privilege and exceptionalism over all the rest. In Paul's case, it was his own Judaism. But as a Jew who had embraced Christ, he believed (as did countless other

[112]　Caird, *Paul's Letters from Prison*, 186.
[113]　Wright, *Colossians*, 92.

Messianic Jews) that this Messianic era now opened the family of God to all who believed in Christ. They were grafted into the great olive tree of Abraham's family (Rom 11:7–24). They indeed were "in" by faith, not by race.

This insight was absolutely profound, and it shaped the course of the church's life. If gentiles were "in," then everyone was invited in. If faith was the key to the locked door, then anyone could possess that key. This stone, tossed into the lake, would create ripples reaching every shore. The old lines of division and exclusion were finished. Paul makes this utterly clear in Col 3:11 (also Gal 3:28) and so draws a picture of a wildly diverse church following a God who was not tribal but instead was global. This was a great theme that belonged to Paul and to his friend Luke, whose story in Acts reinforced this idea of wide inclusion in the church.

The application of this mystery, or, perhaps, the realization of this reality, is not in the confession of some orthodox belief (though this is important), nor is it affiliated with a social movement in the world. This mystery is defined (**1:27b**) as "Christ in you," a phrase of seminal importance for the apostle. Elsewhere Paul will refer to being "in Christ" as the unique experience of the believer (Gal 3:14, 26, 28; Eph 2:13, 15–16, 21–22, etc.), but here the same idea is viewed simply from the other direction. In the Spirit, the person of Christ indwells his followers. "You" is plural in this phrase, and, for some, this then has a corporate meaning ("Christ among you"), mirroring the similar phrase "among the Gentiles" earlier in the sentence. But this misses the meaning entirely. Paul commonly referred to Christ indwelling individuals (Gal 2:22; 2Cor 13:5; Rom 8:10; Eph 3:17), and here the plural can support that meaning. "In each one of you, that is all of you" gets at the meaning as well.[114] No doubt Paul has in mind the interior experience of Christ-in-Spirit that marks the believer as in Rom 8:10.

The outcome of this indwelling is the hope of glory, the same glory richly promised in 1:27a. This is the third time in Colossians that hope is mentioned and linked to the gospel (1:5, 23, 27), and we need to see it as critical to our understanding of what this mystery offers. If glory is a natural attribute of God's own person, it also describes the wonder of humanity's creation, sharing God's image, and this was true of Adam. But

---

[114] McKnight, *Colossians*, 199; Moo, *Colossians*, 158.

it was sin that led to the loss of this glory (Rom 3:23). The promise here in Colossians is for restoration, the resumption of a human life as it was divinely intended, a life freed from the frailties and brokenness of ordinary life in this world.

For Paul the core of his message is not the new unity of Gentiles and Jews or, as in 1:27, the hope for societal renewal. These are themes at the center of Ephesians. These important ideas are secondary to Paul's primary message that Christ is the center of the gospel. Paul's message is Christocentric, and it will permit no compromise. History has been intersected by God himself, who in Christ has revealed his purposes for his world. Christ is the one whom "we proclaim" (*kataggellō*, **1:28**), Paul says emphatically, as if to contrast himself against those teachers in Colossae who might be offering a different message.[115] But even this verb stands out. It is not synonymous with "to preach the gospel" (*euaggelizomai*) or proclaiming (*kēryssō*).[116] Its uses in the Hellenistic period normally occur in formal declarations, such as imperial announcements, religious festivals, or honoring emperors. This word lives in the realm of the grand herald. The gospel is a proclamation bearing authority because of the person it introduces to the world. It is not one announcement among the many announcements we may hear; it is *the announcement*, the dispatch from heaven that will concern everyone.

Because of its gravity, this proclamation demands a wide audience. This is not a message only for Jews. Nor is it a message for those who claim to be spiritually elite – as the false teachers in Colossae seem to view themselves.[117] Three times Paul refers to "all people" (*panta anthrōpon*), making the universality of the gospel ring right through the paragraph. The audience is not selective. It is neither for the elect nor for one ethnicity. Everyone is admonished, everyone is taught, so that anyone may become mature in Christ. The first two verbs in this string are closely related and come from the Hellenistic world of the classroom. This proclamation does not simply warn or admonish. *Noutheteō* means to bring something to mind (*nous*) or to awaken someone's thinking – hence, to advise, exhort, or chastise (Job 40:4 LXX). In this sense, it could mean "setting someone's

---

[115]   The pronoun "we" is emphatic in Greek (*hēmeis*).
[116]   TDNT 1:70–73, noted in Dunn, *Colossians*, 123.
[117]   Martin, *Colossians*, 65.

mind into proper order"[118] – or to clear up confusion. This is what Paul needed to do in many of his churches (1Thess 5:12, 14; 2Thess 3:15). The second verb (*didaskō*) points to the conveying of information, teaching properly understood. A strong teacher does both to succeed.

The aim of these efforts – expressed here at the end of 1:28 as if it were a conclusion – is to present every person complete (*teleios*) in Christ. This is a well-known and widely used term (from the noun *telos* meaning final or end) that has an array of meanings. It refers to bringing something to perfection, completion, or fulfillment. Its adjective (*teleios*) can describe a sacrifice, for instance, that is unblemished or acceptable, an animal that is not compromised. Thus, it can infer being "whole," which can metaphorically point to moral character – thus, "mature." The aim, then, of this gospel now echoes what we saw in 1:27: namely, the return of glory. The aim is not simple fealty to God but *participation with God in Christ*, bringing our humanity to the place it was meant to be. This task in Paul's mind cannot be achieved by human ingenuity or moral discipline. It requires the inbreaking of God to arrest our minds and give us direction for the path toward redemption. It requires Christ to live *in us* so that we might acquire his *teleios* humanity.

If we think about *teleios* as perfection, then this too will resonate within the Colossian controversy. Perfection or completion have always served as religious terms in faiths promoting an interior, mystical experience. Through these activities, beliefs, or experiences we will at last be perfect. *Teleios* was used widely among Greek philosophers and promoters of mystery religions to describe the restorative perfection every person seeks. It could describe virtue (as in Stoic philosophers and Aristotle) or it could describe transforming enlightenment (as in the mysteries). Here Paul is saying clearly that there is one path by which *all people* will become who they were meant to be. And that path begins with Christ.

It is easy to forget how much Paul sacrificed for his vocation. He had once been an esteemed student in one of the most respected schools in Jerusalem. Mentored by the well-known Gamaliel, Paul was entrusted with enacting synagogue discipline on behalf of the Sanhedrin. But as he says so poignantly in Philippians 3:1–11, he was willing to discard his professional

---

[118] Wright, *Colossians*, 93.

rank, his educational advantages, and his entire future for the unsurpassing worth of knowing Jesus Christ. "For his sake I have suffered the loss of all things" (Phil 3:8). This keen sense of vocation is similarly reflected in **1:29** (see 1:23). He writes, "for this I toil," and we see in Greek that the antecedent to "this" is *teleios*. Paul toils so that he may present to all persons the marvel of this mystery – so that he may bring completion or maturity for all persons, offering them almost as a sacrifice to God. He then describes this effort using two colorful verbs. The noun *kopos* meant weariness, which the LXX uses for exhaustion after battle (2Sam 23:10) or fatigue in work (Josh 24:13). Its verb (*kopiaō*) refers to work that is arduous or grueling. Paul often uses this for the labor of toiling on behalf of the gospel. Thus, in Rom 16 Paul can describe his associates such as Mary or Tryphaena as people who did not just work but *toiled* for the gospel in this manner. Paul describes his own work in this way (1Cor 15:10; Gal 4:4; Phil 2:16). One simply needs a description of what travel, lodging, and accommodation looked like in Roman antiquity to get a sense of what Paul endured.[119]

A Stanford University tool called Orbis now allows us to measure the time, distance, and cost of travel in the Roman world.[120] Some estimate that Paul's travels as outlined in Acts may have spanned 10,000 miles – much of it on foot under conditions that were challenging to say the least. After looking at these distances and understanding what it means to traverse the Taurus Mountains or the dangers of sailing across the Mediterranean, Paul's own capacity for strenuous work becomes clear. His second term, strive (*agōnizomai*), comes from the stadium (an *agōn* was an assembly place for athletic contests).[121] This verb describes any struggle – athletic, legal, personal – that assumes conflict (see also 2:1; compare the Arabic *jihad*). This is the struggling hero in many stories, and in the LXX it often described the martyr fighting against his own vacillating desire to avoid death. This *agōn* word group appears frequently in most of Paul's letters, being used to describe the conflicts and troubles that

---

[119] See B. Rapske, "Acts, Travel and Shipwreck," in B. Winter, ed., *The Book of Acts in Its First Century Setting. Volume 2: The Book of Acts in Its Graeco-Roman Setting* (Grand Rapids: Eerdmans, 1994), 1–48.

[120] For using the Stanford Orbis tool, consult https://orbis.stanford.edu.

[121] TDNT 1:135–140.

followed him (1 Thess 2:2; Col 2:1). We might imagine Paul saying that his ministry has been an "arena of conflict."[122]

Together these terms offer a profile of Paul at work pursuing the vocation Christ had given him. In the second half of the sentence (**1:29b**) he elegantly says that his successes have been a combination of his striving in concert with "(God's) energy that he energizes in me with power." Or as Caird puts it: "The toil is Paul's, but the energy is Christ's."[123] This doubling of noun and verb is typically a Jewish idiomatic style that has found its way into Paul's speech. But it underscores the point: namely, how Paul's achievements should be credited. He owns a divine call on his life and he senses a divine power in his work, and these are the sources of his unyielding efforts on behalf of the Gentiles.

2:1–5 Paul's Ministry to the Colossians

2:1 For I want you to know how greatly I strive for you and for those in Laodicea and for all who have not seen me face to face.

2:2 I want their hearts to be encouraged and united in love, so that they may have all the riches of assured understanding and have the knowledge of God's mystery, that is, Christ,

2:3 in whom are hidden all the treasures of wisdom and knowledge.

2:4 I am saying this so that no one may deceive you with plausible arguments.

2:5 For though I am absent in body, yet I am with you in spirit, and I rejoice to see your orderly conduct and the firmness of your faith in Christ.

While Paul had been speaking generalities, now he is beginning to focus on the realities present in Colossae and its place in the Lycus Valley.[124] He has had pastoral interests all along, but now he is warming to the subject that is on his mind. The linking conjunction "for" (*gar*) solidly connects this short paragraph with what has been said in 1:24–27 and could be translated "for

---

[122] Lightfoot, *Colossians*, 171.
[123] Caird, *Colossians*, 187.
[124] There is debate among scholars as to where this section division should be drawn. Is 2:1–5 a part of Paul's polemic beginning in 2:6 or does it conclude the previous section? The majority view 1:24–2:5 as unified, particularly as they see thematic links between 1:23 and 2:6.

you see . . ."[125] He has disclosed personal things about his own work so that the Colossians who have not met him personally will realize that his endeavors have also been for them. No doubt through a report from Epaphras, he is now letting on how much he knows about the difficulties in the church. There are some eloquent speakers there who are trying to persuade the Colossians to follow a different path. To this Paul answers that the Colossians need to acquire a clear understanding of what is at stake (2:2). He digresses (as he did in 1:15–20) into Christology (2:3), reiterating that Christ is the center of all knowledge. He then returns to pastoral concerns in 2:4–5, drawing up a profile of the church that can weather this sort of storm: standing united together and holding firmly to their convictions.

When Paul says, "I want you to know," he is employing a rhetorical device that was well known in his day (2:1). He uses it often (Rom 1:13; 11:25; 1Cor 10:1; 11:3, etc.). It alerts the reader that what he is saying is crucial to the argument he is making. When he refers to his striving (*agōnizomai*), he again is drawing an image from the arena and its contests, as he did in 1:29. With this comes a hint of the struggle he is anticipating in Colossae. We forget that Paul experienced hostilities and conflicts in a number of his churches. His first effort in Pisidian Antioch concluded with Paul and Barnabas being driven out (Acts 13:50–52). Even within some churches he saw conflict. After Paul began the church at Corinth, it suffered a major internal schism led by rival leaders (1Cor 1:10–17). Things truly erupted after Paul had moved on, and in his second letter he describes revisiting the church and experiencing public rejection (2Cor 10–13). In 2Cor 2:1–4 he describes his anguish regarding this church. He "suffered pain from those who should have made him rejoice" (2:3).

Now his concerns reach beyond Colossae. Paul is in prison, and so his ministry is limited by his lack of freedom. He is thinking not just about the churches he planted, like Corinth, but also about those that have never met him, believers who have not been with him "face to face."[126] For the

---

[125] BDAG, 189–190 §2 refers to it as an explanatory use (Rom 7:1; 1Cor 16:5), supplying a reason for what has just been said.

[126] The full phrase in Greek is "those who have not seen my face in the flesh." It is an idiom that means seeing someone "face-to-face." See TDNT 6:776.

present, Paul is thinking about the three cities in the east Lycus Valley (Colossae, Laodicea, Hierapolis), since we know that Epaphras, who is with Paul, served in founding churches in each (4:13; see earlier). These three formed a triangle, were about a dozen miles apart, and no doubt knew each other well. In 4:16 we learn that Paul wants this letter (Colossians) read in the church of Laodicea, and he notes that the Laodiceans have received their own letter (which Paul wants read in Colossae). No doubt Tychicus, the courier of these letters, will orchestrate all of this (4:7). We can only speculate about this second letter.

In **2:2** Paul explains his purposes in reaching out to the Colossians.[127] Four pastoral gifts that are interwoven stem from Paul's heartfelt yearnings for these believers he has never met. As he does in his other letters, Paul writes hoping to bring *encouragement* to them (Rom 12:8; 15:4–5; 2Cor 1:4; 13:11). In some cases, encouragement (*parakaleō*) can refer to exhortation or admonishment, as Paul uses it in Eph 4:1. The word can also refer to "comfort," but that is likely not strong enough. This meaning only works if we understand comfort in its more ancient connotation of strengthening (Latin *confortare, advocatus*). Joined here as it is with "hearts," translating as encouragement is likely best only if we carry in the notion of strengthening, which is a common connotation with the Greek term.[128]

When Paul refers to "hearts" we have to reframe this, since it had a different meaning in antiquity. Ancient Hebrew anthropology explained that life was in blood (Hebrew *lēb, lēbāb*; hence blood sacrifice at the altar). The heart (*kardia*) was the center of a person's life and thought. Therefore, the heart was the "focus of his being and activity as a spiritual personality, the seat of their moral and intellectual life."[129] This is why, for instance, in Rom 1:21 Paul can describe pagans who have abandoned interest in God as

---

[127] This is introduced by *hina* plus the subjunctive *paraklēthōsin*, creating a purpose clause.
[128] The Greek term belongs to the word group linked to *paraklēsis*. Its root is in the idea of calling someone alongside (TDNT 5.774). Friendly exhortation or encouragement easily becomes consolation or comfort. In rabbinic writing in this period the noun *paraklētos* became a Hebrew loanword for an advocate who could accompany you and defend you (m.'Abot 4:11). This is the Johannine meaning of the Spirit-Paraclete in the farewell discourse (John 13–17). TDNT 5.802; G. M. Burge, *The Anointed Community. The Holy Spirit in the Johannine Tradition* (Grand Rapids: Eerdmans, 1987), 6–31.
[129] TDNT 3.609. The LXX sometimes translates the Hebrew *lēb* with the Greek *psyxē* (soul). Thus the NT emphasizes this Hebrew distinction (against the Greek) and makes the *kardia* the "main organ of psychic and spiritual life," 3.611.

having "their hearts darkened." As the balance of Romans 1 shows, their problem is a complete collapse of religious sensitivity, moral integrity, and reason. In 1Cor 7:37 the NRSV rightly translates *kardia* as "mind," recognizing that this is the source of thought and decision-making. God tests the heart (1Thess 2:4) and judges the heart (1Cor 4:5). Thus, to encourage someone's heart is to strengthen their resolve and fortitude and not entirely their emotions (compare 1Thess 3:2–3; Rom 1:11–12).[130]

This encouragement (which is Paul's main thought) now takes on a series of subordinate ideas that weave together the notion of encouragement: Paul wants these churches to be encouraged as they (1) experience unity in love and, in this unity, (2) experience all the riches of assured understanding as well as (3) the deepest knowledge of the mystery of Christ Jesus.

Paul refers to unity frequently in his letters (Phil 2:1–4), but here the idea is linked grammatically to the encouragement mentioned at the beginning of 2:2. The encouragement of their hearts is found in this unity of love, which then brings about a flourishing community. One difficulty is that this verb (*symbibazō*) can mean either "being united," as it is here in the NRSV, or "being taught," which we find in Acts 9:22 and 19:33 and in 1Cor 2:16. This is also the standard translation in the LXX. But the reason most translations point to "unity" in Col 2:2 is the parallel with Eph 4:16, which links the word with being "joined" (NRSV "knit together"). In Col 2:19 Paul uses it again, and this time the theme of unity is obvious from his metaphor of the body working together in unison ("the body ... held together by its ligaments and tendons"). Therefore, our translation of "united in love" makes good sense.

This unity is a unity of love (*agapē*, see 1:4), which we have seen before and will see again (Col 1:4, 8; 2:2; 3:14, 19). The temptation for a modern reader is to sentimentalize this idea, but for Paul and his contemporaries this type of love expresses something specialized: It is about intentionality and investment, a commitment that focuses on behavior rather than affections. It could convey sympathy, mercy, honoring someone, or

---

[130] The emotions in Hebrew thought were located in the lower abdomen (*splagchnon*). Thus 2Macc 9:5–6 LXX refers to a seat of feelings (also Prov 26:22). In 1John 3:17 John warns against those who "close their hearts" – but the actual noun here is *splagchnon*. Curiously, the ancient world focused much on the heart but was utterly unclear about the function of the brain.

showing esteem. Among Greek authors writing about emotive love, the word was deemed colorless, which is why it was rarely used in the centuries prior to the NT.[131] In contrast, the NT made enormous use of it and took advantage of its moral imperatives. Thus, when Jesus tells his followers to love their enemies (Matt 5:43–44) he is describing a disposition or outlook that will treat the enemy differently, and, in this sense, the Parable of the Good Samaritan (Luke 10:29–37) becomes a prime illustration of loving behavior. This sort of love, then, is something qualitatively different, a love that will encourage and enrich the community in which it lives. Given the controversies that were at work in Colossae, this encouragement had to be rooted in a disciplined choice to respect, support, and aid all those in their fellowship.

This encouragement rooted in *agapē* love leads to good things. We can take the next words to explain the purpose of this encouragement-in-unity. Paul writes, "The riches of assured understanding," but this disguises a very complex Greek difficulty (see 1:19–20). It is literally "all the riches of assurance (*plērophoria*) of understanding (*synesis*)." The issue is how assurance and understanding work together in this string of run-on modifiers. *Plērophoria* as a compound noun describing "fullness brought" (*plērēs*, full; *pherō*, to bring) and can refer to the full measure of something now completed (Rom 11:25). Its verb can mean *to convince*.[132] This means *plērophoria* can mean conviction, certainty, or assurance ("fullness of mind"). In Eph 4:13 it is aligned with maturity.

Box 2.9 A Closer Look: United in Love

Every community enjoys a shared vocabulary that unifies it and sets it apart from those who live nearby. Occasionally this vocabulary is cryptic so that outsiders might find it incomprehensible. But certainly, any community that fails to build insider codes for itself is likely disunited or indistinguishable from its world.

We sense that within Paul's writing there are key words that are being used to distinguish the Christian worldview from all others. For instance, Paul's use of "faith, hope and love" – the well-known Pauline triad – is used with enough frequency that it had become recognizable to his readers (Gal 5:5–6; 1Cor 13:13; Col 1:4–5; 1Thess 1:3; 5:8). These were to be the hallmarks of what it meant to

---

[131]　TDNT 1:36–37.
[132]　BDAG 827–828.

belong to the community of Christ. This was the foundation of Christian ethics. This is what set the church apart. Among these the term *agapē* is likely the most provocative. Of its 116 uses in the NT, 75 appear in Paul's letters.[133] But what is striking is how rarely this word was used by Paul's contemporaries. The uses of it in non-biblical Greek in this era (until the third century) are limited. Nevertheless, the NT has drawn from this word an essential meaning that lived at the heart of Christian identity. With Dunn, this word "gave distinctive weight as a carrier of one of the important and far-reaching emphases marking out Christianity among other religions of the time."[134] Jesus' use of this in his great commandment (Mark 12:28–32) is well-known. But the centrality of love belongs to Paul as well (Gal 5:6, 13, 22; Rom 13:10; 1Cor 13; 16:14; Eph 5:2; 1Tim 1:5, etc.). Both in the writings of Judaism in this era and in the NT, discussions of love begin with how God loves his people, a theme reinforced relentlessly in the LXX.[135] In both the OT and the NT this love is expressed by a covenant relationship and thus cannot be viewed as sentimental. It is about commitment and protection and stability (Gen 12; Exod 19–24). And for the NT the supreme expression of this can be found on the cross (2Cor 5:14–15; Rom 5:6–8; 8:31–35).[136]

If this covenantal framework is what grounds the Christian notion of love, it becomes easier to understand why Paul can expect and celebrate when the Colossians love *all the saints* (1:4) and how in 2:2 he can expect unity anchored in love. He tells us in Gal 3:28 and Col 3:11 that this is a love not based on affections – because now Jews will love Gentiles and slaveholders will love slaves – but rather it is anchored to a love mirroring what we know about God and in particular what we know about Christ. This love, expressed by *agapē*, represents an ethical choice that surely sweeps up our feelings but is not undone by their absence.

This is perhaps the test of how deeply members of the church understand love. If it is not tethered correctly to what has been seen and experienced in Christ, it will quickly dissipate when loving becomes too difficult.

Paul's thoughts now begin to come clear. He aspires for these Christians that they have encouraged hearts inspired not only by loving unity but by living in full confidence that what they know is true. Understanding (*synesis*; also 1:9) is knowing that can synthesize the whole.[137] In secular

---

[133] If we include other forms of the word such as the verb *agapaō* and the adjective *agapētos*, the number of uses surpasses 300.
[134] Dunn, *Colossians*, 57.
[135] TDNT 1:39.
[136] McKnight, *Colossians*, 93; Witherington, *Colossians*, 121.
[137] LouwNida, 32.6, *synesis*.

Greek it meant bringing (ideas) together, and so it might mean a conflu-
ence, and thus comprehension at the deepest level. It is someone that does
not simply recite the creeds but comprehends their inner logic and so
becomes confident, assured, in where they stand. However, we cannot
forget that Paul has tied this assurance to the heart, and so this
understanding is personal, profound, and not simply intellectual, or a
cataloging of theological information. In 1:9 this understanding is acquired
through the Spirit.

But, in addition, Paul seeks for them to have knowledge (*epignosis*, 1:9,
10). Here the nuance is different. While *synesis* pointed to comprehending
the coherence of a subject, this now refers to knowing anchored to facts,
things that can be tested and recited (in a Roman school perhaps). This
knowing is the ability to manage the basic truths – in this case, about the
mystery of God (i.e., Christ). This is an abrupt and surprising ending.[138]
But perhaps this is precisely what Paul intends. The aim of everything he
has been saying is Christologically focused. The faith is not a regimen of
beliefs; it is a person, Christ, in whom the mysteries of God have been
revealed. We have seen already how this mystery was defined in 1:27 – it is
"Christ in you," an invitation that welcomed Gentiles, who now share in a
divine inheritance (1:12). However, while in 1:12 the mystery was Christ in
you, here it is about God in Christ – that is, "the Christ who lives on in the
church and is himself the embodiment of God's wisdom ..."[139] The
indwelling of Christ in this story is not a mystery separate from God
himself; it is God himself. This knowledge thus joins with the comprehensive understanding that can be celebrated in loving unity in the church.
This assurance-in-community, in Paul's mind, will fortify the Colossians
against those teachers who are pushing them in new directions.

Mention of Christ in 2:2 now draws Paul into another Christological
digression in **2:3**. We saw the same digression in 1:15–20, which sprang
from words of praise for Christ in 1:13–14. Now we hear words that are

---

[138] Scribes found Paul's grammar in 2:2 impossible (or intolerable) at this point. Over a
dozen variants attempt to smooth the abrupt sentence: *the knowledge of the mystery of
God, Christ*. This reading is found in two important manuscripts (P46, B). Still, the
grammar is strained. Scribal emendations include: *the mystery of Christ, the mystery of
God, the mystery of God and of Christ, the mystery of God who is in Christ,* and *the
mystery of God the father of Christ* (Sinaiticus*).
[139] Caird, *Colossians*, 187.

reminiscent of 1:15–20 but sound different notes. The verse begins with "in whom" (*en hō*), and this refers not to the mystery of 2:2 but to Christ whose name ends 2:2. For some, this verse is the high point of the letter.[140] It does not match the exalted language of 1:15–20 but it concentrates the main theme that Paul has been driving home. "Christ is the one in whom is to be found *all* that one needs in order to understand spiritual reality and to lead a life pleasing to God."[141] The imagery of hidden treasures of wisdom and knowledge was commonly applied to Wisdom in the Jewish tradition (Prov 2:3–6; Wis 6:22; 7:13–14). And as we have seen, the Jewish Wisdom tradition was fertile ground where Paul began to frame his understanding of Christ's identity. A similar thought is in 1Cor 2:7, where Paul speaks of God's wisdom as "a hidden mystery which God decreed before the ages for our glory." But this hidden mystery – and this is Paul's central point – has not been left disguised or incomprehensible to the world. This mystery is now in the open in the gospel, and the failure of many is that they neither believed nor understood what was happening before them.

This allusion to wisdom within Christology in 2:3 is different than the other references to wisdom in Colossians (1:9, 28; 2:23; 3:16; 4:5). Generally, wisdom is a characteristic of sound teaching (1:28; 3:16, "teach in all wisdom"). But here it is an attribute of Christ himself. And this may give us some insight into the controversy in the church. Evidence today points away from an early gnostic of a pagan emphasis on wisdom in this text.[142] Instead, Paul may be anticipating a debate with those in the Jewish (-Christian?) community who had elevated Torah-as-Wisdom as a means to possess these eternal properties of divine mystery. This is particularly true in Jewish apocalypticism (1Enoch 46:3; 2Bar 44:14–15) but also in the OT itself (Dan 2:19–21; Prov 2:3–6). See Isa 33:5–6: "The Lord is exalted; he dwells on high ... He will be the stability of your times, abundance of salvation, wisdom, and knowledge; the fear of the LORD is Zion's treasure."[143] This may have evolved into a Torah mysticism claiming access to

---

[140] Moo, *Colossians*, 169; Beale, *Colossians*, 157–158.
[141] Moo, *Colossians*.
[142] M. Bockmuehl, *Revelation and Mystery in Ancient Judaism and Pauline Christianity*. WUNT 2/36 (Tübingen: J.C.B. Mohr, 1990).
[143] Cited in McKnight, *Colossians*, 212.

these mysteries that were inaccessible to the ordinary person.[144] This mystery, this wisdom, these treasures that had been at the very heart of God now have been revealed in Christ, and any other claimant to such revelation will be deemed in error.

In sum, Col 2:2–3 provides a vital reminder to anyone standing for the truth of the gospel in a setting where that truth is questioned or new teachers wish to supplement it – or where the church is distressed because critics want to deny what the church holds dear. Paul wants Christians in Colossae or in any context to be strengthened and encouraged by a loving unity based on a confident, shared understanding of what the mystery of the gospel actually says. Jesus Christ lives at the very center of God's self-revelation in history. To have Christ-in-you is to have God indwelling our deepest selves. And to demote Christ or to view him as bearing incomplete access to God, a half-filled treasure, obsolete perhaps, indicates someone whose wisdom and knowledge are fallible. This is to upend the very essence of the most profound mystery of what God has done for us.

To be sure, Paul knows that critics to this absolute and uncompromising idea will abound (2:4). They will be eloquent, persuasive, even cynical. They will stand alongside the narrow path and call believers to abandon the presumption of claiming to have the only "way" (Matt 5:13–14). These, Jesus says, are false prophets (Matt 5:15). Such voices always make a case that is plausible; they are often compelling, and they will always have their followers. They will argue that the popularity of their message demonstrates that it cannot be wrong, that God is blessing them – but this is the wide gate, the way of deception.

For the first time in this letter, we have clarity about what is happening in Colossae. Paul confronted such teachers in other settings such as Galatia or Corinth, but here Paul's words sound a warning. "I am saying this so that no one may deceive you . . ." These opening words are a form of gentle reinforcement to strengthen the message. Paul's word for deception (*paralogizomai*) was widely used to express fraudulent behavior or deceit.[145] But the key to the warning is the character of this teaching: It will seem plausible (*pithanologia*). This term is rare in the NT (only here) but well-known in Greek rhetoric. Dunn points out a fascinating comparison in

---

[144] Arnold, *Colossian Syncretism*, 270–274.
[145] BDAG 768. It occurs fourteen times in the LXX and twice in Josephus (11.275 and 17.8).

Plato between a *plausible* argument and a *demonstrated* argument.[146] The latter leads to a sound conclusion that is compellingly based on its evidence. The former is an argument that seems specious on its face. It offers cunningly told falsehoods presented so well that the hearer is beguiled by the form of the speech, not its content. But we also have to imagine that these critics were sufficiently sophisticated (2:8) that they could pose a substantial challenge.

A major question in the balance of this chapter is the nature of this teaching. It may, of course, have simply been popular religious speculation that would have circulated in any Roman town, and so Paul's warning is broadly generic. It could have been teaching *within* the Colossian church that led to internal strife. Or it may have come from a synagogue in Colossae where teachers were not only contradicting Paul's Messianic message but revealing that they were caught up in a form of Hellenistic mysticism. The details of circumcision (2:11), dietary rules and festivals (2:16), or angel worship suggest a hybrid worldview anchored in Judaism but also receptive to Hellenistic religions.

Paul has just delivered a strong warning to the Colossians, and they might have inquired about the authority Paul assumes he has.[147] He is in Rome; they are in Roman Asia. He recognizes that he is absent but argues that he is also present, not simply within the letter they are holding, as if his "voice" here penned in ink brought him to Colossae. Nor is he suggesting that he is simply empathic, feeling one with them in their struggle (e.g., "I am with you in spirit"). Much as he does in 1Cor 5:3 ("For I, though absent in body, am present in spirit . . ."), Paul here does not mean that his human "spirit" in some manner has relocated itself. Paul's use of *pneuma* (spirit) generally refers to the Holy Spirit.[148] And with the Colossians together Paul believes that they can experience unity and presence together inasmuch as they both share in the Holy Spirit.

The main point in 2:5 is that Paul wants to be with them as much as possible, despite his imprisonment. And in this unity he finds consolation. He sees their "orderly conduct" and the "firmness" of their faith in Christ,

---

[146] Dunn, *Colossians*, 133. He cites Plato, *Theaetetus*, 162e and sees the same distinction in Aristotle, *Ethica Nicomachea*, 1.3.4; Epictetus 1.8.7; and Philo, *De cherubim*, 9.

[147] This argument follows Moo, *Colossians*, 173, and Martin, *Colossians*, 70.

[148] G. Fee, *God's Empowering Presence* (Peabody: Hendrickson, 1994), 645–646.

which are two antidotes to the challenges facing their community. Orderly conduct (*taxis*) points to something well-organized and having a purposeful appearance much as Paul uses it in 1Cor 14:40, where he tells the Corinthians that "everything must be done properly and in good order (*taxis*)." But it is also a military term describing an array of troops standing in well-regimented form.[149] The second word, firmness (*stereos*), describes something that is rigid, hard, or solid – something substantial. Thus, in 1Tim 2:19 this is the "firm foundation" consisting of the promises of God. In the LXX the word appears in Genesis to describe the "firmament" (Gen 1:6; Ps 19:2). Together these two words (*taxis, stereos*) join to create a military image of troops standing in formation such as a phalanx of soldiers whom Paul, their leader, is now addressing. This use of *stereos* spilled over to the strength of one's faith, as we see in 1Pet 5:9: "Resist him [the devil], steadfast in your faith …" (also Acts 16:9), and therefore it implies stability and immovability.

Before Paul begins his more detailed examination of the teachings at Colossae (2:6–4:6), he therefore has in mind the spiritual defenses he aspires to see in them. Paul is with them "like a general standing before his troops reviewing the battlelines."[150] A church united, standing shoulder to shoulder, a church knowing what it believes confidently – such a church will not be uprooted in any generation.

THE CONCERNS OF THE LETTER, 2:6–4:6

2:6–7 A Grounding Theological Statement

2:6 As you therefore have received Christ Jesus the Lord, continue to walk in him,

2:7 rooted and built up in him and established in the faith, just as you were taught, abounding in thanksgiving.

Col 2:6 opens Paul's careful discussion of the mistaken teachings at Colossae that have been reported to him. And since Paul wants this letter read also at Laodicea (4:16), we can assume that these teachings were widespread in the Lycus Valley. He begins by warning them against

---

[149] Lightfoot, *Colossians*, 176, with citations from antiquity: 1Macc 4:19; 10:50.
[150] Martin, *Colossians*, 70, citing Lohmeyer, *Colossians*.

novelty. Their faith should not be an unmoored set of beliefs that may be reshaped from time to time, but it should be anchored to the handing on of the tradition that Epaphras has given to them.

The language Paul uses here (and elsewhere in his letters) was a routine reminder of the importance of adhering to an apostolic message that originated with the earliest teachings among Christian leaders about what the followers of Jesus believe. This suggests that during the earliest periods of Christian history, while Paul was alive and before the gospels were written, the church had developed some fundamental agreements about the faith. This is not to say that there were no differences in the early church. The Johannine communities had a very different vocabulary for the faith than, say, the Pauline communities. However, within this diversity there was consensus as well about the centrality of Jesus Christ, his relation to God, and the importance of his entry into human history both as revealer and savior. Thus, Paul can remind the Colossians that they "received" Christ and that they had been "taught." This teaching had content, it was centered on Christ, and it required an unflinching commitment to critical ideas that might be challenged by others. Is this a movement toward orthodoxy at its earliest stages? Orthodoxy is likely too strong a word. But it at least shows that from the very start Christians began to find a degree of agreement on what they should believe (and not believe) and how they should live.

These verses set the tone of what is to follow and underscore that what Paul is about to say must be taken to heart as a lived reality within the church. A similar preliminary exhortation can be found in Gal 1:11–12 or perhaps Rom 1:16–17. Here we should read Col 2:6–7 together with 2:4: "I am saying this so that no one may deceive you with plausible arguments." This echoes the "firmness of faith" and the stature of their demeanor mentioned in 2:5. These comments are preparatory for the debate that is about to be engaged.

Paul begins (**2:6**) with a comparative conjunction (*hōs oun*, therefore, just as), which continues his previous thoughts and then ties an opening verb to an imperative: *Just as you received Christ Jesus the Lord, (continue to) walk in him.*[151] Adhere, therefore, to the Great Tradition Epaphras

---

[151] Paul does not complete the comparison with the usual *outōs* ("just as . . . so") but instead opens the sentence with it, giving the sense of cause ("insofar as . . . walk"). BD §453.

delivered to you. What does it mean to receive Christ Jesus? In many Protestant (Evangelical) circles where personal conversion and rebirth are emphasized, this might describe the moment when a person accepts the lordship of Christ, receives the Spirit, and commits to a life of obedient discipleship. It could also be accompanied by baptism. Of course, some of these emphases were true for Paul; however, this verb (*paralambanō*, receive) is never used by Paul for conversion. Here in 2:6 Paul is emphasizing how the Colossians embraced Epaphras' teachings and how they need to show fidelity to the truth of the gospel.[152] This concern is echoed in 1:7, "as you learned from Epaphras ..." and in 2:7, "as you were taught ..."[153] This teaching no doubt included narratives about Jesus (1Cor 11:23–32), ethical instruction from him (1Cor 7:10; 9:14), as well as teachings Paul had advanced throughout his career.

The language of reception here recalls the transmission of sacred teachings well-known in Judaism. This was a world where the preservation, handing on, and receiving of sacred texts were critical duties and obtained a technical language. But in communities such as the early church without formal custodial communities where texts could be preserved, such transmission and reception were delicate matters that had to be carefully handled. It was a religious obligation to transmit and receive tradition faithfully. We see this awareness of transmission illustrated in the Mishna's opening of the tractate *The Sayings of the Fathers* (*Pirke Avot*).[154]

A. Moses received Torah at Sinai and handed it on to Joshua, Joshua to elders, and elders to prophets,

B. And prophets handed it on to the men of the great assembly.

C. They said three things: (1) "Be prudent in judgment." (2) "Raise up many disciples." (3) "Make a fence for the Torah."[155]

This is the opening overture found in the vast collection of sayings that had been transmitted within Judaism from the Second Temple period until

---

[152] Campbell, *Colossians*, 32.

[153] Similarly, 1Thess 4:1; 1Cor 15:1, 2; 9:23; Gal 1:9, 12; and Phil 4:9, where the received and learned stand together.

[154] Cited by McKnight, *Colossians*, 217, and Caird, *Colossians*, 189.

[155] The fence refers to supplementary laws that keep the Jew from infringing on the Torah itself. If the Torah specifies limits to work on the Sabbath, a fence would exceed that limit to protect one from breaking the law.

about 200 CE. Since Paul lived within this period, we are correct to imagine that he understood such transmission. Paul uses this language of tradition transmission in 1Cor 11:23: "For I *received* from the Lord what I also *handed on* to you, that the Lord Jesus on the night when he was betrayed took a loaf of bread ..." Here we have Paul citing a text from the Lord's Supper with close linguistic parallels to Luke and alerting the Corinthians that these are words he "received," and he is now "handing them on" to them. Both Col 2:6 and 1Cor 11:23 use *paralambanō* to describe this tradition "reception" (also 1Cor 15:3; 1Thess 2:13; 4:1; 2Thess 3:6).[156] How did this instruction take place? In both the Christian and Jewish settings, transmission was likely oral and overseen by so-called custodians of the faith. In the church, these might be elders, apostles, or those appointed by them.

The language "Christ Jesus the Lord" (*ton Christon Iēsoun ton kurion*) can be taken in a variety of ways. The question is whether Christ is a proper name or a title.[157] Did the Colossians receive "Christ Jesus" as (their) Lord (so TNIV) or "Christ Jesus, the Lord" (NRSV, ESV)? Or was this a title and they received "Jesus" – as Christ and Lord (NEB) or the "Christ, even Jesus the Lord" (Lightfoot)?[158] These distinctions are perhaps less important than we imagine. At the heart of the earliest Christian confessions was the signal announcement that Jesus was Messiah (Christ), and this evolved into a name: Christ Jesus (which occurs in Paul eighty-nine times). But it is not only that Jesus (of Nazareth) is embraced as Messiah, but that he is also Lord, the one to whom full obedience was due. Thus, the climax of Peter's speech in Acts 2 reaches this point: "Therefore let the entire house of Israel know with certainty that God has made him both Lord and Messiah, this Jesus whom you crucified" (2:36). Similarly in Phil 2:10–11, Paul announces that "every tongue should confess that Jesus Christ is Lord, to the glory of God the Father."

In this Roman context, such an announcement was arresting. Lord (*kurios*) suggested a hierarchy and created a framework of masters and servants or a king and his subjects. It is an astounding claim. *Kurios* was

---

[156] The verbs *paradidōmi* (to hand over) and *paralambanō* (to receive) may have become technical terms in Hellenistic Judaism for transmission (corresponding to Hebrew *qibbel* and *masar*). Caird, *Colossians*, 189; Dunn, *Colossians*, 138.

[157] See numerous options, e.g., Harris, *Colossians*, 80.

[158] Lightfoot, *Colossians*, 173; Harris, *Colossians*, 80.

commonly used for the emperor, and more, it is the usual way that the LXX translates the divine name of God (Yahweh). This is an exhortation to the Colossians to be sure to live lives of full obedience. But it was also an announcement that had wider implications. Jesus was not simply a Jewish messiah so designated for Jews around the empire. Jesus *as messiah* also had a universal authority that was greater than Judaism. Imagine the implications this bore for any in the Roman Empire where allegiance to the emperor as *kurios* was assumed.

Reference to the lordship of Christ now takes on a concrete form: *walking* in him. This present imperative (*peripateite*) following the past tense verb ("as you received") gives the phrase a continuous force: *As you have received, now (continue) walking in him.*[159] Here walking refers to a life lived in obedience and is peculiarly Greek but also a natural Hebrew expression (Exod 18:20; Deut 13:4–5; Ps 86:11). This echoes Col 1:10 (". . . walk worthy of the Lord, fully pleasing to him") and implies that the believer is not simply giving mental acknowledgment of Christ's position but is living a life in conformity to Christ's position. This is a continuing proposition (here emphasizing the continuous force of the imperative) and assumes an unyielding discipleship for the long term. But this also is not simply conformity to the traditions given by Epaphras. This takes on something personal and inescapable: *walking in him.* This is not only adherence to a doctrine but a living relationship with Christ, a spirituality motivated from within.[160] It might be compared with Gal 5:16: "Live (or walk, *peripateite*) by the Spirit, I say, and do not gratify the desires of the flesh." This is a life of discipleship grounded in the inner presence of Christ-in-Spirit. As in 1:27, this is "Christ in you, the hope of glory."

Here we have an important pastoral insight. Paul's hope for the Colossians is that they will have the twin experiences that together will anchor them. They conform to the traditions as received ("an assured understanding," "having received Christ") – and are led by Christ-in-Spirit ("walking in him"). Whenever the church has concentrated on either of these to the exclusion of the other, difficulties arise.

This notion of living or walking *in Christ* and possessing an assured understanding of their faith now finds fuller explanation in three

[159]   Harris, *Colossians*, 80.
[160]   Dunn, *Colossians*, 140.

metaphors (**2:7**, *rooted*, *built up*, and *established*) that all serve the same purpose, tying back to the imperative *to walk*.[161] Walking "in him" is not simply moral obedience or spiritual experience; it is knowing what we believe with confidence and conviction. The first metaphor, being rooted (*hrizoō*), comes from agriculture for a tree whose roots have moved deep into the soil (also Eph 3:17). It suggests health, growth, strength, and vitality, tapping into depths that will sustain. This too is a Jewish metaphor. Ezekiel imagines Israel as a tree finding abundant water at these depths (Ezek 31:7). Jeremiah describes the faithful Israelite whose roots find such water and so is unafraid of the desert heat or drought but instead continues to yield fruit (Jer 17:8; see Col 1:10).

The second metaphor, built up (*epoikodomeō*), comes from construction (we can see the term for a house or building: *oikos*) and means to build on (*epi*) something, such as a house built on rock (Matt 7:24). In 1Cor 3:10 it refers to building on a foundation that is already laid. In Eph 2:20 Paul describes the church as built on the foundation of prophets and apostles (cf. 1Pet 2:5). And here he implores the Colossians to be built up *in Christ*, the one foundation of the church.[162] Jude 20–21 shares a similar thought: "But you, beloved, *build yourselves up* on your most holy faith; pray in the Holy Spirit; keep yourselves in the love of God; look forward to the mercy of our Lord Jesus Christ that leads to eternal life."

Paul's third metaphor points to stability and involves a quick shift of images. A person who is *bebaios* is someone who is reliable, steadfast, or steady (Heb 6:19; 2Pet 1:10). In 2Cor 1:7 Paul refers to "unwavering" (*bebaios*) faith. In Rom 4:16 this term is used to refer to the "certainty" of the promises God has given in Abraham. Its verb (*bebaioō*) describes making something certain or firm and was used widely in the market or for legal purposes. It is a price or an agreement that is solid or confirmed.[163] So in 1Cor 1:6 Paul can describe how "the testimony of Christ has been *strengthened* (or confirmed) among you ..." Here in Col 2:7 Paul wants to see the Colossians grounded and strong, stable and steady, in their faith.

---

[161] These are three participles creating subordinate ideas to the imperative that precedes it.
[162] Note that this second participle is in the present, implying ongoing growth. The first participle, rooted, is in the perfect tense, suggesting something that has happened and now has ongoing implications. This rootedness may well refer to their baptism. See further Martin, *Colossians*, 72–73.
[163] TDNT 1:602–603.

This would be knowing the nature and content of the apostolic teaching but also comprehending its logic and implications fully (1:28; 2:2; 3:16).

"Abounding in thanksgiving" is Paul's closing to this exhortation (a final participle joining the previous three). To abound (*perisseuō*) refers to someone having plenty, such as in Mark 12:44 when Jesus describes the widow who gives money to the treasury: "They contributed out of their *abundance*, but she out of her poverty." Of course, the abundance Paul points to is their thanksgiving (also 1:12), and behind this is the assumption that gratefulness – along with rootedness, strength, and stability – now complete the picture of the believer who is walking in Christ. This thanksgiving is not directed generically to the good things in life. It is directed toward the blessing of having lives changed by Christ and living lives anchored thus to his lordship. The NIV brings this together well, "overflowing with thankfulness."

2:8–23 An Exhortation and a Warning

2:8–15 *The Claims of This Philosophy Are Wrong*

2:8 Watch out that no one takes you captive through philosophy and empty deceit, according to human tradition, according to the elemental principles of the world, and not according to Christ.

2:9 For in him the whole fullness of deity dwells bodily,

2:10 and you have come to fullness in him, who is the head of every ruler and authority.

2:11 In him also you were circumcised with a spiritual circumcision, by the removal of the body of the flesh in the circumcision of Christ;

2:12 when you were buried with him in baptism, you were also raised with him through faith in the power of God, who raised him from the dead.

2:13 And when you were dead in trespasses and the uncircumcision of your flesh, God made you alive together with him, when he forgave us all our trespasses,

2:14 erasing the record that stood against us with its legal demands. He set this aside, nailing it to the cross.

2:15 He disarmed the rulers and authorities and made a public example of them, triumphing over them in it.

In the previous sections of Colossians, the nature of the opposition has only been implied. Paul warned against the deception of these teachers in 2:4 but here comes very close to naming them and describing what they say. We can read lengthy discussions about the origin of these teachings (see earlier), but today most scholars believe that the fundamental posture of the teachers comes from Judaism. And yet there are numerous hints that this is a Judaism with a difference, a Judaism that has assimilated some of the religious trends well-known in Phrygia. This could be Jewish mysticism or even popular Hellenistic mystery religions. But the common thread is that this was a movement that was likely syncretistic and blended spiritual disciplines for aspiring adherents. The disciplines of Judaism (feast days, circumcision) lived alongside speculation about ascent into spiritual planes populated by angels and spiritual forces. In 2Cor 12:2 Paul shows his interest in this: "I know a person in Christ who fourteen years ago was caught up to the third heaven – whether in the body or out of the body I do not know; God knows." In Gal 1:8 he says that even "if an angel from heaven" brought a new gospel, it should be accursed! Paul can give this hypothetical situation because his audience held a worldview in which such angelic visitors were capable of doing such things.

Much will depend on how we interpret "the elemental principles of the world" in Col 1:8. The name for these so-called principles is *stoicheia*, and, as we will see, the NRSV has taken one view of interpreting them. But it was a term native to Hellenistic religions and no doubt was used liberally and without technical precision among the popular religions of Paul's day. Paul refers to this teaching as a "philosophy" that in some manner is opposed to his teaching about Christ, and with this we can assume that some level of religious elitism is also at work here. A system has been proposed offering good things to those who learn these mysteries, and for those who are spiritually zealous what is offered surpasses what Paul offers in Christ.

The language of 2:8–15 is notoriously difficult to organize. Paul's thoughts seem to weave back and forth as he both promotes the primacy of Christ while warning the church of what is at risk. He doesn't want them taken captive – like a prisoner captured in a military campaign – but instead he wants them to build their defenses and resist this teaching. He reminds them of the benefits that have accrued to them in Christ and ends by saying that not only is Christ greater, but that Christ has defeated these "powers" (2:15) as an army defeats an enemy, taking them captive.

Paul often uses opening exhortations to sound an alarm (1Cor 8:9; 10:12; Gal 5:15; Phil 3:2). "Watch out" conveys this tone nicely (imperative *blepō* followed by *mē*) and implies: *Look out lest someone . . .* or *Take heed!* In **2:8** his warning refers to an unnamed person (*tis*, someone) who will capture them. Paul is not being intentionally ambiguous here, and we should assume he knows who this entity is.[164] Paul also uses the future (*someone will attempt this*) to underscore the imminent threat. The term for "captive" (*sulagōgeō*) appears only here in the NT and describes someone who can carry (you) away (*agō*) as booty (*sulēma*).[165] It can suggest kidnap, exploitation, or making prey – and it could describe someone "capturing your mind" and taking you away before you know it. Harris suggests a literal translation: "Take care lest there will be anyone who carries you off as spoil . . ."[166] Dunn imagines a clever speaker, perhaps a market preacher, gathering disciples through his persuasive speech and then taking them off "for a fuller exposition and induction."[167] Paul's decision to use this rare word might even be provocative. It may be a pun playing on the word synagogue (*sulagōgeō*, *synagōē*), since it is teachers from the synagogue who may try to take you captive.[168]

This threat of captivity – or perhaps of unrelenting, captivating persuasion – is alarming and identifies philosophy (*philosophia*, only here in the NT) and empty deceit (*kenēs apatēs*) as the culprits. Paul here is not demeaning philosophy as we understand it today. Christians have promoted philosophy for centuries as an intellectual discipline worthy of any believer. The term had a long history in Greek reaching back to Plato and Aristotle to describe a comprehensive explanatory system that carefully studied life, its origins, its meaning, and its duties.[169] These explanations stood in opposition to the ancient mythologies that had done the same

---

[164] Contra M. Hooker, "Were There False Teachers in Colossae?" in B. Lindars and S. Smalley, eds., *Christ and Spirit in the New Testament: Studies in Honor of C.F.D. Moule* (Cambridge: Cambridge University Press, 1973), 315–331. As Lightfoot (*Colossians*, 178) pointed out, Paul will use *tis* when speaking about opponents he knows well (Gal 1:7). Lightfoot also points to Ignatius, *Smyrn* 5 as a parallel. See Arnold, *Colossian Syncretism*, 185–186.
[165] Harris, *Colossians*, 83.
[166] Ibid.
[167] Dunn, *Colossians*, 147.
[168] Wright, *Colossians*, 100.
[169] TDNT 9:172–179.

thing. The term simply means "love of wisdom" and was picked up by many to categorize their systematic efforts. Hellenistic religions used this term as well as Judaism, and in Paul's era the OT law was viewed as a *philosophia* and its practical directions valued. Philo refers to Judaism itself as a philosophy (*Legat.* 33.245). In the Jewish *Letter of Aristeas* (c. 200 BCE) an appeal was made to include the OT (in Greek translation) in the Royal Library of Alexandria to stand alongside the great philosophies of antiquity (*Let. Aris.* 1–12). Even the rabbis turned it into a loanword in Hebrew to describe their great scholars (2Macc 1:1–2; 5:22–24). In fact, Josephus uses *philosophia* to label the religious movements of his own day: The Pharisees, the Sadducees, and the Essenes each represented "philosophies" (*War* 2.119; *Antiq.* 18.11).

But the key here is that philosophy could be a systematic *religious* presentation, and this is likely what Paul must confront in Colossae. It is a Jewish philosophy no doubt, and in 2:16–17 Paul will indicate some of the unique Jewish teachings it contained. But the word "philosophy" itself does not express criticism; it is simply descriptive of a "school of thought" that the church has encountered. But in this case, Paul sees this teaching as deceitful (he uses a double negative: *empty/foolish deceit*). As in 2:23 this teaching has the "appearance of religion" but is in fact untrue despite its promoters. In Eph 5:6 Paul describes teaching that deceives with empty (*kenēs*) words. In secular Greek, *kenēs* refers figuratively to words that were frivolous, futile, boastful, even specious; words that are opinions but not true.

Paul also refers to this teaching as a "tradition." It is not problematic to have a religious tradition passed from generation to generation by respected leaders. Synagogues and churches have always had religious traditions. This was the origin of the Colossian gospel (2:6): The apostolic tradition had been passed to them by Epaphras. The problem is the source of that tradition and its successful claim to be revelation originating from God. Paul can say pejoratively that here he must confront *human* tradition (not a divine tradition), which is in itself a rebuke. This contrasts with the divine self-disclosure gained through Christ who presented God's own voice in the world. This of course is a timeless debate that was alive in antiquity and appears even today. All religions claim some degree of transcendent authority. And the debate will center on the source of that authority. For Paul (and the church) the arrival of Christ in history is unprecedented because he is not a courier of ageless human ideas but a bearer of God's own word, God's own person in the world (1:15–20).

In contrast, these rival traditions now have a named source: *the elemental principles (stoicheia) of the world* (NRSV). This phrase represents an ambiguous and frequently debated word: *stoicheion*.[170] The problem is that its many uses make it difficult to apply here. Essentially the word group *stoich-* refers to something belonging to a series or row, such as an element in a list – or something or someone who is in rank. It could refer to a syllable (a part of a word), the alphabet's letters, a musical note on a scale, or a number, such as "first principles."

The term appears only four times in Paul's letters (Gal 4:3, 9; Col 2:8, 20) and has been debated for years. Two options are usually proposed to explain its use in 2:8.

(1) *Cosmic elements: Stoicheia* could refer to the impersonal four elements of the universe: earth, air, water, and fire (2Pet 3:10, 12; also Wis 7:17; 4Macc 12:13).[171] These elements were primal, eternal, and incorruptible, and everything in creation owed its existence to them. Humanity, trees, animals, mountains, and so on – each consisted of a remixing of these same elements. As primary instruments of creation, they took on a religious or spiritual dimension and held properties viewed as sacred. They could be seen as spirits and were usually divinized.[172] We cannot be certain if the *stoicheia* also referred to heavenly bodies such as the stars,[173] but this was a natural extension of this cosmology: The stars were made of fire, which of course had spiritual properties.

(2) *Cosmic spirits: Stoicheia* could also describe personal spiritual powers such as the gods who appeared in pagan worship. This, of course, is a crossover from the cosmic elements discussed earlier, but now it acquires a highly personal feel. However, even this distinction is strained, since the cosmic elements were deemed personal to some degree. The stars were living beings – in fact, the world itself lived

---

[170] See the lengthy discussion in TDNT 7:670–687 and Arnold, *Colossian Syncretism*, 158–194.
[171] TDNT 7:672.
[172] Dunn, *Colossians*, 149, refers to Philo, *Comtempl. Life*, 3, *Decalogue*, 53.
[173] The late *Testament of Solomon* 8:2–4 makes this connection, but we have yet to find this in the pre-NT era.

under a hierarchy of such beings (*stoicheia*) who controlled its fate. Arnold illustrates this with a description of initiation into the Isis cult in Asia Minor. Here *stoicheia* are heavenly beings, "gods and goddesses," who will control or guide or condemn the journeying dead.[174]

Many Jews held views that were little different. Jubilees 2:2 says that there are angels of the spirit of fire as well as the winds – once again the primal elements. Here too the cosmos was populated not simply with spirits, but the Torah itself lived as a divine entity overseeing human life exactly like the *stoicheia* of the pagans. The Jewish Book of Jubilees describes the creation of heavenly bodies on the fourth day, and in one text variant we read how the *stoicheia* were created as well. Most believed that these *stoicheia* were angels, whom many viewed as stars in the heavens. As Jews tried to present their faith to Romans, they would adapt that faith to Hellenistic ideas of fate, astrology, and "modern" philosophies. This returns us to Col 2:8. Paul is likely contending with a Jewish mysticism that has promoted heavenly "elements" (*stoicheia*) as necessary components in spiritual enlightenment. And more, these Jewish apologists were teaching that Jewish practices had a mystical power that increased this spiritual power. But to this was added the worship of angels (2:18), which were the *stoicheia* to which this Jewish teaching – far on the fringes of Jewish orthodoxy – now required obedience. This is similar to the worldview found in Galatians. When Galatians refers to the Jewish law as *given by angels* (3:19) or the temptation Paul sees of the Galatians regressing into an enslavement under the *stoicheia* (4:1–3, 9–10), we are likely encountering the same Jewish mysticism that has embraced a Hellenistic cosmology and populated it with a hierarchy of angels.

Of course, for Paul, this is absolutely unacceptable for one reason alone: *This does not accord with the authority and revelation given to us in Christ.* And rather than seeing Christ as preeminent over these cosmic forces, this new teaching required the Colossians to placate them in order to find advantages in this life and protection from evil. This is a veneration of angels and spiritual practices that has virtually evolved into the practice of magic.

A paraphrasing of this important verse might sound thus: *Be alert so that no one entices you into their web of deceit and makes you a captive to*

---

[174] Arnold, *Colossian Syncretism*, 174.

this religious system. Their teachings are not in line with what you learned about Christ. Such teachings belong to the pagan world, but more, they have been shaped by those cosmic powers, those angels and spirits, you know so well from the pagan world around you.

The deeper inadequacies of this teaching can now be explored (**2:9**). Its problems are twofold: First, the Colossians were committing a theological error by substituting inferior, created beings for God himself (2:9–10); and second, there was the practical error of thinking that ritual practices would advance their spirituality.[175] Both were wrong. The first will be dealt with in 2:9–15; the second will be dealt with in 2:16–19.

Paul's explanation in 2:9 echoes 1:19: ". . . for in him, the fullness of God was pleased to dwell." This is why Jesus is preeminent: Because he descends from God himself, bearing in bodily form the fullness of God's divine life, and thus he can bypass the *stoicheia* that have been promoted as intermediaries. Paul does not write that Jesus bears the fullness of "God" but rather the "fullness of deity" (*theotēs*, only here in the NT). *Theotēs* expresses Christ's divine essence (from *theos*, god) rather than his divine qualities (which would be *theiotēs*, Rom 1:20). This is an ontological description, a link between Christ and the very being of God now given in the abstract. In fact, Colossians does not refer to Christ as God, but what is clear is that Paul "could not reflect on God without reflecting also on Christ."[176] That is, Paul views Christ as participating in God's divine life, and this participation was without parallel. None of the *stoicheia* could say this. In 1:15 Paul says that Christ is "the image of the invisible God" – which means making God's "presence visible and God's power effective since images in antiquity not only reveal but also channel the effectiveness of their 'prototype.'"[177]

Translations attempt to reflect this literally as "God in all his fullness" or the "full measure of divinity." This is an affirmation that leaves no room for compromise, that refuses to let Christ be anything other than above all creation and all the *stoicheia*. Above all, he does not fit into the hierarchal orders of the *stoicheia*; he is beyond them. He is not another God, nor does he seem to be like God; he is a person who is above creation, who

---

[175] Lightfoot, *Colossians*, 181.
[176] Barclay, *Colossians*, 81.
[177] Ibid.

originated creation (1:16), whose life and identity are found with God himself.

But in addition to this Christological clarification (2:9a), Paul adds that this same person in whom God's divine life is present appeared in history in bodily form (*sōmatikōs*). This has been interpreted variously.[178] It could refer to the incarnation itself, where Christ is embodied in flesh (John 1:14). Less likely is the proposal for this referring here to the church, which Paul refers to as the body of Christ (1:18, 24; 3:15). Or *sōmatikōs* could refer to the physical reality, the tangible character of Christ, as opposed to the nebulous and uncertain *stoicheia*.[179] Dunn warns how difficult it is for English speakers to grasp the nuances of "the body" (*sōma*, *sōmatikōs*) when we see this as meaning mere physicality.[180] For Paul, *sōma* refers to more than the physical (such as "corporeality") and instead refers to *presence* or *relationality*, and so Dunn suggests embodiment as the superior translation. In 1Cor 6 Paul uses *sōma* eight times, and here we see its many nuances (see esp. 6:18–19). One can join the body to a prostitute (6:13), but we also must remember that our bodies are "members with Christ" (6:15), and this body is a temple of the Holy Spirit (6:19).[181] The nuances of this distinction are apparent particularly in Paul's discussion of the body in 1Cor 15:33–44, where he can imagine the destruction of one body – and the resurrection of another. In sum, Paul is expressing the essential character of human life – not apart from its corporeality – but knit to it fully. The popular expressions "She is all in" and "She is all here" express something similar: Being here physically is one thing; being fully here, present and available, is quite another but still requires that physical presence.

In this thinking, the dualistic instincts of Hellenism are being upended. The body (*sōma*) is a category of creation required for anyone to encounter anyone else. The body is the instrument that enables us to see and know

---

[178] For the range of options, see Barth and Blanke, *Colossians*, 312–315; for the history of *sōma* in Hellenistic thought and Paul, see Dunn, *The Theology of Paul the Apostle*, 55–61. Beale, *Colossians*, 177–178, argues for Temple typology in 2:9, but few have followed his lead.

[179] So Caird, *Colossians*, 191; Garland, *Colossians*, 146; Abbott, *Colossians*, 249; Wright, *Colossians*, 103.

[180] Dunn, *The Theology of Paul the Apostle*, 55–61.

[181] Note how Paul can say that "Abraham's body was dead" (Rom 4:19), but what he means is that Abraham was impotent; ibid., 59.

and love one another. Therefore, this indwelling of God in Christ included an indwelling *into* the world, which puts this verse in the company of John's Christology (John 1:14; see also Col 1:19).[182] We are therefore very close to the credal notion of incarnation with an emphasis on accessibility and availability.[183] Christ in whom the Father dwells has fully appropriated a creaturely body and so presents us with the Father in terms we can understand. Ferguson explains, "The Son of God has come to our side without leaving the side of his Father."[184] Translations attempt to express this creatively. The NET Bible offers, "For in him all the fullness of deity lives in bodily form." The NLT gives, "For in Christ the fullness of God lives in a human body." Phillips paraphrases, "Yet it is in him [Christ] that God gives a full and complete expression of himself (within the limits that he set himself in Christ)."

Of course, this is an exclusive claim for Christ that is controversial. Thompson summarizes well:

> While some philosophers of religion label (and also reject) as "exclusivist" this claim of Christian faith, other have pointed out that it is properly called "particu-laristic." That is, the primary claim of the Christian faith is a positive one, namely, that God has become manifest in the *particular* person of Jesus of Nazareth and therefore known in the particular narrative of this man's life, death and resurrection.[185]

If Christ enjoys the fullness (*plērōma*, 2:9) of God's divine presence, so, too, now we learn the benefit of attaching to Christ (**2:10**): We, too, have been filled (*plēroō*) with the presence of Christ that was once unimaginable. This noun and verb (*plērōma*, *plēroō*) suggest completion or satisfaction, or an abundant measure.[186] The parallel uses of this in Ephesians make this even stronger: ". . . and to know the love of Christ that surpasses

---

[182] Here we are close to the language of Chalcedon (451 CE), where *homoousios* (same essence) explains Christ's unity with the Father (established at Nicaea in 315 CE) as well as Christ's unity with humanity: ". . . consubstantial [*homoousios*] with the Father according to the Godhead, and consubstantial (*homoousios*) with us according to the Manhood . . ." (*homoousion tō Patri kata tēn theotēta, kai homoousion hēmin ton auton kata tēn anthrōpotēta*).

[183] Dunn, *The Theology of Paul the Apostle*, 205; Moo, *Colossians*, 194.

[184] S. Ferguson, "Chalcedon: A Defining Moment for the Doctrine of Christ," www .desiringgod.org/articles/chalcedon (accessed January 2024).

[185] Thompson, *Colossians*, 54; cited (in part) by McKnight, *Colossians*, 230.

[186] *plērōma*, *plēroō* appear in Colossians five times: 1:9, 19, 25; 2:9; 4:17.

knowledge, so that you may be filled with all the fullness of God" (3:19; cf. 1:23; Rom 15:13–14). Paul imagines how *in Christ* God plans to "flood the lives of men and women, and ultimately all creation, with his own love, power and richness" – and that this is already begun to unfold in the coming of Christ and the Spirit.[187] But the focus here cannot be on *what they obtain* through association with Christ. The focus is on *the one to whom they are connected.*[188] And this, perhaps, is a fundamental difference from the practices of the pagan religions of Paul's day or of the mystics who may be coming from a Colossian synagogue. The center of Paul's message is not on obtaining power – which was central to all ancient religions. Paul's message centers on a person, and this sets Paul's message apart. We are made full not by spiritual practice but "in him," in his living presence. Certainly, there is power to be had here (1:11, 29), but it is not something to be had outside of Christ.

In a world of competing claims for divine encounters or strategies to control those spiritual forces that influence the world, Paul returns again to the status of Christ in that world as he did in 1:15–20. Christ is the head (*kephalē*) of every ruler and authority. The idea of headship here (and throughout Paul) must be carefully nuanced. We are quick to imagine this as Christ ruling, directing, or leading as a corporate head might lead a business. In Hellenistic Greek the fundamental idea of *kephalē* has to do with prominence, supremacy, or primacy. Such a head may be one who rules and leads (Deut 28:13; Isa 9:13–14 LXX), but not necessarily. Here the idea is prominence and power by virtue of Christ's position in relation to God. As a Roman column was "crowned" by its capital (its *kephalē*), so, too, Christ presides over all spiritual forces arrayed beneath him. They can make no claim on him; he, however, can make every claim on them. In fact, as we will see in 2:15, he has conquered them, displayed them in defeat, and removed from them any supposed power they once claimed.

We can assume that these "rulers and authorities" are the same as the "thrones, dominions and rulers" of 1:16 over which Christ is first and above all (1:15). These are also the "elemental forces" (the *stoicheia*) of 2:8. Knowing that Christ's rule supersedes any other rule, that his power is unsurpassed in the cosmos, provides the Colossians with the assurance

---

[187] Wright, *Colossians*, 103.
[188] McKnight, *Colossians*, 231.

they need to be free from those powers that can control the world. Paul refers to this assurance frequently in this letter ("all endurance," "assured understanding," "steadfast in faith," "firmness of faith," "established in faith," 1:11, 23; 2:2–4, 6), and no doubt this is a feature of the fullness described in 2:10. To be so filled with the power of God leads to spiritual confidence. And this can defeat fear – a central feature of life in antiquity: fear of loss, of death, and of the cosmos itself, which is arrayed against human life.

What follows is a complex set of phrases (**2:11–15**) that every translator tries to break up into coherent sentences. Paul is piling on phrase after phrase, attempting to describe fully the significance of what Christ has done as before in 2:8–10 he described who Christ truly is. But as he does this, he speaks directly against practices that were promoted by these teachers from the synagogue. In Paul's mind, if we have "come to fullness" in Christ (2:10), mechanics of religious ritual such as circumcision make little sense (**2:11–12**).[189] Circumcision, of course, was a biblical command (Gen 17:1–14) and evolved into a constant marker for fidelity to the Jewish covenant.[190] But it was also a cultural marker promoting separation between Jews and Gentiles. Circumcision was acknowledged throughout the Greek and Roman worlds as something unique but offensive in Jewish culture (they saw it as mutilation). For them, the intact penis was a sign of masculine beauty and virility; exposure of the glans, however, was improper, and this is what circumcision did.[191]

In a diatribe against Judaism, the Roman historian Tacitus writes, "They [the Jews] adopted circumcision to distinguish themselves from other peoples by this difference. Those who are converted to their ways follow the same practice" (*Histories*, 5.5.2). But also, Jewish leaders shared this

---

[189] This verse is actually a clause linked to 2:10: "... who is the head of every ruler and authority, *in whom also* you were circumcised ..." Notice how the NRSV helpfully begins 2:11 by turning the prepositional phrase (*en auto*, in him) into a new sentence.

[190] McKnight, *Colossians*, 234, points out how circumcision may have been a countermovement by the ancient Hebrews to end child sacrifice, which was prohibited by God. Thus circumcision only "wounds" the older son. See J. D. Levenson, *The Death and Resurrection of the Beloved Son: The Transformation of Child Sacrifice in Judaism and Christianity* (New Haven: Yale University Press, 1995).

[191] J. Neusner, *Approaches to Ancient Judaism. New Series* (Atlanta: Scholars Press, 1993), 149; thus sculpture artists were very careful in how they approached this part of male anatomy, giving the foreskin remarkable detail. Athletes, fearing that the glans might be improperly exposed, could wear a *kynodesme* (*kunodesmē*), which tied the foreskin shut.

same understanding. Josephus describes how the posterity of Abraham would be kept pure from Gentiles: "Furthermore, [so] that his posterity should be kept from mixing with others, God charged him to have them circumcised and to perform the rite on the eighth day after birth" (*Antiquities*, 1.192).[192] In the Maccabean Revolt circumcision was elevated among Jews as a mark of separation from Hellenistic cultural corruptions and as a sign of Jewish loyalty. But for Jews, to remove the marks of circumcision surgically (called *epispasm*) was considered a profound betrayal of Jewish faith (1Macc 1:5, 48; 2Macc 6:9–10). This dividing marker was so common that Jews such as Paul could easily refer to Gentiles and Jews as the "uncircumcised" and the "circumcised" (Acts 11:3; Rom 2:25–27; Gal 2:7–8; Eph 2:11), and everyone knew what they meant.

But circumcision could also be a metaphor. Deut 10:16 can say, "Circumcise, then, the foreskin of your heart, and do not be stubborn any longer." And in Deut 30:6: "[T]he Lord your God will circumcise your heart and the heart of your descendants, so that you will love the Lord your God with all your heart and with all your soul, in order that you may live." This metaphorical use persisted through the Second Temple period as well. In a rewriting of the story of Moses, the Jewish Book of Jubilees records God telling Moses what he will do for his recalcitrant people: "I shall cut off the foreskin of their heart and the foreskin of the heart of their descendants" (Jub 1:22–23). This is the language of spiritual renewal expressed in ancient ritual terms.

This is all useful to us in Col **2:11** because here we find Paul referring to circumcision metaphorically and reinterpreting it in Christian terms and applying it to baptism. It also signals to us how common this metaphor was within the early church and how it could be used to symbolize the competing prospects of religious traditions. Unfortunately, the NRSV and the NRSVue lead us astray here: "You were circumcised with a *spiritual circumcision*," when the older RSV has it exactly right: "[Y]ou were circumcised with a circumcision *made without hands*." The *acheiropoiētos*

---

[192] Others in the ancient world also practiced circumcision, notably the Egyptians. Thus Strabo writes in *Geography* 17.2.5, "One of the customs most zealously observed among the Egyptians is this, that they rear every child that is born, and circumcise the males, and excise (remove portions of *nymphae*) the females, as is also customary among the Jews, who are also Egyptians in origin . . ."

(handless or without hands; elsewhere only Mark 14:58; 2Cor 5:1) is the opposite of *cheiropoiētos*, which means "hand-made." This is a circumcision-without-hands, and it is being juxtaposed to ordinary circumcision that was done ceremonially "by hand." The Colossians, Paul is reminding them, have been circumcised in a manner that their critics cannot approach: *This is a divine circumcision given by God.* And in this sense, the NRSVue is pointing in the right direction with its paraphrase: It is spiritual marker, a work of God, something that human hands promoting a physical ritual could not achieve.[193] This sounds very much like an echo of Paul's use of circumcision in Rom 2:28–29: "For a person is not a Jew who is one outwardly, nor is circumcision something external and physical. Rather, a person is a Jew who is one inwardly, and circumcision is a matter of the heart, by the Spirit . . ." This circumcision as a work of the Spirit is precisely now what Paul has in mind. This is "the circumcision of Christ" (2:11b), which will be more closely defined in 2:12.

What can Paul mean that the circumcision of Christ is a "removal (*ekduō*) of the body (*sōma*) of flesh (*sarx*)?" This "removal" translates the verb *ekduō*, which means to strip something away, such as when Jesus is violently striped of his garments at the cross (Matt 27:31; Mark 15:20). Of course, a nod to literal circumcision with the removal of the foreskin is obvious. But our verb, *apekduomai*, is rare, and it only occurs here and in Col 3:9. Paul has added a seemingly redundant prefix (*apo*, here as *ap-*) on top of another prefix (*ek* giving us *ap* + *ek*) to reinforce that something has been completely, utterly *taken away* and there is no possibility of returning.[194] We might think of how we could use *super* as a modern modifier (thus: "This meal is super-delicious"). This is a colloquial expression, but we know exactly what we mean despite its unusual form.

But what is this "body of flesh" that is removed? And how does this happen in the "circumcision of Christ"?[195] We need initially to determine the use of the genitive in "circumcision *of Christ*." Greek has two major uses of the genitive, which are just as ambiguous in Greek as they are in

---

[193] It may be no accident that in the LXX *cheiropoiētos* (handmade) is used for making idols. TDNT 9:436: "In the LXX *cheiropoiētos* almost always . . . describes the gods made with men's hands." Lev 26:1; Isa 46:6; Sib 3:606.

[194] TDNT 2:318–319.

[195] Moo and McKnight suggest that there are three ways to interpret this. Moo, *Colossians*, 198–200; McKnight, *Colossians*, 232–233.

English. It could be a subjective genitive, which means Christ is the actor or subject bringing this circumcision to others. This removal of the body then is an activity on the believer. Or this could be an objective genitive, in which Christ is acted on. In this case, the removal of the body of flesh refers to Christ and what happened to him.[196]

Some have opted for the first (subjective use) and made this removal a reference to a metaphorical circumcision experienced in our conversion.[197] Flesh, by this reading, refers to the "believer's unregenerate nature which would tyrannize over him and hold him in bondage" (see Rom 7:24, "the body of this death").[198] This body is then the "body of sin" in Rom 6:6. In 2:12 Paul refers to baptism with words reminiscent of Rom 6:1–11, seeing the circumcision of Christ happening when the believer is "buried with him in baptism."

Others view this as an objective genitive and argue that this stripping happens to Christ, and while it could be his own literal circumcision (which is unlikely), it is also a symbolic reference to the cross.[199] In this case 2:11 is echoing 1:22, where Christ's death is a work done on "his body (*sōma*) of flesh (*sarx*)." By this interpretation, believers are attached to Christ and to his physical death on the cross through which he gained resurrection life – as believers will likewise. The circumcision of Christ is *life-giving* in this sense because of what occurred on the cross. A similar use of this literal stripping occurs in 2:15.

We can surmise that the Jewish opponents in Colossae were using identity language common to Judaism. And they urged the Colossians to adopt circumcision as a spiritual practice (see 3:11). Paul concurs, reaching into his Jewish vocabulary and saying that they should do so – but then he upends its terms: We have a circumcision "not made with hands," a circumcision that bonds us to Christ, that disrupts our old identity and makes it new. This suggests that the subjective genitive is the right meaning for Paul.

---

[196] These genitives are easily illustrated when we say in English "the preaching of Christ" in Rom 16:25. Is this Christ who preaches (subjective)? Or is it our preaching about him (objective)? Another possibility is the possessive genitive, where the noun owns this activity; hence, this is Christ's circumcision.

[197] Lightfoot, *Colossians*, 183–184; Arnold, *Colossians Syncretism*, 296–297; Caird, *Colossians*, 193–194; Abbott, *Colossians*, 250–251; Bird, *Colossians*, 78. The NIV makes this explicit in its translation: "Your whole self, ruled by the flesh was put off when you were circumcised by Christ."

[198] Martin, *Colossians*, 77; also Moo, *Colossians*, 200; Lightfoot, *Colossians*, 182.

[199] Dunn, *Colossians*, 157–158.

Box 2.10 A Closer Look: The Circumcision of Christ

The idea that circumcision should be a deep symbol for renewal is found throughout the OT and Judaism (Deut 10:16–17; 30:6–7; Lev 26:40–41; Jub 1:22–24; 1QS 5.5). But here something new is given in the circumcision that is given by and belongs to Christ. This is a Messianic gift that only Christ has provided. Paul's reference to baptism in 2:12 makes this view compelling. This is a spiritual circumcision that Christ as Messiah brings to his people, and it is found in baptism, with Lightfoot explaining it as "the grave of the old man, and the birth of the new."[200] Therefore, if literal circumcision was a marker for religious identity in the synagogue, so, now, baptism *as spiritual circumcision* was a marker of religious identity in the church. Or with Calvin (who took great interest in these verses), circumcision *prefigured* the Messianic baptism that was to come. "Where the reality [the circumcision of Christ] exists, that shadowy emblem vanishes."[201]

The idea of spiritual or religious markers is difficult for us to understand in any ecclesial context that has been influenced by the Western church. We have been indelibly shaped by a modern Platonism that cannot see how activities in this world – activities that occur on our bodies – could have any permanent significance. Circumcision was not a passing marker for Jews. It had profound implications for lifelong identity and attachment to God's covenant. Paul is transposing those values onto baptism as a parallel marker of spiritual consequence.

Friends who have spent their entire careers in the Middle East often explain to me how in Islamic-majority cultures respect for baptism is remarkable. In cases of Sharia law where Muslim judges need to determine whether a family can make a claim on the children of new converts, the question of religious markings appears unexpectedly. "Has the child been baptized?" becomes a question with legal implications. And judges have ruled in favor of the parents simply on this basis alone. Spiritual markings such as circumcision and baptism tell us how we are bound and to whom we belong.

Baptism (**2:12**) thus becomes a burial – this is the stripping off – in which something dies and, through the power of God, something new is raised. It is a full attachment to Christ wherein we join him in both his burial and in his resurrection (Rom 6:1–11). In much of the NT this twin attachment to Christ's death and resurrection is separated: In baptism we are buried, but resurrection is still to come (Rom 6:5; 8:11; 1Cor 15:47–49; Phil 3:10, 21). This suspends the Christian life in a tension between the two,

---

[200] Lightfoot, *Colossians*, 184.
[201] Accessed through the Christian Ethereal Library (www.ccel.org): Calvin, *Colossians* Translated from the Latin by John Pringle (1851).

always awaiting the promise. But here in Colossians note that *both* burial and resurrection are past (or aorist) tense. We have been buried – and we have been raised. Christian life, therefore, is a sharing in Christ's death *and a sharing in the present in eschatological life*. It is a present encounter with the life-giving power of God. Thus, Paul can write in 3:1 that it is due to their present resurrection that they are able to seek "the things that are above." We can imagine the importance of this reality (over promise) when the power of the Christian life is presented in a world populated with religious claimants, Jewish or pagan. The church is not simply promising realities; it is presenting realities worked out in the power of God.

Box 2.11 A Closer Look: Death, Burial, Resurrection, Rebirth

One remarkable feature of early Christian thought was a vocabulary that presented discipleship as death and rebirth. Thus, in Romans 6:4, Paul writes, "Therefore *we were buried* with him [Christ] by baptism into death, so that, just as Christ was raised from the dead by the glory of the Father, so we also might walk in newness of life." In Colossians 2:12 we read the same: "*You were buried with him* [Christ] in baptism, you were also raised with him through faith in the power of God, who raised him from the dead." In 2 Tim 2:11 we can find a similar idea, now cited as a part of the Christian tradition: "The saying is sure: *If we have died with him*, we will also live with him." Titus 3:5 is similar: "[H]e saved us, not because of any works of righteousness that we had done, but according to his mercy, through *the water of rebirth* and renewal by the Holy Spirit." Union with Christ is achieved through the ritual of baptism, which represents the believer's death and the emergence of a new life and present-resurrection.

The many Hellenistic religions of Paul's world were well acquainted with this language of death–burial–rebirth. And from Schweitzer through Bultmann we can see how many scholars in the twentieth century assumed that the origin of this thinking was Hellenistic mysticism.[202] For Schweitzer, this is "resurrection-mysticism" that Paul had brought to Christian thinking. For Bultmann, this became a ritual no different than Hellenistic magic. Today these views are rarely heard.[203]

---

[202] A. Schweitzer, *The Mysticism of Paul the Apostle* (English translation) (New York: Macmillan, 1960), 12–15; R. Bultmann, *Theology of the New Testament*, 2 vols. (English translation) (London: SCM, 1952), 141–144. Bultmann: "Baptism imparts participation in the death and resurrection of Christ. This interpretation undoubtedly originated in the Hellenistic Church, which understood this traditional initiation-sacrament on analogy with initiation-sacraments of the mystery religions" (140).

[203] See the survey of A. Copenhaver, *Reconstructing the Historical Background of Paul's Rhetoric in the Letter to the Colossians*. LNTS 585 (New York: Bloomsbury, 2018), 1–39.

At the center of Christian proclamation was the paradoxical claim that *in Christ's death and resurrection* God had achieved his plan for the redemption of the world. Thus, Christ's own crucifixion–resurrection introduced into the language of discipleship the need to attach to Christ's reality (being "in him"), to become one with him *in his death–resurrection*. Burial and resurrection (Col 2:12) are therefore about attaching to Christ because it was his burial–resurrection that could give the believer life. In Paul's concise, near-creedal saying in 1Cor 15:3–8, Jesus lived, died, was buried, raised, and exalted. Discipleship meant joining him in this narrative.

Arnold points out that it is at this moment that we revisit the Hellenistic religious environment well-known to the Colossians. Christ's death and resurrection demonstrated his victory over the powers (the *stoicheia*) that threatened their lives. Their conversion – their union with Christ's death and victory – meant God had "rescued them from the authority of darkness and transferred them to the kingdom of his Son." This was a "decisive separation from the powers of darkness."[204]

This new attachment was ceremonially achieved in baptism, as Paul makes clear in Colossians and Romans. But as an initiatory ritual Paul also found a clear parallel in Jewish circumcision – yet one more initiatory ritual he knew well.[205] This parallel is not insignificant. Circumcision took on a new meaning similar to Paul's treatment in Romans 2, which points to spiritual circumcision. There is now the new vehicle for moving into the activity of God in Christ. Baptism does not convey an automatic result as if it were magic. It must be joined by faith (Col 2:12, *through faith in the working of God*) and celebrated as a work of God's grace.

Discipleship therefore embraces the cross of Christ and makes his death a foreshadowing of our own: Christians therefore are marked by the cross. And they live lives of rebirth and resurrection. This rhythm of attachment to the cross is often presented as *cruciformity*. That is, discipleship is not simply imitating Christ's life, but imitating Christ's death. A "cruciform" life understands how we relinquish attachments to the world and reattach ourselves to Christ *in his death and resurrection*. This is in stark contrast to church settings that merely see conversion–initiation–baptism as a change in belief or the washing away of sin. It is a death. It is a burial. It is our baptism into Christ's death (Rom 6:3), so that through this death we can become one with him and live as he lives.

---

[204] Arnold, *Colossian Syncretism*, 191.
[205] D. Moo, *A Theology of Paul and His Letters* (Grand Rapids: Zondervan Academic, 2021), 590. This correlation between circumcision and baptism opens the door for accepting the baptism of infants. As Jewish communities circumcised their infant boys, so the early church practiced household baptisms, in which all who were attached to the family participated (Acts 10:47–48; 16:15, 30–31; 18:8; 1Cor 1:16). Less convinced is J. D. G. Dunn, *The Theology of the Apostle Paul* (New York: T&T Clark/Continuum, 2003), 457–459.

It is interesting how casually Paul can refer to baptism. By the writing of this letter, baptism was already established in the early church as a boundary marker, an identifier of what it meant to be a part of the Christ-community. This tradition was old, reaching back to the gospel tradition, when the account of Jesus' baptism was regularly taught, when baptism and the work of the Spirit were connected (Mark 1:8), and when Jesus viewed his own baptism-in-death as a prelude to the disciples' baptism-in-death – both included a resurrection (Mark 10:38–39).

If 2:12 described the transforming and empowering experience of baptism-as-dying-and-rising, now **2:13** centers on Messianic forgiveness as another avenue of transformation. We might think of this as Paul's summary of the story of redemption as applied to his Gentile audience at Colossae. Paul describes their status in two ways: They were dead in sin and the uncircumcision of their flesh. And yet God not only made Christ alive in his resurrection, but also he makes us alive together (*suzōopoieō*) with him.[206] This language finds a close parallel in Eph 2:1–5: "You were dead through the trespasses and sins . . . but God, who is rich in mercy, out of the great love with which he loved us . . . even when we were dead through our trespasses, made us alive together with Christ."

Col 2:13 appears to present two separate problems, but they are in fact one. The central issue for the Colossian Gentiles ("you were dead") is that they had been living outside the covenant of God. Eph 2:12 defines it more closely: "[R]emember that you were at that time without Christ, being aliens from the commonwealth of Israel and strangers to the covenants of promise, having no hope and without God in the world." Being outside meant finding themselves without access to the grace of God found within this covenant. They were estranged much like the Prodigal Son "who was lost and made alive again" (Luke 15:32, 35).[207] Immediately this echoes another theme for Paul: that Israel *within* the covenant had this access and therefore enjoyed advantages because of their election. Nevertheless, they too were guilty of sin and in need of forgiveness, as Paul signals when he

---

[206] *Su-zōopoieō* is another instance of Paul's use of *syn* (here *su-*, together, with) as a prefix in this chapter. This compound verb combines the words for making (*poieō*) alive (*zaō*). The NT refers to the resurrection routinely as "making alive" (John 5:21; Rom 8:11; 1Cor 15:22, 45; 1Pet 3:18).

[207] Wright, *Colossians*, 109.

includes himself *as a Jew* in his change of pronouns, "he forgave us (not 'you') all our (not 'your') trespasses."

Thus, Gentiles were *dead in trespasses* – a phrase commonly used for Gentiles who violated the law of the OT (see also 1:21). Therefore, the jeopardy of the Gentile was not simply that they had sinned,[208] but that they were living outside the covenant, a charge reinforced by their status as uncircumcised *in their flesh*. The remedy therefore was inclusion, unexpected Messianic inclusion, brought about by Christ's spiritual circumcision that brought them into the Messianic covenant. And since they could now through their forgiveness join with God's covenant, they were no longer alien to the covenant community. "So then, you are no longer strangers and aliens, but you are fellow citizens with the saints and also members of the household of God" (Eph 2:19). Jews were not "in" nor Gentiles "out" (Eph 2:13). The Messianic covenant belonged to all who were marked with the Messianic circumcision, both Jews and Gentiles.

Forgiveness is now explained through legal metaphors (**2:14**). The work of God in Christ on our behalf is now seen as an erasure of a record, an accounting, that stood against us. This is now the fourth of four metaphors to describe the transformed identity offered in Christ. Paul has referred to a spiritual circumcision (2:11), burial and resurrection (2:12), death and new life (2:13), and now the removal of a legal document (2:14). These four create a collage that may fit together awkwardly but gives multiple views of how reconciliation works. Here Paul imagines charges – written charges – that could appear in court as a part of a prosecution. The document (or *cheirographon*) is something formal like a personal legal decree. Or it could also be a promissory note or a bond used to confirm an arrangement. The key is that it is a binding document with power behind it.[209] Some think it is a document of indebtedness, much like an IOU. Moo points to Job 11:11 to illustrate where Job brings notes of indebtedness, reads them, and cancels them.[210] Judaism in this period made extensive use of this idea, suggesting heavenly records of each person's life that were awaiting the

---

[208] Moo, *Colossians*, 206, points out that the difference between trespass (*paraptōma*) and sin (*hamartia*) may be marginal. The first word refers to a "false step," which Paul uses often (Rom 4:25; 5:15, 16, 17, 18; 2Cor 5:19; Gal 6:1; Eph 1:7, etc.).

[209] TDNT 9:436. The word appears only here in the NT and twice in the LXX (Tob 5:3; 9:5).

[210] Moo, *Colossians*, 209.

judgment.[211] This development was not missed by the patristic church, which made fantastic claims about this verse, thinking about debts signed by Adam for all humanity. Today these ideas are best left aside.[212]

Box 2.12 A Closer Look: The Roman Cheirograph

When Paul refers to the work of Christ erasing or destroying "the record that is set against us," he is using a technical term: the *cheirographon*.[213] This is a handwritten document giving financial guarantees (such as a debt repayment promise) or a transaction receipt. The documents were widely used from the second century BCE to the Byzantine period and had become so formalized that they had proforma sections that had to be completed much like any legal form. The Oxyrhynchus Papyri collection from Egypt has even offered a template for completing these (P.Oxy. 33.267):

Someone (*tis*), son of someone (*tinos tou tinos*), son of someone whose mother is someone from somewhere. Greetings! I admit to having received from you through a hand in the registry such-and-such money which totals such-and-such an amount which I shall repay to you as soon as you should make the request. If I do not, I will pay in full in accordance with the deposit law, whatever the exaction of debt is, from my property and from all that I own, just as it is required. The hand, which is mine – the autograph of so-and-so – written twice over is validation of receipt in whatever place it might be brought and to anyone you might bring it. Year.[214]

Generally, these documents were written entirely in the personal hand of the debtor (hence its name, *handwritten*), but where the debtor was illiterate a scribe could produce the document. However, it always required some "signature" such as we find in P. Merton 1.14, as well as in the Oxyrhynchus Papyri regarding the loan of corn: "This deed, written by the hand (*hē idiographos*), of me, Diogenes, also called Sarapion, is valid wherever it is produced and to whomsoever may produce it. Seventh year of Imperator Caesar Nerva Trajanus Augustus Germanicus Dacius, Hathur 29."[215]

---

[211] Dunn, *Colossians*, 164; and Bird, *Colossians*, point to Exod 32:32–33; Ps 69:28; Dan 12:1; Jub 4:23; 39:6; 1Enoch 81:2–4; 89:61–64, 70–71; 96:7; 97:5–7; 104:7; 108:7; 2Enoch 44:5–7; 50:1; 52:15; 53:2–3; Apoc. Ab. 7:108; Apoc. Zeph. 3:6–9; 7:1–11).

[212] A popular patristic and medieval view was that this document of debt was signed by Adam (or all humans) and held over us by Satan. See Moo, *Colossians*, 209–210. Lightfoot, *Colossians*, 188, provides a list of patristic options.

[213] N. Elder, "This Hand Is Validation: Philemon as a Pauline Holograph," *NTS* 70 (2024) 324–339.

[214] Ibid., 326.

[215] Accessed at https://papyri.info/ddbdp/p.mert;1;14. Cited by Elder, ibid., 327. This papyrus document (with translation) can be viewed at https://cblo1.intranda.com/viewer/image/MP_14/1/. It was written November 25, 103 CE, on papyrus with ink.

> In Col 2:14 Paul is referring to something any Roman would recognize: a cheirograph. We possess a "debt guarantee" that God now holds. And yet, thanks to the work of Christ, that document has been destroyed and cannot be used against us.

This document that Paul has imagined has made legal demands (*dogmata*), specifics, a list perhaps, particulars about what is owed or required – and this "stood against us," placing us in jeopardy. Christ has erased (*exaleiphō*) this document, which we have learned is a "handwritten" record (*cheirographon: cheir*, hand) and so may be undone, wiped clean from a slate, blotted out from vellum, or rubbed new if a wax tablet. This phrase appears in the OT with some frequency. Ps 69:28 remarks: "Let them be blotted out of the book of the living; let them not be enrolled among the righteous."

It is likely that Paul is also thinking about the Torah, the law, which embodies God's expectations and becomes the test by which righteousness is measured. In 2:1–22 Paul's opponents actually make use of the law to leverage their demands over the church. So Paul here can say that this leveraging of the written requirements and of our failures has been addressed. But a key here is not that the law itself is a problem even though it is linked to wrath (2Cor 3:6–7), sin (Rom 5:20), death (1Cor 3:6–7), and imprisonment (Rom 7:6). The law is good (Rom 7:12), but the lingering problem is our inevitable and persistent disobedience of it. This is where we find Messianic relief: Our failings are now gone, but with Dunn, the law remains "God's yardstick of right and judgment."[216]

The graphic resolution to these accusations now takes another turn. The written accusations have been erased, set aside, and also crucified ("nailed to the cross"). This last term is actually "to nail" (*proseloō*), but given Paul's deep awareness of the work of the cross (Col 1:20) in Christ's crucifixion, the more elastic meaning holds.[217] Since crucifixion served as a public warning against crime, Romans would lead the victim to the site of death with a plaque (Latin *tabula*; Greek *pinax*) indicating the crime, and this could be posted on the cross itself. Jesus' crucifixion shows this pattern

---

[216] Dunn, *Colossians*, 166.
[217] BDAG 880.

clearly (John 19:19–22), and John provides the correct Greek term for the written accusation: the *titlos* (Latin *titulus*). Blinzler imagines this as red or black lettering on a white gypsum board that was then nailed above the victim.[218] Eusebius provides a helpful image of this in the martyrdom of Attalus of Pergamum. He was paraded about his city led by a placard saying "Attalus the Christian" (*ChHist.* 5.1).

For Paul, this is a splendid play on images. The document listing our sins – the fair accusations held against us – now becomes the *titlos* that is crucified with Christ. The concept assumes ideas of Christ's death as a substitutionary sacrifice that has absorbed the guilt of the one who has just been absolved.

The fifth and final metaphor (**2:15**) explaining the achievements of Christ and the dramatic benefits he brought to his followers now presumes a cosmic setting. In one of Paul's most celebrated sentences, he describes the disarming and public shaming of "rulers and authorities," leading to Jesus' full triumph over them. Wright correctly points to another profound irony here. The great rulers of Rome and Israel had taken Jesus by force to the cross. "These powers, angry at his challenge to their sovereignty, stripped *him* naked, held *him* up to public contempt, and celebrated a triumph over *him*."[219] But here we see that the reverse happened.

There are three important steps in this. First, these powers and authorities are disarmed. The verb here is "strip off" (*apekduomai*), and it is used again in 3:9 (cognate noun, 2:11) for stripping off the old self. This is a rare word that does not appear in Greek before Paul and rarely after him, but its sense it clear enough. In Matt 27:28 we read how the soldiers "stripped" Jesus (*ekduō*, a shortened form of our verb). However, its grammatical form is difficult. It is a participle using the Greek middle voice where the subject acts reflexively on itself (the shorter, *ekuomai*, means to undress oneself). Moo points out that since 2:13 God has been the subject and there has been no change.[220] This leaves us with the awkward notion of

[218] J. Blinzler, *The Trial of Jesus: The Jewish and Roman Proceedings against Jesus Christ Described and Assessed from the Oldest Accounts* (English translation) (Westminster: Newman, 1959), 254; R. Brown, *The Death of the Messiah* (New York: Doubleday, 1994), 963; C. Keener, *The Gospel of John: A Commentary* (Peabody: Hendrickson, 2003), 1137.

[219] Wright, *Colossians*, 116.

[220] Moo, *Colossians*, 213.

God stripping himself. It was natural for patristic writers to introduce Christ as subject here, and if they were right, the cross became a place where Christ was stripped of his life and power. Or with some, Christ stripped off these powers from himself. But in NT Greek the middle voice can also serve as active (called "deponent use").[221] If God remains the subject, it means that he is acting directly. Thus God (or Christ) has acted decisively on the rulers and authorities, *stripping them* – or, following another meaning of the verb, disarming them, removing their defenses, making them powerless.[222]

But who are these rulers and authorities? We have seen this reference already in 1:16, and it occurs as well in Eph 1:21, 3:10, and 6:12. In our texts (see discussion of 1:16) these are likely the spiritual powers that served as intermediaries, populating the cosmos, living in opposition to God. In 1:16 we learned how Christ's dominance over them was determined by his authority over creation. And now in 2:15 we learn that his triumph over them was completed at the cross. It is difficult for us to imagine a worldview such as this. In 2:8 Paul refers to the *stoicheia*: those forces arrayed in the cosmos that could determine the fate of every person. And this is likely happening here. However there was never a divorce between these powers and the powers of this world. These *stoicheia* empowered and protected them. Rome was ordained by and prospered by the gods. These were viewed as genuine beings that demanded control of the world.

The second step is that they have been shamed in public. This is implied by their stripping and is reminiscent of Roman soldiers who would parade their captives naked through the city as they were led to a public death. This verb (*deigmatizō*, to exhibit) means to make something public or to display it. It appears only here in the NT and in Matt 1:19, where Joseph decides not to shame the pregnant Mary publicly. Thus the idea is not simply exposure, but shaming exposure that led to disgrace and spectacle, which deepens the irony of this story. "This strange but wonderous act of God turns typical Roman brutality on its head ... here God exposes the

---

[221] This is the well-known deponent or middle-deponent use. See D. M. Harris, *An Introduction to Biblical Greek Grammar* (Grand Rapids: Zondervan Academic, 2020), 70. A typical common deponent verb is *erchomai*. Most English translations view this participle as active, with Christ as the subject.

[222] So BDAG 100; see BD §316.

hideousness of systemic evil by means of crucifixion."²²³ Paul adds that this
was done *parrēsia* or openly, underscoring their shame. But this word has
another fascinating connotation: *boldly.* God has boldly defeated these
powers at the cross.

Finally, Paul says that God not only stripped and shamed these powers,
but he triumphed over them. Similarly in 2Cor 2:14 he can write: "But
thanks be to God, who in Christ always leads us in triumphal
procession ..." The picture here was well-known to every Roman, since
it portrayed a returning military legion, cheered by its city, headed by its
officers, and followed by its troops and their captives.²²⁴ The word
thriambeuō means to "lead in a triumphal procession"²²⁵ and implies the
defeat, pacification, and conquest of one's enemies. Paul uses this image in
Eph 4:8 (citing Ps 68:18) and opens to us the enormous irony of this scene.
With Lightfoot, "The paradox of crucifixion is thus placed in the strongest
light – triumph in helplessness and glory in shame. The convict's gibbet is
the victor's car."²²⁶

Col 2:15 is one of the literary climaxes in the letter. Paul and Timothy
have concluded their multi-metaphor tour of the exploits of God in Christ
defeating the powers of the world. It is not that the triumph happened only
at the cross (NRSV *in it*, 2:15b), although this was the decisive battle; but it
happened *in him* (*en autō*), the fifth reference to *in him* (namely, Christ)
since 2:9.²²⁷ Christ represents the totality of God's invasion of this world
from his incarnation (1:15–19) to his resurrection. But at the cross, the
decisive blow was struck that made the powers of this world yield. The
gospels reflect this as well. It is at the cross where Satan arises and acts
either to tempt Jesus away from it or to inspire Judas' betrayal. But we
cannot miss the drama of this message. Dunn says, "To treat the cross as a

---

²²³ McKnight, *Colossians*, 256.
²²⁴ R. Yates, "Colossians 2:15: Christ Triumphant," *NTS* 37 (1991) 573–591, argues that the
    triumphant procession did not consist of defeated captives but liberated Romans and
    dancing crowds.
²²⁵ BDAG 459.
²²⁶ Lightfoot, *Colossians*, 192, as cited in Garland, *Colossians*, 153, and Martin, *Colossians*,
    82. McKnight, *Colossians*, 257–259, cites at length Plutarch's vivid account of the
    triumphal procession of the Roman Aemilius Paulus over King Perseus, the king of
    Macedon, which is one of the best descriptions on record of a Roman triumph.
²²⁷ The pronoun *auto* can be either masculine (referring to Christ) or neuter (referring to
    the cross or the triumph itself).

moment of triumph was about as huge a reversal of normal values as could be imagined, since crucifixion was itself regarded as the most shameful of deaths."[228] The early Christians were not simply telling a heroic story in which the death and resurrection of Jesus turned the tables on Rome; they were telling a story about how God at work in Christ had turned things upside down, not only in Jerusalem at Golgotha and the tomb, but in the cosmos itself. The powers that dominated and controlled, that threatened and killed had been fatally undermined and shown up for what they were: powerless.

2:16–19 *The Demands of These Teachers Are Wrong*

2:16 Therefore, do not let anyone condemn you in matters of food or drink or of observing festivals, new moons, or Sabbaths.

2:17 These are only a shadow of what is to come, but the body belongs to Christ.

2:18 Do not let anyone disqualify you, insisting on self-abasement and worship of angels, initiatory visions, puffed up without cause by a human way of thinking,

2:19 and not holding fast to the head, from whom the whole body, nourished and held together by its ligaments and tendons, grows with a growth that is from God.

At this point Paul has established that the claims of this new philosophy are mistaken. Christ is not merely an addendum to the normal course of this world and its religious philosophies; Christ is their end – he is the unexpected messiah-king now come to take back his creation and establish a new kingdom, a Messianic kingdom. This is no provincial effort only affecting Judea or Jewish interests (though the impact on them is formidable), but it is cosmic, or today we might say "global" if by that we understand not only things observable in this world but all of creation, including spiritual forces we can barely perceive but know are there. Claimants to ongoing power – including Rome or any political or religious system – are now put on notice. A greater king, a more powerful reality, the Son of God himself has now asserted his dominance over all.

---

[228] Dunn, *Colossians*, 170. On crucifixion in this context, see M. Hengel, *Crucifixion* (London: SCM, 1977).

This clearly makes any other religious system (as with other political systems) obsolete. Something – or, better, someone – so remarkable has entered the stage of history that any religious rules that they might impose seem quaint, unnecessary, even impediments to a rightly ordered life. Paul must now draw out the consequences of his previous section and resist any calls that might pull the Colossians back into old religious habits or newly invented spiritual practices. Only one thing matters: *holding fast to the head* (2:19) – which, of course, is Christ.

The truest index of the Colossian freedom was found, in Paul's mind, within their routine religious disciplines. What follows, therefore, is a result (*oun*, therefore, 2:16) of what came before. In Col 2:16–21, however, we have had difficulty understanding some of these except to say that these teachers were imposing rituals and requirements on the Colossians that focused on diet (eating and drinking) and ritual calendars (festivals, the moon, sabbath). This was joined to mystical experiences that promised to connect them with beings in the spiritual world. This is likely a Jewish framework – a fastidious one to be sure – that had indulged in syncretistic practices. But here Paul will reject it all in exchange for centering ourselves entirely and completely on Christ's supremacy.[229]

Clearly the Colossians had made steps in the right direction (**2:16**). They had changed their way of living and questioned some of the accepted religious rules that had been imposed on them. And this had led to criticisms – condemnations, really – about their choices. It is not as if they had been indulging in sin or unrighteousness. They simply changed their habits and had not conformed to expectations; they had chosen to live into the freedom from fear and rules that Christ had won. Naturally the custodians of the old ways would not be happy.

Tensions about dietary rules were not exclusive to Colossae. In Rom 14 and 1Cor 8–10 we can read about other debates over food that divided the community. We should not think these odd. Throughout the world today, dietary regulations appear in countless religions (Islam, Judaism, Hinduism, and Mormonism are simple examples) where piety or asceticism are displayed publicly by what one will or will not

---

[229] Caird, *Colossians*, 197.

consume. The Christian faith generally (then and now) stands out as absent such rules.[230]

Clearly "someone" (*tis*, 2:16a; also 2:18a) is judging these believers, but precisely who they are is not indicated. Since the first concern is about food law, we can speculate that this is a Jewish issue. Restrictions on Jewish diet are anchored solidly in OT law (Lev 11; Deut 14), and the attitude of Jewish adherents was to judge those not in compliance. The NRSV reflects this: *Do not let any condemn* (krinō) *you*, but the nuance is someone pointing out a violation to an obvious rule. Thus, in the LXX *krinō* is a common legal term either expressing God's judgment on human sin or judgments we make on others' misbehaviors.

In this period, Judaism viewed dietary rules along with circumcision and sabbath observance as critical markers of self-identification within the Roman world. They were classified with purity laws and seen as expressions of faithfulness to God. But their concern was not just the prohibition of food groups such as pork (most famously). They also required that blood be drained from meat properly (Lev 7:26–27; Deut 12:16), and they watched for any meat that may have come from a Gentile market that once was used in pagan sacrifice (a common source of meat in Roman antiquity). References to Jews in the Second Temple period refusing to eat such meat even on pain of death abound.[231] Even food extremists when imprisoned by Rome refused to eat anything but figs and nuts (Josephus, *Life*, 13–14).[232]

The same restrictions followed drink. Diaspora Jews worried about wine that may have come from a libation offering in a pagan temple – or oil that could have had a similar history. Or what if the oil came from an olive grove owned by a pagan temple?[233] All of these scruples were viewed as

---

[230] In most Arab Muslim cities such as Damascus or Amman, everyone knows that if you wish to buy wine or pork, you simply go to the Christian quarter of the city. However, there are exceptions. Ethiopian Orthodox and Eritrean Orthodox Christians – along with Seventh-day Adventists – avoid pork. Muslim grocery stores in Dubai and the United Arab Emirates have meat sections set apart and labeled: "Pork for Non-Muslims."

[231] Dan 1:3–16; Tob 1:10–20; *Jos. Asen.* 7:1; 8:5. See Sanders, *Jewish Law from Jesus to the Mishnah*, 23–28; also E. Sanders, *Judaism: Practice and Belief* (London: SCM, 1992), 214–218.

[232] Sanders, *Practice and Belief*, 24. The Mishna shows how the houses of Hillel and Shammai debated the strictures surrounding food.

[233] Here see Josephus, *War*, 2.591; *Life*, 74; *Antiquities*, 12.120. Sanders, *Practice and Belief*, 216.

Jewish resistance to a Roman culture saturated with paganism and immorality (as they saw it). It should not surprise us to find diaspora churches wrestling with this as well when Jews and gentiles mixed. In 1Cor 10:27 Paul tells his readers not to inquire as to the origin of the food when they are a guest. And, of course, this is central to Peter's vision in Acts 10 at Joppa (see Gal 2:11–14). In Rom 14 we have a very close parallel to what we see here in Colossians. Both food (*brōsis*) and drink (*posis*) appear in 14:17.

Romans 14 also indicates that observing feast days was equally a divisive issue: "Some judge (*krinō*) one day to be better than another, while others judge (*krinō*) all days to be alike" (14:5). We can imagine that living in a Roman world might mean deciding not to participate in the countless Roman festivities – and experiencing public criticisms for it. But it also could mean not openly celebrating the Jewish calendar and risking the scrutiny of Jewish neighbors. Sabbath, in particular, set Jews apart and in many cases led to public disapproval.[234]

But why were these criticisms even germane in this setting? Dunn observes that this suggests that the Colossian Christians could only be subject to these Jewish criticisms *if they viewed themselves as inheriting a place in the people of Israel* (see on 1:12). Jews would not impose these sorts of judgments on Gentiles strictly speaking, but they would quickly impose them on those claiming a shared biblical religious heritage.[235] At once we see here the practical implications of a theme that resonates throughout Paul from Romans to Ephesians: Gentiles in Christ could now claim a spiritual legacy from Abraham and were heirs to Israel itself.

The reference to Sabbath makes it clear that here we are looking at a debate with a Jewish context. Sabbath observance was a signature Jewish practice (Exod 20:8–11; 31:16; Deut 5:15; Isa 56:6; Ezek 20:12). Josephus records that as early as the fourth century BCE purists in Jerusalem sought out those who either ate impure food or violated the Sabbath.

---

[234] An easy comparison to this is the modern celebration of Christmas among devout Christians: What do we do with the secular images? And how much do we promote the religious images in public?

[235] Dunn, *Colossians*, 174. Lightfoot is often cited here: "The contrast between the ordinances of the law and the teaching of the gospel, as the shadow and the substance respectively ... implies both the unsubstantiality [sic] and the supersession of the Mosaic ritual." *Colossians*, 194–195.

Now when Alexander [the Great] was dead, the government was parted among his successors; but the temple upon Mount Gerizim remained; and if anyone were accused by those of Jerusalem of having eaten things common [*koinophagia*, used in Rom 14:14 for prohibited food] or of having broken the Sabbath or of any other crime of the like nature . . .

they fled. We assume they fled due to the severe judgment that would inevitably fall on them.

Since Paul has referenced the Jewish Sabbath, "new moons" should also be taken as a Jewish motif.[236] The Jewish festival calendar was organized around the calendar months (indicated by the moon), so here the criticism likely was about matters such as Passover or Sukkoth. In fact, sabbaths, new moons, and festivals when listed together were a common way Jews might refer to the festival practices of their faith (1Chron 23:31; 2Chron 31:3; Neh 10:33; Isa 1:13–14; 1Macc 10:34).[237] Still, however, we also must remember that these contested teachings had also absorbed influences from Hellenistic systems, as 2:18 makes clear. Still, the basis of this complaint is principally Jewish, no doubt stemming from the synagogue.[238]

Moo rightly wonders if this verse tells us something about early Christian observance of the Sabbath.[239] Was the problem that the church viewed the Sabbath as optional? Or did it disregard it altogether? "Only Sabbath observance that is connected inappropriately to a wider religious viewpoint is here being condemned." He is right. The issue throughout these charges is that Gentiles are making claims *as Christ-followers* and making decisions about things sacred to Judaism. It is their faith in Christ that is likely at issue. Still, with Moo, we are likely right to conclude from the argument of 2:17 and elsewhere in the NT (Rom 14:5) that Sabbath observance was "no longer a requirement of God's people in the new realm."

---

[236] Caird, *Colossians*, 197. However, this is disputed by some who think that the false teachers had fully integrated Jewish ritual into pagan custom, making a hybrid, syncretistic proposal.

[237] Lightfoot, *Colossians*, 193; Moo, *Colossians*, 220; McKnight, *Colossians*, 267.

[238] We should assume that, while it is not mentioned, circumcision is somewhere within these expectations of the teachers. Along with food laws and Sabbath, circumcision stood out as one of the chief markers in Judaism, and it is the center of debate in Galatians, where Gentiles are being confronted with the need to complete their Jewish identity. See Dunn, *Colossians*, 175.

[239] Moo, *Colossians*, 221.

The principal reason these many rituals must fade (**2:17**) is because they are a shadowy representation of what is real and true.[240] They prefigure Christ; they do not compete with him. This is the Platonic dualism that was repeated in Hellenistic Judaism to compare things in heaven and on earth. Hebrews represents this well, comparing the law (a shadow or *skia*) to the truer forms we have in Christ: "Since the law has only a shadow of the good things to come and not the true form of these realities" (10:1). And with this phrase Hebrews can dismiss the sacrifices of the temple *as a shadow* of what we have in Christ's death. In 8:5 he can dismiss the earthly tabernacle because the genuine temple resided in heaven. Philosophers such as Plato used *skia* frequently to make these contrasts: A shadow (*skia*) might precede a person coming toward you and give a faint hint of its origin. To be sure, the reality makes the shadow unnecessary. "What is to come" (NRSV; *mellō*) describes something about to happen.[241] And it was used commonly in Jewish writing to describe the new age (*ho aiōn mellōn, the age to come*) anticipated in the future (Isa 9:6 LXX; Eph 1:21). Here Paul echoes this phrase but gives it a new application: Christ is the embodiment of that Jewish expectation. He is the reality that makes the shadow interesting but secondary. Christ presents what the shadow only represents. The substance (translating *sōma*) "is found in Christ" (NIV) or, with the NRSV, "belongs to Christ." Harris concludes, "The implication is that the shadows not only are now superfluous but actually disappear with the appearance of the 'substance.'"[242]

Paul now returns to his warning that began two verses earlier (**2:18**). Few verses in the NT present such a number of difficulties and rare words as this. For some, it is the most difficult verse in the NT.[243] A referee or umpire in a sporting event was a *brabeus* and the prize awarded was a

---

[240]   The Greek sentence is not a new sentence as in the NRSV. It is a clause beginning with a plural neuter relative pronoun (*ha*) that refers to food and drink or the three terms for festivals – or all of these. A literal translation would be ". . . festivals, new moons, or Sabbaths *which are* a shadow of what is to come . . ."

[241]   The language is unusual. See Matt 20:22: "Can you drink the cup I am about [*mellō*] to drink?" When *mellō* appears as a participle, it refers to the future or something to come. Matt 12:32; Eph 1:21; 2Clem 6:3; Ign. Pol. 5:2. See BDAG 627. Similarly it can point to the future: *ti melleis?*, "why delay?"

[242]   Harris, *Colossians*, 106.

[243]   E. Percy, *Die Probleme der Kolosser- und Epheserbriefe* (Lund: Gleerup, 1946), 143, cited by I. Smith, *Heavenly Perspective. A Study of the Apostle Paul's Response to a Jewish Mystical Movement at Colossae* (London: T&T Clark, 2006), 119.

brabeion. To make "a call" as an empire (*brabeuō*) was neutral but adding *kata* described a call made against you (*katabrabeuō*).²⁴⁴ Here Paul warns the Colossians not to let anyone "call you out" – or disqualify you because, in some manner, you were not doing as you should. Or we might translate: "Don't let anyone cheat you out of your prize."²⁴⁵

What follows is a maze of challenging Greek terms, but happily we can reconstruct the general drift of Paul's intentions. These false teachers were judging or condemning the Colossian's behavior as being remiss or negligent (2:16). And now they would rob the Colossians of the life they treasured in Christ. Paul offers five ironic descriptions of how these teachers have approached the church. He does not want the Colossians to be disqualified by people promoting (*thelō*) this list.

But is this simply a self-description of what they want for themselves?²⁴⁶ Or is it proscriptive of things they want for the Colossians?²⁴⁷ The first might translate Paul's advice as: "Do not let anyone disqualify you, delighting (as they do) in ..." The second is translated, "Do not let anyone disqualify you, insisting on ..." The NIV follows the first; the NRSV the second. Either way, even if these teachers hold these practices for themselves, their position is polemical or apologetic. They do these things and promote these habits as a witness to persuade the Colossians to imitate them.

In false humility: The first term (*tapeinos + phrosynē*) stems for the idea of lowliness or weakness (*tapeinos*; Latin *humilis*, humility) and is a compound, pointing to a mind that has lowered itself. Usually in Paul humility is a virtue (in Phil 2:3 he expects this of the church). In Col 3:12 he does the same. But here something is amiss, as it joins a list of clearly unacceptable behaviors in the rest of the sentence. In the LXX the word is used for ritual behavior – self-mortification, perhaps – that had a cultic dimension (Lev 16:29, 31; 23:7). It can even refer to fasting (Ps 35:13; Isa

---

²⁴⁴ See C. Beetham, *Echoes of Scripture in the Letter of Paul to the Colossians.* Biblical Interpretation Series 96 (Leiden: Brill, 2008), 202–203.
²⁴⁵ Martin, *Colossians*, 91.
²⁴⁶ So Lightfoot, Lohse, Moule, Dunn, Beale, and Moo. Abbott and Dunn explain that Paul is using a Hebraism that makes the Greek verb self-referential.
²⁴⁷ So Pao, Harris, McKnight, and Martin, as well as F. O. Francis, "Humility and Angelic Worship in Col 2:18," *Studia Evangelica* 16.2 (1962) 109–134. Abbott (*Colossians*, 267) points out that the fatal argument against a Hebraism here is that Paul never uses them when they violate Greek grammar.

58:3, 5; Jdt 4:9). Since we know that these teachers also prohibit certain foods and drink as well as severity to the body, they suggest some form of rigorous spiritual discipline. When linked to the worship of angels we likely have the description of a posture of subordination that sets itself beneath the cosmic powers whom they adore. In Jewish literature there is often a connection between fasting and mystical experiences. In Philo, Moses fasted for forty days on Mt. Sinai (*Dreams*, 1:35–37; *Mos.* 2:67–70). It is a recuring theme in much of Jewish literature (Dan 10:2–3; Apoc Abr 9:7–10; 12:1–2; T Issac 4:1–6; 5:4; 2Bar 5:7; Apoc Ezra 1:1–5). In *Joseph and Asenath* we read about Asenath's religious humility and the sudden appearance of the angel Michael.[248]

What we likely have here is a form of asceticism or simply a spiritual outlook that says: If you are genuinely pious, if you do not argue and resist but join with us, you will have what we have: access to a mystical encounter with the heavens. But first, initiates must be lowly and humble (humiliated?) in order to gain access.

The worship of angels: This phrase continues to be a crux in the quest to define these Colossian teachers. Much turns on how we understand this genitive (... *of angels*). Is this the worship practice belonging to angels who worship God (subjective genitive)[249] or the worship directed to angels by humans (objective genitive)?[250] The strongest case belongs to the latter since in the folk religion of the day angels populated the cosmos and could serve as intermediaries with God. While the term for worship here is rare, Arnold has carefully shown the range of its meanings and suggests that *worship* is only one possible translation. Others include veneration, conjuring, or magical practices that engage or pacify these angels. We find this pattern in the liturgical texts of Qumran (esp. 4Q400–407 and 11Q17), where thirteen liturgies help believers commune mystically with angels and thereby have access to ecstatic experiences. "The communal mysticism of the angelic liturgies thus enabled the Qumran community, separated from the impure worship of the Jerusalem temple, to participate in the sacrificial cult of the

[248] Smith, *Heavenly Perspective*, 122.
[249] F. O. Francis and W. A. Meeks, *Conflict at Colossae*, 2nd edition (Missoula: Scholars Press, 1975), 176–183; Dunn, *Colossians*, 180–182. Arnold, *Colossian Syncretism*, 91, writes that in his exhaustive study of all uses of *thrēskeia* with the genitive he failed to find one example of a divine being described as the source (not object) of worship.
[250] Harris, *Colossians*, 107–108; Arnold, *Colossian Syncretism*, 90–93.

heavenly temple itself."[251] In other words, the Qumran sect could *ascend* mystically to divine regions. The upshot of this is that we are listening to Paul critique Jewish mystics who have indulged in and are promoting magical liturgies that promise access to the range of spiritual beings – the *stoicheia* (see 2:8) – that populated the cosmos and who could either aid or defeat one's access the heavenly realities. And by indulging these strategies, Christ's dominion over them and his superiority over all creation is diminished.

Initiatory visions: This phrase, according to Arnold, is the "single most perplexing exegetical problem of the letter."[252] We can even see the confusion among copyists who, in one textual tradition, insert a negative between the relative pronoun (*ha*, things) and the verb (*heoraken*, seen), suggesting that these initiates had *not* seen anything. But this is of little help.[253] The key here is undoubtedly the verb *embateuō*, which is not only rare but can have many uses. Essentially it means to step into (a temple) or enter into an experience or even an inheritance. But, above all, it appears in initiatory rituals in Hellenistic mystery cults (such as the Apollo temple at Claros, north of Ephesus). If the verb was a technical term, it could be that the teachers at Colossae were involved in a mystery cult and that this described their entry to the mysteries.[254] We also have to imagine that new converts were entering the Colossian church, and that many had come from the Hellenistic mystery religions. The coin evidence alone from Colossae shows that innumerable deities from the Ephesian Artemis to Athena to Isis were all worshiped there. A recent discovery of a ring at Colossae depicts the city as the cult center of Tyche Protogeneia (goddess of luck)[255] and "proclaims Colossae as the center of comic

---

[251] Arnold, *Colossian Syncretism*, 96, summarizing C. Newsom, *Songs of the Sabbath Sacrifice: A Critical Edition.* Harvard Semitic Studies 27 (Atlanta: Scholars Press, 1985), 17–21; and M. J. Davidson, *Angels at Qumran. A Comparative Study of 1Enoch 1–36, 72–108, and Sectarian Writings from Qumran* (Sheffield: JSOT Press, 1992), 237.

[252] Arnold, *Colossians*, 104.

[253] Lightfoot, *Colossians*, 254, provides the textual evidence and defends the common reading. But he is also convinced that something is still amiss and that the words of Paul here have been lost to us.

[254] This view was first defended by Dibilius (1917), cited in Arnold, *Colossian Syncretism*, 105n8; this view was further defended by Lohse, *Colossians*, 114–120. For the fullest treatment, see Arnold, *Colossian Syncretism*, 104–156; TDNT 2:535.

[255] The phrase "good luck" (*agathē tychē*) stems from her cult and, of course, is widely used today. In modern Greek it survives as *kalē tychē* for a young girl seeking a good match. OCD 1566.

energy."[256] In other words, religion of every variety was present throughout the city.

The problem with this view is that it is too limiting. Over 100 years ago, Ramsay and others underscored the prevalence of syncretism in Hellenistic cities and urged that some Jewish contribution was a part of this picture.[257] The Jewish character of this Colossian teaching now seems obvious to most. But it does not mean that these Colossians were not indulging in pursuits similar to their pagan neighbors. Visionary or mystical experiences were common in Judaism (1Enoch 14:8–13; 2Enoch 3; 3Baruch 2:2; 3:1–2; TLevi 2:5–7; Rev 4:1–12).[258] And even here *embateuō* appears to describe entry into heavenly realms. Paul himself had taken such a journey (2Cor 12:2–4). But for Jews the goal of these visions was heaven itself – another "promised land" – that they were entering and, in it, perhaps could be ushered into the very presence of God.

The essence of this teaching now becomes clearer. The verb *embateuō* was likely a popular term for religious initiation into visionary experiences. The Colossian teachers not only were promoting (and experiencing) the worship of angels but also were entering into "what they had seen," engaging in a journey into mystical realms that could reveal things no other could imagine. They were truly mystics, Jewish mystics, swimming in a Hellenistic religious setting. They had glimpsed behind the curtain but also entered in fully to join what was behind the stage. But the Colossian church was also populated by people who knew other religious experiences from their pagan backgrounds. And this is what made them susceptible to the teachers. This is echoed by Paul in 1Thess 1:9: "[Y]ou turned to God from idols to serve a living and true God." This was the true Colossian experience as well.

Puffed up without cause: Paul now lands his stinging criticism of this religious behavior without reserve. They are "inflated" – *phusioō* – which takes on a rich variety of meanings: puffed up, conceited, arrogant, or haughty. This is preceded by an adverb *eikē* (Rom 13:4; 1Cor 15:2; Gal 4:11), which usually means vanity or purposeless, but here (as in Matt 5:22)

---

[256] A. H. Cadwallader, *Colossae, Colossians, Philemon: The Interface.* Novum Testamentum et Orbis Antiquus/Studien zur Umwelt des Neuen Testaments, Band 127 (Göttingen: Vandenhoeck & Ruprecht, 2023), 231.

[257] See W. Ramsay, *The Teaching of Paul in Terms of the Present Day* (London: Hodder & Stoughton, 1914); E. R. Goodenough, *By Light, Light: The Mystic Gospel of Hellenistic Judaism* (New Haven: Yale University Press, 1935).

[258] Dunn, *Colossians*, 183, offers extensive evidence.

it refers to the absence of reason or thoughtlessness. This is pointed because the teachers are claiming superior spiritual wisdom, but instead they are informed by a mind "of his flesh" (*sarx*). This is loaded with irony: Persons highlighting the depth of their spirituality now are described as vacuous and pointless. Of course, *sarx* carries with it pejorative suggestions and is the antithesis of an elevated spirituality. Rather than being profound, they were egotistical. Their claims to access knowledge of the "elemental spirits of the universe" (2:8), to venerate angels, and to possess visions are all part of the slogans they employed in Colossae. Martin writes, "Those who were making this proud boast were vainly inflated by reason of their worldly way of thinking."[259]

Not holding fast to the head: This, of course, is their great and final failing (**2:19**). They were not holding firmly (*krateō*) to Christ (the head, 1:18; 2:10). This sort of holding implies something strong – *kratos* refers to strength or power (Deut 8:17; Ps 62:11 LXX).[260] This is "holding on for dear life" or gripping something with no intention of letting go. It can mean "seize," such as when John the Baptist is arrested (Mark 6:17). Similarly, as we find it in Acts 2:24, death could not "hold" Jesus.

But this opens another question about this Colossian philosophy: Were they Christians? Were they teachers who assumed some attachment to Christ but had not held on sufficiently?[261] Who let go? The NIV suggests this (they had "lost connection to the head"). Or, on the other hand, were they Jews who were not holding on to Christ and never had (NRSV) and so were misguided?[262] The language is ambiguous, but we can assume – Christians or not – that Paul sees their failure to maintain a strong grasp on Christ as having led to their error. If they did not belong to the church, they then "never grasped" Christ in the first place, which leaves them as, Wright colorfully says, "like a torso without a head."[263]

Viewing Christ as head of the church was common imagery for Paul (Col 1:18; 2:10; 1Cor 11:3–5, 7, 10; Eph 1:22; 4:15; 5:23). With it the apostle sees Christ as the unifying principle of the church. The head (*kephalē*, see

---

[259] Martin, *Colossians*, 94.
[260] We can think of the famous Greek krater (*kratēr*), the two-handled heavy jar at any Greek banquet such as a symposium that held mixed wine and was placed at the center of the room. Its weight and strength are underscored. The term for mixing (*krasis*) comes from this word group: Wine was mixed with water in the krater.
[261] McKnight, *Colossians*, 278.
[262] Wright, *Colossians*, 123; Dunn, *Colossians*, 185.
[263] Wright, *Colossians*, 123.

on 1:18) suggests something that is prominent, central, or elevated, and this is the rightful place of Christ over his people. But the head/body metaphor now takes on a fuller usefulness as Paul stretches it to include more anatomy. The parts of the body (*sōma*) – particularly, here, ligaments and tendons – are given exactly what they need (*epichorēgeō*, NRSV: *are nourished*; 2Cor 9:10; Gal 3:5). And this leads to its growth and well-being. Paul provides more detail in Eph 4:15–16: "Christ – from whom the whole body, joined and knit together by every ligament with which it is equipped, as each part is working properly, promotes the body's growth in building itself up in love" (also 1Cor 12:14–16).

Therefore, the loss facing these Colossian teachers is that they have lost Christ and so have also lost the very body that he sustains: the church. Or, said differently, it is not possible to belong to the church without being nourished by its head, by Christ. And in some manner these teachers have lost their way, indulging in mystical visions and the veneration of angels, hoping to gain access to divine encounters, but they have done so without the one glorious ruler over all these: Christ himself (1:18). But the body metaphor brings more than this. The falsehoods of these teachers have also threatened ecclesiological damage. The head/body image underscores unity and interdependence; any teaching that undercuts the centrality of Christ damages the "the body of Christ" because it dismisses its head who nourishes it.

Colossians 2:8–19 summarizes for us the types of challenges that were weighing down the vitality of the Colossian church. And these challenges were formidable. In 1939, W. L. Knox summarized the issues before the Colossians well:

The Colossians must not allow themselves to be impressed by the assumed superiority of those who sought to impose on them a system of ordinances, of rules as to eating and drinking and the observance of special days as sacred . . ..Nor must they let themselves be impressed by those who sought to impose on them higher standards of special fasts, enjoined as a means of propitiating the angels, whose appearance to them in a vision would mark the stages of their progress to higher things . . .. Access to the heavens was only to be obtained by union with Christ who, as head of the church and the cosmos, provided to everything in it that life which enabled it to grow with a divine increase.[264]

---

[264] W. L. Knox, *St. Paul and the Church of the Gentiles* (Cambridge: Cambridge University Press, 1939), 170; cited in Martin, *Colossians*, 95.

2:20–23 Jewish Practices Are Unnecessary

2:20 If with Christ you died to the elemental principles of the world, why do you live as if you still belonged to the world? Why do you submit to regulations,

2:21 "Do not handle! Do not taste! Do not touch!"?

2:22 All these regulations refer to things that perish with use; they are simply human commands and teachings.

2:23 These have indeed an appearance of wisdom in promoting self-imposed piety, humility, and severe treatment of the body, but they are of no value in checking self-indulgence.

The logic of Paul's exhortation in 2:20–23 centers on the new identity that the followers of Christ at Colossae should have attained by now. In joining the Messianic community, some things were left behind while other things were elevated. And some religious regulations were among those that needed to be abandoned. The problem, of course, is that practitioners of these rules were persuasive and, in some cases, threatening, implying that without obedience to these regulations, spiritual growth would be limited. But what they had to offer – engagement with angelic powers, visionary experiences, dietary secrets, and ascetic denials – these must now be denied fully and forcefully.

Rather than comparing the cosmic rule of Christ to these alternative spiritualities, Paul assigns them to their rightful home: They belong to the world. They are human attempts to ritualize our religious instincts in order to gain access to heaven – to rebuild the Tower of Babel; to take charge of our good and wholesome spiritual instincts and exploit and harness them within a well-crafted religious system. Of course, it all looks profound (having the appearance of wisdom), but it is false, from its worship to its disciplines.

When Paul says, "If with Christ you died to the elemental principles of the world" (**2:20**), we should hear echoes of things he has already covered. First, Paul employs a type of conditional clause here that in Greek assumes something to be true (*ei*, if).[265] We often translate this "false condition" with *since* because it assumes the truth of the assertion (see NIV 2:20).

---

[265] Known as a "condition of fact." BDF §372[1]; Harris, *An Introduction to Biblical Greek Grammar*, 218–220.

Therefore, he doesn't wonder if they have died with Christ; he is affirming that *since* they have died with Christ, their behavior makes little sense. Something happened to them, and here we should imagine that their baptism is in view. In 2:12 Paul described discipleship as dying (being buried) with Christ and being raised with Christ. Here Paul refers to dying, and in 3:1 he will return to resurrection. This means that discipleship is a departure from one sphere and entry into another. This is quite naturally the dramatic meaning of baptism: death and resurrection. In Rom 6 Paul describes this fully: "We know that our old self was crucified with him so that the body of sin might be destroyed . . ." (6:6). And "if we died with Christ, we believe that we will also live with him" (6:8). A consciousness that has been fully shaped by Christ and his death and resurrection will be insulated from the pull of the world. This is why Paul is surprised that they are still susceptible ("Why do you submit?").

Paul writes not that they have "died to" something but that they have died "from" (*apo*) something.[266] This underscores the idea of separation from something (echoed in the verb *apothnēskō*, to die) and its inability to control you. The phrase might mean, "Since you were freed from . . ." reflected in the translation of the REB, "Did you not die with Christ and pass beyond reach of . . .?"[267] Thus if they have died-and-are-free, from what are they free? The NRSV "elemental principles" is again the "*stoicheia*" of Col 2:8 (cf. Gal 4:3, 9), and, as we saw earlier, these are not principles (if we are thinking about rules or laws); these are the forces of the cosmos that can have full effect over human life. Viewing life as subject to these means living life threatened by powers that are *less than* the powers possessed by Christ. And from such a system, religious regulations had emerged either to protect or empower people who live in the world.

But this is Paul's urgent message: These forces and their attendant religious systems have nothing to do with those who belong to Christ, who have joined his Messianic kingdom and no longer fear such forces. Christ's death has rearranged the meaning of the world, for the cross is the place where the fullest activity of God can be found. And this is what believers join. For Paul this might be called "co-crucifixion," and it should

---

[266] Generally this construction would find the verb followed by the dative. See Rom 6:2, 10 for examples.

[267] Harris, *Colossians*, 112; also BDAG 111.

be a natural part of the "circumcision of Christ" (2:11), which is their baptism and identification with Christ's death.[268] This idea of full conformity to the person of Christ – Christoformity – which includes his death, is a theme that appears not only in the gospels (Mark 8:34–37) but also in Paul throughout his writings (2Cor 4:10–12; 2:8–13). "The order is vital: Christ died, the believer dies in Christ's death, and as a result of that death the believer is to put to death the deeds of the flesh."[269]

Notice how Paul expresses this in Philippians, where he defines the new heavenly citizenship that belongs to disciples. Conversion does not simply mean salvation; it means transformation of who we are today: "He will transform the body of our humiliation that it may be conformed to the body of his glory, by the power that also enables him to make all things subject to himself" (3:20–21). The power that enabled Christ to subject *all things* to himself is also the power that is available to the Colossians in the present moment.

The regulations listed in **2:21** each have to do with purity. They are not unusual, and they belong to religious rituals that are commonly used to maintain (with Dunn) "harmony with the spiritual forces behind perceptible reality. This is the Colossian philosophy's version of a 'sacramental universe.'"[270] The list of three regulations belong to the false teachers' rules, and so many translations such as the NRSV place these in quotes lest anyone think these directions belong to Paul.[271]

The words are sarcastic and have a descending order of significance. The first, *haptō*, refers to grasping or touching something with intention or conscious effort. It can mean lighting a fire (Luke 22:55), it can connote sexual touch (1Cor 7:1), or it can mean causing harm (Ps 104:15 LXX).[272] But it also refers to defilement, touching something that brings impurity (2Cor 6:17). Food law was central to this religious preoccupation, and this is likely the meaning here since the second prohibition refers to "tasting" (Luke 14:24). Lastly, they have been told not to "touch" (*thigganō*), which

---

[268] McKnight, *Colossians*, 281.
[269] Ibid.
[270] Dunn, *Colossians*, 190.
[271] Lightfoot, *Colossians*, 203, refers to Latin commentators who believed these were Paul's prohibitions, "thus making a complete shipwreck of the sense." Augustine, Jerome, and Tertullian all viewed it rightly, but their understanding ran counter to popular views of severe asceticism in their day.
[272] LouwNida, §14.65; BDAG 126.

is similar to *haptō* but has a more generic or casual sense. However, the three together form "a descending series,"[273] and, dripping with irony, the list shows the preoccupation with purity rules that end in the slightest taste or touch.

Such purity concerns that measured exposure to things that were clean and unclean, of course, were the preoccupation of Judaism in this period. We should expect that such rules were doubtless "not only enacted but exaggerated by the Colossian false teachers."[274] This understanding of ritual in Second Temple Judaism has been confirmed by the remarkable discoveries of ritual baths (*mikva'ot*) throughout Israel from this period, the writings from Qumran, which held to such rules strictly (1QS 6–7), and the Mishnah, where they were codified later. Simply put, one's status as impure could disqualify someone from a variety of religious activities and so place them in spiritual jeopardy.

This is a form of asceticism with Jewish roots that we already met in 2:16 (food, drink, festivals, new moons, Sabbath), but here Paul is providing one last jab. Paul is promoting a freedom from fear of the *stoicheia* but also freedom from ritual that may be binding and non-liberating. The measure of purity that believers possess was won at the cross, not achieved at the table.

The deeper problem of these regulations (**2:22**) is not simply that they belong to religion built by the world but that they are ephemeral, not eternal. They are a part of a human religious landscape and not originating with God. *This is the theological basis for undoing these religious systems.* They will perish; they are human ideas, fading over time. The idiomatic phrase here (*ha estin panta eis, which are all destined for*) implies the inevitability or perishability of the things of this world: They cannot be eternal because they are human systems with real human limitations. Using the metaphor of perishing (*phthoran*) is a not-so-subtle hint at the food laws of 2:16 and 21, whose food disappears with consumption (1Cor 6:13) – or perhaps spoils. This does not mean that these religious systems simply wear out but that, when employed, their usefulness evaporates. *They are of no use. And using them proves this.*

---

[273] Lightfoot, *Colossians*, 203. Older translations such as the KJV viewed these words in reverse ("touch not, taste not, handle not"). But this has now been shown to be incorrect.
[274] Abbott, *Colossians*, 273.

But the reason for this impermanence is that they are human commands and teachings. Remember that Paul is confronting a basically Jewish teaching, and now with good reason he reaches for the OT. Col 2:22 finds a close echo in Isa 29:13 (LXX), where the prophet critiques the false worship of Israel, describing it as filled with "the commands and teachings of people" rather than directed by God. In Col 2:22 Paul repeats this rebuke and dismisses these regulations with the same language: They are "commands and teachings of people."[275]

Dunn points out how this text from Isaiah also appears in the Jesus tradition (Mark 7:1–23/Matt 15:1–20). And it is also in a context concerning ritual purity and the table, food preparation, and eating, similar to the rules of 2:21. This not only demonstrates that the early church leaders like Paul were aware of the Jesus tradition in Greek, but that they were grounding their teaching in things expressed by Jesus himself. In Mark 7:9 Jesus makes this clear: "You have a fine way of rejecting the commandment of God in order to keep your tradition!" And, of course, in 7:19 Jesus gives his full critique of food laws.[276]

This pejorative view of ritual as human teaching was intrinsic to Paul's debate with his Jewish critics. Such human tradition included circumcision, which, in its historic form, pales next to the truer "circumcision of Christ" (2:11). But this critique certainly included festival participation, purity laws, ritual bathing, calendars, conduct – an entire catalog of regulations that were preserved and taught by many synagogues. For Paul the connection to Christ was to gain access to purity, wisdom, and worship that no other system could match.

Box 2.13 Bridging the Horizons: Legalism

Of course, the religious rules listed in 2:16–19 have their own cultural context in antiquity. Some were from the synagogue, while others merged with that Jewish world from Hellenistic religious traditions. No doubt most people in the Colossian church would have recognized these things as ordinary habits that any religious person should follow. But it is easy to dismiss these rules as having limited value for us today.

---

[275] The word order is different in the LXX (command of people – and teachings) versus Paul: "commands and teachings of people."
[276] Dunn, *Colossians*, 194.

Religious settings constantly generate rules that create captives to the sort of legalism we find in 2:16–19. I have had a long career in Christian higher education in both colleges and seminaries, and I have been amazed to learn how frequently my students came from churches that burden them with rules. These were churches that no doubt preached about the grace of God seen in Christ. But their lived reality in particular was something I never expected. These were devoted Christians who lived with performance anxiety that robbed them of the joy of the gospel.

I frequently thought that the more conservative or traditional the church, the more demanding its expectations. And to a degree this seemed true. Perhaps it was because these churches took their faith very seriously that their pursuit of righteousness or purity or holiness became a necessary condition for membership or identity. In Reformed theological settings, it was a confirmation of their election. In many other churches, such obedience to rules was a precondition for "being saved." It became clear with time that many of these students had lost any idea of what the gospel could mean for them. Paul calls these rules "simply human commands and teachings" that appear to be wise but have limited value.

My awareness of this legalism evolved over time. When students told me that they came from a religiously saturated environment, I suspected that a degree of legalism was at work in them. And I was rarely wrong. This is Paul's chief concern. Paul wants his followers to "walk" as Christ walked (2:6) – which implies faithful obedience – while at the same time experiencing a life filled with thanksgiving (2:7; 3:17).

The catch, of course, is that many of us are drawn to the complexity and mystery of spiritual disciplines or the asceticism that comes with the rigors of a strict religious life. *Doing something hard means that we are moving forward, progressing toward someplace promising, climbing a rewarding path.* This is what the philosophy (2:8) is promising. Paul knows this (**2:23**).[277] The severity and subtlety of these disciplines can become ends in themselves, leading us into our own spiritual preoccupations. Ultimately, we can become spiritually indulgent. He writes that "such things" (likely the regulations of 2:21) have the appearance or form (*logos*)

---

[277] The syntax of 2:23 is extremely obscure and has posed difficulties for many. Here the verb (*estin*) and participle (*echonta*) work together in expressing how "such" (rules) have a "form" (*logos*) of wisdom. The intervening *men*, widespread in classical Greek but rare in the Hellenistic period (BDAG 629–630), increases the contrast between *logos* and *sophia*. See Harris, *Colossians*, 115.

of wisdom (*sophia*) – and the implication is explicit: But they are not wise. They do not carry us where we seek to go.

These religious rules come with empty promises, and Paul lists three. First, they seem to (falsely) promote a religious fervor to which we give ourselves freely. This peculiar Greek noun (*ethelothrēskia*) occurs in no other known text, but we can discern its meaning. This is religion, spiritual endeavors, or cultic practice (*thrēskia*, see 2:18, *the worship of angels*) that are willingly and eagerly embraced (*ethelo-*, from *thelō*, such as a "willing slave," *ethelo-doulos*). Paul is describing spiritual practices that spring from our self-interest, that we cherish for our own experiences, or "piety that orders its own nature."[278] Or, as some have said, these are self-made religions that end in spiritual conceit.

Second, this philosophy requires "humility" (see 2:18) but of a sort that lowers the self in subjection to those who demand submission (the verb *taipainō* can refer to being weakened or humiliated). This is not the humility that Paul regularly promotes in his letters (Eph 4:3; Phil 2:3). In this list, it carries a hint of inferiority, whose embrace promises to make us open to greater spiritual experiences. Or it might demand an attitude of receptivity that includes no discernment. We then become susceptible to teachers or prophets who can lead us as they wish.

Third, this philosophy requires "*apheidia*," a term rarely used in Greek. Its meaning evokes ideas of severity and asceticism, a strict or harsh treatment of the body that hopefully will promote spiritual depth. Fasting or self-denial comes into view, particularly practices that might give us visions or ecstatic states. But it can be anything that disciplines the body in order to elevate the spirit.

Paul quickly dismisses all three of these outcomes.[279] While they seemed to promote wisdom, now it is clear: They have no value (*timē*) for "restraining sensual indulgence" (NIV). The target of Paul's criticism is that these practices do not address "the flesh" (*sarx*). His phrase is a well-known problem for interpreters. Literally Paul writes that such things

---

[278] K. L. Schmidt, TDNT 3:159; Martin, *Colossians*, 97, refers to the noun as "a composite term meaning 'self-made religion' or 'would-be religion.'"

[279] The syntax of 2:23b is extremely difficult. The phrase "having no 'value'" likely completes the earlier Greek *men* (that would seek a completing adversative *de*). Thus 2:23a: "[S]uch things [indeed, *men*] have the form of wisdom ... but [now, *de*] we see they have no value for anyone." However, the expected *de* is missing.

"have no value in *gratifying* (*plēsmonēn*) the flesh (*sarx*) or physical needs." Three options are possible. (1) The church fathers saw *sarx* positively as natural needs of the body, but this is an unlikely use here. The sense then would be "these practices do not satisfy what we need naturally." (2) Or *sarx* could hold Paul's usual meaning of *sinful flesh* (Gal 5:16–17). This would echo Paul's use in 2:18. This makes *plēsmonēn* a negative term (*indulging* the flesh). (3) Dunn suggests that this "gratification" of the flesh refers to the Jewish context of satisfaction in their ethnic status as Jews (*kata sarka*).[280] Most modern translations opt for the second view and in various ways make the phrase negative. Thus, in the NIV, "they lack any value in restraining sensual indulgence." Or in the ESV, "they are of no value in stopping the indulgence of the flesh." And in the NRSV, "They are of no value in checking self-indulgence." Essentially, as spiritual disciplines they do not deliver what they promise.

For Paul and Timothy this is a catalog of what is fundamentally wrong with the promises of these false teachers. If we are not "holding fast to the head" (Christ, 2:19) or if our lives are not "hidden with Christ in God" (3:3), then we are susceptible to religious experiences that are "of the world" (2:20), "simply human" (2:22), from "the flesh" (2:23), or "of the earth" (3:2).[281] Our sight is not fixed on "things above" (3:2), nor are our imaginations shaped by Christ and his glorious place with God. This makes us susceptible indeed to self-generating religious appetites, desires for spiritual experiences promoted by teachers who do not know what it means to be immersed in Christ's presence. They call such a spirituality wisdom, but it is not. It promotes a "self-ordained piety," and it has "no (true) validity and simply serves to satisfy (pious) self-seeking."[282]

3:1–4:6 How We Live in Christ Matters Deeply

3:1–4 A Grounding Ethical Statement

3:1 So if you have been raised with Christ, seek the things that are above, where Christ is, seated at the right hand of God.

---

[280] Dunn, *Colossians*, 197–198.
[281] Delling, TDNT 6:134.
[282] Ibid.

3:2 Set your minds on the things that are above, not on the things that are on earth,

3:3 for you have died, and your life is hidden with Christ in God.

3:4 When Christ who is your life is revealed, then you also will be revealed with him in glory.

There are two ways that we can look at these four verses. They might be a summary of Paul's theological presentation in chapter 2. In this case, they sum up his argument and these words connect particularly with 2:6–15. The opening phrase, "if therefore you have been raised ..." then echoes 2:20, and 3:1 is a continuation of his earlier argument. This is also suggested by the conjunction *therefore* (*oun*) that opens 3:1. "Therefore [given what you have just learned and] since you have been raised with Christ ..." This view has much to commend it.

But the passage also looks forward. The aim of this section is to underscore what a resurrected and transformed life looks like. Here again we see Paul's use of a condition (*ei*) that assumes a fact that is true (see on 2:20), which is why translators will commonly use *since* rather that *if*: "since you are have been raised..." Or: "Having been raised, seek the things that are above ..."

Given this new spiritual reality worn by the Colossian Christians, Paul now opens a discussion about ethics within the church. In this second view, these verses are a *grounding theological statement* from which Paul's ethical arguments can be launched. Wright remarks that since Paul has drawn out the implications of dying with Christ (2:20–23), he "now draws out the implications of having also risen with Christ. They have entered the new age, and, belonging there by right, do not have to struggle to attain the status of membership in God's people: they already have it. They must now simply allow its life to be worked out in them."[283]

Paul already hinted at this in 2:6: "As you therefore have received Christ Jesus the Lord, continue to walk in him, rooted and built up in him ..." But it is also embedded in the idea that there has been a very real death ("If with Christ you died ..." 2:20; 3:3). Death and new life frame Paul's understanding of the Christian life going forward. Now we learn that the newly gained spiritual identity offered in Christ comes with genuine

---

[283] Wright, *Colossians*, 130–131.

expectations. We are to live as Christ lived, walk as Christ walked, exhibiting a life to the world the bears all the marks of Jesus' life *because* our lives have been attached to his.

Two verbs organize Paul's exhortation. We now must ground our *desires* (to seek, *zēteō*, 3:1) and our *understanding* (to comprehend, *phroneō*, 3:2) in Christ alone. This is where the Christology of the letter begins to show its full effect. Note how Paul repeats five times the fuller name with the definite article, *ho Christos*, rather than the usual *Christos*, giving a rhythmic cadence to the verses and reinforcing them.[284]

If the identity and successes of Christ that Paul has outlined so far are true, then our goal is no longer finding our own spiritual paths – or, as some might (unfortunately) say today, finding our personal "truth." We do not need to decipher religious or philosophical possibilities in life, nor do we need to navigate a cosmos populated with spiritual beings such as angels that we barely comprehend. Religions no longer need to be weighed to test their veracity or effectiveness. Christ is our one true guide and his path the one true faith. In joining him we begin to live his risen life in us, thereby shaping our desires and our thinking. *It is this changed reality that then can fuel the fully transformed life* (3:5–4:6). Ethics for Paul is never grounded in the efforts of *sarx*, in the compromised humanity we all inhabit, in the strivings of *this world*. Paul might say that we have seen enough of that in all its failings – and with this most of us would concur. Instead, ethics springs from attachment to Christ, and in this sense its grounding is fully mystical or, better, inspired and formed by the Spirit.[285] For example, Paul will call for compassion (3:12), but this is a compassion that is not commonplace, not ordered by the world; rather, it is the compassion moving *from* Christ *into* us, and then – and only then – it is exhibited in the world.

Paul begins (**3:1–2**) by describing the flip side of the death and burial we experience in our conversion (2:12). We are now raised with Christ. Discipleship refers to our death to sin and our resurrection to new kingdom-life, as in Eph 2:4–6: "But God, who is rich in mercy, out of the

---

[284] Two uses employ the article in the dative, *tō Christō*.
[285] Paul's understanding of the work of the Spirit can be presumed in these verses even though the Spirit is not mentioned directly (but see Col 1:8, 9; 2:5; 3:16). Rom 8:5 echoes Col 3:1 closely and uses the language of the Spirit.

great love with which he loved us even when we were dead through our
trespasses, made us alive together with Christ – by grace you have been
saved – and raised us up with him and seated us with him in the heavenly
places in Christ Jesus . . ."

This "raising" should not be confused with the future expectation of
resurrection life promised after our physical death. This is not a future
eschatological promise. Paul understands that well. Here he is using
resurrection as a metaphor to describe a new reality born with Christ's
resurrection: It is perhaps our "co-resurrection," where we join Christ in
his resurrection in the present. The uniquely Christian rhythm of death/
resurrection, which had its literal realities in Jerusalem, now has given birth
to a new kingdom reality that belongs to Christ's followers, who are led and
shaped by the Spirit. The gospel always brings an announcement of death
(of Christ, of us, Rom 6:8) along with an announcement of resurrection (of
Christ, of us). That is to say: Something has died *so that* something new
can emerge. "If a single grain of wheat falls to the earth and dies . . . it will
bear much fruit" (John 12:24).

Resurrection in this setting (*egeirō*) literally meant to awaken or stir
someone (possibly from death). Therefore, as Christ was raised and lives *in
the present* a transformed resurrected life, we too are raised by the same
powers that raised him; we are raised "with him" (*syn + egeirō*). Caird
writes, "Christianity offers a more radical and effective solution to man's
ethical and spiritual problems than an ascetical legalism. It allows the old
human nature, with its unruly passions and bad conscience, to die, nailed
to the cross of Christ, so that it may be raised with him to a new life."[286]
Christ's resurrection in Jerusalem can thus be mirrored in our present
resurrection achieved by the work of the Spirit. This co-resurrection of
Christ and us is a unique feature, certainly, of Colossians and Ephesians –
but this is an idea found throughout Paul.[287]

This "shifted reality" in us is not automatic nor mechanical, as if once we
become a follower of Jesus or once we have been baptized we suddenly
metamorphize into something new. The believer must also lean into this

---

[286] Caird, *Colossians*, 201.
[287] On the controversy as to whether this theme of co-resurrection betrays that Paul was
not the author of Colossians and Ephesians, see the succinct dismissal of this this claim
by McKnight, *Colossians*, 290.

transformation, participate in what has happened, and welcome this new perspective into their thinking. This is the not-so-surprising feature of this transformation. A gift has been given and reciprocity follows. Transformation is not automatic. This change *in us* comes about by God's grace, and this forges a change in how we begin to see ourselves and the world. But we participate as well. Paul urges us to *keep seeking*[288] or focus our attention as a spiritual discipline on things that are "above" – that is, on realities that are in heaven.[289] This exhortation has often been misunderstood as promoting an otherworldly life, one that is so focused on heaven that it has lost any investment in this world. This is not a mystical separation from the world but a life lived in this world "on the basis of the rule of Christ over all powers."[290]

Such seeking – or, perhaps, this quest – is a yearning for higher things. It is not a self-seeking for our own edification or glory (Gal 1:10) but a desire to concentrate ourselves so fully on Christ that his values, his thoughts, and his priorities infuse our thinking completely. Perhaps we can say that this is about our desires: those things we yearn for in this life. Perhaps it is about our insatiable appetites for treasures that we think can be found in this world. The NIV translates 3:1 as "set your hearts on things above." This rendering has now become legendary. But if this is taken to mean that our effort is to be focused on our inner selves, our own emotions, or perhaps our impulses, the NIV has misled us ("hearts" is not in the text). But if we see this as an idiom that illumines the fullness of our deepest yearning for Christ himself, then it might serve us well. This is about desires – rightly ordered desires that aim us to rightly ordered ends.

The focus of this disciplined gaze is singular: It is Christ himself, who lives in heaven and is seated in a place of authority. These are two coordinate ideas: Christ is in heaven, where our attention is directed ("the above"), and Christ is located at God's right hand.[291] This right-hand position was known throughout antiquity as a place of privilege and honor, such as a person sitting with a king (1Kgs 2:19; Ps 98:1; Mark 10:37). It is reflected in Ps 110:1: "The LORD says to my lord, 'Sit at my right hand'" (cited in

---

[288] The verb is an active present imperative (plural), which can carry a continuous aspect.
[289] TDNT 1:376.
[290] McKnight, *Colossians*, 290.
[291] The Greek here is an abbreviation: "where Christ is seated on God's right," *en dexia cheiri*, meaning on the right hand.

Mark 12:36; Acts 2:34–35; Heb 1:13, with various allusions elsewhere, Eph 1:20), making it the most cited OT text in the entire NT.

However, the idea resting behind this description of Christ's place opens a window into a constellation of ideas that set Christian thinking completely apart. This place – God's right hand – refers to rule. From this position Christ has not disappeared into heaven awaiting the eschaton, but now he has an active role, intimately connected to God, demonstrating divine power over all creation (Acts 2:33–36; 1Cor 15:25). *He has been enthroned.* And if this is the case, he is now the Christian's Sovereign in the world. The spiritual powers (the *stoicheia*, 1:18) that populate the cosmos and the political forces of Rome, including Caesar himself, now have become secondary in light of Christ's enthronement. With Caird: "To seek the things that are above is to give Christ an allegiance which takes precedence over all earthly loyalties."[292]

In **3:2** we have a coordinate idea that Paul is using for emphasis: "Set your minds (*phroneō*) on things that are above." In its earliest form, *phrēn* referred to the seat of thought, considered to be in the abdomen (hence, *diaphragm*, *dia + phragma*, through a fence). But it evolved to mean more than merely thought. It pointed to comprehension, insight, or cleverness.[293] It meant having a settled mind, a conviction, an opinion, or an attitude (Rom 8:5; 14:6; 1Cor 13:11). Therefore, we are grounded, fixed in our understanding of Christ and our lives under his rule (Phil 2:5; 1Cor 2:16), attached inflexibly to a commitment that does not waver. But unlike 3:1, this verse presents the alternative to be avoided: We should not let our minds be shaped by the earth (*gē*). Paul does not say "world" (*kosmos*, used forty-six times in Paul), which for him generally refers to the sphere of human life bound up in sin (Rom 3:19; 5:12). The *kosmos* and its spiritual forces are the opposite of "the heavens." So Paul can write to the Corinthians, "We have received not the spirit of the world (*kosmos*) but the Spirit that is from God, so that we may understand the gifts bestowed on us by God" (1Cor 2:12).

But here in 3:2 it is creation – *gē* – the commonplace matters of living and thriving and, in some cases, surviving; perhaps good causes that spring

---

[292]   Caird, *Colossians*, 202.
[293]   TDNT 9:220–229; in Josephus (*Antiquities*, 16.380) it was often paired with *nous* or mind. In *Antiquities*, 1.37, the tree of knowledge if the tree of knowing (*phronēseōs*).

from the commonplace can be the distraction that disguises itself as a heavenly vision. This is the language Paul uses for his opponents in Philippi (Phil 3:19): "their minds are set on earthly things (*epigeia*)."

These may be good, but they are from below, from creation and all of its limitations. This is the counterpoint to heaven but does not imply a dualism between the two. Paul is warning that our identity in Christ can be sabotaged by the rhythms of life in this world. To be sure, even spiritual or religious efforts – the church and all of its functions – may be victims of this pull. Paul may even have in mind the rival religious community competing with the Colossian church itself. Instead, the believer's values and deepest orientations are shaped differently: They see things differently, and this has led to a transformed understanding of everything around them. In a sense, this is a command to meditate, to look so completely at Christ that we begin to absorb the vision of who he is in all of his glory – and with that vision see the world through a different lens. This heavenly vision then permits us to "begin on earth to reflect the very life of heaven."[294]

Paul has now said what he needs to say: We should seek the things that are above and set our minds on things above. This is a reorientation of everything. But the catalyst for this shift is what has happened to us. "You have died" (**3:3**). Paul of course has already said this in 2:20. He likely is thinking of baptism/conversion, which created the marker separating a life into two halves: one that was apart from Christ and belonged to sin; and one that has died as Christ died, sheltered in Christ's life, and now reflecting the life of the resurrected Christ. The verb in this case evokes an important nuance: Something has happened once and for all, and there is no going back.[295]

This death is, of course, metaphorical – no one has died *as Christ died* – but it nevertheless conveys a truth. Something is gone and in the past. But this now becomes the basis for the exhortation that follows (3:5). If something has died, things that were attached to that old life must go as well. The follow-on from this death is once more resurrection, but it is framed differently: "Your life is hidden with Christ in God." Paul's use of

---

[294] Wright, *Colossians*, 132.
[295] The verb *apethanete* (*apothnēskō*) is in the aorist tense, which bears the aspect of a singular event.

kruptō (hidden) is unusual for him and has inspired wide speculation: Is this mysticism, Jewish apocalyptic, and hidden divine secrets?[296] The principal idea, however, is sheltering: Your life is sheltered. This means removal to a place of safety and a promise of protection so that no harm may come. It also means that as Christ has been drawn into the divine life of the Father, so, too, Christ's followers now have a place of refuge and sanctuary. They, too, have been drawn into a place of safety; they are sheltered like Christ, in God himself.

Once again, the idea is not removal from this world; it is living in the world with a life that is empowered by a "hidden resource" (Rom 6:4; 2Cor 4:10–11; 13:4).[297] Discipleship for Paul builds on the notion of not simply a renewed identity but a new one. This is a life that is utterly changed by both death and life. In 2Cor 4:10–11 Paul expresses this in unexpected forms: "[W]e [are] always carrying around in the body the death of Jesus, so that the life of Jesus may also be made visible in our bodies." We live with both death and life working their way out in the daily affairs of the world. Using a different construction, Paul can say we are citizens of heaven (Phil 3:19–20), and yet we live in the world, bearing both identities at once.

The mystery of our dying and rising and our divine sanctuary in heaven will appear to many as invisible and unpersuasive (**3:4**). And naturally the cynical will mock these things. Paul now shows that vindication will be found at the conclusion of time. The flip side of this hiddenness is the future unveiling of who Christ truly is. This is a future (eschatological) hope that refers to Christ's second coming (Mark 13:26; Acts 3:19–21; 1Thess 4:15–17). Moreover, it also means that as Christ is revealed for the world to see, so, too, his followers, safely hidden in God, will likewise be revealed.[298] This revealing (using the rarer *phaneroō* rather than *apokaluptō*; but see 1Pet 5:4; 1John 2:28) means a joint revelation at the end of time that will make clear the truest nature of God's efforts *in Christ*

---

[296] The verb does not appear in the so-called authentic Paulines. It occurs only here and in 1Tim 5:25. However, the cognates *apokruptō* and *apokruphos* do appear in Colossians, and *apokruptō* is in 1Cor 12:7.

[297] Dunn, *Colossians*, 207.

[298] A minor variant appears in 3:4. Many commentators prefer "our life" (*hē zōē hēmōn*) to the more common English version translation "your life" (*hē zōē hūmōn*). This second reading has stronger textual support, and the second-person plural appears in the phrases before and after it. See Harris, *Colossians*, 122, for textual evidence.

throughout the world. How will this revelation work? Christ – in his Jerusalem resurrection – already provided the model for the person who is both a "man from heaven" and a "man of earth." There will be genuine continuity but also substantial discontinuity.

This idea of the Second Coming of Christ – the Parousia – has been with the church from the beginning and appears in all of its creeds. "He is seated at the right hand of God the Father almighty and from there he will come to judge the living and the dead" (Apostle's Creed); "He ascended to heaven, and is seated at the right hand of the Father. He will come again with glory to judge the living and the dead. His kingdom will never end" (Nicene Creed). Or we could point to the Memorial Acclimation that follows the eucharist in countless churches around the world: "Christ has died. Christ is risen. Christ will come again."

The return and rule of Jesus are the final steps in his incarnational mission to redeem the world. And its eschatological assumptions are simple: "History has a goal, God is in control, and history will come to its fitting conclusion when Christ is exalted above all and when he hands over the kingdom to the Father, who will then be 'all in all'" (1Cor 15:35–37).[299] Therefore Christ's rule will be public, and the world will no longer be able to resist it (Phil 2:6–7). But the surprise is that as we have joined Christ in his death and resurrection, likewise we will join him in his great self-revelation to the world.

Recall that in Paul's mind the great fall of humanity recorded in Genesis can be summed up by the collapse of Adam as the exemplar of God's efforts in creation. And in Christ this Adam – or (with Dunn) an Adam Christology – is now being revisited in the NT.[300] The loss incurred by Adam was a loss of glory (Rom 3:23), and Christ, the new Adam, has now taken this up and revived the glory of God in his incarnate life (John 1:14; 2:11; Rom 8:29–30; 2Cor 3:18). He has also invited his followers to be immersed in this glory (John 17:22; Rom 9:23; 1Cor 2:7; 1Thess 2:12). Indeed, Christ's followers are glory-bearers who manifest this glory both now in this life and, most importantly, at the great conclusion of the human story. Even within our suffering and loss, this revelation of glory glows most clearly. Paul states, "For we who are living are always being handed over to

---

[299] McKnight, *Colossians*, 296; Garland, *Colossians*, 202–203.
[300] Dunn, *Colossians*, 208–209.

death for Jesus's sake, so that the life of Jesus may also be made visible in our mortal flesh" (2Cor 4:11). The glory of Jesus is an endowment given to his followers, and it is most clear as his followers live faithfully even under duress in this world. Glory was one of the gifts of Christ provided at the completion of his life. "The glory that you have given me I have given them . . ." (John 17:22). This is what it means to be drawn into the life of Christ: It is to be drawn into the glory that radiates from God himself.

3:5–17 *General Guidelines for Conduct*

3:5 Put to death, therefore, whatever in you is earthly: sexual immorality, impurity, passion, evil desire, and greed (which is idolatry).

3:6 On account of these the wrath of God is coming on those who are disobedient.

3:7 These are the ways you also once followed, when you were living that life.

3:8 But now you must get rid of all such things: anger, wrath, malice, slander, and abusive language from your mouth.

3:9 Do not lie to one another, seeing that you have stripped off the old self with its practices

3:10 and have clothed yourselves with the new self, which is being renewed in knowledge according to the image of its creator.

3:11 In that renewal there is no longer Greek and Jew, circumcised and uncircumcised, barbarian, Scythian, enslaved and free, but Christ is all and in all!

3:12 Therefore, as God's chosen ones, holy and beloved, clothe yourselves with compassion, kindness, humility, meekness, and patience.

3:13 Bear with one another and, if anyone has a complaint against another, forgive each other; just as the Lord has forgiven you, so you also must forgive.

3:14 Above all, clothe yourselves with love, which binds everything together in perfect harmony.

3:15 And let the peace of Christ rule in your hearts, to which indeed you were called in one body. And be thankful.

3:16 Let the word of Christ dwell in you richly; teach and admonish one another in all wisdom; and with gratitude in your hearts sing psalms, hymns, and spiritual songs to God.

3:17 And whatever you do, in word or deed, do everything in the name of the Lord Jesus, giving thanks to God the Father through him.

These lists – moral warnings in 3:5–11, virtues in 3:12–17 – can be found in other Jewish and Hellenistic settings, making them some of the best-known teaching tools of antiquity. If Paul's lists seem burdensome, Philo has his own list in *The Sacrifices of Cain and Abel* (§32) that contains 150 vices, making Paul's prohibitions seem miniscule. Even Paul's language of "putting off" (3:8, 9) and "putting on" (3:10, 12) was common in Paul's day.[301] The Jews at Qumran had a parallel list (1QS 4:2–6) that is surprisingly similar to Paul's. But it is important to note how Paul "Christianizes" these discussions. While we may find echoes of these warnings and virtues elsewhere, Paul is thinking about them Christianly, expecting that, even here, followers of Christ bear some degree of uniqueness. Paul anchors these thoughts in Christology.

This ethical instruction begins with *therefore* (*oun*), linking the theological conclusions of the previous paragraphs to what Paul is about to say. Given our new theological realities, so, too, must we expect new ethical realities. It is Christ who rules in our hearts (3:15), and it is the word of Christ that dwells in us (3:16). The phrase "in the Lord" abounds throughout these paragraphs. Thus, the ethics of the church are not celebrated because they fulfill or surpass the secular standards of the world or the virtues of "religions." They are celebrated because they carry some semblance of Christ within them. They bear the imprint of Jesus, which means each virtue will take on a characteristically Christian feature. Thus, Paul will conclude the section with a summary exhortation: "Do everything in the name of the Lord Jesus" (3:17). The imitation of Christ (*De Imitatione Christi*) must have been central to the earliest ethical teaching of the earliest church.

Death now returns as a metaphor for Christian living (**3:5**). The entire sentence recalls Gal 5:23: "Those who belong to Christ have crucified the flesh with its passions and desires." Something dramatic and shocking must accompany how we see ourselves. This death concerns not simply a

---

[301] Dunn, *Colossians*, 213, and Bird, *Colossians*, 100n19, point to such Jewish sources: *Wis* 14:25–26; 4Macc 1:26–27; 2:15; 1QS 4:9–11; Philo, *De sacrificiis*, 32; 2Enoch 10:4–5. Even Jesus easily produces such lists, Mark 7:21–22. Also Paul: Rom 1:29–31; 1Cor 6:9–10; 2Cor 12:20; Gal 5:19–21.

disconnection from the things of this world (2:20; 3:3), but it means that we now have an entirely different relationship with sin (Rom 6:1–6). Our union with Christ demands such a realignment – but, in addition, that union empowers it and achieves it. Moo remarks, "Ultimately, then, the imperative 'put to death' in this verse must be viewed as a call to respond to, and cooperate with the transformative power that is already operative within us."[302]

What dies? Paul says that we put to death *parts* (*melē*) of who we are, parts of us that belong to the natural order of this world (*gē*). Similar language can be found at 3:2. Ordinarily *melē* referred to body parts, but this was used generally for parts that orchestrated a natural order together: the human body, a choir (where every "part" played a role), or even a city (where the *polis* is sustained by parts of each citizen).[303] Paul might say, *There are parts of us, deeply connected to creation with its wild mix of virtue and evil that now need realignment and rethinking.*

Thus, discipleship does not simply cultivate a mystical, otherworldly connection with God, but it requires that, *as we are in creation*, those parts of us that engage with this world require attention. *Melē* is thus here a metaphor: The bodily life we lead continues to have a connection to the world and its values. *Union with Christ does not aim to disconnect us from the world.* Union with Christ now sharpens that connection with the world, giving it a perceptive and acerbic posture, an antagonism to values that are deeply opposed to Christ. The list that Paul will open in 3:5 undoubtedly springs from this very world he wants the Colossians to see with fresh eyes. This list likely describes the world where they live – even now. But those days of participating with such values must be over.

What is striking is that when Paul considers those features of ordinary life that should exhibit dramatic change in Christ, sexual morality comes immediately to mind. We forget how much the worlds of Judaism and Hellenism differed on this score. Cities like Colossae and most other Roman cities in this period displayed a public sexuality – from garments to statuary – that surprised the Jews. Sexual license (with some firm limits for households) was common. Husbands might have "procreational sex" at home with their wives and then pursue "recreational sex" in public

---

[302] Moo, *Colossians*, 255.
[303] TDNT 4:556.

spaces.[304] And this "recreation" could include everything from the sexual use of young boys (pederasty), prostitution, and banquets offering sexual orgies. Same-sex relations were common. A quick look at the erotic poetry of Ovid or the graffiti of Pompeii makes this clear. Mosaics, pottery, inscriptions, and erotic artifacts each illustrate this sexual freedom in ways that surprise modern students of Rome.

Imagine the reaction of Jews in Colossae encountering a wealthy man who "owns" a prepubescent boy dressed in feminine attire.[305] Or imagine seeing the easy integration of temple service with fertility metaphors that were nothing less than explicit. Idolatry was the deepest offense a Jew saw in Roman society, and often it appeared laced with sexual innuendo that no one could miss.

Paul then begins by saying firmly that a gulf should separate *this feature* of the world and the community of Christ. Each of his initial terms – sexual immorality, impurity, passion, evil desire, and greed (which is idolatry) – can be applied to this setting of illicit sexuality. As a Jew, Paul's context for understanding these five terms was Leviticus 18, which became the common guide to understanding sexual morality. Its list of prohibitions is long, and if assume that this is Paul's wider understanding, words like *porneia* take on this wider meaning.

We can assume that the Colossians knew this world well and indulged in it, and their conversion to Christ meant that a shift in their understanding and experience of sexual practice was necessary (3:7). Sexual immorality (*porneia*) may suggest a prostitute (*pornē*), but more broadly it refers to sexual activity that is unlawful (Mark 7:21; Gal 5:19) or, as a Jew, sexual activity that violates Torah. Paul uses *porneia* or its cognates frequently (twenty-one times). To the Corinthians he writes, "It is actually reported that there is sexual immorality (*porneia*) among you and the sort of sexual immorality that is not found even among gentiles" (1Cor 5:1).

Paul commonly follows *porneia* with *akatharsia* (impurity), as he does in Gal 5:19: "Now the works of the flesh are obvious: sexual immorality

---

[304] These two terms come from McKnight, *Colossians*, 303–305. On sexuality in Rome and Greece, see M. Skinner, *Sexuality in Greek and Roman Culture*, 2nd edition (Hoboken: Wiley-Blackwell, 2013). On same-sex practice, see R. Hubbard, ed., *Homosexuality in Greece and Rome: A Sourcebook of Basic Documents* (Berkeley: University of California Press, 2003).

[305] See Seneca the Younger, *Natural Questions*, 1.16; *Moral Epistles*, 47.7.

(*porneia*), impurity (*akatharsia*) ...." Impurity here refers to uncleanness (*katharos*, clean), and its origins were in cultic, religious life: It was a status, a disordered condition, prohibited by the temple. In Hellenistic Judaism its meaning broadened to include immorality (1Enoch 10:11; Matt 23:25–26). Given Paul's use of *porneia* with it, the word's meaning is clear: This is an impurity linked to sexual misconduct. Passion (*pathos*) has so many positive English connotations that every translation needs to use a phrase to show its underlying meaning in a list like this. Paul uses it in Rom 1:26 and 1Thess 4:5 in discussions of sexual morality, and here it would have the undertone of wrongly directed erotic feelings that express themselves in sexual behavior.

Desire (*epithumia*) can be as positive in Greek as it can be in English. Yet in 1Thess 4:5 and Gal 5:24 Paul combines passion with desire, which narrows its meaning. In vice lists such as this Paul is referring to sexual appetites or perhaps sinful longings,[306] and in Hellenistic literature it could mean lust.[307] Greed (*pleonexia*) could be any unregulated desire, and so it joined many vice lists in antiquity (Rom 1:29; Eph 5:3). In Plato's *Symposium* (182B) we read about men whose extreme power permits them to satisfy their greed any way they wish.[308] This, of course, can refer to the desire for anything. But Paul may be describing people whose sexual appetites consume them, as we might describe an addiction today. Paul adds that this is idolatry, an elevation of sex to a level of fascination and importance that consumes one's life. Idolatry, of course, was enormously important in Jewish thought (Exod 20:4–5), but when Jews encountered the Hellenistic world they met a religious setting where sexual practices met religious devotion. Idolatry and sexual immorality were thus often linked (Num 25:1–3; Hos 4:12–18; 1Cor 6:9–11; 10:7–8; Rom 1:18–32).[309] Typically, Jews found this reprehensible.

It is indeed stunning that sexual immorality owns a central place in Paul's list as the first of many markers of the new life in Christ. Is this the signal test of the Spirit-led transformation of the human heart? Paul shares

---

[306] Dunn, *Colossians*, 212.
[307] TDNT 3:168–195; cf. LXX Nu 11:4–34; Deut 9:32; Prov 6:25 and Sir 4:22. Dunn (*Colossians*, 215) adds Plutarch, *Moralia*, 525AB; Josephus, *Antiquities*, 4:130, 132; and Plato, *Laws*, 9:854A.
[308] Dunn, *Colossians*, 215. See Loeb 166:176–177.
[309] Dunn, *Colossians*, 215.

parallel words with the Thessalonians: "For this is the will of God, your sanctification: that you abstain from sexual immorality; that each one of you know how to control your own body in holiness and honor, not with lustful passion, like the gentiles who do not know God" (1Thess 4:3–5). Sexual purity likely became a marker in the earliest Christian communities.

Paul knew (and we know) how often these sins can appear in the church. They lead to dishonoring Christ and discrediting his followers. And this is why (**3:6**) Paul can point to the judgment of God as focused on sins such as sexual immorality or idolatry (Rom 1:32; 1Cor 5:9–13; 6:9–10; Gal 5:19–21). God is not simply dismissive of these things; he is angry (*orgē*) – which puts a sharper edge on this than the NRSV "wrath." In Biblical thought, this idea is not peculiar. God's anger is expressed toward Israel for its unresolved sins including immorality and idolatry (Exod 32:10–12; Num 25:1–4). Likewise in the NT, God's anger is fully and ultimately expressed in judgment (Gal 5:19–21; 1Thess 4:3–6). These are the consequences, the inevitable results of a life lived in direct opposition to God's will. Thus, Paul can describe these not simply as violators of a law but as "disobedient" as if to a person.[310] Their conduct is not only offensive; it is in violation of his expectations for his people's moral life. It is their demeanor before this law that matters as much as their sin.

This exhortation suggests that Paul did not simply bring the pious or religiously inclined into his circles of discipleship (**3:7**). What he has just described is familiar to his readers in Colossae. The Colossian believers were no more immune to the temptations of their culture than we are. The text, using a semitic idiom, says that they had "walked" in these ways – but this should be behind them. After another long list of prohibitions written to Corinth (1Cor 6:9–10) Paul can say, "And this is what some of you used to be!" The church at Corinth – viewed through Paul's first letter – may give us a window into how fully his churches could be shaped by their surrounding culture.

Because of this verse, Paul may know more than we realize about this church (as he seems to in other letters). Or he may be speculating. There is

---

[310] The NRSV includes a variant: "wrath of God *on the sons of disobedience*." This is a semitic phrase ("sons of") typical of a bilingual speaker such as Paul but it does not appear in a number of important, early manuscripts. Many commentators remove these words, thinking that a scribe knew Eph 5:6 or 2:2, which are close parallels (and which have no variants). Thus Beale, *Colossians*, 288, contra Abbott, *Colossians*, 281.

every possibility that the Colossians not only had absorbed the religious inclinations of their culture, but they might also have absorbed its moral failings. Paul's letter may be as much a declaration of Christlike righteousness as it is a suggestive rebuke about how their lived experience differed from what it should be.

Paul's list of prohibited behaviors, however, is not complete. Col **3:8** opens with Paul's always-significant "but now" (*nuni de*, see 1:22), which leads to further exhortation. *But now – now that you (emphatic plural, hymeis) have moved from darkness to light, abandoned the troubled world of failed spiritual quests, fear of powers, and endless religious ceremonies – but now that you have attached yourself to Christ, have the courage to abandon as well the practices of this world.* Paul does not say that they have abandoned these things in their conversion, but he uses an imperative verb, a call to action, saying in effect that that they too must apply effort. This parallels Paul's words in 3:1 ("Seek the things that are above!" also 2:6), which present cooperation or participation between the believer and God. Human effort is successful because of divine participation.

What follows is a catalog of behaviors that is reminiscent of Paul's "works of the flesh" in Gal 5:19–21. As in 3:5, Paul now offers another list of five vices, this time centering on failings that lead to disunity: anger, wrath, malice, slander, and abusive language. And this is followed by a more generalizing vice in 3:9. But notice how 3:8 begins: We must get rid of all such things. We must remove everything that belonged to our previous life. "Put to death" now is replaced with "get rid of" (NRSV, *apotithēme*), but the image here is closer to taking off a garment. Something we have been wearing must be shed. Some wonder if this was a word that harked back to baptism when a candidate may have had to remove clothes to enter baptismal water, signaling that a new life and identity had been gained.[311] There are many things that Paul could have listed, but in this case he recognizes the destructive capacity of interpersonal relationships inside the Christian community, and for him this is of supreme concern.

Two principal words expressed anger – *orgē* and *thumos* – and Paul lists both: We are to do away with anger and wrath. They are nearly synonymous, but the second, *thumos*, likely evokes a more emotional, explosive

---

[311] McKnight, *Colossians*, 306.

anger. Cognates use it for *violent movement* and apply it to things that are boiling, agitated, or smoking.[312] Warnings about anger appear in a number of Paul's letters (2Cor 12:20; Gal 5:20; Eph 4:31). Malice (*kakia*) simply points to deeds that are evil or repugnant, vicious perhaps. Slander is the familiar term "blasphemy" (*blasphēmia*), but here it has an application of speech that is false *regarding another*, that harms and is basically a form of lying to one another. This same deceit is reinforced in **3:9**, which shows the seriousness of Paul's concern.

The NRSV "abusive language" (*aischrologia*) is more complex than the rest. These are words (*logia*) that are shameful or disgraceful (root: *airsch-*), not simply abusive, though this would be included. The verb *aischunō* means to shame someone or to be shamed or disgraced, and it is attested widely in the LXX and Hellenistic Judaism, since shame and honor were pivotal culturally (Luke 14:9; Did 4:11). In fact, in this world, shame was like a contaminant that stains both the speaker and the hearer. But this virtue requires someone to be alert to what could be shaming or honoring, and these are culturally derived values. The best treatments describe this as "filthy speech"[313] or perhaps speech that is obscene.[314]

We can imagine Paul urging that, in the gathering of the church at least, there should be charity and harmony rather than strife (1Cor 5:8). Paul similarly tells the Ephesians, "Put away from you all bitterness and wrath and anger and wrangling and slander, together with all malice" (Eph 4:31). Therefore, this is about mutual respect, honor-sharing, and unity. But this change in behavior only happens once one decisively commits to forging a life that is set apart from the usual reflexes in the world. Here again in **3:9** Paul talks about stripping away (only here and in Col 2:15). This sinful behavior belongs to the old self – and here again see how Paul understands that the Christian life has two chapters: the old self (**3:9**) and the new (**3:10**), one anchored to this world and dressed in shameful attire and the second reclothed with righteousness (**3:10**).

But Paul does not exactly say this: It is not old garments that are lost – it is the *old person* (*palaios anthrōpos*) that must be stripped away; the person

---

[312] TDNT 3:167.
[313] Moo, *Colossians*, 163–164.
[314] BDAG 30; LS 22. From the root *aisch-* we find *aischrologia* (foul language or abuse) and *aischunē* (shame), synonymous with *aidōs*. Both spellings (*aischr-* and *aischu-*) are common in the Hellenistic era.

linked to Adam, to sin, to the compulsive and inevitable behaviors of this world. This is a more profound movement than a change in garments. My truest self – indeed, my soul – has been renewed, and the old self, complete with its sinful reflexes, has been obliterated. Without losing who I am, I now have become what my creator has meant me to be from the beginning. The old self is gone; the new self now can emerge thanks to the grace of God.

Thus, it is *this new self*, this new person rebuilt in Christ, that will require new garments (3:12). New garments are now placed on the new person. If the old self was based on the image of Adam – and in this image we had nothing but death (1Cor 15:22) – this new self has been built on the image of its creator: God himself. Here the image is clearly taken from Gen 1:26–27. This redemption found in Christ is therefore a *restoration*, a recovery of what God had intended from the beginning. Like the renovation of an old home, God peels away centuries of decay and returns us to our original beauty. In Genesis the fall was not only the loss of God's glorious image in us, but it was also linked to Adam's failure to act rightly on the knowledge he possessed (Gen 2:17; 3:5). We should expect that Paul, who is fully aware of the tragedy in Genesis, writes that this restoration includes a renewal of knowledge – the knowing that was distrusted, misused, and abused in the Garden. These words represent the fuller explanation of what Paul prayed in 1:9: "that you may be filled with the knowledge of God's will in all spiritual wisdom and understanding." This is not, then, a life that is wiser; it is a life that is wise in divine things, that embraces God's will eagerly and obeys it with joy.

Paul's theology of restoration is not individualistic – which is so often the temptation of the modern church. We can privatize spiritual experience and disregard the communal or social dimensions of spiritual life. The gospel is not simply about my transformation, my renewal, my "newness-in-Christ." Cultures in Paul's day were communal, and religious communities produced a shared life. To live as a follower of Christ *without* a community would have been unimaginable to Paul.

Therefore, Paul envisions a new community of restored and renewed people, men and women who are revisiting creation, and as Christ is a new Adam (1Cor 15:45), so, too, those who belong to him share in this new Adam's life. The restoration of creation means the restoration of the human family and the dissolution of humanity's endless divisions. Dunn writes that this new community has made "irrelevant ethnic, cultural and social distinctions" that no longer carry the importance they once did in the old world controlled by the old self (**3:11**).[315] The church thus has the prospect of creating a new world without the old hierarchies and hatreds.

Greek culture had won over Paul's world beginning with the spread of Alexander's empire in the fourth century BCE. By Paul's time, Greek was the language of commerce, education, and "high culture," despite the conquests of Rome two centuries later. Rome may have won battles, but Greece owned the imagination. This is why Paul, even though he is a Roman citizen and living in the Roman Empire, is writing in Greek. Hellenism, the Greek cultural force under Roman rule, had never been defeated.

To refer to "Greeks" as Paul does in 3:11 is probably a signal of high culture, an elite outlook, a sophistication that others could not attain. At least it is a signal of someone who sets themselves apart. The Jew (from the Greek perspective) represented the marginal, the provincial, or the less sophisticated – much as we might imagine a speaker of French in the nineteenth century listening impatiently to a speaker of Swahili. This was a cultural presumption of superiority. From a Jewish perspective the world was divided into the circumcised (Judaism) and uncircumcised (everyone else – the "nations" or Gentiles).[316] This was a theological presumption that spilled into a worldview that promoted the entitlements, privileges, and superiority of one ethnicity that was uniquely blessed by God.

"Barbarian" was a slur directed at people who could not speak Greek launched by Greek-speakers who spoke (they thought) a refined language. In another era these were scorned people who lived "in the provinces." Literally the word meant someone who lacked eloquence, who "stammered," or was crude and uncivilized. The Greek noun *barbaros*, with its harsh consonantal rhythm, imitated odd foreign sounds. Scythians (*scythēs*) were the barbarian cliché. These were Iranian nomads who moved from the Russian steppes into Asia Minor 700 years before Paul. They had marched through Judea to Egypt and terrorized these countries

---

[315] Dunn, *Colossians*, 175.
[316] The term "Jew" (*Ioudaios*) described people from Judea (*Ioudaia*). An awareness of Judaism as a "religious system" appears in this period (*Ioudaismos*) for the first time in 2Macc 2:21; 8:1; 14:38. This was often in response to "Hellenism" (*Hellēnismos*). See ibid., 224.

for decades.[317] They epitomized the crude, repugnant barbarian that had become a stereotype in Paul's day (2Macc 4:47; 3Macc 7:5).[318] From a Hellenistic perspective, it is no surprise that Jews could be considered barbarians.

And, of course, the slave/free division was enormously significant in Roman society. It is widely accepted that in Rome 20–30 percent of the population was made up of slaves. This could be a threatening presence to the socially advantaged – the Roman citizen. But here that powerful line of demarcation has been erased *because in the church* things were different (see Philemon). Christ had changed everything. He was the One who now defines identity, and all other identifiers must fall away.

Paul's interest in the new Messianic community he called the church is well-known. In 1Cor 12:13 he writes, "For in the one Spirit we were all baptized into one body – Jews or Greeks, slaves or free – and we were all made to drink of one Spirit." In Gal 3:28 he can write a close parallel to Col 3:11: "There is no longer Jew or Greek; there is no longer slave or free; there is no longer male and female, for all of you are one in Christ Jesus." But in each of these lists, "Jew and Greek" and, in Colossians, "circumcised and uncircumcised" stand out and suggest to some scholars that this may reflect pressure by the synagogue to promote Jewish religious experience as a requirement to fully access God.[319] Certainly this is clear in Galatians, and, to a degree, the heresy in Colossae had significant Jewish features. Paul would object to all who might elevate Jewish experience as a necessary feature of the gospel. Bird writes:

Paul's statement implies a breaking down of the covenant boundaries separating Jew and non-Jew, and, in a sense, expands the currency of Israel's election by

---

[317] TDNT 7:447.

[318] This is the only such reference in the NT. But in the later apologists they become the premier example of the reach of the gospel "even to Scythians." "Under these conditions even a member of such a rude and immoral people can become a friend of God," *Dialogue Tryph. 28* (TDNT 7:450). See Herodotus 4.1–117 for a severe description of Scythia from an early Greek perspective. A remnant of Scythian history in Israel today is OT Beit She'an (Arab Beisan; Israeli Beth-shean). In the NT era it was named Scythopolis or "city of the Scythians," and it was the leading city of the Decapolis and the only one west of the Jordan River. See H. Maier, *Barbarians, Scythians, and Imperial Iconography in the Epistle to the Colossians.* WUNT 2.193 (Tübingen: Mohr Siebeck, 2005) and Sumney, *Colossians*, Excursus 2, 208–209.

[319] Dunn, *Colossians*, 224; Moo, *Colossians*, 272–273; Lightfoot, *Colossians*, 216–217.

including Gentiles in its purview. By transforming the inherent value of "Jewishness" and its chief covenant boundary marker of circumcision, Paul was implying that the ethnic and ritual distinctions marking off Jew from Gentile had been removed. Consequently, the rationale for separateness from and any sense of superiority over the Gentiles has been nullified by the coming of the Messiah.[320]

This does not mean that distinctions disappear. *There are still men and women in Christ. Paul continues to view himself as a Jew.* But rather hierarchies and privileges fall away. Paul is creating a theology of the church in which no one race, no social class, no nationality has priority over another. No ethnicity can make a *theological* claim of election that sets it apart in the workings of the kingdom because members of the church now are called "elect" (3:12). This strikes at the heart of the colonial attitudes that have dogged the church for centuries. And it questions ethnic movements within the church that claim a blessed status not shared by others and has resulted in a unique sort of spiritual narcissism. *Christ is all and in all.* Other identifiers must fall away.

Box 2.14 A Closer Look: The Church as the People of God

When Paul imagines the church as the people of God, how does he imagine the church's relationship to historic Israel in the Old Testament? What is striking about his writing is the number of times Paul uses language originally intended for Israel, which he now applies to the church. As Paul argues in Ephesians 2, the older categories of Jew and Gentile – those who are near and those who are far – now have been upended by Christ. There is now "one new person" in place of the two because in Christ this new body – the church – is playing an unexpected role. The divisions between Jew and Gentile, Paul understands, have ended because of a new Messianic reality that has emerged in Christ. This, Paul believes, is a dramatic "mystery" that has changed the course of Israel's history.

During and after Israel's exile to Babylon, the Old Testament prophets provided hope to Israel by predicting a return to the land. Jeremiah is typical. In a letter to the exiles in Babylon, he wrote expressing God's hope for them (29:10–14):

This is what the LORD says: "When seventy years are completed for Babylon, I will come to you and fulfill my good promise to bring you back to this place. For I know the plans I have for you," declares the LORD, "plans to prosper you and not to harm you, plans to give you hope and a future. Then you will call on me and come and

---

[320]   Bird, *Colossians*, 103–104; also Wright, *Colossians*, 139.

pray to me, and I will listen to you. You will seek me and find me when you seek me with all your heart. I will be found by you," declares the LORD, "and will bring you back from captivity. I will gather you from all the nations and places where I have banished you," declares the LORD, "and will bring you back to the place from which I carried you into exile."

Other prophets such as Ezekiel promised the same. Note that as a part of this promise there would be an "ingathering." The dispersed Jews would return.

This ingathering was well-known in Paul's Jewish world, and some believed that it took place in Israel's return from exile. However, many features of the return were not fulfilled. In fact, Israel continued to live under a series of occupying powers that seemed to invalidate it. For some, their post-exilic life was so difficult that it appeared Israel still lived in exile.

Paul, however, makes an extraordinary theological move in his letters. He knows the OT promises of ingathering, and he cites them and alludes to them. But in Eph 3:2–6 he makes explicit what he understands. The "mystery" given to him by revelation is that the ingathering is not about Jews rebuilding a nation; it is about the ingathering of Gentiles into God's people who build the church. Paul takes these promises and applies them to the church: "This mystery is that through the gospel the Gentiles are heirs together with Israel, members together of one body, and sharers together in the promise in Christ Jesus" (Eph 3:6).

Dunn has argued that Paul examined the great promises to Abraham that were so well-known (Gen 12:3; 18:18; 22:18).[321] God's promise of land and nation were foremost in Israel's thinking. However, a third promise – a neglected promise – to bless the nations Paul now saw as completed in Christ. This blessing only now realized in the Messiah meant that the character of the people of God had welcomed into its ranks *the nations* that had embraced belief in Jesus Christ. This is why he can describe the barrier between Jew and Gentile as removed (Gal 3:28; Eph 2:19). Gentiles are now fellow citizens of Israel. In Ephesians 2 Paul writes about those who were far but who are now near (2:13, 17) and how this movement results in their new citizenship in Israel and their membership in God's household (2:19–20). The end result is a new humanity (2:15) consisting of Jews and Gentiles who, together in Christ, find unity.

Therefore, Paul's gospel is not simply about grace or Christ's life-giving death on the cross. It is also about the re-creation of human possibilities, a new order of life, a redefining of what it means to be the people of God forged by the work of the Spirit. This worldview and mystery would upend everything Paul knew about his own

---

[321] J. D. G. Dunn, "Paul as Apostate or Apostle of Israel," *ZNW* 89 (1998) 256–271.

religious history and the ongoing role of Israel in God's plan. God had surprised everyone. Christ was an agent of reconciliation in ways few expected.

Paul's language in Colossians echoes these same themes. In 3:12 he refers to the gathered Colossian community as "God's chosen ones, holy and beloved." These are terms used in the OT for Israel. But Paul's expression of these themes is also subtle. In 1:2 when Paul (as a Jew) can write to the Christians of Colossae (who are Gentiles) that they share together the same Father in God, he is expressing something not heard before. The Father/child relationship was an exclusive privilege of Israel in the OT. Now it is held jointly with believing Gentiles. In 1:12 and 3:24 Paul refers to the inheritance that these Gentile believers will receive. But inheritance is also an OT term, and Paul's use of it for Gentiles is a not-so-subtle hint that Gentiles who have faith in Christ now hold a place never known in the OT (see also Eph 1:11, 14, 18; 5:5). Even Paul's use of "church" (*ekklēsia*) in Col 1:18, 24 and 4:15–16 may have its origin in the LXX name for the community of Israel. And in 2:13 Paul can describe Gentiles who were dead due to sin and uncircumcision but who now have come alive, and who now have joined those whose lives are enlivened by God.

It is hard to underestimate what Paul is doing in these verses. Paul is using language that presupposes the metaphor he employs in Rom 11:17, where Israel's life is depicted as a great olive tree with the patriarchs at its root. In the Messianic era now unfolding, the great mystery that God has revealed is that Gentiles who were once outside God's family now belong to it. He writes, "You, a wild olive shoot, were grafted among the others to share the rich root of the olive tree."

If pressed, Paul would no doubt say that the Messianic community, made up of believing Jews and Gentiles, now represents the people of God whose history began with Abraham and moved directly to Jesus. This is the very essence of Paul's Abrahamic mission to bless the Gentiles. He does not imagine a parallel community alongside Israel; he reimagines Israel now as a permeable, living community based on faith in Christ, not based on ethnicity. This is the fulfillment of Abraham's blessing of the nations (Gen 12:3). This is why Paul can now refer to Gentiles as children of Abraham (Gal 3:29, Rom 4:11). An unimaginable Messianic miracle was unfolding, and the Colossians needed to know that they were a part of it.

"Therefore" (**3:12a**) tells us that Paul is beginning a new section that will continue the theme begun in 3:10. Those who belong to Christ have clothed themselves anew, and now 3:12–17 will describe what that clothing will look like. Paul begins with an affirming endearment: These believers are chosen, holy, and beloved – each is a title that cannot be understood outside of the OT. These are terms employed exclusively for Israel, and, with Caird, "they constitute a claim that the church is the new people of

God."[322] Similarly, with Lightfoot, "All three terms *eklektoi, hagioi,* and *agapēmenoi* (chosen, holy and loved) are transferred from the Old Covenant to the New, from Israel after the flesh to the Israel after the Spirit."[323]

Throughout the OT Israel is called "Israel my chosen" through its covenant with God (Deut 7:6; Ps 33:12; 105:6). Isaiah says, "But you, Israel, my servant, Jacob, whom I have chosen, the offspring of Abraham ..." (41:8; 45:4). Israel is also called "holy" because it has been set apart from the nations (Exod 19:6) and is dearly loved (Ex 19:5–6; Deut 7:6–7; Isa 44:2; Jer 31:3). *In a remarkable turn of events, Paul has now applied this status of Israel to the Messianic gathering of believers he calls "the church" (also Rom 8:33; 2Tim 2:10; Titus 1:1).*

This threefold self-understanding of Israel made a claim of exclusivity on Israel's relationship with God. Paul is claiming that the exclusivity of this claim has expired with the arrival of the Messiah. He has redefined the scope of what it means to be chosen, and attachment to Christ makes this possible. This is the same logic that Paul employs in Gal 3:6–9 and more fully in Rom 4:1–25. Abraham's blessing of the nations (Gen 12:3; 17:5) is fulfilled as Messianic faith attaches gentiles to Christ and thus makes them children of Abraham (Rom 4:11). The larger program of "Israel" no longer belongs exclusively to Jews; gentiles-with-faith also belong to Israel, and this variegated community of Jews and Gentiles, each retaining its cultural uniqueness, now makes up the Messianic community. Paul offers another metaphor in Rom 11:17: Gentile believers in Jesus have been grafted into the great olive tree of the patriarchs, with Jewish and Gentile branches now growing together attached to the great patriarchal foundation while also attached to Christ.

However, the language of this transition must be carefully nuanced. Paul is working to resolve the identity of Israel and the identity of the Gentile believers, but this must be distinguished from his comparison of "Jew" and "Gentile." Jew was an ethnic (or geographic) identifier. Jews (*Ioudaioi*) were from Judea (*Ioudaia*). But he appears to understand Israel to be something altogether different though related. Israel was a *theological*

---

[322] Caird, *Colossians,* 207. See also Sanders, *Practice and Belief,* 262–275; and N. T. Wright, *Paul and the Faithfulness of God* (Minneapolis: Fortress, 2013), 774–1042.
[323] Lightfoot, *Colossians,* 221.

status stemming from the covenant of Abraham in the old covenant reserved for Jews. It is impossible for Gentiles to becomes Jews; but, for instance, in Rom 9–11 Paul introduces the name "Israel" in his argument to show how Gentiles have joined Israel through Christ.[324] Gentiles now belong to Israel – and this is where covenant blessing and privilege belong. However, this inclusion of the Colossian Gentiles does not necessarily imply the exclusion of unbelieving Jews. They continue to be beloved due to the unwavering covenant love of God (Rom 11:28). But something has changed, and *some in Israel* have missed their Messiah. Those in Israel's remnant who (like Paul) embrace the Messiah represent a faithful remnant (Rom 9:1–13) and thus are advancing the new work of God through Jesus the Messiah.

From the beginning of chapter 3 Paul's concern has been for the life and vitality of the church. He listed five sins chiefly centering on sex (3:5) as well as five speech habits that would destroy the church's unity (3:8). After making clear that Gentiles are not marginal members in this new Messianic community but share the center with believing Jews, he wants to offer five virtues that will heal, strengthen, and enrich the community's life (**3:12b**). Earlier he had described the new person who now, having lost the garments of sin, must be reclothed with garments of righteousness. Clothe yourselves, Paul writes, with compassion, kindness, humility, meekness, and patience. His first attribute here is literally entrails (*splagchna*) of compassion. The Hellenistic world assigned emotions to the organs below the stomach (bowels, intestines, etc.), and this is its meaning here.[325] These were not a person's passing impressions but rather profoundly felt, "moving" feelings that carried significant weight. Many translations are right to think of the English idiomatic use of *heartfelt*, which is not exactly correct for this noun but carries the right meaning. What we mean by "heartfelt" a Greek might refer to as *splagchna*. But what is felt is merciful caring (*oiktirmos*) for one another.[326] This is compassion, empathy, and perhaps mutual support (Phil 2:1). As the Colossians struggled with opponents and witnessed division, their first task was a profound,

---

[324] Dunn, *The Theology of Paul the Apostle,* 504–509.
[325] BDAG 938 provides numerous contextual examples.
[326] Paul uses this term for *eleeō* (showing mercy) in Rom 9:15, parallel LXX Exod 33:19. *The Testaments of the Twelve Patriarchs* use this phrase prominently, even in the heading of *Test. Zebulun.*

nurturing care for one another, perhaps a protective care. The quality of this care now is given a short list of accompanying features.

Kindness (*chrēstos*) describes a high virtue that appears in Paul's lists of godly conduct. In both Gal 5:22 and 2Cor 6:6 it is an outworking of the Spirit that should show itself among believers who are living in community. Thus Eph 4:32: "Be kind (*chrēstos*) to one another, tender and forgiving." An interesting use of the word is Matt 11:30, where Jesus says, "[M]y yoke is easy." But "easy" here is *chrēstos*, meaning that his yoke is kind or beneficial, not harmful. In Rom 2:4 a form of the noun describes one of God's essential attributes: He is kind.[327] Humility (*tapeinophrosynē*) was used negatively by Paul in Col 2:18 and 2:23 to describe the compliance or subordination (a false humility) that the opponents wanted from the Colossians. But here Paul is elevating the virtuous aspect of this, which we understand as well. Humility can lead to self-depreciation that is unhealthy, or it can describe a willingness to lower oneself as a choice of virtue – not to self-promote but to let go of position to promote another. Its close partner is meekness (*prautēs*), which expresses the attitude accompanying this humility (Rom 2:4; 2Cor 6:6; Gal 5:22). Both attributes are linked to Jesus in 2Cor 10:1, which is likely their origin for Christians. This disposition is all the more striking given the Roman pursuit of honor and disdain for humility or meekness. The surrounding culture viewed these Christian virtues as weak and shaming; but in the church, which was taking its moral views from Christ *in whom descent to the cross* was a model, humility was pursued as a matter of course.

Patience is a quality that God holds for each of us (of God, Rom 2:4; 9:22; of Jesus, 1Tim 1:16). It is thus another high virtue for Christ's disciples. It is also another fruit of the Spirit (Gal 5:22) and should join with the other character virtues already listed. Humility and kindness appear with patience in Eph 4:2 and 1Thess 5:14, and Paul exhorts the church to be kind and patient even with those who are difficult. Perhaps that is the chief point: These first four virtues become difficult when people are difficult, and patience is the prerequisite that makes the others possible.

---

[327] BDAG 1090 shows how the noun could also point to abstract morals: something that was good or someone who had a good reputation. The noun (*chrēstotēs*) appears widely Aristotle.

The reality of this shopping list of social virtues is that it is difficult to love the less lovable. Being kind to the overbearing is almost a supernatural gift of the Spirit. But Paul continues this exhortation (**3:13**) by adding two more commands that likely connect with patience. We are to bear with one another and forgive. Bearing (*anechō*) with someone points to endurance, tolerance, or restraint – "put up with" gets to its meaning well – or perhaps accepting someone fully (2Cor 11:1; cf. Mark 9:19), particularly when this is hard (sometimes the verb is used for enduring suffering, 2Thess 1:4). This is the opposite of being reactive, especially when complaints are uttered. Dunn points to an excellent case study of this in Rom 12:9–13:10, where there were significant disagreements.[328]

And assuming that wrongs have been committed, forgiveness should be the immediate reflex, just as – and this is the grounding of each of these commands – Jesus set the model for how we live: *as the Lord has forgiven you* (Eph 4:32; 5:2, 25, 29). In this case, the subject of Lord is likely God, who, throughout the NT, is the one who forgives sin (Col 2:13). However, in the gospels we do have a record of Jesus forgiving sin (Mark 2:5–7; Luke 7:47–49), but even in these cases Jesus' forgiveness is viewed as presumptuous and inspires criticism: "Who is this who forgives sins?" Despite this, it was Jesus who brought forgiveness to the center of his teaching, urging its extent: We should forgive "seventy times seven" (Matt 18:22).

Certainly, the principal idea here is that those who have experienced forgiveness ought to reflect that grace on others. This is the climax of the account of Jesus in the home of Simon the Pharisee: Those who have been forgiven greatly will exhibit love that is dramatic. The same lesson is in the Parable of the Pharisee and the Tax Collector: The latter was *affected* by his sin and God's grace, and this changes his prayer (Luke 18:9–14). The same lesson is in Matthew's Parable of the Unforgiving Servant (Matt 18:23–35).

In Col 3:13 the verb for forgiveness is *charizomai*, and we can see its root is the important noun *charis*, grace. This is the second of two verbs in Greek covering the same idea of forgiveness: The first is *aphiēmi* (see 1John 1:9 and over 140 other times in the NT), and it can be seen typically in Mark 2:5: "When Jesus saw their faith, he said to the paralytic, 'Child, your sins are forgiven.'" *Aphiēmi* suggests that you are letting something go or

---

[328] Dunn, *Colossians*, 230.

releasing them. Our verb in 3:13, *charizomai*, is transactional. A harm has been done or a debt is owed – and now you are freeing them from the consequences; offenses set aside, debts forgiven.

The final garment to be acquired ("above all") is possibly the most important (**3:14**): "Clothe yourselves with love, which binds everything together in perfect harmony." The NRSV smooths out a slightly more complex phrase: Paul literally says, "And [*put on* from 3:12] love which is the bond or tie (*syndesmos*) of completion/perfection (*teleiotēs*, from *telos*)."

In Paul's mind, love is the most highly valued attribute of the Christian life. We see this from his exhortation in 1Cor 13 to its prominence in Galatians (5:6, 14, 22). In Rom 13:9–10 he writes that all of the commandments are summed up in this: "You shall love your neighbor as yourself. Love does no wrong to a neighbor; therefore, love is the fulfilling of the law."

We see the same in Jesus' response to the scribe who pressed him on the most important commandment: Love God and love your neighbor: "There is no other commandment greater than these" (Mark 12:29–31). Paul here is continuing his clothing metaphor for one last use. This final garment is the "crowning grace" of all the graces listed here.[329] Paul may have in mind a garment such as a cloak (the Roman *pallium*?) that is wrapped over everything else and completed this new dressing-in-virtue. It could be the clasp (*syndesmos* can mean clasp, chain, or cable) worn in front of the shoulder to keep the cloak in place, thereby also keeping all other garments in place. Love brings completion (*telos*) to the body of Christ and achieves the ever-evasive unity Paul desires for all of his churches. The aim, as Paul says in Ephesians, is for the church to come to maturity (*telos*), unified in faith, knowing the Son of God fully, and reflecting the "measure of the full stature of Christ" (Eph 4:13). Love is the one gift that rules them all. And without it, the others become performative and unconvincing. We cannot imagine kindness or patience without love *because* this sort of Christlike love makes them possible.[330]

The result of all these charitable efforts should bring about peace (**3:15**), which in Eph 4:3 is connected to love and now becomes another source of

---

[329] Bruce, *Colossians*, 106.
[330] Martin, *Colossians*, 123.

unity. This entire effort is a work of the Spirit moving the church toward the "perfection" (3:13) it seeks. However, this is not simply a cessation of hostilities or a truce. It is a peace that comes from our attachment to Christ, and it is related to everything he has said thus far. The sentence begins with *kai* ("in addition," or "also"), meaning that, in addition to putting on these many virtues, we should also acquire the peace of Christ as yet one more signifier of how faith changes who we are. And this change results in the well-being of the church.

Paul introduces a word from the athletic arenas to dramatize what should happen: *Let the peace of Christ take charge* (brabeuō) *of your hearts*. This term is used only here in the NT but was common in Greek for the work of an empire (a *brabeus*) who judged games (a *brabeion* was a prize, 1Cor 9:24; Phil 3:13–14). Thus, *brabeuō* could mean to judge or arbitrate, or even to govern or take charge. But Paul's aim is again unity and cooperation within the church. Bruce writes, "For if the members are subject to Him, the peace which He imparts must regulate their relations with one another" (cf. Eph 4:4).[331] And in a context where there is conflict, this peace "braces us" – hence the famous "rules in our hearts" – and sustains us. When someone generates continuous conflict in the church, it likely signals how far they are from "the peace of Christ" that should center them. And because they are not governed by Christ, all of the virtues listed here have evaporated.

Paul ends these thoughts with thankfulness: *And be thankful*. This phrase is a short footnote added to his long, preceding sentence. He does not use the usual noun (to be, *eimi*) but instead chooses *ginomai* (to become) because the ideal of this thanksgiving "has not been reached."[332] Paul is not imagining a disposition that is simply cheerful; he is thinking about a life that is so grounded in God and his promises that thankfulness springs from the hope and serenity that God's love provides. Thankfulness changes who we are and becomes another gateway to the graces Paul has listed since 3:12. For those thinking that life has held few gifts for them, thankfulness has often become a spiritual discipline that helps us reimagine our lives and discover new growth in discipleship.[333]

---

[331] Bruce, *Colossians*, 106.
[332] Abbott, *Colossians*, 290.
[333] On thanksgiving in Paul, see also 1Thess 1:2; 2:13; 5:18; 2Thess 1:3; 2:13; 1Cor 1:4, 14; 10:30; 14:17–18; 2Cor 1:11; 9:11–12; Rom 1:8; 14:6; 16:4; Phlm 4; Eph 1:16; 5:20; Phil 1:3; 4:6; 1Tim 2:1; 4:3–4.

Gratitude is underrated among the virtues we know. It recognizes the generosity of a giver and the remarkable good fortune of the recipient. It erodes feelings of entitlement and gives birth to joy. In Rom 1:21 Paul describes the problems of the irreligious world and elevated this one idea: They intuit something about God but could not glorify him as God; neither did they give thanks. The inability to recognize a gift leads inevitably to life that cannot imagine thankfulness.

In **3:16–17** Paul offers wisdom providing guidance for a life centered on the gospel. He begins with a mirroring phrase from 3:15: "Let the peace of Christ rule …" and "let the word (*logos*) of Christ dwell …" The noun *logos* of course means "word," but we have to imagine that this was a time when the words of Jesus as we have them in the gospel were rare. *Logos* can also mean the *message* about Christ, and, rather than words *from* Christ, Paul is describing the message about him (see also 1:5, 25).[334] This word is to dwell (*enoikeō*; see *oikos*, house) *in you*, and here Paul uses a plural pronoun (*hymin*, with the TNIV, "among you"), which imagines that the church is a community in which the gospel is richly shared. For Paul the idea of God residing within us was common (the Spirit: Rom 8:11; 2Tim 1:14; God: 2Cor 6:16; faith: 2Tim 1:5). A similar idea is in John 14:23: "Those who love me will keep my word, and my Father will love them, and we will come to them and make our home with them." Note how Paul emphasizes this experience: The indwelling and life of the gospel (the Messianic message) should happen "richly." Moo comments that "this constant reference to the word of Christ should not be superficial or passing but that it should be a deep and penetrating contemplation that enables the message to have a transforming power in the life of the community."[335]

Paul's imperative (*let dwell*) is now followed by three participles that give full expression to what this indwelling should look like. Teaching, admonishing, and singing are each presented as natural occurrences in a community where the word of Christ is thriving. However, translations differ in how they handle this long sentence. Is this one idea (the word of God

---

[334] This means viewing the genitive *of Christ* as objective: This is a message about Christ. Some manuscripts offer *the word of God* (*tou theou*), but *Christou* has the stronger support. See Harris, *Colossians*, 144.

[335] Moo, *Colossians*, 286.

dwelling) or a set of coordinate ideas? We are also uncertain if "psalms, hymns and songs" modify "teaching and admonishing," thus explaining how this admonishing works (TNIV, ESV, NASB). Or do "psalms, hymns and songs" belong to the following participle, "singing" (NRSV, NLT)? The phrases in their literal sequence can be seen thus:

(1) Let the word of Christ dwell in you [plural] richly,
(2) in all wisdom <u>teaching</u> and <u>admonishing</u> one another [;]
(3) *with psalms, hymns, and spiritual songs* [;]
   with thankfulness <u>singing</u> in your [plural] hearts to God.

The decision of the TNIV and ESV to blend this stream into one thought makes excellent pastoral sense. The indwelling of God's word then expresses itself richly in how teaching, admonishing, and singing appear in the community. *This is the life of the word-among-us.* This view then makes the participles modifiers of the main verb.

In Greek these participles could be viewed as adverbial modifiers, but this is not necessary. They can also take on the function (mood) of the main verb: in this case, the imperative in 3:16a.[336] This is the decision of the NRSV, which lets all three participles work as imperatives and separates the thoughts with a semicolon:

(1) Let the word of Christ dwell in you richly;
(2) <u>teach</u> and <u>admonish</u> one another in all wisdom;
(3) and with gratitude, in your hearts <u>sing</u> psalms, hymns and spiritual songs to God.

This is a fully acceptable way to construe the sentence, and it has much to commend it. Teaching and admonishing then work closely together, and singing now stands as a separate but coordinate thought. Advocates for keeping the songs with admonishments can point to Eph 5:18–19, where

---

[336] This is often called an "attendant circumstance participle" or "imperatival participle." An example of its use is Matt 28:19: "Therefore go [present participle] and make [aorist imperative] disciples." Here the participle pairs with the imperative verb to say: *Go and make disciples.* See further Harris, *Colossians,* 146. For extensive examples, see BDF §468 (2): In some cases, "the participle is more or less independent, so that it receives the meaning of an independent statement or exhortation according to the situation." This use creates a style that is "popular and energetic." See also N. Turner, *Grammatical Insights into the New Testament* (Edinburgh: T&T Clark, 1965), 166–167, who discusses how often participles may have been used in moral code lists.

Paul says something similar: "But be filled with the Spirit, as you sing psalms and hymns and spiritual songs to one another."

The word of Christ now richly living in the community finds expression through the regular discipline of teaching and admonishment. As we saw in 1:28, these are terms that come from the Greek classroom, which emphasized both instruction and warning (*noutheteō*).[337] That is, the substance of the gospel must be known completely so that faith in Christ is anchored to genuine understanding about what God has done in Christ. But, in addition, admonishing points to moral instruction or the problem with straying from the truth that every new convert in the church needed. How to believe is accompanied by how to live. One difference from 1:28 is that earlier this task belonged to the apostolic leadership, but now Paul is urging that it has become a corporate duty: teaching and admonishing *one another*. It is hard to think that Paul imagines a church without offices that are equipped by the Spirit. He explains the need for these in Eph 4:11–12 and sees their work as strengthening the body (also 1Tim 3:1–13). Nevertheless, here Paul charges every member to have some capacity for this (Rom 12:7; 15:14; 1Cor 14:26; Gal 6:1–3).

If the gathering of the community sees the full expression of the word of Christ in teaching, so, too, another hallmark was and still is its communal worship. Paul uses three words, but we should be careful about distinguishing them too sharply. Psalms (*psalmoi*) likely originates in a Hebrew expression (to pluck or play a stringed instrument) and occurs only here and in Eph 5:19 but is used in the LXX frequently. It may refer to the Psalms of the OT or it could be simply written hymnic songs used liturgically. Hymns (*hymnoi*) and songs (*ōdai*) are almost synonyms, but the first may be set songs that we may have hints of in the NT. Here, for example, we could point to Eph 5:14 or Phil 2:5–11 as providing fragments of hymns that were creative expressions of songwriters in the early church. Songs may describe informal, spontaneous singing "in the Spirit" that used creativity and informality regularly. In more charismatic circles, this reference to the Spirit is worship-led and inspired by the Spirit – possibly singing in tongues. But grammatically "spiritual" (*pneumatikais*) might apply to all three words. Worship is to be done not for performance or

---

[337] Or literally in Greek, *noutheteō* suggests awakening the mind by exhortation.

for *our celebration* but with God as our audience and the Spirit as our guide.

But these words – together with the presence of the Word of Christ, and the use of baptism and the Lord's Supper – probably give us a full-orbed picture of what the early Christians did as they gathered. They had a worshipping tradition that had both formal (liturgical?) and informal features that together celebrated Christ's presence in their midst. They sang from hearts filled with thankfulness (*charis* can mean "thanks") and thus anchored their worship to the grace and goodness they had experienced in Christ (note how thanksgiving is mentioned three times in 3:15–17).

Paul ends this exhortation in **3:17** with something universal that could be applied in a number of settings. And it is a continuation of what Paul began in 2:6–7: "As you therefore have received Christ Jesus the Lord, continue to walk in him, rooted and built up in him and established in the faith, just as you were taught, abounding in thanksgiving." Bruce notes how the NT does not supply us with long lists of specific rules for conduct as we find in the growing rabbinic teaching of the period.[338] Rather Paul views such codes as for the immature (Gal 3:23–4:7) who are under the guardianship of the law. But now the church needs universal principles (see 1Cor 10:21) that may address any new situation. The conversation about worship now moves to ethics or praxis. How we live is as integral to worship as how we sing. Divine worship and daily living cannot be separated. In Rom 12:1–2 Paul defines spiritual worship as the presentation of every feature of our lives to God and as refusing to be shaped by this world. This results not in obedience to a catalog of rules but discernment: knowing the will of God and instinctively knowing (in the Spirit) "what is good and acceptable and perfect." This type of exhortation avoids the pitfall of forming immature believers who view their discipleship as rule-following rather than mature wisdom.

Paul writes: *Whatever you might do*[339] – *whether in word or in deed* – everything then is a feature of our identity in Christ. Or we might say: Every word and every deed, therefore, must be held captive under the lordship of Jesus. "Word and deed" was a common way to refer to every

---

[338] Bruce, *Colossians*, 108.
[339] Note that *ean* is used rather than *ei* to underscore uncertainty.

aspect of someone's life (Luke 24:19; Rom 15:18; 2Thess 2:17). This develops Paul's reference to Jesus and *the Lord*. Of course, this initially is a Christological affirmation that we saw throughout chapters 1 and 2, but it also implies *lordship*, someone who rules, someone who holds authority over his subjects. Thus, when men and women become Christians and this is formally sealed through baptism, they move under the lordship of Christ. This means that no activity happens independent of Christ's rule. We have moved into union with Christ (Gal 3:27; Rom 6:3) and therefore we are no longer free; we belong to him.[340]

But this is not an ominous and burdensome relationship. And this perhaps sums up the essence of how we should view our life in Christ. "The center of Christian living is grateful worship."[341] We see in Christ the hand of the Father who has achieved this victory over the powers that have held the world captive. Thanksgiving should define the rhythms of our worship as loyalty and obedience to Christ define our living. This thanksgiving is *through Christ* ("through him," *di' autou*). Here we are reminded: Christ is not only the agent of the Father's victory over the world but also our mediator who both shelters us and provides our only access to the Father.

3:18–4:1 *Life at Home*

3:18 Wives, be subject to your husbands, as is fitting in the Lord.

3:19 Husbands, love your wives and never treat them harshly.

3:20 Children, obey your parents in everything, for this is your acceptable duty in the Lord.

3:21 Fathers, do not provoke your children, or they may lose heart.

3:22 Slaves, obey your earthly masters in everything, not with a slavery performed merely for looks, to please people, but wholeheartedly, fearing the Lord.

3:23 Whatever task you must do, work as if your soul depends on it, as for the Lord and not for humans,

3:24 since you know that from the Lord you will receive the inheritance as your reward; you serve the Lord Christ.

---

[340] Moo, *Colossians*, 291.
[341] Wright, *Colossians*, 145.

3:25 For the wrongdoer will be paid back for whatever wrong has been done, and there is no partiality.

4:1 Masters, treat your slaves justly and fairly, for you know that you also have a Master in heaven.

These verses reflect "household codes" or regulations that were common in Roman society.[342] Such lists were as old as Aristotle[343] and Plutarch.[344] Josephus[345] provides a similar list, as does Philo.[346] In each of these, rules outlined the roles of husband and wife, parent and child, and, finally, master and slave. Aristotle's ideal family consisted of husband/wife, father/child, and master/slave, with the father playing a role in all three pairings (husband, father, master).[347] Paul knows that his Roman readers would expect such a "household code" in any moral exhortation, and so he regularly supplies one (Eph 5:21–6:9; 1 Tim 2:8–15; 5:1–10; Titus 2:1–10; cf. 1 Pet 2:18–3:7). These codes were even developed for subsequent generations of Christians (Did 4:9–11; Barnabas 19:5–7; Ignatius, *To Polycarp*, 4:1–6:2 and *To the Philippians*, 4:2–6:1).[348] In each case, the codes give similar guidance for the same three categories: husbands and wives, children and parents, slaves and masters.

The Roman world focused almost entirely on the household as the central organizing unit of society (the *oikos*, or house). If the household was sound, they believed that society itself was sound. This was even projected onto government itself. The emperor was the father (*patēr*) of the state – and even the financial officers of that state were seen as household "managers" (*oikonomoi*).[349] Like Caesar, the father of an *oikos* had supreme authority over its members. Their obedience and loyalty to their "father" (or lord, *kurios*) were assumed, and, in return, they benefited

---

[342] See my previous treatment, G. M. Burge, *Galatians and Ephesians through Old Testament Eyes* (Grand Rapids: Kregel Academic, 2025). For summaries and a bibliography, see P. H. Towner, "Households and Household Codes," in G. F. Hawthorne, R. P. Martin, and D. G. Reid, eds., *Dictionary of Paul and His Letters* (Downers Grove: InterVarsity Press, 1993), 417–419; especially helpful is the discussion in Dunn, *Colossians*, 242–246; and the bibliography in McKnight, *Colossians*, 336n197.

[343] Aristotle, *Politics*, 1.3, 6–7, 12–13.

[344] Plutarch, "Advice on Marriage," 11; and "Advice to Bride and Groom."

[345] Josephus, *Contra Apion*, 2:199, 206, 215–217.

[346] Philo, *Decalogue*, 165–167; *Special Laws*, 225–227.

[347] See D. deSilva, *Ephesians* (Cambridge: Cambridge University Press, 2022), 275–277.

[348] McKnight, *Colossians*, 336.

[349] Towner, "Households," 417.

from an identity and security elsewhere unavailable. A father (*patēr or paterfamilias*) was a patron to his family (*patria*) – and he had patrons to whom he was indebted, and from whom his household members could benefit as well. But, above all, he was responsible for the well-being of his family and its connections to the larger society.

Roman codes focused entirely on honor and how this was acquired and distributed given one's position and authority. Their assumption was that those who were subordinate had less ability to reason and understand moral order, and so this built a firm hierarchy: husbands, wives, children, and slaves. There was little interest in mutuality, and the primacy of the husband/father was central in the cast of family roles.[350] All of this sounds very foreign to us who live with individual autonomy and an interest in the rights of the person. But these modern ideas of personhood did not exist in antiquity.

Paul's churches likely adopted this vocabulary of the *oikos* not only because it was universally familiar but also because they met in houses (his *ekklēsia* likely meant house churches), and this may explain why household language (see *oikos*, *oikia*, or *oikonimos* in Paul, twenty-eight times) and membership names (brother, sister) came from the *oikos*. But, in addition, the gathered Christian community that met for worship and fellowship looked for and promoted the same sense of security, benefit, and attachment as any thriving natural household might. Paul can conclude his letter to the Galatians saying, "So then, whenever we have an opportunity, let us work for the good of all and especially for those of the family (*oikos*) of faith" (6:10). The church worked *like a family* bringing benefit and blessing to its members. Paul even views his own ministry as "stewardship" (*oikonomos*, 1Cor 9:17; Col 1:25), which is a leading member of a household entrusted with oversight.

What we miss when we read these Pauline codes is how different Paul's guidance is from the surrounding context. Paul is viewing these old categories through the lens of the new transformation that was being

---

[350] However, a major movement to empower women was growing in the first century CE. See M. Barth, *Ephesians*, 2 vols. (New York: Doubleday, 1974), 2:655–662; also L. Cohick, *Women in the World of the Earliest Christians: Illuminating Ancient Ways of Life* (Grand Rapids: Baker Academic, 2009); C. Westfall, *Paul and Gender: Reclaiming the Apostle's Vision for Men and Women in Christ* (Grand Rapids: Baker Academic, 2016).

realized in Christ. McKnight is right in saying that Gal 3:28 and Col 3:11 should be the touchstone verses from which we understand all of Paul's household regulations. Those positions that were presumed to have power or privilege (ideally, the free Roman citizen or the circumcised Jewish man) now were diminished. Identity in Christ changed everything about privilege. "Oneness in Christ revolutionized all relationships toward mutual participation in 'Christoformity'[351] with a noticeable emphasis on limiting power."[352]

Our world focuses on rights: Do women have rights? Do children? And how can anyone remove all rights from a person and make them a slave? The Roman world did not think in these categories. It was a world in which honor – its acquisition and its distribution – was primary. One's position increased as one accumulated honor. Thus, for some interpreters, we should note that the Pauline ethic in these codes is not interested in rights per se in the modern sense but in targeting honor and power and how these can be employed *not for the benefit of the holder* but for the benefit of those "below." This is the upside-down ethics of the kingdom: The first shall be last and the last first (Matt 19:30).[353] And this is what we need to look for. In what sense is Paul inverting the accepted norms of his day in which self-interest and self-promotion were ordinary features of life? What if your entire world has taught you that the greatness of your *patēr* and the growth of *his honor* were key to your benefit – and now, in some manner, in Christ, his care for his subordinates and their protection and honoring should be his central concern? What if he worried about their honor more than his own?

Col 3:12 then should also be another touchstone verse. Paul knows the cultural forces of his Hellenistic world (3:7), but he upends these with ideas that were antithetical to Rome's normed values. He writes, "[C]lothe yourselves with compassion, kindness, humility, meekness, and patience" (3:12). These were not honor-acquiring virtues; these were honor-distributing virtues, attributes that reflected the life of Christ in his

---

[351] For McKnight this is the life that is formed entirely by an identity with Christ. Compare: cruciformity, having a life shaped by the cross.

[352] McKnight, *Colossians*, 337.

[353] Ibid., citing B. Witherington and G. F. Wessels, "Do Everything in the Name of the Lord: Ethics and Ethos in Colossians," in J. van der Watt, ed., *Identity, Ethics, and Ethos in the New Testament* (Berlin: DeGruyter, 2006), 303–333.

sacrifice – and came with the loss of position or power in the conventional Roman manner.

Above all, the Christian innovation was to promote humility by putting others first. Humility was never promoted in Roman virtue lists. Paul's writing would have sounded revolutionary to any Roman reading these verses since Paul's code inverts these traditional values so drastically. Romans would be comfortable with the notion of submission in certain circumstances (slaves/masters, subjects/kings), but mutual submission, as Paul says it in Eph 5:21, made little sense: *Be subject to one another out of reverence for Christ.* Submission was the role of the subordinate, never the "superordinate," such as the *patēr*. This call to serving one another and loving one another "demands readiness to renounce one's own will for the sake of others, i.e., *agape*, and to give precedence to others."[354]

Note how in 3:18–25 Paul repeatedly frames his exhortation with reference to "the Lord" (3:18–19, 22–24). This is the new calculus – the new way of seeing everything – that would affect the dynamics of every relationship. Paul begins his guidance by discussing husbands and wives (**3:18–19**), much as he does in Ephesians 5:21–22. This was the first level of order within the *oikos*. But note carefully that while she is called to submit, he is called to love – all of this is ordered as is "fitting in the Lord." To be sure, her submission is not that of a slave – as Wright asserts, "The equality of men and women before the Lord, of which Paul wrote in Galatians 3:28, has not been retracted."[355] This is not a call for subjugation.[356] What this subordination means remains to be seen.

It is also important to note that the pairing of her with her man or husband (*anēr*) makes certain that the words *gunē* and *anēr* do not mean "women and men," but rather wives and husbands.[357] Thus – and here we must be clear – Paul is not writing about women universally in their relationship with men but about women in marriage, and how both she and her husband forge a relationship in Christ.[358]

---

[354] TDNT 8:45; cited in Lincoln, *Ephesians*, 365.
[355] Wright, *Colossians*, 148.
[356] Dunn, *Colossians*, 247.
[357] These two terms can take on either meaning in Greek.
[358] Research on gender in Paul is enormous. Notable surveys should include Cohick, *Women in the World of the Earliest Christians* and especially Westfall, *Paul and Gender*, the latter of whom supplies an extensive bibliography, 316–332.

The Roman view of gender is beyond the scope of this study, but some of its chief results are essential for us.[359] One problem we have with understanding Paul and gender in passages such as this is that we project onto the text assumptions about how Western nuclear families are built. The Roman "household" was not a husband, wife, and a few children. It was a complex community composed of a large extended family, various children, and slaves. Some view it as an economic unit. As with Roman society, patronage controlled the flow of honor and authority within the household. Husbands were the patrons of wives, who were their clients. Women and children were patrons, and the slaves were their clients. Women could be the patrons of slaves as well as all her children. And benefaction flowed among these parties: The clients benefited as they honored their patrons. Authority did not necessarily follow gender, since women exhibited enormous authority within the household. A woman could be the head of her household (*materfamilias*): She could be in authority over sons, a patron of men, and a master of all slaves. She could own property as well as businesses. When we meet Lydia in Acts 6:14 we probably gain a small glimpse of a woman with remarkable independence and authority.

Moreover, as men were understood to have authority in the public arena, their wives held authority in the domestic sphere. Thus, to disrespect female authority within the household was completely unacceptable. Everyone lived within a patron–client relationship – including men – and therefore, in the Roman view, these categories of order and honor had to be sustained. The aim of society was not to establish patriarchy, although patriarchy was the chief mechanism of stability and authority; the aim of society was to preserve order so that patrons and clients could mutually benefit.

Westfall notes that what is striking about the early church is how it convened in households – which was the domain of women's authority.[360] This explains why we have descriptions in the NT of churches hosted by women (Lydia, Acts 16:14–15; Phoebe, Rom 16:1–2; Chloe, 1Cor 1:11; and

---

[359] See Westfall, *Paul and Gender*, 243–277, and A. Batten, "Gender," in Z. Crook, ed., *The Ancient Mediterranean Social World* (Grand Rapids: Eerdmans, 2020), 141–158, on which these paragraphs depend.

[360] Westfall, *Paul and Gender*, 268–277.

Nympha, Col 4:15) and of women occupying roles such as deacon, coworker, and prophet in the NT. The key here is that we have presumed a stereotype of male dominance *in all things*, but this springs from our own assumptions about gender. And this stereotype is foreign to Paul.

Therefore, Paul is respecting the ordering of society for the church's very survival in this Roman world while at the same time subverting it. When we read Col 3:18–19 we undoubtedly must include the close parallel we find in Eph 5:22–33, which comes from the same setting as Colossians. Paul likewise calls for the submission of wives and for the love of husbands but precedes this discussion with his wider exhortation in 5:21: "[B]e subject to one another out of reverence for Christ." The following verse on submission (5:22) has no verb and assumes that we bring that forward from 5:21: "Submit to one another … wives to your own husbands." Everything said in 5:22 presumes the moral premise given in 5:21. Mutual submission is the dramatic about-face in the NT churches of Paul.

While Ephesians shows us a mutuality that upends any Roman code, Colossians has no parallel. But it conditions this submission by the Christ-altering reality under which this couple lives: *as is fitting in the Lord*. In some manner, social rules now were to be seen through the Lordship of Christ. We might take Paul's words thus: *Given the new reality we have in Christ, discern how we should now live within the order of Roman society*. Paul is not upending this order entirely, but he is certainly transforming it by placing new Christ-centered coloring on its operation. Paul is not providing a universal prescription; he is calling for broad wisdom that assesses the culture.

Box 2.15 A Closer Look: Roman Marriage and Paul

We possess abundant evidence about Roman perceptions of marriage from the first century CE.[361] For instance, the papyri tell us that in Roman households girls were often married between the ages of twelve or thirteen. In epitaphs for girls who died unmarried, only one has been found who was over twenty. Jewish and Christian girls were married at fifteen or sixteen. But it is the tributes on tombs that are most striking. Here we see a variety of eulogies giving praise to a family's wife or mother. From Herculaneum, we find this:

---

[361] This follows B. Witherington III, "A Closer Look: Paul on Marriage and Slavery in Context," *Colossians*, 188–190.

Here lies Valeria, daughter of Marcus, of freeborn status from Caesarea in Mauritania. She was kind, affectionate, dignified blameless; she loved her husband and her children, and was faithful in their marriage. Out of respect and love for what is good, her husband, Lucius Dexios from Herculaneum, buried her.[362]

The epitaphs highlight how each woman is praiseworthy because she embodied the ideal role of the Roman wife. Husbands routinely refer to their wives' faithfulness, reverence, hard work, and devotion. All of this fits the Roman patriarchal ideal. Paul, on the other hand, does not exhort women to abide by these ideals, but in each case he is "seeking to revise the patriarchal situation."[363] Paul wants to reframe marriage virtue not in reference to patriarchy but instead in reference to Christian faithfulness. The hallmark of Christian marriage is in how both husband and wife reflect the ideals of Christ in their mutual service and subordination in love for one another.

Nevertheless, we need not soften Paul's words. The family in Roman society was entirely patriarchal, as were most institutions in this world. Paul – as he does with slavery – recognizes this reality but aims to rethink it through the gospel. Dunn reminds us helpfully that those who are critical of Paul and expect to find in him the full emancipation of women should remember that it has only been in the last 100 years that the status of women and wives has been changed in Western society.[364] Those who want to exploit Paul to confirm the subordination of women today have to remember not only Eph 5:21 and Gal 3:28 but also how Paul understands the evolution of patriarchy and how Christ should change it.

Paul's exhortation to husbands to love their wives (3:19) is also stunning in the Roman context. Roman men were not brutes: We have ample evidence of their deep respect and love for their wives within the cultural context of their day. Funerary reliefs and epigraphs of couples can be particularly moving. Nevertheless, this love should also fall under the domain of Christ's lordship, as it does in Eph 5:25: "Husbands, love your wives, just as Christ loved the church and gave himself up for her." The

---

362 *Supplementum Epigraphicum Graecum*, 1536.
363 Witherington, *Colossians*, 189.
364 Dunn, *Colossians*, 247.

reciprocity of respect and love is the hallmark of Christian marriage, and here no doubt this call to love invites us into a Christlike call – a sacrificial call – that does not indulge power or authority that is harmful or abusive.

Paul's third subject is children (**3:20–21**). We live in a culture that nurtures children in the extreme, wants to see the world "through a child's eyes," and projects full personhood on children at their youngest ages. It might be alarming to learn how different this was in the Roman period. We have plentiful evidence of caring love for children. Nevertheless, this was a different culture and time, and we should not project our experiences onto antiquity. Children's lives were difficult, many of them died young, and their disadvantages were enormous: From diet to disease, it is difficult for us to romanticize their lives. In Gal 4:1 Paul can even compare them to slaves, which likely describes their possibilities until they reached an age when education and training could begin. Others made the same comparison. Interest was largely focused on male children and how they contributed to the family honor. Childhood for boys ended at sixteen with a ritual (the *lustratio* or purification) and a ceremonial wearing of the white toga (the child's toga had a red border).[365] There are no records of puberty rituals for girls.

The child's situation was so tenuous that the Norwegian scholar O. M. Bakke can question whether children were even viewed as "persons" until they were much older.[366] When a child was born – and the preference for male children was common – the child was shown to the *patēr* of the family, and he alone had the power to accept it into the household or reject it. This took place over the first nine days of life, and if the child was rejected, it could be subject to "exposure" (*expositio*) – that is, leaving it outside the city, where it could either be killed or taken. Children with deformities, slave children, and girls were more likely to be rejected.[367]

---

[365] Ibid.

[366] O. M. Bakke, *When Children Became People* (Minneapolis: Fortress, 2005). Bakke's thesis is that it was within the context of the church that rethinking children's lives and value emerged. Children could also be abused sexually. On this, see L. Zelyck, "Matthew 18:1–14 and the Sexual Abuse and Exposure of Children in the Roman World," *Biblica* 98.1 (2017) 37–54. See also P. Balla, *The Child–Parent Relationship in the New Testament and Its Environment* WUNT 155 (Tübingen: Mohr Siebeck, 2003).

[367] OCD 322; W. V. Harris, "Child-Exposure in the Roman Empire," *The Journal of Roman Studies* 84 (1994) 1–22.

Therefore, the Roman family's expectations for children were utterly different than what we see today. Children were valued for what they could give "to the larger social whole."[368] Their caregivers were usually nurses, teachers, and slaves who held deeply trusted positions within the family. But their mortality rate was remarkable. By some estimates, 30–35 percent of children did not survive their first month. Possibly 50 percent of children died by age ten.[369] For most Romans, children lacked the essential things that were valued in adulthood: reason, courage, and self-control. They were often viewed as a "wax tablet," fresh and not yet marred but ready to be written on as a teacher or caregiver might desire.

Paul calls for children to obey *in all things* (*kata panta*), a phrase that sweeps up the widest of possibilities (see Col 1:20). However, it is a command that must be led by wisdom. This is obedience that is full and comprehensive but must require discernment in every matter. Jews in this period considered the limits of such filial devotion. Thus Philo comments on the fifth commandment (Exod 20:12) that we are called "to obey [our parents] in everything that is just and profitable."[370]

Both in Col 3:20–21 and in Eph 6:1–4 Paul places responsibility for the child's well-being on the father of the family (a typical Roman understanding), but this leadership must be viewed as Paul sees it: reforged in its new identity in Christ. Children's obedience is a duty *in the Lord*, and in Ephesians we read that a father's discipline likewise aimed at promoting growth in the knowledge of the Lord (Eph 6:4). The child's duty was to be obedient and honoring, but rather than giving license to the father to use strict discipline (as was the custom in Roman households) Paul calls for fathers to exhibit restraint. In Col 3:21 they are not to provoke (*erethizō*) their children, which refers to "stirring up" or "exciting" in them hostility or resentment. In Eph 6:4 Paul warns against angering them (*parorgizō*). But the aim of all this is avoiding discouragement, or, in the NRSV, so that they do not lose heart. Losing heart is a useful paraphrase for Paul's *athumeō* (*thumos* means spirit or passion), and negatively it would

---

[368] L. Cohick, "Women, Children, and Families in the Greco-Roman World," in J. B. Green and L. M. McDonald, eds., *The World of the New Testament: Cultural, Social and Historical Contexts* (Grand Rapids: Baker Academic, 2013), 183.

[369] Bakke, *When Children Became People*, 23; also C. Lae, *Children in the Roman Empire: Outsiders Within* (Cambridge: Cambridge University Press, 2011), 26.

[370] Cited in McKnight, *Colossians*, 353.

describe someone who has given up. Are these children (older children?) who now find their family's attachment to this new Christian movement embarrassing or distressing? Paul hopes for fathers who encourage and shape their children's lives without breaking their spirit.

The absolute authority of the father in Hellenistic Jewish settings could be represented by Ben Sirach (Ecclesiasticus): "He who loves his son will whip him often so that he may rejoice at how he turns out. An unbroken horse turns out stubborn, and an unchecked son turns out headstrong. Pamper a child and he will terrorize you, play with him and he will grieve you" (30:1, 8–9). When we consider the near-absolute authority of the father in these family settings, calls to exhibit love and to show restraint *in the Lord* certainly stood apart from Paul's culture. In many respects, Paul is asking how a new identity in Christ might shape the manner of a household living together. To be sure, the gospel suggested freedom to many: freedom from Jewish legal obligations and freedom from equally strict Hellenistic religious duties. However, this freedom, however it is imagined, cannot be used to diminish the importance of the family and its order. But, in addition, Paul is using guidelines for fathers that temper their approach to children. He does not reinforce their authority over children that would make them reactive and angry. He imagines an environment that nurtures and loves. With Moo, "Paul, in effect, is exhorting fathers to raise their children in such a way that they do their utmost to avoid provoking this kind of rebellious attitude in them."[371]

Paul's exhortation for slaves and their masters (**3:22–4:1**) is no doubt the most troubling for us who find slavery utterly incomprehensible and objectionable. Slavery, however, was a constant in classical antiquity and remained so up until the modern era. Slavery was so thoroughly woven through Roman society that it was impossible to avoid it. But our mistake is often to compare Roman slavery with what we have seen in the modern world in the last 300 years. There are parallels, to be sure, but there are important differences (see Chapters III and IV). Above all, the slave was a part of the Roman household and could provide a variety of roles from field labor to the instruction of children. But we should not romanticize slavery, for being owned by another has its inherent moral problems. But

---

[371] Moo, *Colossians*, 307.

here, as Paul imagines the new Christian household in Christ, its realities shaped the role of slave as well as every other household member. No doubt Col 3:11 was the stunning headliner that presented the new order: *In Christ there is no longer slave and free.* Those institutions remained, but something dramatic had changed. And as Philemon is told, his runaway slave now should be welcomed back as a loved brother (Phlm 16). Even here in Col 4:1 Paul tells masters to have a benevolent approach to slaves *because* the master will be held accountable to God in heaven.

Nevertheless, Paul is not dismantling an institution that we would like to dismantle. But we also have to keep in mind the social limits of this fledgling Christian movement. They were not powerful, and quite likely they felt vulnerable because any new religious movement like the church that spoke openly about the dissolution of slavery was certainly going to see a ferocious Roman response. Dunn has important wisdom for us that has been cited by many:

> [Paul's views] should not be criticized today as merely social conformism; those who live in modern social democracies, in which interest groups can hope to exert political pressure by intensive lobbying, should remember that in the cities of Paul's day the great bulk of Christians would have had no possibility whatsoever of exerting any political pressure for any particular policy or reform. In such circumstances a pragmatic quietism was the most effective means of gaining room enough to develop the quality of personal relationships which would establish and build up the microcosms (churches) of transformed communities.[372]

Dunn is right when we look at the first century CE. But today we who live in places that have genuine access to social power wonder how to employ a paragraph like this. The best avenue is to look closely at how in virtually every social issue Paul's response is to ask, "In what manner will Christ make a difference here?" In what manner will a life shaped by the cross alter our position in relation to someone who has been relegated to powerlessness? In a thoroughgoing patriarchal world, Paul still calls for women to sustain their traditional roles, but then he offers the subversive idea: *Something in Christ will erode what we think is normative.* How is submission to a man who is living a life shaped by the cross – a man who

---

[372] Dunn, *Colossians*, 253. See also McKnight, *Colossians*, 357.

loves like Christ and who has relinquished his patriarchal entitlements – going to look? So here: Something about Christ will interrupt this social category as well.

There is sufficient evidence to suggest that Colossians and Philemon were written at the same time. They used the same courier (Tychicus, 4:7), and with the mention of the slave Onesimus, the subject of Philemon (4:9), we can assume that this letter came to the Lycus Valley along with the letter to Philemon. This means that Paul's instructions here in Col 3:22–4:1 must be read in light of Philemon – and vice versa. As this was read aloud, we must imagine Philemon and other slaves in the church listening attentively, wondering how all of these instructions apply to them as well as to the runaway slave.

Many have assumed that the early church had many slaves in its ranks, and that these represented an important aspect of Christian life in the first century CE: Society's disadvantaged found a home here (Rom 12:14–21; 1Pet 2:11–25). Of course, this is one of the famous Roman criticisms of the church, cited for us by Origen: that the church consisted only of "slaves, women, and little children" (*Against Celsus*, 3:44). This is likely a polemical exaggeration, but, like every polemic, it may hold a bit of truth: The church was not filled with the elite of society. Perhaps this is why Paul shows a remarkable interest in addressing slaves. In 1Cor 7:21–23 he describes slaves who became followers of Christ *as slaves* and are now wondering about their status. He encourages them to gain their freedom, but his reassurance leans into their new identity: *Yes, you may be a slave, but in the Lord you are free*. In 1Cor 12:13 Paul describes the church as a wild mix of various backgrounds, all baptized and joined in one Spirit. But then he singles out the principal categories: *Jews and Greeks, slaves and free*. Perhaps these are the great social dividers of Paul's lived experience in the church: *How will Jews and Gentiles share the same spaces? How will slaves and free persons likewise find any unity given their stark differences?* Paul and his colleagues are so comfortable with the simple idea of slavery that they adopt it for themselves. Slave (*doulos*) is Paul's esteemed title for his new role in Christ: "Paul, a *slave* of Christ Jesus" (Rom 1:1); "Paul and Timothy, slaves of Christ Jesus . . ." (Phil 1:1). Epaphras, a Colossian himself, is likewise introduced as a slave (4:12), and he joined Paul in his imprisonment.

Both in Col **3:22** and Eph 6:5 slaves are called to be obedient, which is the same command he used for children in 3:20.[373] At the very least Paul is calling for slaves to respect the present social order, much as he does in 1Cor 7:20 when he tells slaves to remain in their role (but still seek freedom). This obedience should be comprehensive ("in all things"), which is also parallel to the command for children in 3:20. There and here, the proviso we suggested applies equally. This is full obedience that lives within the Lordship of Christ, which means there are certainly ethical boundaries that should not be crossed. And he expresses the limitations of the master's role by reminding slaves that their masters are temporal and limited in their reach, and that they are "according to the flesh" (*kata sarka*, NRSV earthly masters). This is similar to his words in 3:22b and 3:23b telling slaves that they must have a new consciousness. The master here is called the *kurios* (lord or master), but of course this same word (*kurios*) is used for Christ (1:3; 3:18), creating a dramatic contrast. *You have a* kurios *who is of flesh* (sarx) *and a* kurios *who is in heaven.* And between these our fullest identity is in the Lord Christ. This dual identity is also true of masters who live under the supervision of the Lord (4:1), who is watching for justice and fairness.

Box 2.16 A Closer Look: Slavery

Paul's call for slaves to be obedient *in everything* both in Col 3:22 and in Eph 6:5–6 is certainly disconcerting for anyone living in the modern world. He even compares this obedience in Ephesians with obedience to Christ (6:5). In 1Cor 7:21–22 Paul says similar things: "Were you a slave when called? Do not be concerned about it." We are understandably more concerned than Paul on these matters.

In the OT world of the ancient Near East, the idea of slavery was extremely common and widely accepted. Slavery was such a common idea that Israel used it as a metaphor for its relationship with God: Israel was God's slave and owned by him (Ex 32:13; Ps 31:16). But Israelites also owned slaves. They are listed as property (Ge 12:16) and could be bought and sold. Sarah owned an Egyptian slave, Hagar, and Abraham owned many others (Ge 17:23; 21:12). The Israelites were slaves in Egypt, and this tempered their view of slavery but did not end it. Deuteronomy 20:10–14 typically gives directions for conquering cities: If the city surrenders, all are put into slavery; if it resists, all the males are killed, and the women and children, like cattle,

---

[373] In 3:18 Paul calls for wives to submit. In 1Pet 2:18 submission is applied to slaves.

become Israel's slave property. Israel also knew debt slavery, which held a person for a limited time (implied in Prov 22:7). Thus, in Exodus 21:1–6 we find directions for an Israelite father who sells his family into slavery (no doubt due to debt). The law stipulated that they should be freed in six years.

Modern scholarship today recognizes that slavery in Rome was more complex and violent than we imagined. Slaves were treated as property: They had no autonomous rights, were subject to the whims of their owner, and had limited hope for freedom. The origins of slaves were many. Slaves could come through conquest as prisoners of war or be born into slavery (from parents who were slaves). There was debt slavery as well.

Slavery was widespread in the Hellenistic and Roman periods. By some estimates, 16–20 percent of the Roman Empire, or 12 million people, were enslaved in the first century CE. In the capital Rome, possibly 30 percent of the population were slaves.[374] Greek and Roman households commonly held slaves. What is surprising is how frequently domestic slaves held positions of privilege in their wider society. They could serve as educators or physicians, and their services were often sought. But many – and perhaps this is the majority – worked in "industrial" jobs such as agriculture or mining, and for this reason the economy of the Roman Empire was deeply dependent on them. Aristotle defined a Greek slave as a "living tool," and, judging them by their physical strength, he believed that many were "slaves by nature" (*Politics*, 1252a–1255b).[375] This sentiment was widespread, and few gave moral arguments against slavery as a common practice.

Second Temple Judaism was completely familiar with slavery to such an extent that even Jesus can tell stories using slaves as characters (Luke 14:15–24). In Lk 12:47–48 Jesus describes the duties of a slave that any Roman would champion: "That slave who knew what his master wanted but did not prepare himself or do what was wanted will receive a severe beating. But the one who did not know and did what deserved a beating will receive a light beating."

The weight of this enormous cultural assumption about slavery helps us understand the difficulty for Paul or any NT writer to swim against the tide. The societal assumptions were so enormous it is hard to imagine any early Christian imagining a world without slaves. And this is what makes Paul's writing so surprising. It is clear

---

[374] See T. E. J. Wiedemann, *Greek and Roman Slavery* (London: Routledge, 1981); O. Patterson, *Slavery and Social Death: A Comparative Study* (Cambridge, MA: Harvard University Press, 1982); J. Byron, *Recent Research on Paul and Slavery* (Sheffield: Sheffield Phoenix Press, 2008); S. Joshel, *Slavery in the Roman World* (Cambridge: Cambridge University Press, 2010); recently C. Cobb and K. Shaner, *Ancient Slavery and Its New Testament Contexts* (Grand Rapids: Eerdmans, 2025).

[375] S. Bartchy, "Slaves and Slavery in the Roman World," in Green and McDonald, *The World of the New Testament*, 170.

that Paul is promoting a rearrangement of the slave–master relationship (Gal 3:28; Philemon). And yet, in passages such as 1Cor 7:20–24 he sustains the traditional roles. The early church even adopts the name "slave" for its own membership (Rom 6:16–17; see Rom 1:1, 2Cor 4:5) and recognizes slaves in its communities (1 Cor 7:21) while encouraging them to gain their freedom. A trajectory is therefore in place that should have led to a critique of slavery on theological grounds, but the closest we get to this is Philemon. Here in Colossians we see a hint of this. In 3:22–25 Paul reframes the slave–master relationship as conditioned by their relationship to "the Lord." And in 4:1 he calls masters to treat their slaves "justly and fairly" because the master's behavior is observed by "the master's Master," who is in heaven.

Some scholars have suggested a "story of ascent," arguing that the rise of Christianity gradually caused the decline of the institution of slavery. If true, this took centuries. We might point to the gradual erosion of slavery, but this is weakly attested. Within two generations of Paul, the apocryphal writing *The Didache* presents a view of slaves and masters that seems to erode the Roman view but still sustains the institution: "And you slaves shall be submissive to your masters in respect and fear, as to a symbol of God" (4:11).

For more on this subject, see the "Slavery" section in Chapter III.

Slaves who are attached to Christ should be known for their integrity (**3:22b**). Paul warns against service that is only meant to "catch the eye" (*ophthalmodoulia*, from service for the eye) and likely means working only when watched, when credit can be gained, rather than working with honor. The idea is repeated in the next words: working as "people-pleasers" (*areskō*, to please, hence *anthrōp-areskos*) – that is, working to curry favor (REB).[376] The contrast is stark: Slaves who belong to Christ work "whole-heartedly" (NRSV) or, rather, with "sincerity of heart." Together these instructions are meant to inspire a demeanor within this position that is fully aspirational such that, despite their circumstances, the slave gives to the master honor and good character. The following phrase, *fearing the Lord*, introduces the same wordplay we noted earlier. Slaves who might exhibit a servile fear of their master (*kurios*) now live with an awareness of their true master (*kurios*). However, we must nuance this idea of fear

---

[376] Both of these words are very rare: The first occurs only here in the NT, and the second occurs here and Eph 6:6.

carefully. This term was a regular feature of Jewish moral exhortation such as Ps 111:10: "[T]he fear of the Lord is the beginning of wisdom," pointing to piety, respect, and reverence more than anxiety. This is Paul's routine use (Rom 11:20; 2Cor 5:11), and we should think of it as combining some measure of relational respect with the awe that God necessarily deserves.[377]

Box 2.17 Bridging the Horizons: Surviving as a Modern Slave

Paul's words for slaves – as well as his words for wives – look forward to a Christ-centered change that can only take place when genuine transformation in the Spirit takes hold. We have to imagine that these cultural orders were so ancient – so solidly fixed – that their upending or their modification were nearly impossible, unless God upended a person's views. I have already said that these verses must not be used to endorse slavery today. That would be to misunderstand Paul completely and to fail to see how he desires to subvert the very order he is forced to acknowledge. A Christian should find unimaginable the idea that he or she would own another under any circumstance.

But there is one thread we might pull linking ancient slaves and modern forms of slavery. The slave was powerless and, in many cases, hopeless. And we can plausibly assume that some did not live with a Christian master. Without glimpses of hope and Spirit-led transformation in their household, the slave's only hope could be in God. Of course, as Paul tells slaves in 1Cor 7 to gain their freedom if they can, so, too, pursuing freedom might take other forms to interrupt modern forms of oppression. But this is not always possible, and to say otherwise means we have not seen how profound powerlessness can be.

Of course, we know that slavery has not disappeared. The United Nations (UN) estimates that there could be as many as 50 million slaves in the world today.[378] However, I have heard this language of Paul elsewhere in contexts in which Christians live in hopeless, powerless situations. They might be locked in overwhelmingly complex poverty (New Delhi, India; Cairo, Egypt; Ndola, Zambia; or Jackson, Mississippi) or living under tyrants who use shocking cruelty (Iraq, Syria, Myanmar). Or they may struggle to survive under violent military occupations (Gaza, West Bank). I witness their circumstances as a tourist might: I stand on the margins of their world as a safe, wealthy, privileged American having no fear.

---

[377] An excellent example of this nuanced use of *phobos* is in the last sentence of Mark (16:8). Once the disciples witnessed the empty tomb, they "were afraid." They are not entirely fearful, but they experience fear-inducing awe because a divine work was before them.
[378] "50 Million People in Modern Slavery: UN Report" (2022), www.un.org/en/delegate/50-million-people-modern-slavery-un-report (accessed October 2025).

I own a passport and a return plane ticket. But I look and I wonder if I could survive what they endure. But consistently I hear something else: how their faith mediates a profound reality to them that I barely possess. A one-hour worship gathering in a Cairo slum showed me this for the first time.

For these modern powerless, it seems that their faith increases as their situation worsens. This doesn't always happen, but it may. They know where they truly belong; they know to whom they are most completely faithful; they have one *kyrios* who reigns in heaven and who will judge the architects of their circumstances that they are powerless to change.

This spirituality of hope-within-hopelessness is represented in the American context most powerfully in the Black Gospel tradition that was formed under slavery. In it we find an honest acknowledgment of terrible circumstances and a powerful eschatological hope. The slave hymn "Glory Land" reflects this fully:

> If you have friends in Glory Land, who've left because of pain, there'll be no pain in Glory Land, they'll suffer not, again.
> So weep not friends, I'm goin' home; up there, we'll die no more; no coffins will be made up there, no graves on that bright shore.

Paul is reinforcing these ideas in **3:23** with sayings that almost sound proverbial. Slaves might withdraw their commitments or only work when watched (3:22). A literal translation might be: *Whatever you do, work from the heart* (pseuchē) *as if you were working for the Lord and not for people.* The Greek *pseuchē* is generally taken as "soul" (in the LXX it is the usual translation of the Hebrew *nephesh*) and was the vital seat of living. It is what makes a person who he or she is. It is what disappears when someone dies or is lost to dementia. It is not just life; it is the person within that life. Today our metaphor for this is the heart. So to follow Paul's lead, this is work that comes from the center of our commitments rather than the periphery. This is work that sees passionate investment in what we do. The NEB may represent it best: *Put your whole heart into it.* This means the slave's effort is not grounded in their fear of the master but in their own inner worth and integrity, their dignity, and because God is alert to all their circumstances.

Therefore, the basis of this working is not grounded in elevating the master. This work is not centered on the hierarchy or subordination inherent in the slave's status. Paul anchors this theologically by suggesting that all such work be done in honor of the Lord, who will be pleased with the slave's good behavior. Working with one's "whole heart" *as for the Lord* echoes another command in the OT. In Mark's rendition of the great confession of Deut 6:5, Jesus says, "[Y]ou shall love the Lord your God with all your heart (*kardia*) and with all your soul (*pseuchē*) and with all your mind and with all your strength." Here then is a profile of life that is conscious of the Lord so fully that it diminishes the situation in which the slave lives.

But there is more. This spiritual perspective includes hope that is anchored to the future (**3:24**). *You will receive the inheritance as your reward.* This is striking because slaves could not by law inherit anything. They inherited nothing within their household. Nor did they inherit anything from their patron, the master of the household. Even what they owned was not truly theirs. But in this case they become heirs from their truest patron, the Lord Christ, who will reward them for a life lived with integrity. The Greek word order makes this clearer: *You will receive "the reward of an inheritance."* The term for inheritance (*antapodosis*) occurs only here in the NT (though variants of it are in Luke 14:14; Rom 11:35; 12:19). It has a double emphasis: getting back from (*apo*) in return (*anti*), regarding something given (*didōmi*). Positively this is a reward; negatively it could also be a retribution (as in Rom 11:9).

But here it is encouraging, since what is given will be an inheritance (*klēronomia*, a *klēros* was a lot drawn, Mark 15:24). The idea of inheritance is very Jewish and appears widely in the LXX for the land of Canaan in the Abraham promises (Gen 12:1–5; Exod 3:7–8; Num 26:52–56). This promise was more than incidental to Israel. It was a promise on which it developed enormous theological hope. But as an idea this promise could also become elastic. It could also describe a future promise held for God's people in various forms. Thus the "inheritance" became eschatological and moved beyond the land of promise.[379] It could refer to life with God following death. Therefore, inheritance with this broader meaning now could provide a slave with a new avenue of thinking: The slave too was moving to a promised land, now spiritualized, as a place with God in heaven (PsSol 14:10; Eth Enoch 40:9; Test. Job 18).[380]

It is difficult to determine the audience for Paul's warning in **3:25**. Who is the subject of wrongdoing: the slave or the master? The parallel in Eph

---

[379] TDNT 2:779.
[380] Ibid., 780.

6:8 clearly points to the misconduct of the slave, and some believe Phlm 18 is relevant because here Paul refers to any wrong that Onesimus might have done toward his master. Even the same word (wrongdoing, *adekeō*) is used in Phlm 18 as it is in Col 3:25. In his letter to Philemon Paul certainly is trying to reassure the slave owner that Onesimus will be an obedient and respectful member of his household. In no manner does Paul want a Christian slave to exploit his faith and use it as justification for misconduct toward his master. However, the evidence could just as easily point to the master as warned. The final clause (*there is no partiality*) suggests strongly that Paul is thinking about the master, for in such discussions the master might well think that he is above any exhortation and is privileged in his conduct with slaves. It is also significant that the following verse (4:1) explicitly refers to masters. Scholars are almost evenly divided on the verse's audience, and some have suggested that the warning works both ways: to masters and servants equally.

The warning is also a play on words, which gives it a lyric sense. Those who "do wrong" (*adikeō*) will be repaid for what they have done wrong (*adekeō*) – and there is little difference (i.e., no favoritism) for who you are. This then is about accountability, and we are reminded that conduct in this matter is *observed conduct*. All behavior is seen by the Lord and not done independently.

The direct word to masters in **4:1** appeals to justice: *Grant to your slaves what is just* (dikaios) *and what is fair* (isotēs). The Greek text moves the nouns (justice, fairness) forward in the sentence, giving them special emphasis. While the notion of justice is well-known, Paul's use of *isotēs* is striking. *Isotēs* (translated as equality) was an enormously important word in Greek legal writing (Plato, *Laws*; Aristotle, *Politics*), and it was understood to belong to all citizens.[381] This one idea was viewed as fundamental and lived at the center of any democracy. But if Paul is echoing this tradition for slaves ("justice and equality"), he would be calling for the dissolution of slavery itself. There was no room in Roman law for slaves to have anything approximating equality with free persons. Nevertheless, Paul is willing to push this limit. In 2Cor 8:13–14 he argues for the generosity of rich Christians toward their poorer brothers and

---

[381] Dunn, *Colossians*, 259; TDNT 3:343–355.

sisters because within the church there is *isotēs*. Is this equality? Is Paul arguing that there can be no unequal distribution of God's material blessings "in order that there may be equality?" But if there were slaves in these churches – and we can assume there were – the implications are profound. If in Christ there is no longer "slave nor free" (Col 3:11) and *isotēs* describes their community, the implications are monumental.

A second meaning for *isotēs* is fairness or equity. This was something that could be expected for all persons, even slaves (Seneca, *Epistles*, 47). Paul is not appealing to the master to view the slave as a peer or to give him or her the rights of a free citizen, but rather that there would be equitable treatment for them.[382] Fairness (*isotēs*) and its adjective *isos* were commonly applied to judges: An excellent judge is a fair (*isos*) judge.[383] In Plato (*Laws*, 12.957c) fairness and justice together share an important mutual dependence. Fairness in justice leads to equity. Justice without fairness leads to justice that is not impartial.[384] But Paul might also add that the master cannot decide what is just and fair. This is decided by God alone – as Paul says in Eph 6:9 – since both "have the same Lord in heaven, and with him there is no partiality." These words are an example of how Paul is undermining or subverting the usual way his Roman world viewed slaves. In these two words, just and fair, "the power differential of slave and master was diminished dramatically."[385]

As in Eph 6:9, the leverage for this appeal is theological: *knowing that you have a master in heaven*. In this case, it is provocative and certainly best to translate *kurios* (lord) as master, since Paul is reminding the master that he himself lives under another master, God himself, and this brings accountability. We thus have an interesting symmetry: *Masters . . . grant to your slaves . . . knowing that you have a master in heaven*. Paul's argument implies that he is assuming the master is a Christian, perhaps someone who is attending the Colossian church alongside his slave. And we can imagine that a slave community in that church would hear this with keen interest: Christians with slaves are living under an obligation that is both moral and spiritual – God is attending to their behavior.

---

382 Harris, *Colossians*, 162.
383 TDNT 3:354.
384 Ibid.
385 McKnight, *Colossians*, 367.

The modern reader of Roman history is always astonished to learn what a Roman master could do to his slave. Examples of unjust treatment in the vast literature on Roman slavery describe abuse that is astounding by any modern standard. The sexual use of slaves is today a widely discussed subject, since some wonder whether Paul's silence about this implies that he sees it as morally neutral – as Romans often did.[386] If slaves had no rights, were not protected by Roman law, and were the property of another, then their mistreatment was above criticism. This has brought sharp disagreement from those who argue that Paul's discussion of slavery in Colossians and Ephesians must be seen within the wider guidelines that Paul employs. Thus the sexual ethic Paul uses in Col 3:5 ("put to death ... sexual immorality, impurity, passion, and evil desire") surely means that treatment of slaves will fall within these rules.[387] Moreover, the slave's obedience in "all things" (3:22) excludes sexual demands, since these belong to the very sinfulness that must end.

The grounding idea prevalent in Paul's household codes is the spiritual transformation – and thus the moral transformation – that emerges when a person is shaped by the power of Christ through the Spirit. Paul is not writing an inspiring tract and providing one more human vision for a life that could be lived well. His starting point is the *new creation* that is beginning to be seen in the church. And he would likely question that if such transformation is absent from the church (or from a person), one may rightly wonder whether the presence of Christ is at work there at all.

4:2–6 Life in the Community

4:2 Devote yourselves to prayer, keeping alert in it with thanksgiving.

4:3 At the same time, pray for us as well, that God will open to us a door for the word, that we may declare the mystery of Christ, for which I am in prison,

4:4 so that I may reveal it clearly, as I should.

---

[386] J. Glancy, *Slavery in Early Christianity* (Oxford: Oxford University Press, 2002). See Seneca, *Epistles*, 47.8, who describes this sexual use of slaves. The male slave "must remain awake throughout the night, dividing his time between his master's drunkenness and his lust."

[387] M. MacDonald, "Slavery, Sexuality and House Churches: A Reassessment of Colossians 3.18–4.1 in Light of New Research on the Roman Family." *NTS* 53 (2007) 94–113.

4:5 Conduct yourselves wisely toward outsiders, making the most of the time.

4:6 Let your speech always be gracious, seasoned with salt, so that you may know how you ought to answer everyone.

These few verses find Paul giving final admonitions before he turns in 4:7 to extend greetings from friends and to recognize the recipients of his letter. Paul begins by underscoring the importance of prayer as a routine spiritual discipline and then asks for prayers for his own unfolding work. Just as he has been faithful in praying for the Colossians (1:3), so now he asks of them the same favor. This request for prayer is something he does regularly (Rom 15:30–32; Phil 4:6; 1 Thess 5:17, etc.), and in this manner he is connecting his followers to his own efforts. He finally ends this section with a short exhortation about public decorum: conduct, speech, apologetics. These read like notes that have sprung to mind as he thinks about wrapping up.

Paul's urging about prayer in **4:2** only becomes dramatic when we set it alongside common Roman religious practices in the period. The imperative *devote* comes from a Greek verb for strength – *kartereō*, and in the LXX this can mean "endure" (Job 2:9; Isa 42:14; cf. Heb 11:27). Thus, the more intensive *proskartereō* that we see here suggests a fierce devotion, an enduring commitment, a practice that is unflinching. In Mark 3:9 Jesus says in Gethsemane to be "ready" using the same verb: Do not just be ready, *but be diligent*. Therefore, Paul has in mind a life that is continuously and diligently devoted to prayer – and with this he adds a descriptive participle: one that is watchful and alert as well. This is no casual devotion; this is prayer that is disciplined, focused, sustained.

What is striking different about Paul's exhortation compared with Roman practice is that there is no cultic dimension. A devout Roman convert would likely see this at once: no temple, no ritual utterances, no magic practices, no intermediaries, and no sacrifices to Christ. And there was no deference to priests either – at a temple or within the household (the *paterfamilias* was viewed as the household priest). This would have been noticed because religion in Rome followed ritual expression that was generally centered on temple and sacrifice.[388] There were informal prayers,

---

[388]　See R. L. Wilken, *The Christians as the Romans Saw Them* (New Haven: Yale University Press, 2003); J. Rüpke, *Religion of the Romans* (Cambridge, UK: Polity, 2007); J. Rüpke,

to be sure, but most prayer was formulaic.[389] The ordinary person could address the gods, but this was done as a vow or was accompanied with a sacrifice at the local temple. Household altars could even provide a ritual context for such vows and requests. Nevertheless, the spoken word of the faithful was viewed as powerful, and without it even rituals could lose their power.

Paul's understanding of prayer mirrors what we find in the gospels and throughout the NT. And what stands out is the personal immediacy of the connection one is assumed to have with Christ. This is not a prayer uttered, say, following a walk to a local shrine. Paul is describing prayer as a spiritual rhythm that carries an immediacy that was typical of Christian discipleship. We could describe it as persevering prayer, much as Paul describes it in Rom 1:9 on behalf of the Romans: "For God, whom I serve with my spirit by announcing the gospel of his Son, is my witness that without ceasing I remember you always in my prayers . . ." He concludes Ephesians with similar words of exhortation: "Pray in the Spirit at all times in every prayer and supplication. To that end, keep alert and always persevere in supplication for all the saints."

Prayer with alertness is reminiscent of someone who is "on guard" and watchful. The term refers to standing up or being alert, watching for some surprise, as in Matt 26:41, where it suggests staying awake. But in this case it is connected to thanksgiving. It may then suggest a "threefold rhythm: intercession, 'watching' for answers, and thanksgiving when those answers appear."[390] There may even be an echo here of the Garden of Gethsemane when the disciples are warned against sleep while Jesus prays (Mark 14:32–42). "Simon, are you asleep? Could you not keep awake one hour? Keep awake and pray that you may not come into the time of trial; the spirit indeed is willing, but the flesh is weak" (Mark 14:37–38). Possibly this story was known in Paul's church and was repeated along with the early passion accounts. But if so, these words to Simon Peter could have been repeated as a proverbial warning about the difficulties of prayer and why discipline was needed.

A Companion to Roman Religion (London: Blackwell, 2009); J. Rüpke, *On Roman Religion: Lived Religion and the Individual in Ancient Rome* (London: Cornell, 2016).

[389] H. S. Vernel, OCD 1243; Rüpke, *A Companion*, 235–236.

[390] Wright, *Colossians*, 152.

But it could also be a caution. Jesus' disciples are praying protective prayers as he prepares for the cross. But what lurks in the background are soldiers and their plan to arrest him. So, too, the earliest Christians may have needed similar awareness, because in many cases they would also be in jeopardy. This more defensive or combative tone concludes Ephesians, and it no doubt adds color to Paul's understanding of spiritual disciplines such as prayer.

Finally, be strong in the Lord and in the strength of his power; put on the whole armor of God, so that you may be able to stand against the wiles of the devil, for our struggle is not against blood and flesh but against the rulers, against the authorities, against the cosmic powers of this present darkness, against the spiritual forces of evil in the heavenly places. (6:10–12)

Paul then asks for the Colossians to pray for him (**4:3–4**). He does this as well in the ending of Ephesians: "Pray also for me, so that when I speak a message may be given to me to make known with boldness the mystery of the gospel" (6:19). When we read the closings of each of Paul's letters, we get the sense of his own vulnerability and the tenuousness of his ministry (compare Rom 15:30–32; 2Cor 1:11; 1Thess 5:25; 2Thess 3:1–2; Phlm 22). He had experienced severe opposition from Jewish synagogues as well Roman officials. Jewish-Christians devoted to adherence to Jewish law even debated him. At the time of this letter, he is in prison (4:4b). In Phil 1:19 his request in light of his risks is clear: "I know that through your prayers and the help of the Spirit of Jesus Christ this will turn out for my salvation." But it is not just physical risks that are before him. His own work itself was always in jeopardy. His churches were fledgling communities that, once he departed their cities, could easily collapse and be reabsorbed into their old religious settings.

Box 2.18 Bridging the Horizons: The Vulnerable Pastor

Paul is expressing in these verses remarkable vulnerability. He is in prison, he needs people supporting him, and he is asking the Colossians to pray for him.

Pastors have always felt vulnerable. Some will tell you that this feeling surfaces particularly after preaching a sermon: So much of their heart, values, and commitments are displayed in public that Sunday afternoon feels risky. We might be surprised to hear what church members will say to their pastor during the coffee hour following worship.

But for the last ten years I have heard something new. We live in an era of cultural polarization, when social media has given us permission to say things we ordinarily would never say, using a tone that once embarrassed us. And much of this is directed to the pastor. As a seminary professor, I have pastors confide in me about verbal and written comments that even made them reconsider their chosen vocation. They have shown me emails that were absolutely shocking. And it has made me wonder whether this phenomenon contributes to the remarkable number of mid-career men and women who are leaving the ministry. In some surveys, 45 percent of American pastors have considered a vocational change since 2020. For me, this points to a vulnerability that at some point has become toxic.

What would happen if a church committed itself to praying for its pastor *daily*? The pastor might feel embarrassed by the idea – but here Paul was not embarrassed. He understood his own vulnerability at every level: from theological disputes to political charges. In 2Tim 4:14 Paul refers to a long-forgotten man named "Alexander the coppersmith" who once did him great harm. Pastors can be harmed. But a praying congregation that took this effort seriously would change things. Not only would this change the church itself, but it would also protect the pastor, for whom vulnerability and stress represent an ever-present reality.

But Paul is not alone. Here he says: *Pray for "us."* While the theme of 4:2 was thanksgiving, this is now a plea for intercession. Of course, Timothy is working closely with him and is a signatory to this letter (1:1). And as we read in 4:10–17, there are others who are sharing in this mission, such as Epaphras, Luke, and Demas. For this reason we should likely not imagine Paul as a solitary evangelist who moves from city to city like an itinerant preacher. Through the years he has built a network and a team. And this probably helps explain the successes of his work that were sustained long after his passing. Solo pastors who lack such a team are uniquely vulnerable, and Paul knows this.

Therefore, this prayer is not only for his own protection. Since he is in prison, this would make sense. But Paul is also thinking about his life's work, the evangelistic effort to bring the gospel to the world. He is asking that God will give him opportunities (*a door might be opened*) so that he might explain the mystery of Christ. As we learned earlier (see 1:26–27; 2:2), this mystery centers on the remarkable and unexpected arrival of God in a person, Jesus Christ. And we may confidently say that this is the theme of this letter. Jesus Christ was not simply another Jewish teacher interpreting the Jewish law. Nor was he a sage to be welcomed by Roman philosophers. Even "Messiah" does not exhaust his meaning. His life was an event on which all history turned: He was "the image of the invisible God" (1:15), the source of all creation (1:16), and thus his dominion reached over all powers on earth and beyond. And this included spiritual powers that dominated the cosmos, but also it included the political powers centered in Rome. As a man arrested and now held in Rome, this teaching about the lordship of Christ that swept up every domain certainly caused a stir in places that had authority over Paul's fate.

According to Luke, Paul had various brushes with the law. In Ephesus, for instance, there was a controversy about Paul's teaching and its economic impact on those who built religious artifacts for the goddess Artemis (Acts 18). But the definitive controversy erupted in Jerusalem when Paul arrived after his third journey and he was accompanied by various Hellenistic believers. Some of Paul's opponents had seen him with a Gentile named Trophimus the Ephesian, and they assumed Paul had taken this Gentile into the Temple, thus defiling it (Acts 21:27–32). These "Asian Jews" (27) were likely from Ephesus, and they would have recognized Paul from his visit there (19:1, 10). This is why they identified Trophimus, whom they called "a Jew from Ephesus." Paul's teaching had split their Ephesian synagogue, and the animus toward him must have been enormous.

A riot ensued: Paul was attacked and thrown out of the temple, and the temple itself was shut down. Such a reaction was not uncommon. The sanctity of temples was a given throughout the Roman world, and Roman writers describe similar crises in their temples where deaths occurred.[391] Josephus tells of a Roman soldier who exposed himself lewdly in the Jerusalem temple and thousands were trampled in the ensuing riot (*War*, 2.224–227).[392]

At once, Roman soldiers intervened and assumed Paul was a revolutionary from the militia called the Assassins (21:28). But when this was found not to be the case, Paul was freed. He then addressed the crowd in Hebrew, telling the story of his conversion. But this did not appease them. They called for Paul's death (22:22). When the Romans decided to interrogate Paul using torture, he at once declared his Roman citizenship to the

---

[391] C. Keener, *Acts: An Exegetical Commentary* (Grand Rapids: Baker, 2014), 3.3149.
[392] Ibid., 3.3145.

centurion in charge. "Is it legal for you to flog a Roman person [a citizen] who is not condemned" (22:25)? Immediately everything stopped. Paul was sent into protective custody in a military prison in Caesarea (on the Mediterranean Sea) while he awaited audiences with both Jewish and Roman leaders. Each of them found him innocent. But his earlier appeal to citizenship triggered a Roman law requiring his appearance before a Roman court. As the Jewish Agrippa told the Roman governor Felix, "This man could have been set free if he had not appealed to the emperor" (26:32).

We know a great deal about the severity of imprisonment for accused persons in the Roman Empire.[393] This was unlike imprisonment we see today in which the prison experience is a feature of the punishment. Roman prisons were custodial as the prisoner awaited their trial. A criminal judgment then resulted in punishments such as execution, exile, work in mines, decapitation, or crucifixion. Nevertheless, the imprisonment itself was severe: dark fortified rooms, little or no hygiene, meager rations, and chains connected to manacles around ankles, wrists, or the neck. This was designed to keep the prisoner from fleeing. In many cases, prisoners emerged from prison barely alive.[394] In Paul's case, described in Acts 21:33, the soldier who arrested Paul immediately no doubt followed protocol when he put Paul in two chains before he learned of his citizenship.

Acts 28:16 tells us that Paul was permitted to "remain by himself" in Rome, which likely means he could have private quarters at his own expense. This means that he rented his own lodging (likely an apartment) somewhere in the city.[395] In Acts 28:23 his place of residence is called a *xenia*, which refers to hospitality or hospitable lodgings.[396] Thus we believe that Paul enjoyed "free custody" in Rome as he awaited his judicial appointment. He was still guarded, but because this was a disputed charge with conflicting witnesses he was presumed innocent and was likely not chained. See Phlm 1 for typical living conditions in apartments in Rome.

---

[393] See B. Rapske, *Paul in Roman Custody*, volume 3 in the series The Book of Acts in Its First Century Setting, ed. B. Winter (Grand Rapids: Eerdmans, 1994).

[394] Ibid., 195–223.

[395] Ibid., 179.

[396] BDAG 683. The Greek root *xen-* can either refer to strangers or guests (*xenoi*), and the connection assumes the hospitality shown to strangers who are welcomed guests. In the NT most uses refer to strangers (Acts 17:20).

Paul could see visitors, write letters, and live under a "house confine-ment" until his appointed court date. Luke ends Acts by telling us that this continued for two years, all at Paul's own expense (Acts 28:31). But Luke never tells the story of this trial or its results. However, when Paul writes Colossians, the apostle is deeply aware of his condition. He describes himself here as "bound" (*deō*), which literally means to wrap or tie something together, especially clothes or even grain (Matt 13:30; John 11:44). But it could also serve as a metaphor for being *bound in chains*. This is true in the story of the Gerasene demoniac (Mark 5:3–4). But it also had the general sense of imprisonment (Mark 6:7; Acts 20:22). Paul's creative use of the term appears in 2Tim 2:8, where he describes his experience: "I suffer hardship, even to the point of being chained (*deō*) like a criminal. But the word of God is not chained (*deō*)."

Paul's description of the compulsion he has to reveal the mystery of Christ bears the urgency of a prophet. He asks them to pray "so that" (*hina*) a door might be opened and "so that" he might reveal this mystery *as I am compelled* (hos dei me) *to speak*. Thus, Paul is never free from the necessity or the requirement to speak about Christ, and this compulsion in the NT is generally the description of a prophet.[397] This language using *dei* ("it is necessary") describes a compelling destiny (also Mark 9:11; Luke 4:43; Acts 3:21), and Paul uses it three times in his writing (1Cor 11:19; 15:53; 2Cor 5:10).

Before giving his personal greetings, Paul's final words (**4:5**) are directed toward the community's public decorum and how the city of Colossae might view their behavior. In his other letters he might close with repeated concerns about internal conflicts as he does in Corinthians. But here we have to imagine that this is a very small community of believers no doubt surrounded by other competing interests and probably threatened by the much larger Colossian synagogue. Already the letter hints at the many ways these two communities wrestled over major ideas. Therefore, they needed "to be both circumspect in their dealings with others and be ready to respond when questions were raised by their own faith."[398]

---

[397] Beale, *Colossians*, 340; Dunn, *Colossians*, 264.
[398] Dunn, *Colossians*, 265, citing M. MacDonald, *The Pauline Churches: A Socio-Historical Study of Institutionalization in the Pauline and Deutero-Pauline Writings*. SNTSMS 60. (Cambridge: Cambridge University Press, 1988), 100–101, 108–109.

This speech within the public setting needed to be wise (*sophia*). We have already seen this word multiple times in the letter (1:9, 28; 2:3, 23; 3:16). On the one hand, it may simply be a call for discretion, prudence, or self-awareness. But in Colossians wisdom is directly related to the gospel itself. Paul says he prays "that you may be filled with the knowledge of God's will in all spiritual wisdom and understanding" (1:9). In 4:5 we likely do not have a reference to discretion, but it is wisdom that comes from the Holy Spirit. It is this engagement with Christ-in-Spirit that will unlock the treasures of wisdom that then will give us what we need to say (2:3). A better translation might be that the Colossians should conduct themselves *in wisdom*, and this means that they are bearing an enlightened comprehension of the mysteries of God so that these can be parlayed in the wider community. In the Greek text, *in wisdom* leads the sentence: *in wisdom* walk before outsiders. In Eph 4:29 Paul gives further guidance on speech, and in this case he tells the church to avoid speech that would offend or alienate others.

It is curious that Paul refers to those who encounter the Colossians as "outsiders" (*hoi exō*, those outside). This gives the sense that already the Colossian church has developed a sectarian response to their world. There were those who were *inside* and those who were *outside*. But this would accord with Paul's own understanding of the significance of his message. There are those who are in step with what God has done in Christ and there are those who are either oblivious or hostile. But the Colossians are not to be avoidant, staying away from those outside. They should "make the most of the time." The verb here (*exagorazō*) means to buy something back or to redeem something.[399] Here they are to "redeem" the time (*kairos*, not *chronos*), which is not an oblique reference to time in general but *unique time* designated for a purpose – hence, an opportunity, an occasion that should be used carefully.

In Paul's final exhortation in the letter, he writes that speech should be gracious (**4:6**). If the theme of these verses is evangelism, then Paul's use of *ho logos humōn* (your word) could refer to a message or even preaching. On the other hand, it more likely has a general meaning for speech in general and its manner (*en chariti*, in grace, *charis*). It should be "full of

---

[399] BDAG 343. The verb is related to *exagō*, to lead something or someone out.

grace" (NIV), "with grace" (NASB), or "gracious" (NRSV), Paul says, *at all times*. It describes a demeanor that is kind, respectful, amiable, similar to the thoughts in Ecc 10:12–14: "The speech (*logoi*) in the mouth of the wise [brings] grace or favor [*charis*]."

> Words spoken by the wise bring them favor,
> but the lips of fools consume them.
> The words of their mouths begin in foolishness,
> and their talk ends in wicked madness,
> Yet fools talk on and on.

In classical writing *logos* and *sophia* were commonly used together to depict a manner of speech that was edifying, that brought honor to the speaker.[400] This reinforces Paul's thought in 4:5. The church is not to be separated from society as if it must stay apart from the world, nor should it be antagonistic. The church should be engaged with its community but in a manner that does not lead to harsh divisions or insulting speech. It is redemptive. This is a posture in the world that does not relish polemics and arguments but instead works to bring generosity and clarity. Caird says that "Christians should give an attractive impression of the faith they profess," and that certainly is the very least Paul expected.[401] If outsiders are considered personal threats or if they are viewed as hostile to the gospel, Christians do not have license to speak similar hostility. Bruce comments, "If they practice grace of speech, it will not desert them when they find themselves suddenly confronted by the necessity of defending their Christian belief."[402]

Box 2.19 Bridging the Horizons: Where Angry (Authentic) Speech Is Encouraged

In the opening decades of the twenty-first century, social media has given many people permission to speak in a manner we only rarely used to hear in public. It was always there in society; but now something has shifted. Anonymous written speech (in text, webpage, or narrative) now has become personal public speech that may lack every measure of personal decorum. For many, this is a mark of authenticity or honesty – a moment to provide the "unvarnished truth" about a matter.

---

[400] Lightfoot, *Colossians*, 232; See also Ps 45:2; Sir 21:16; Luke 4:22.
[401] Caird, *Colossians*, 210.
[402] Bruce, *Colossians*, 175.

Remarkably, Christians have followed this trend more than they realize. And we are likely becoming acclimated to it. High-conflict, abrasive speech now can be seen coming from public Christian figures as well as ordinary church members who feel aggrieved about something and have decided that aggressive speech is the best way forward. The NLT provides a colorful translation of Eph 4:29: "Don't use foul or abusive language. Let everything you say be good and helpful, so that your words will be an encouragement to those who hear them." This advice accords with what Paul is saying here in Col 4:6. Speech should be tuned to grace (*charis*), and this alone will set us apart in a world where wounding speech has become common.

Paul's image for this is speech that it is seasoned with salt (Luke 14:34; Job 6:6; Mark 9:50). In antiquity salt was used either to preserve or to flavor, and here the latter is in view. The term for seasoning is exactly what it seems to be: This is the language of the kitchen. This is to season (*arturō*) food to enhance its flavor. However, there is a nuance that often follows this metaphor. In speech, this is not simply colorful language; this is language that has wit, cleverness, or shrewdness.[403] Perhaps it is speech that has discernment or imagination, particularly when speaking with those who do not share the faith. Thus, Paul adds that the purpose of this is *so that* we will know how to answer anyone.

We can imagine that this is wise counsel for those who are living inside a society that may not tolerate faith in Christ. It may have been foremost on the minds of early Christians, for whom opposition from "outsiders" was common. The words of 1Pet 3:15–16 may be apt: "Always be ready to make your defense to anyone who demands from you an accounting for the hope that is in you, yet do it with gentleness and respect. Maintain a good conscience so that, when you are maligned, those who abuse you for your good conduct in Christ may be put to shame."

FINAL GREETINGS, 4:7–18

4:7–9 Paul's Messengers

4:7 Tychicus will tell you all the news about me. He is a dear brother, a faithful minister and fellow servant in the Lord.

---

[403] Ibid. refers to Latin *sales Attici*, meaning "Attic wit" (*Attic salt*).

4:8 I am sending him to you for the express purpose that you may know about our circumstances and that he may encourage your hearts.

4:9 He is coming with Onesimus, our faithful and dear brother, who is one of you. They will tell you everything that is happening here.

In most of Paul's letters – and certainly in all of the undisputed letters – Paul ends his correspondence with personal concerns and greetings. In these notes he always tells of his travel plans, provides greetings, gives final instructions, adds a personal note or two, and provides a personal blessing or benediction.[404] For those who are skeptical about Paul's authorship, the personal character of these sentences presents a difficulty. Some scholars have suggested that these notes belong to Timothy, who is a cowriter of the letter and who Paul has given his final endorsement in 4:18. However, as soon as we recognize a more complex understanding of authorship in the ancient world (see Chapter I), we can begin to give authorship the elasticity it deserves. There is no convincing reason to set apart these verses from the body of the letter. Both stem from the same author: Paul and Timothy.

These final verses also give us some insight into Paul's relationship with his coworkers. Every experienced minister – including Paul – knows that ministry must have cooperation, friendship, and mutual support if it is to be successful. Tychicus is a beloved brother. Onesimus is also a beloved brother. Tychicus is a faithful minister and servant/slave of the Lord. And the slave Onesimus is a faithful follower of Christ and is "one of you" – that is, a Colossian himself. This is the language of immense shared respect. These two men are also being endorsed. Paul is "sending Tychicus" to them, and this is the language of commissioning telling the Colossians that he is Paul's authorized emissary. But Onesimus will also arrive under the authority of Tychicus' commission. Both men will speak on behalf of Paul and tell the church the circumstances of his life and very likely explain the letter itself.[405]

But the description of Paul's community continues as he sends greetings from a variety of colleagues: Aristarchus, Mark (Barnabas' cousin), Jesus/

---

[404] See Dunn, *Colossians*, 269, for careful closing parallels between Colossians and the other Pauline writings.

[405] Note that Paul does not speak of his own circumstances himself, although he could easily have done so. McKnight, *Colossians*, 387–388, notes what a contrast this is to the way self-disclosure works in modern social media networks.

Justus, Epaphras (also a Colossian), Luke, and Demas. These are among the people who are standing with Paul in prison despite the threats that face him and the consequences that they could incur. In Colossae itself Paul knows Nympha, the woman who is hosting the house church there. He is known in Laodicea nearby. And he knows one man, Archippus, sufficiently well that he can send a coded message to him (4:17), which surely the church pestered him about as soon as they heard it.

Col 4:7–18 displays the wide circle of Paul's social network, and it was as diverse as we might imagine. It is almost as if the principles of Gal 3:28 and Col 3:11 have now come to life among his friends: We have Jews (Aristarchus, Mark, Jesus/Justus) and Gentiles (Epaphras, Luke, Demas).[406] We have a physician (Luke) and a slave (Onesimus). Many want to be known as "slaves of Christ" and join Paul and Timothy in this remarkable title (Rom 1:1; 2Cor 4:5; Phil 1:1). And this diverse community of Christ-followers in Colossae are meeting in the home of a woman.

Tychicus (**4:7**) was a native of the Roman province of Asia (in western Anatolia, Acts 20:4) and may have come from Ephesus (possibly 2Tim 4:12). Paul has him return to this area multiple times, and this further points to this being his home. He originally joined Paul during his third tour and was a part of a growing company of delegates from various churches who supported him and carried donations for the poorer churches in Judea. Then he reappears in the prison letters (Eph 6:21; Col 4:7) now serving as the courier of these three: Colossians, Ephesians, and Philemon. Finally, we see his name at the close of Paul's life as an envoy to Ephesus (2Tim 4:12) and Crete (Titus 3:12). Lightfoot speculated that perhaps Tychicus was the unnamed famous disciple Paul mentioned in 2Cor 8:18.[407] If so, as Paul says in these verses, he was a well-known preacher. His name (*Tykikos*) was not common in this period, although numerous inscriptions near Colossae and Ephesus have it listed.[408]

What stands out is the way Tychicus is described. He is a beloved brother, a faithful minister, and a fellow servant. We should likely imagine him as one of Paul's most senior, deeply trusted colleagues, similar to Silvanus, Timothy, and perhaps Epaphras (who is also "beloved"). Being a

---

[406] Based on Acts 20:4, some conclude that Aristarchus was a Gentile.
[407] Lightfoot, *Colossians*, 234.
[408] Ibid., 235.

dearly loved brother reflects the common tendency in the church to use familial language. But this is the same title as Paul uses for Timothy (1:1), and so this elevates Tychicus status significantly. And this is important because he is being accompanied by someone the Colossians may not trust (Onesimus), and his illicit escape from Colossae may be well-known in the other churches in the Lycus Valley.

When Paul refers to Tychicus as a faithful minister, this does not carry the meaning we assume today. He is a *diakonos*, which could be taken as "deacon," meaning that he is someone committed to serving and no doubt has done this fully with Paul in his imprisonment. We should not think of this as an office at this point but as a role providing service to his imprisoned friend. He is also described as *faithful* (*pistos*), which carries a sense of trustworthiness. But, above all, he is a co-slave in the Lord (NRSV, fellow servant, *syn-doulos*), meaning that he shares an identity and vocation with Paul of full slavery in his service to Christ.

All of these words together provide Paul's courier with a strong commendation because Tychicus will represent the apostle when he arrives. He will bring greetings and instructions to Laodicea (4:16), Colossae, and, we can imagine, Ephesus as well. But, in addition, as any trusted representative would do, he will teach and interpret what Paul and Timothy have written. We must imagine this correspondence being read aloud to a gathering of believers in a home setting and then Tychicus fielding questions and expanding upon meanings.

When Paul writes "I have sent him to you" in **4:8** he is employing the formal language of "sender and agent," making Tychicus Paul's authorized representative. This is a relationship between two persons in business, diplomacy, or even personally, when the "sender" commissions their "agent" to complete the sender's affairs as if they were present. The Colossians would have been quick to recognize this. Tychicus should be received as Paul would be received. He and Onesimus should be welcomed and given generous hospitality and, if needed, money if he makes the return trip to Paul. Paul says this explicitly for Timothy when he is sent to Corinth (1Cor 16:10–11).

The tasks of Tychicus, however, are not simply instructional (explaining the letter); he will also update the church on the circumstances of the esteemed apostle. But note how restrained Paul is in this verse when he describes his condition. He is reticent to say it, but Paul is actually in a place of jeopardy: He is on the threshold of his trial, and its outcome could severe. Compare the difference in his tone with 2Tim 1:15–19 and 4:9–18, where Paul tells a trusted colleague how dire his situation is. But in this case he has instructed Tychicus that no such talk is allowed. The report will be upbeat and encouraging so that the church will come away from this visit confident in their faith and relieved that Paul is safe.

The note about Onesimus (**4:9**) was no doubt unexpected. Remember that this letter did not arrive in advance of this visit. Tychicus read this aloud after the slave has been seen and greeted – and now Paul is providing some context. We also have to remember that Tychicus is carrying the Letter of Philemon, and we can assume that its contents would make its way around the church, since it too would be read by a group of believers (Philemon, Archippus, and Apphia) and their house church. But, above all, Onesimus is a Colossian. He is "one of you," just as Epaphras was (4:12). So this means that the person (Philemon) from whom he escaped is likely to be in this congregation seeing Onesimus and hearing things like 3:11: *In Christ there is no longer slave and free.* The arrival of the gospel now reframes Onesimus' relationship with Philemon, and here we have our first hint at one of Paul's intentions. It was a bold decision to send the newly converted Onesimus back home, and yet Paul is doing so with theological assumptions that now must surface socially. Notice that Paul does not describe Onesimus as servant or fellow slave, as he does Tychicus. He is not in Paul's inner circle of leaders (Phlm 10–22 will tell us more). Onesimus is Paul's "brother," and so if Philemon considers himself as a part of this Christian family, Onesimus is his brother as well. Onesimus is faithful. But so are Tychicus and Timothy. This slave now stands in esteemed company as a believer.

Box 2.20 Bridging the Horizons: Onesimus Returns Home

I can barely imagine the many conversations between Onesimus and Paul when they discussed this slave's future. Paul believed both that a slave should seek his freedom (1Cor 7:21) but also remain if he must in his position as a slave (1Cor 7:24). But in this case Paul's pastoral advice was that, despite Onesimus' artificial freedom in Rome – artificial because he could still be caught and prosecuted – Paul believed that in order to go forward in his life, he must first go back.

It is remarkable advice. And perhaps there is something universal in this. An error once made cannot be ignored or suppressed. Going forward requires going backward *so that* our histories are seen clearly and addressed bravely. Here

Paul is relying on the power of the gospel to pave the way for Onesimus so that his master will not immediately hand him over to the authorities. But also, by making this return public, Paul has leveraged the social pressure of the community on Philemon and openly expects him to do what is right. Does this mean Philemon should free his slave? We cannot know. But, certainly, Philemon should become a different sort of master, just as Onesimus has become a different sort of slave.

The second feature about Onesimus in this verse is that he will also serve as a reporter to the congregation regarding Paul's circumstances. This is what Tychicus will also do (4:7), and it means that Onesimus is not just a convert but a trusted disciple who will stand shoulder to shoulder with Tychicus telling private stories about Paul. In other words, Onesimus is an insider to some degree, and with that position he deserves respect as someone who is a personal disciple of the founder and leader of this fledgling Christian movement. Philemon could barely say that about himself. And so we can imagine, as Onesimus returns to his status as a slave, all of the categories of slave/free were upended, and Philemon might be relying on Onesimus for insights into the faith they both share. Such a reconstruction is both plausible and revolutionary.

4:10–14 Greetings from Paul's Companions

4:10 My fellow prisoner Aristarchus sends you his greetings, as does Mark, the cousin of Barnabas. (You have received instructions about him; if he comes to you, welcome him.)

4:11 Jesus, who is called Justus, also sends greetings. These are the only Jews among my co-workers for the kingdom of God, and they have proved a comfort to me.

4:12 Epaphras, who is one of you and a servant of Christ Jesus, sends greetings. He is always wrestling in prayer for you, that you may stand firm in all the will of God, mature and fully assured.

4:13 I vouch for him that he is working hard for you and for those at Laodicea and Hierapolis.

4:14 Our dear friend Luke, the doctor, and Demas send greetings.

These verses indicate to us that early Christianity thrived through a strong network of friendships and working relationships. Paul was not a solitary evangelist, and his success relied on the work of others. A glance at the long list of names included in Rom 16 gives us an even better insight into this network. Who were Rufus who is "eminent in the Lord," Tryophaena, Persis, and Phlegon (Rom 16:11–16)? And what about Stephanas, Fortunatus, and Achaicus (1Cor 16:17)? This is just a sample of names that come from Paul's concluding words in other letters. This network included women (Euodia, Syntyche, and Prisca, Phil 4:2–3; Rom 16:3) as well as men (Epharoditus, Clement, Phil 2:25; 4:3). These are the many leaders in the church who are unrecognized by us today, and, like in most churches throughout history, they carried on the work of the church uncelebrated.

Here in Colossians Paul refers to eight names, which is remarkable, since he either has not been to Colossae (2:1) or has met only a few members of the church perhaps when he visited Laodicea. Five of these names also occur in Phlm 24 (Epaphras, Mark, Aristarchus, Demas, and Luke), and the last four are called Paul's "co-workers" (*synergoi*), which was Paul's common name for his colleagues (Rom 16:3, 2Cor 8:23; 1Thess 3:2). Here we are tapping into the circle of leaders who reside in the east Lycus Valley, and Paul wants them to know that he is aware of them and their efforts. No doubt Epaphras and Onesimus have named them; Tychicus may also be a source.

Sending greetings (**4:10**, *aspazomai*) refers to offering a gesture of welcome (*aspasmos*), which could include an embrace, kiss, or words of friendship. In the culture of Jesus' world, such greetings were expected (Mark 9:15; 15:18–19; Luke 1:29). Hellenistic writers used the same set of terms for greetings, and so it is not surprising that this verb appears in Paul's letters forty-seven times, and in these few verses here it appears four times. Aristarchus is first listed, and, while it was a common name, we likely have another reference to him in Acts during the crisis in Ephesus (Acts 19:29). He is called a Macedonian there, but then Acts 20:4 more closely describes him as coming from Thessalonica, a city in Macedonia (also Acts 27:2). On his third tour, Paul was traveling with a delegation that aimed eventually to go to Jerusalem (where Paul would be arrested). Aristarchus was among his companions. On this third trip, Paul traveled from Asia Minor west to Macedonia and then south to Greece, but then he returned to Macedonia to embark on his final trip to Judea. His delegation went ahead of him (to Troas), where Paul eventually met them after he sailed from Philippi (Acts 20:4–6). From Troas Paul and his entourage continued south and east, eventually arriving in Judea (21:17). Aristarchus was among the few who remained with Paul in Jerusalem and likely continued with him into his imprisonment for two years in Caesarea. Aristarchus traveled with Paul by ship under guard as they headed to Rome (Acts 20:7), and eventually we find him in Rome supporting Paul in prison. This explains why Paul describes him as a "fellow prisoner of war" (*syn-aichmalōtos*). It is an odd word (only Rom 16:7; Col 4:10; Phlm 23) and implies that possibly – just possibly – Aristarchus may have been taken into custody with Paul. But we cannot be sure. However, he says something similar in Phlm 23 about Epaphras, who is in Paul's service *while* Paul was in prison. Since Paul does not use the term for others who are with him, it increases the likelihood that Aristarchus was set apart by the authorities or "under suspicion." A natural reading of 4:11 also suggests that Aristarchus was among the Jewish believers working with Paul (along with Mark and Justus).

Mark was "the cousin of Barnabas."[409] This was one of the most common names in the Roman Empire. The reference here links Mark with the narrative in Acts, where he appears in 12:12 as a resident of Jerusalem with Paul and Barnabas. Luke tells us that his mother was Mary, and he was also was called John (hence, John Mark).[410] The beginning of Paul's second journey in Acts 15 finds Barnabas eager to be accompanied by Mark. However, Paul disagreed with this decision, and he and Barnabas parted company over it. Paul traveled north into Syria with another colleague named Silas, while Barnabas and John Mark went west to Cyprus. This close connection with Barnabas (even used in Col 4:10 as an identifier) likely explains in part how John Mark became well-known.

The story of Mark and Paul should be remembered as a broken relationship that found some level of restoration with time. Over a decade later Mark was in Rome with Paul (Phlm 23). Timothy knew him so well that

---

[409] This term, *anepsios*, usually refers to the child of someone's uncle or aunt. Ibid., 236–237.

[410] The use of double names was common among Hellenistic Jews. Here John was a common Jewish name, while Mark (*markos*; Latin *markus*) was Roman. J. Marcus, *Mark 1–8* (New York: Doubleday, 2000), 18. Romans would have probably found *markos* far easier to pronounce than the more difficult *Iōannēs*. C. Keener, *1Peter. A Commentary* (Grand Rapids: Baker Academic, 2021), 406.

when Paul was captive in a later imprisonment – his most desperate – Paul can tell Timothy to go and find Mark and bring him to Rome because Paul values him as "useful in ministry" (2 Tim 4:11). Mark's wide recognition may explain the reception of the second gospel written, according to tradition, by John Mark himself. Eusebius wrote of him: "Mark became Peter's interpreter and wrote accurately all that he remembered . . .. For he had not heard the Lord, nor had he followed him, but later on, as I said, followed Peter" (Eusebius, *Church History*, 3:39, 14–16). Most surviving Greek manuscripts of the second gospel, despite their anonymity, find scribes adding *kata markon* (according to Mark), supporting the authorship tradition.

If he was a cousin of Barnabas and a follower of Peter, this shows him as well-established at the center of Christian leadership. In 1 Pet 5:13 Peter can refer to him affectionately as "my son," but this is likely a fictive kinship. This language could refer to a teacher–disciple relationship or even an elder–younger relationship (1 Cor 4:17; Phil 2:22; 1 Tim 1:2, 18; 5:1–2; 2 Tim 2:1; Phlm 10).[411] Nevertheless, John Mark eventually became a close and trusted coworker with Paul, Peter, Barnabas, and Timothy.

Perhaps most intriguing is Paul's short parenthetical remark about Mark: "concerning whom you have received instructions." The word here is stronger than the NRSV implies. They had received "commands" (*entolē*) regarding him. Paul can use this term for divine commands (Eph 2:15; 6:2), and rarely does he use it for human instructions (Titus 1:14).[412] It is likely that Mark is not traveling under Paul's direction, but it is unnecessary to conclude that their relationship was strained.[413] Paul is reminding the church of their duty (*entolas* as an order) to show him hospitality "if he comes." The note suggests a separate, earlier correspondence about Mark, and we cannot know who wrote it. It may have been Paul himself or a letter from Peter or Barnabas that Paul is endorsing.[414] Or perhaps Mark was traveling with Peter at this time and so the visit was coming from outside Paul's circle of friends. Does this mean that Mark was working for someone as a separate courier? Did Mark's influence grow

---

[411] Keener, ibid.
[412] BDAG 340.
[413] Contra Dunn, *Colossians*, 277.
[414] Bruce, *Colossians*, 180.

to such an extent that churches welcomed him openly and were eager to hear from him? Most of all, if Mark had already begun his own archive of stories and teachings about Jesus that would result in his gospel, was he already bringing this material from the Jesus tradition to churches?

These questions we simply cannot answer. But this short sentence does give us a window into the network of Christians in this period and the expectation of hospitality that was incumbent on every church.

The third greeting (4:11) is from Jesus, who is also called Justus. Like Aristarchus and John Mark, he too is from the circle of Jewish believers. This indicates an obvious but needed restating: Paul had many contentious debates with the so-called "circumcision party" (or Judaizers) who wanted Gentiles to embrace Jewish religious customs such as circumcision as they embraced the Messiah. But here we have examples of three ordinary men who refused this premise. They are colleagues of Paul's *from the synagogue* who shared in these early Messianic debates but joined with Paul fully.

The name Jesus is simply a Greek rendering of the Hebrew Joshua and was common in Judaism at this time.[415] For example, when the Jewish *Epistle of Aristeas* (48, 49) lists the names of the LXX writers, three of the seventy-two have the name Jesus.[416] Josephus refers to twenty men named Jesus who appear in his story in the first century CE. Ossuaries and burial inscriptions show even more widespread use of the name. Having a second name was also common in the first century CE. And in this case Justus was another common name. We know Joseph Barsabbas Justus in Acts 1:23 as well as Titius Justus in Acts 18:7. Jesus Justus is someone we know nothing about. The other five companions of Paul are mentioned in Philemon, but Jesus Justus is not.

Like Paul, these three men were Jewish by background and provided Paul with comfort and support in his imprisonment.[417] We can imagine the shared cultural habits they all had and how significant this was for each as they lived under this duress. But also, during these years they were learning from Paul how to interpret the messiahship of Jesus and the nature of Jesus' kingdom in a manner that made sense in the synagogue.

---

[415] TDNT 3:285–286.
[416] J. Charlesworth, *The Old Testament Pseudepigrapha* (New York: Doubleday, 1985), 2:16.
[417] Paul here uses the usual Jewish name for these men: They are among "the circumcision."

These three, therefore, give us a window into how Paul replicated his own work by living and studying closely with others who shared his convictions. After Paul's death in the first century CE, there were others who sustained his passions.

Epaphras (**4:12–13**) is one name that the Colossians would recognize immediately. Paul referred to him in 1:7 as the founder of this Colossian community and therefore as someone well-known (see also Phlm 23). This also explains why Paul can give increased attention to his importance. As a slave of Christ (a title Paul uses frequently for himself), his prayers for the Colossians and his service not only for them but for the nearby cities of Laodicea (see 2:1) and Hierapolis (4:12) each point to his devotion and spiritual discipline, which Paul clearly admires. His commendation of Epaphras is similar to the way Paul describes himself. Epaphras, like Paul, does not simply pray but strives or struggles (*agōnizomai*) continuously (*panta*) on behalf of those he serves (1:19; 4:12). Both men have one aim: that the Colossians would "stand mature" (*teleios*, 1:28), fully conscious of the threats in this city that could jeopardize their faith. In this sense, Epaphras has become an intercessor on behalf of this community in the Lycus Valley while he has been away. He knows these believers well. He knows how they began, he knows the potent threats of their own setting, and he knows that this is a struggle that requires hard work (4:13).

Luke and Demas (**4:14**) are Gentiles like Epaphras who now send their greeting. This verse is where we learn that Luke was a physician ("the beloved physician"). From at least the second century he was identified with the third gospel, and some have argued that the style of Acts betrays medical knowledge that might support this understanding.[418] But this is contested. However, in Acts Luke uses the first-person plural ("we") to indicate that he is traveling with Paul (16:9–10; 20:4–21:19; 26:32–28:17), and this carries to the end of Acts ("... and so we came to Rome," 28:14), which fits with Luke's appearance here. We can infer from this that here again, like Epaphras, there was a close relationship between Luke and Paul.

---

[418] Bruce, *Colossians*, 181n57. See also Eusebius, *Church History*, 3.4.1–7; 3.24, 14–15; 5.8.3; 6:25.6.

Demas has always remained a mystery. His name was also common and likely was a shortened form of a name like Demetrius, Democritus, or Demosthenes.[419] He is mentioned here and in Phlm 24. But we may have a foreshadowing here of what is to come.[420] Following Paul's warm praise for Luke, the spare introduction of Demas may point to what unfolded in a later imprisonment represented in 2 Timothy. In 2Tim 4:10 Demas is mentioned again, but this time critically. Demas will abandon Paul and go to Thessalonica because, as Paul says, he was "in love with this world." Paul clearly sees this as a betrayal. History has no other records of him, and perhaps he represents something that few of us are willing to admit: There are disciples like Epaphras who are resilient and faithful, and there are disciples, like we meet in the Parable of the Sower, who are not. Of the latter, once loyal, their commitments diminish, and soon they are no longer the people we assumed them to be.

4:15–18 Paul's Own Greeting

4:15 Give my greetings to the brothers and sisters at Laodicea, and to Nympha and the church in her house.

4:16 After this letter has been read to you, see that it is also read in the church of the Laodiceans and that you in turn read the letter from Laodicea.

4:17 Tell Archippus: "See to it that you complete the ministry you have received in the Lord."

4:18 I, Paul, write this greeting in my own hand. Remember my chains. Grace be with you.

The final greeting belongs to Paul himself (**4:15**). While six names are mentioned sending greetings, only two names are given as recipients, which may strengthen the idea that Paul has not been to this church but that Epaphras has. Note the reciprocity Paul expects between the churches of Laodicea and Colossae. The first was hosted by Nympha and the second by Philemon (Phlm 2).

---

[419] Lightfoot, *Colossians*, 242, believed his full name was Demetrius. The use of shortened names was extremely common. Lightfoot points to Artemas for Artemidorus (Titus 3:12), Zenas for Zenodorus (Titus 3:13), Olympas for Olympiodorus (Rom 16:15), etc.

[420] Abbott, *Colossians*, 303.

The name Nympha is attested both as a female name (Nympha) and as a male name (Nymphas). The text has the accusative: Nymphan.[421] The following pronoun (the church in *her* house) might dictate whether this is male or female but here, we also have variants: The church in her (*autēs*) house and the church in his (*autou*) house. Some scribes tried to resolve this by writing, "Greet Nymphan and the church in their (*autōn*) house." The decisive reason for reading Nymphan as feminine should be taken from the context of the early church's gatherings. These groups met in homes, and as Westfall has argued successfully, the Roman home belonged to the domestic sphere that presumed women as hosts. Hospitality, food preparation, and rituals of domestic worship were under her purview in every Roman family.[422] This is why we find many women such as Priscilla/ Prisca hosting house churches in their homes in Rome, Ephesus, and Corinth (Rom 16:3; 1Cor 16:19). Chloe led a house church in Corinth (1Cor 1:11). Lydia hosted in Philippi (Acts 16:14–15, 40). Phoebe not only hosted in her home but is described as a patron (Rom 16:1–2). With Westfall: "Women who functioned as patrons and opened their homes and shared their table and food with the Christian community were crucial to the churches' success, and Paul showed appreciation for the patronage and hard work."[423] In cases where couples are mentioned (Prisca and Aquila), still domestic hosting would fall to her as a cultural duty.

The cities of Colossae and Laodicea were only ten miles apart in the eastern Lycus Valley, and they shared a legacy through Epaphras' work there. Today the archaeological remains of Laodicea are on display. These can be compared with the new residential quarters recently excavated in Ephesus. These show residential spaces that could easily host as many as fifty people. But it was not the location or the building that mattered. Above all, these were communities of believers who worshipped together. They had no designated building, and likely their formal identity was fragile. It was their commonality as followers of Messiah Jesus that set

---

[421] The masculine name, Nymphãs, forms the same accusative as the feminine. Nymphas is an abbreviation of Nymphodōros. Abbreviated names generally ended in *-as* (Theudas for Theudōros, Acts 5:36; Artemas for Artemidōros, Titus 3:12; or Zēnas for Zēnodōros, Titus 3:13). The feminine name, Nympha, is related to *nymphē*, bride. BDAG 680; BD §125.

[422] Westfall, *Paul and Gender*, 230–233.

[423] Ibid., 232.

them apart, and their name often followed their host: There was no "Church of Laodicea," but there was the church hosted by Nympha, which sometimes could move to a new host.

Both were receiving letters that they should share (**4:16**). We can imagine Tychicus reading aloud and interpreting this letter to a Colossian gathering with Philemon and then traveling to Laodicea to read Colossians to that other gathering. He would then bring the Laodicean letter (which had been read there) back to Colossae. While we cannot generalize, it makes sense to consider how the Christian communities circulated materials from Paul – and likely from other sources (Mark? Luke? Peter?). Once this practice was well established, it is a short step to imagine churches creating their own collections of materials – copies of the originals – so that Paul's teachings could be preserved. In perhaps one of the most intriguing verses in Paul, the apostle writes to Timothy much later: "When you come, bring the cloak that I left with Carpus at Troas, also the books, and above all the parchments" (2Tim 4:13). Are these collections of writings? Copies of Paul's letters? Were the early Christian manuscript collectors copying and preserving any writings that came their way?

Paul mentions another letter from Laodicea, and this has proven a mystery. Of course, it could be a letter written by the Laodiceans *to* Colossae, but this seems unlikely. It could also be a letter that has been lost.[424] Some have pointed to Ephesians, and, oddly, Marcion's copy of Ephesians is titled, "To the Laodiceans."[425] Some have suggested Philemon is the letter Paul refers to. But if Onesimus is being recommended to the Colossians as "one of you," the letter of Philemon belongs to the Colossians.

As if Paul's unknown letter from Laodicea were not enough, he ends this letter with one more enduring mystery. In **4:17** he sends a cryptic message to a man named Archippus. In Phlm 2 Archippus is associated with the household of Philemon and described as a devoted worker in the church.

---

[424] The New Testament Apocryphal collection includes *The Letter to the Laodiceans*, but this is centuries later than Paul. See J. C. Edwards, *Early New Testament Apocrypha*. Ancient Literature for New Testament Studies, vol. 9 (Grand Rapids: Zondervan Academic, 2022), 374–394. The text can also be found in Lightfoot, *Colossians*, 274–300 (with analysis).

[425] Bruce, *Colossians*, 184.

And yet here Paul is exhorting him to complete a task that has come "from the Lord."

The theories about this mystery abound. Lightfoot speculated that he was the leading elder of the church at Laodicea and the son of Philemon and his wife, Apphia (Phlm 2).[426] Knox (and others) have held that Archippus was the owner of Onesimus and Philemon was the bishop. Therefore, Paul was sending the slave back to his owner via Philemon and reminding Archippus what he must do for the slave.[427] We can be sure of none of this. But we can guess that Paul knew Archippus and viewed him as one who had worked and struggled in tandem with the apostle in the work of the church. In Philemon he is called a soldier (*sustratiōtēs*), a term whose use points to warfighting or even a siege. In Greek a *stratos* is a military camp, a *strateia* is a campaign, and a *strēgos* is a military leader or officer. Paul uses this term for himself (1Cor 9:7; 2Cor 10:2–6) and clearly sees his efforts as a fight against spiritual powers. He uses the term for Epaphroditus in Phil 2:25 – which means that Archippus was ranked among the foremost of Paul's coworkers.

However, Archippus' task or ministry (*diakonia*) remains a mystery. This must be something Archippus had learned on an earlier occasion or something he has been reluctant to complete. It was certainly dramatic for Archippus to hear this exhortation read aloud before the entire gathering in Colossae (or Laodicea too if the letter had been shared). The social pressure would have been enormous. Archippus likely was answering questions for days. Was Paul's reminder tied to the return of Onesimus? It is tempting to speculate. And with Archippus' name attached as well to the letter to Philemon, this possibility only grows.

At least we can be sure that Archippus' task is in line with the themes we have seen in the letter, particularly since chapter 3. Paul assumes that these worshipping communities shared a communal life in which accountability was common and the values of the gospel – grace , truth, courage – were foremost. It is not farfetched to think that the courier Tychicus knew more about this assignment, and Paul was probably looking for some report on Tychicus' return.

---

[426] Lightfoot, *Colossians*, 245, 308–310; this view was popular among patristic writers such as Theodore of Mopsuestia. See Lightfoot, *Colossians*, 308n7.

[427] J. Knox, *Philemon among the Letters of Paul* (London: Collins, 1959).

It was common for writers of letters to use a professional scribe (or amanuensis) when composing a final draft (**4:18**). This custom promised a skilled finish to the correspondence, excellent writing style, minor corrections to grammar, and, if the scribe was trusted, more active participation in the letter's content. We have one such scribe named in Romans: Tertius. He not only identifies himself, but he greets Paul's readers (Rom 16:22): "I Tertius, the writer of this letter, greet you in the Lord."

In cases in which a scribe was employed, the author would often conclude the letter-writing in his or her own hand. This handwriting, certainly less skilled than the scribe's, was a signature that not only added a personal touch but also protected against forgeries. In one of his letters Paul is worried that letters may be circulating claiming to be from him when they were not (2Thess 2:1–2). A private closing might address this. Such personal final words are well attested in the ancient world.[428] Cicero is a famous example of this. When he used a professional scribe, he generally closed his correspondence in his own hand using the Latin *hoc manu mea* ("this with my own hand").[429]

Paul adds a final phrase exactly like Col 4:18 in 1Cor 16:21 and in 2Thess 3:17. The latter explains Paul's purpose: "This is the mark in every letter of mine; it is the way I write." Phlm 19 is similar: "I, Paul, am writing this with my own hand." In Galatians Paul cues the reader to learn his writing style: "See what large letters I make when I am writing in my own hand!" (6:11).

When he says "remember my chains," the idea of him picking up a pen *while chained* becomes poignant. But the term for chains (*desmos*) could also mean imprisonment generally (1:24; Eph 3:1; Phlm 9). This is Paul's one moment – and they are rare – in which he calls attention to his condition and asks for support. "Remember" refers to prayer, as it does in 1Thess 1:3, and with these words Paul is asking for what he himself does regularly: prayer. Paul prays for his churches (Rom 1:9–10; Phlm 4) and for

---

[428] A. Deissmann, *Light from the Ancient East* (New York: Doran, 1927), 170–172.
[429] Bruce, *Colossians*, 186. See also E. R. Richards, *The Secretary in the Letters of Paul.* WUNT 2.42 (Tübingen: Mohr Siebeck, 1991); J. Weima, *Neglected Endings: The Significance of Pauline Letter Closings.* JSNTSup 101 (Sheffield: JSOT Press, 1994). E. R. Richards, *Paul and First-Century Letter Writing: Secretaries, Composition, and Collection* (Downers Grove: InterVarsity Press, 2004).

his friends: "I remember you constantly in my prayers night and day" (2Tim 1:3).

His final brief words, "grace be with you" (*hē charis meth' hymōn*), must have been his favorite closing. He also uses it in 1Tim 6:21 and 2Tim 4:22. In some cases it is expanded, such as in Rom 16:20 and 1Thess 5:28: "The grace of our Lord Jesus Christ be with you." In Gal 6:18 we find: "May the grace of our Lord Jesus Christ be with your spirit." Ephesians closes thus: "Grace be with all who have an undying love for our Lord Jesus Christ" (6:24).

We should not take casually how grace had become the routine greeting and closing in our early Christian correspondence. One could argue that grace was at the center of most of Paul's letters. Paul's encounter with Christ – no less than the experiences of other Christians both now and then – was an encounter with the love and grace of God. This was the very core of Paul's own ministry. He was eager to announce this grace at every opportunity – and he was quick to defend it strenuously, as he did in Galatians. Paul began this letter with a note of grace: "Grace to you and peace from God our Father" (Col 1:2). Here he closes the letter with the same words.

III Introduction to Philemon

Philemon is the shortest and most personal letter we possess from Paul. The only NT comparison is 3 John, which is similarly addressed – both are personal, private, and short. At 335 words, Philemon is longer than most personal letters from antiquity but is the shortest letter in the NT. When we remember that Paul commonly wrote long public letters we should not be surprised at its length. The Pastoral Epistles are also brief as well as personal.[1] Yet they are discussing matters of church-wide interest that make it certain that they were intended not just for Timothy and Titus but for a public audience.[2]

Philemon has always been attached to Colossians because of the many literary connections they share. Both were written by Paul along with "Timothy our brother." But the context makes clear that this is a private letter written "from Paul to Philemon" because it refers again and again to the two men's personal history and Paul's personal request of Philemon. Its greetings are also similar: Aristarchus ("my fellow prisoner"), Mark, Epaphras, Luke, and Demas send greetings in both letters. In each, Archippus is addressed. Paul also describes those in his company as "coworkers" (Col 4:11; Phlm 24), and a number of times he refers to his imprisonment (Phlm 1, 9, 10, 13; Col 4:3, 10). These parallels have led to the conclusion that Philemon was written from the same setting as Colossians, Tychicus (Col 4:7) was the courier of each, and the letters were

---

[1]   In the Greek text: 1 Timothy, 1,591 words; 2 Timothy, 1,238 words; Titus, 659 words; cf. Jude, 458 words.

[2]   By comparison, Paul's public letters are quite long: Romans, 7,111 words; 1 Corinthians, 6,831 words; Colossians, 1,581 words.

both going to the Lycus Valley in Phrygia, where both Laodicea and Colossae were located. This means that all of the contextual background we outlined for Colossians can just as easily apply to Philemon.

AUTHORSHIP AND VALUE

The earliest collections of Paul's letters usually included Philemon. It does not appear, however, in some of our earliest Greek manuscripts of the NT, but this does not imply its rejection for canonicity. These collections may have been used for public reading, and Philemon was thus not included. Some early papyri (Chester Beatty p[46]) dated to about 200 CE do not have it, but between 150 and 250 CE many ancient writers refer to it, giving it a place in the church.[3]

In the fourth century we hear objections to it because the letter bore limited theological value, especially in the years when major theological issues were being debated. Philemon focused on the very personal problem of the slave Onesimus. Some suggested the author was not Paul or at least was not inspired as scripture. Lightfoot lists the number of patristic writers (especially Jerome) who felt compelled to defend Philemon, suggesting to us that the letter had critics. But its defense was sustained, and for centuries it owned an uncontested place in the canon.[4] It appears in Marcion's collection of Paul's letters and in the Muratorian Canon.

Even through the Reformation Philemon was valued. Luther wrote,

> This epistle shows a right noble lovely example of Christian love. Here we see how St. Paul lays himself out for poor Onesimus and with all his means, pleads his cause with his master . . . . Even as Christ did for us with God the Father, thus also does St. Paul for Onesimus with Philemon . . . . We are all Onesimus, to my thinking.[5]

Many scholars compared the letter to one written by Pliny the Younger to a friend named Sabinianus whose young slave had infuriated him. "You loved the man, and, I hope, will continue to love him: meanwhile it is

---

[3]   Barth and Blanke, *Philemon*, 104–105.
[4]   Lightfoot, *Colossians*, 316–317.
[5]   Ibid., 317–318.

enough that you should allow yourself to yield to his prayers. Do not torture him, lest you torture yourself at the same time."[6]

With the rise of biblical criticism in the early nineteenth century, Philemon was questioned due to its connection with Colossians. Many valued the sentiment of the letter, but scholars such as F. C. Baur rejected the authenticity of the prison letters and thus Philemon as well. It was a "Christian romance in embryo" in which two men, separated under unforgivable circumstances, nevertheless reunited thanks to the gospel, "no longer as slave and master, but as brothers in Christ."[7] But with Caird, this argument could be turned on its head: "The letter would surely not have been preserved at all without a strong tradition that it came from the hand of Paul."[8] Today it is the rare scholar who questions the authenticity of the brief letter.[9]

THE OCCASION OF THE LETTER

There are two central questions about the narrative itself: (1) What was Onesimus' status in relation to Philemon – a slave-fugitive, an abused slave seeking an advocate, or an emissary on behalf of the Colossian church? (2) How did Onesimus gain access to Paul in Rome (or Ephesus) during the apostle's imprisonment? It seems unlikely that Onesimus simply ran into Paul, a friend of his owner, almost 1,000 miles from home (assuming a Roman imprisonment). Of course, coincidences happen, but, as one writer quipped, "this is a coincidence worthy of a Dickens novel."[10]

The traditional view tells us that Onesimus was Philemon's slave who had become a fugitive, had stolen (money?) from Philemon likely to finance his escape, and had made his way to Rome.[11] In Rome the slave became a Christian and was drawn into Paul's circle (who had a liberal

---

[6] Pliny the Younger, *Letters*, 9.21 (Loeb 59.119–120).
[7] Bruce, *Colossians*, 192.
[8] Caird, *Colossians*, 213.
[9] Dunn, *Colossians*, 299–300: "We can be confident, therefore, that Philemon was authored by Paul, elsewhere so well known to current and later generations as the (Jewish) apostle to the Gentiles."
[10] Moo, *Colossians*, 367.
[11] In Chapter I, I argued for Rome as the likely location for Paul's imprisonment. One argument for an Ephesian imprisonment is that Onesimus could have made his way to this nearby city with ease. However, the risk of being identified in Ephesus may have made this destination unlikely. Still, scholars debate this setting. Among modern

form of imprisonment called *custodia libera*), and there he was counseled by Paul to return to his master in Colossae. In the letter, Paul is writing to Philemon, who was not only was the slave's owner but an important benefactor for the church of Colossae.

In the letter Paul intercedes for Onesimus and reminds Philemon that he himself had become a Christian through Paul's ministry (19). Paul describes Onesimus as his child (10) whom he is returning to Philemon, but he implies tactfully that he is of such value to Paul that, if Philemon concurs, Paul would be glad to have him back. In any case, Paul urges Philemon to receive this man "as more than a slave," even as a beloved brother (16). Many have noted that Paul is changing Onesimus' status by putting into practice what he wrote in Col 3:11. In Christ the categories of "slave and free" have been upended, thereby putting in question slavery itself.

This traditional view has a good deal of plausibility. Slaves fled their masters so frequently that it was considered a major judicial issue in Rome. Onesimus would have departed Colossae perhaps with a band of others and then entered the shadowy world of a large city such as Rome. It is difficult to know how he found Paul, but the connection with the Colossian Epaphras is not far-fetched. However, this letter no doubt presented Paul with some difficulties. He was a man facing trial himself, but now he was giving shelter to a fugitive slave and appealing to his master that the slave not be prosecuted. Surely Paul reflected on how this might look if his efforts were discovered by his own prosecutors.

So far, so good. But recently theories have come forward that modify this traditional view and, in some cases, abandon it altogether.[12] The most important are as follows:

Onesimus as Commissioned Aide: In 1935, John Knox suggested that Onesimus was not a slave-fugitive but was commissioned by either Philemon, Archippus, or the church of Colossae itself to bring relief to Paul.[13] Moreover, the owner of the slave was likely not Philemon but

---

    writers, McKnight points to Ephesus, whereas Dunn believes it was Rome. Either way, the setting does little to shape the meaning of the letter.

[12] See J. A. D. Weima, "Onesimus: Still a Runaway Slave," T. Still and J. Myers, eds., *Rhetoric, History and Theology. Interpreting the New Testament* (Lanham: Lexington/ Fortress, 2022), 201–230, whose summary has served the following paragraphs.

[13] J. Knox, *Philemon among the Letters of Paul. A New View of Its Place and Importance* (Chicago: University of Chicago Press, 1935, revised 1959).

Archippus, whose home hosted the Colossian church (Phlm 2). Philemon was the overseer (or bishop) of the church, and Paul was sending the slave home via the church and its leader, Philemon, in order to place leverage on Archippus. This explains the cryptic Col 4:17 (cf. Phlm 13): Archippus' duty was to receive Onesimus and release him to Paul's service. While the "Knox Theory" has enjoyed very limited support,[14] still in recent years it has enjoyed renewed interest.[15] Even if the theory of Archippus' ownership of Onesimus has been widely abandoned, the theory of Onesimus as a commissioned aide for Paul remains.

The substance of Onesimus' mission was the practical care of Paul, which was common in Roman imprisonments where friends or family members supported prisoners. The Philippian Epaphroditus did this very thing for Paul on behalf of his church. He became Paul's "fellow worker, brother, and fellow soldier" as he ministered to Paul's needs (Phil 2:25–40).

One reason why this view has received limited support is because Epaphras had already been sent by the Colossians for this very purpose (Phlm 23; Col 4:12–13), and, besides, Onesimus was not a Christian until after he met Paul, and it is unlikely that he would gain this commission as an unbeliever. But perhaps a fatal problem is Phlm 18–19. Here Paul says candidly that Onesimus had wronged his owner and likely stolen from him. This sets up a context that is a far cry from Onesimus as a trusted emissary for the Colossian church.

Paul as Mediator and Advocate: Slaves had two ways to seek asylum if they had been wronged: They could flee to the home of a free citizen of high standing or they could flee to a temple that was qualified to offer refuge.[16] Roman law carefully legislated this process due to the widely attested problem of fugitive slaves. If the slave gained refuge, he or she was no longer technically a "fugitive" (Latin *fugitivus*) under the law or guilty of flight (*fuga*). This removed them from legal jeopardy.

Some have argued that Onesimus fled his home not as a slave-fugitive but as a slave in jeopardy needing defense from an unfair and threatening situation. In this case, Onesimus has located Paul intentionally in order to

---

[14]   See the full critique by Weima, "Onesimus," 205–206.
[15]   S. C. Winter, "Paul's Letter to Philemon," *NTS* 33 (1987) 1–15. Also see C. S. Wansink, *Chained in Christ. The Experience and Rhetoric of Paul's Imprisonments* (Sheffield: Sheffield Academic Press, 1996), 175–199.
[16]   Barth and Blanke, *Philemon*, 28–29.

enlist his help as an advocate.[17] The idea that Onesimus would be able to locate Paul is explained simply enough, since Epaphras was already with Paul, Onesimus knew Epaphras, and he may have met Paul in some earlier setting during Paul's Ephesian ministry. This would not be surprising. We have records of slaves appealing to leading citizens who then would write letters of acclaim for the slave and request for clemency and a resolution to the problem. We frequently are pointed to one penned by Pliny the Younger, whose letter to Sabinianus we noted earlier: "Pliny to Sabinianus: Your freedman, whom you mentioned as having displeased you, has come to me; he threw himself at my feet and clung to them as he could have to yours. He cried much, begged constantly, even with much silence. In short, he has convinced that he repents of what he did."[18]

This mediator reconstruction of Philemon has enjoyed growing support, and for some it represents a majority view. Critics of this view are uncertain whether Roman texts about theory and practice are reliable guides for our problem. But this seems minor. A major difficulty is that this view assumes that harm has been done by either Onesimus or Philemon, but generally the slave owner is given a negative profile. "If he has wronged you" (18) suggests that Onesimus is the culprit, but he may have fled with cause: Perhaps Philemon had harmed his slave or Philemon was untrustworthy. The text of Philemon does not imply any wrong had been done on Philemon's part.[19]

It is certain that Onesimus has fled, but it is his motivation for fleeing that is at stake here. Viewing the slave as an ambassador seems implausible. And believing that Onesimus fled as a fugitive not wishing to return and just happened upon Paul in Rome seems unlikely as well. Various conditions must be held to be true at once: (1) Onesimus fled without permission; (2) Onesimus damaged his relationship with his master; (3) Onesimus knew about Paul through his service to Philemon; (4) Onesimus also knew Epaphras who lived in Colossae and was now located in Rome; (5) Onesimus came to Rome *with the intention* of locating Paul and gaining his aid in resolving his problem at home; and (6) Onesimus

---

[17] This view has been defended by P. Lampe, "Keine 'Sklavenflucht' des Onesimus," *ZNW* 76 (1985) 133–137; B. M. Rapske, "The Prisoner Paul in the Eyes of Onesimus," *NTS* 37 (1991) 187–303; Barclay, *Colossians*, 98–102; Fitzmyer, *Philemon*, 17–23.

[18] Pliny the Younger, *Letters*, 9.21 (Loeb 59.11).

[19] See further Weima, "Onesimus," 209–212.

became a Jesus-follower when he joined the company of Paul and his companions and – in some manner that we cannot know – something transpired in Onesimus, possibly due to his conversion, and this influenced his return to Philemon.

Weaving these together produces a hybrid that is close to the traditional and the mediator views. It resolves the question of how the slave found Paul, but it also means that Paul was not harboring a legal fugitive, which in his imprisonment, though liberal, could have been perilous.[20] As soon as Paul determined that Onesimus was a fugitive, Roman law unequivocally dictated Paul's course of action. Onesimus must be arrested and/ or returned.

This letter is a result of deep pastoral conversations between Paul and Onesimus that very likely included Epaphras and Timothy; the first had personal knowledge of the situation in Colossae, and the second had become one of Paul's most trusted coworkers. Timothy may also have been well-known in Colossae, which explains why his name joins Paul in the opening verse.

SLAVERY

Paul's letter to Philemon directly opens the subject of slavery in antiquity, and without a clear understanding of this context it is virtually impossible to understand the power dynamics involved in the letter. We frequently soften references to slavery in the NT. The Greek term was *doulos/ē*, and when we translate it as "servant" we lose the force of what this language meant. Imagine the difference in meaning when we translate 1Cor 7:21: "Were you a slave when called?" (NRSV), "Were you a bondservant when called?" (ESV), and "Art thou called being a servant?" (KJV). Slavery itself, or the metaphor of slavery, appears throughout the NT, but once we become alert to the language, at once the prominence of the idea becomes clear.

Slavery was ubiquitous in the Roman world.[21] The entire social fabric as well as the economic system depended on slaves in enormous numbers.

---

[20] Similar views may be found in N. T. Wright, *Paul and the Faithfulness of God* (Minneapolis: Fortress, 2013), 8–9; Wright, *Colossians*, 170–171; Dunn, *Colossians*, 304–306; Beale, *Colossians*, 368–370; Garland, *Colossians*, 298–299.

[21] The literature on Roman slavery is extensive. The following have been most helpful: S. Bartchy, "Slavery (Greco-Roman)," AB 6:64–79; S. Bartchy, "Slaves and Slavery in the

Onesimus was a typical slave, but he was a part of a system that is unimaginable to modern readers of Philemon. Scholars estimate that as many as 12 million slaves populated the Roman Empire. Rome easily had far more slaves living in it than free persons. Half of Corinth's population was slaves. In the Saronic Gulf of Greece, a small island named Aegina (Greek *aigina*) had only forty square miles, much of which was volcanic, yet it played host to 470,000 slaves.[22] In rural areas, large numbers of slaves were held. Caius Caecilus Isidorus, a free Roman, owned an enormous farm with 3,600 pair of oxen and 4,116 slaves.[23] In urban settings, owning slaves was a form of prestige. Pliny the Elder describes how in the Roman senate one household owned more than 400 of them.[24]

Slaves appeared in almost every capacity: from domestic slaves, who could enjoy privileges in their position, to slaves working mines, quarries, and construction sites, where danger was acute. There were estate managers whose slave identity could be invisible, and there were slaves who had been tattooed or were required to wear an iron neck collar. The wide range of slave activity is surprising. In addition to manual labor, particularly in industrial settings, they could be skilled as scribes, accountants, cooks, leatherworkers, managers, teachers, or physicians. Even the Roman emperor used countless personal slaves to manage his bureaucracy.

Roman World," in J. Green and L. MacDonald, eds., *The World of the New Testament: Cultural, Social and Historical Contexts* (Grand Rapids: Baker, 2013), 169–178; Barth and Blanke, *Philemon*, 5–52; K. Bradley, *Slaves and Masters in the Roman Empire: A Study in Social Control* (New York: Oxford University Press, 1984); J. Byron, *Recent Research on Paul and Slavery* (Sheffield: Sheffield Phoenix Press, 2008); C. Cobb and K. Shaner, *Ancient Slavery and Its New Testament Contexts* (Grand Rapids: Eerdmans, 2025); J. Glancy, *Slavery in Early Christianity: Expanded Edition* (Minneapolis: Fortress, 2024); J. Harrill, *Slaves in the New Testament: Literary, Social, and Moral Dimensions* (Minneapolis: Fortress, 2006); C. Hezser, *Jewish Slavery in Antiquity* (Oxford: Oxford University Press, 2005); S. Joshel, *Slavery in the Roman World* (Cambridge: Cambridge University Press, 2010); H. Mouritsen, *The Freedman in the Roman World* (Cambridge: Cambridge University Press, 2011); O. Patterson, *Slavery and Social Death: A Comparative Study* (Cambridge, MA: Harvard University Press, 1982); K. Shaner, "Slavery," in B. Longnecker, E. Shively, and T. J. Lang, eds., *Behind the Scenes in the New Testament* (Grand Rapids: Baker Academic, 2024), 476–483; T. Wiedemann, *Greek and Roman Slavery* (London: Routledge, 1981); T. Wiedemann, *Slavery: Greece and Rome* (Oxford: Clarendon, 1987).

22 Lightfoot, *Colossians*, 321, referring to *Legatio Pro Christianis*, by Athenagoras, a second-century apologist.

23 Pliny the Elder, *Natural History*, 33.47; cited in Bartchy, "Slaves and Slavery," 171; Wiedemann, *Greek and Roman Slavery*, 99–100.

24 Pliny the Elder, *Natural History*, 7.12; cited in Bartchy, "Slaves and Slavery," 173.

Claudius, for instance, made use of 20,000 men who were a mix of slaves and freemen.

The education of slaves was encouraged – this increased their value – and many of the scribes who produced the literature we have today from Rome were slaves. The task of the scribe was highly valued in an era during which illiteracy was common. The ability to use paper, make and use ink and pen, know letters, and take dictation made them invaluable to an aspiring Roman. Some have even argued that Tertius, the scribal writer (or amanuensis) of Romans (Rom 16:22), was a slave.[25]

Slaves came from many sources. The Romans viewed conquered cities and their populations as legitimate sources of them, and in the Roman period armies could be followed by slave traders who bargained with commanders for the "spoils of war" – this time in human capital. Men who survived battle were often taken in as slaves, along with anyone deemed valuable from the defending city or fort. They might be redeemed by their family after the conflict, but this was rare. Sometimes the numbers of captive-enslaved were exaggerated, such as during Julius Caesar's conquest of Gaul, in which the historian Plutarch records that victory after brutal victory resulted in the taking of hundreds of thousands of slaves. However, while captive slaves were important, their numbers declined sharply at the end of Rome's Republic (to 27 BCE), after which Rome's wars of expansion became fewer. Other sources of slaves soon were found.

An ongoing source of slaves consisted of children born to slave parents. These household births increased in importance after the first century BCE, when slave prisoners were few. Many also thought that an estate's "natural" slaves could be socialized more easily and rarely engaged in rebellion or flight. These slaves might come from natural unions between male and female slaves, or they would be the result of the master and his female slaves. Slaves could be married, but this never involved the legally binding marriage contract of Roman law. It was permanent, but it was controlled entirely by their master's whims. There was no guarantee that either married partner might not be sold. And, above all, there was no guarantee that their children might not be sold. These people were legally property, and the needs of the owner's estate were foremost in any

---

[25] Shaner, "Slavery," 476; also see K. Shaner, *Enslaved Leadership in Early Christianity* (New York: Oxford University Press, 2018).

decision. Everything was determined by profits. Rewards, inducements, and punishments all aimed to increase a slave's productivity, obedience, and loyalty.

The possibility of slave revolts worried the Romans. In 73 BCE one revolt led by the gladiator Spartacus stunned and worried the Roman world. At one point this revolt mustered a slave army of 70,000 and defeated numerous trained Roman units. It took over two years to defeat and extinguish the rebellion. Slave numbers were so high in most regions that a slave revolt in one place could ignite widespread rebellion and threaten not simply the local economy but the lives of every slave owner. Many thought that slaves originating from the East were safer bets, and so their value would be greater. A slave market auctioneer would promote the promise of each slave (amiability, history, abilities), and if they were "safe" they could be purchased by temples, large estates, cities, shop owners, or private citizens.[26] Slaves who had any history of rebellion generally were given to more dangerous tasks (mining, road construction) and kept at night in slave prisons (*ergastula* or workhouses).

Infant exposure was yet another source of Roman slaves. Unwanted newborn children – often females – were abandoned outside the city walls and left to their fate. Slavers could take up these children and, when they neared puberty, sell them in the markets. Debt slavery was also common. Roman, Greek, and Jewish parents might sell their children into slavery because of their own poverty, or, in some cases, they might hope that slavery would bring the child benefits if they were attached to a wealthy patron. These were signs of desperation, to be sure, particularly when entire families fell into slavery – such a drastic decision arose only when all hope was lost. Slavery was even a tool of the judicial system. Those found guilty of various severe crimes (murder, theft, arson) could be condemned to slavery, being joined to the city's slave population or sold farther afield.

For most of the nineteenth and twentieth centuries, writers downplayed Roman slavery as less brutal than it was and contrasted it with the Atlantic slave trade in the West. Some would even depict it as a benign form of mass employment.[27] It was common to rely on examples of privileged

---

[26]   Barth and Blanke, *Philemon*, 6.
[27]   J. Byron, "Paul and the Background of Slavery: The *Status Quaestionis* in New Testament Scholarship," *CBR* 3 (2004) 116–139; typical of this more generous approach is S. S. Bartchy, *First Century Slavery and the Interpretation of 1Cor 7:21*.

slaves and to imagine a Roman society dealing humanely with this institution. This gave Christian interpreters of the NT an easy way to live with slavery in their scriptures. But further scholarship since the 1990s has moved in the opposite direction. At its most fundamental level, we now recognize the truly diminished experience of the Roman slave. The slave lacked personhood and agency in his or her own life.[28] Aristotle makes this clear. Slaves, he said, were "living tools," and due to their strength and vigor they clearly were born for purpose, not for personhood. This made them "slaves by nature."[29] The Romans did not go this far and viewed slavery as unnatural, and yet they conceded that every nation they encountered engaged in slavery, making it commonplace. It seemed then to be a natural law. The slave had lost his or her rights by war, birth, sale, or poverty, and this was simply a result of ill fortune. Thus once-successful free persons could have their fortunes reversed and find themselves in debt bondage.

A slave's loss of agency is apparent in simple things such as names.[30] Slaves were renamed either with diminutive forms of a common name or they were given names that their master aspired to (fortune, luck, fertility). Onesimus means "useful," Syntache (Phil 4:2) means "good luck," Euodia (Phil 4:2) means "sweet smell," Eunous means "friendly," and Fortunatus (1Cor 16:17) means "lucky man." Some names are simply numbers: Secundus, Tertius, and Quartos.

More diminishment can be seen in how they were rarely viewed as adults, having no autonomy, much as a child might. Slaves remained "boys" and not men, since had no agency under the law. We can see this in the gospel story set in Capernaum when the centurion pleads for help: "Lord, my servant (*pais*) is lying home paralyzed" (Matt 8:5–6). A *pais* is a child or youth (Matt 2:16; Mark 9:21; Acts 20:12). But we assume he is a

---

SBLDS 11 (Missoula: SBL Press, 1973). These views are represented as well in his entry to the AB 6:65–73. Since these publications, Bartchy's views have changed dramatically as he recognized new research unavailable in 1973, seen particularly in H. J. Harrill, *The Manumission of Slaves in Early Christianity* (Tübingen: Mohr Siebeck, 1995).

28 See Patterson, *Slavery and Social Death*; Bradley, *Slaves and Masters*; R. Horsley and A. Smith, eds., *Slavery in Text and Interpretation* (Atlanta: Scholar's Press, 1998).

29 Aristotle, *Politics*, 1252a–1255b.

30 Here see Barth and Blanke, *Philemon*, 15–18 for extensive details and references.

servant, not a *huios* or son. John's gospel knows this, and in 4:47 it calls the slave "son." Luke simply (and accurately) calls him a *doulos* or son (Luke 7:2). This even appears in Phlm 10 when Paul refers to Onesimus as a *teknon* or child but not as a son or a man.[31]

Violence was also commonplace. Patterson writes, "Slavery was a sentence of execution suspended only as long as the slave acquiesced in his powerlessness to his master."[32] There was almost no limit to what an owner could do to his slaves, since they were viewed as the property of the *paterfamilias*. Beating, whipping, torture, branding, starvation, and exposure to cold were all common. Slaves who killed their masters were by law punished by execution, usually using any excruciating manner they could imagine: crucifixion was common. But no doubt the fate of female slaves in the Roman household was most perilous. In addition to labor, they were subject to sexual abuse.

The female slave was the object of unlimited, at times perverse, sexual exploitation by the master, his male offspring, and his friends. Also she could be hired out to individuals or to a brothel as a prostitute – just as were handsome young male slaves for sodomy. It was assumed that lasciviousness and promiscuity were natural and welcome to all slaves, including those married.[33]

Opportunities to end one's slavery – called manumission – were not unknown. For instance, records indicate that some slaves had terms of service and were manumitted when, for example, their master died, their debts were paid, or, in some cases, when the slave turned thirty years old. But despite their newly gained freedom, in a patron–client society like Rome, manumitted slaves were obligated by law to conduct themselves for the benefit of their owner. They might be required to work for them (but with newfound freedoms). But as "freedmen" (*libertinoi*, Acts 6:9) they never escaped their history, and while they might elevate their social rank, they always carried the "stain of slavery" (*macula servitutis*).[34] By the first century CE, the numbers of these freed slaves grew so enormous that

---

[31] McKnight, *Philemon*, 16; Bradley, *Slaves and Masters*, 21–45.
[32] Patterson, *Slavery and Social Death*, 3, 5. Cited in Byron, "Paul and the Background of Slavery," 120.
[33] Patterson, *Slavery and Social Death*, 17.
[34] H. Mouritsen, *The Freedmen in the Roman World* (Cambridge: Cambridge University Press, 2011).

Augustus put in place laws that limited their number and the age at which they could be set free.[35]

INTERPRETING SLAVERY IN PHILEMON

Slavery in the NT has always presented a major difficulty for interpreters. Thompson rightly says, "The most pressing theological issue raised by the epistle to Philemon for modern readers, although likely not for ancient readers, is that of the relationship of the gospel to slavery."[36] It is a curious truth that Paul's original audience was so acclimated to slavery and the presence of slaves in their communities that Paul's relative silence regarding the institution or Paul's silence about ending it may never have occurred to them. Paul's words in 1Cor 7:20–24 are telling. Slaves are instructed to remain in the social status that they possess: "Do not be concerned about it." Of course, in 7:21b Paul says that if an opportunity arises to gain freedom, then a slave should take advantage of it. And here Paul is likely thinking about manumission. In other words, while people should remain in the social status they began with (7:20, 24), still he does not admire slavery per se ("... do not become slaves of humans"). Nevertheless in 7:24 he can refer to any social status as a calling ("... in whatever condition you were called ...").

This is a perplexing movement in Paul both toward criticism of slavery and toward a defense of the status quo that surrounds it. It seems clear enough that Paul believes that, within his churches, slave status should not be the arbiter of someone's standing. Here Gal 3:28 and Col 3:11 ("... there is no longer slave nor free ...") no doubt represent Paul's ideals and should play a definitive role in clarifying Paul's views. Does he see the church's context as a place where slaves may be "free," and yet that this freedom should not apply to public contexts? These are the critical questions that follow.

Since the late nineteenth century and the abolition of slavery in the USA, most biblical scholars presumed that the NT and, in particular, Paul were essentially opposed to the institution of slavery, and that Paul was making

---

[35] A. A. Rupprecht, *DPL*, 881.
[36] Thompson, *Colossians*, 198.

assertions that would fundamentally undo its institutions.[37] As Lightfoot said in 1879, "a principle is boldly enunciated, which must in the end prove fatal to slavery."[38]

The chief problem with this view is that the NT offers little to support this position. Nevertheless, as Wilson shows, the NT does set our principles that would eventually lead to the abolition of the institution: "in Christ," Paul says,

> there is neither Jew nor Greek, bond nor free (Gal 3:28; 1Cor 12:13; Col 3:11) and both Ephesians (6:5–9) and Colossians (3:22–4:1) as well as Philemon itself, seek to inculcate a new attitude among both slaves and masters, a spirit of Christian charity, since both are servants of the same Lord.[39]

This led to the eventual elimination of slavery in the later Roman Empire and to its eventual disappearance in the West by the time of the Renaissance. "The slave trade in the Americas was a new development under wholly different circumstances."[40]

The burden of slavery's recent history in the West has led to a dilemma among interpreters, and two alternatives remain with us today. Some have been openly critical of Paul, claiming that he says nothing or little about slavery and his silence alone is condemning. Worse, when Paul calls slaves to obey, it appears that he is not simply silent but condoning the practice. If he believes with Gal 3:28 and Col 3:11 that slavery is not a social category that affects one's salvation or one's life in the church, then he should say so – and his test case should be Philemon, where at best he is indirect.

Others are less harsh and recognize the difficulty Paul faced. Slavery was so deeply rooted in Roman society that it would have been impossible if not dangerous to uproot it entirely. In this case Paul would have run the risk of having this fledgling Christian movement viewed as a place for slaves to be free from their masters. And this would have certainly brought the Roman authorities down on their heads. This more sympathetic view also belonged to Lightfoot in the nineteenth century, and it could be represented today by Wright and many others.[41] Of course, this turns on the meaning of

---

[37] J. Barclay, "Paul, Philemon, and the Dilemma of Christian Slave Ownership," *NTS* 37 (1991) 161–162.
[38] Lightfoot, *Colossians*, 325.
[39] Wilson, *Colossians*, 329.
[40] Ibid.
[41] Lightfoot, *Colossians*, 323; Wright, *Colossians*, 173–174.

Philemon itself and what Paul is asking: *Does Paul's announcement of Onesimus' faith affect his status as slave? Is Paul asking with diplomatic nuance that Philemon should manumit his slave?*[42] *And what does Paul expect when he asks Philemon to view his slave as "a dear brother"?*

Many interpreters acknowledge some degree of frustration with Paul. But they also are ready to recognize the very real limitations imposed on him by the power of slavery as a Roman institution. And to this they add that, at some level, Paul is planting an idea about slavery that appropriately could be picked up at some later time to reject slavery altogether on the basis of Christian faith. Paul was certainly able to suspend some of his ideals for the sake of his mission to advance the gospel in his world. We feel this ambiguity in Paul not only in terms of slavery but also regarding women's leadership in the church. On the one hand, he recognizes that the gospel has changed everything and that new kingdom values will affect gender and traditional roles. 1Cor 14:34 and 1Tim 2:12 limiting women's voices and authority will also live alongside Gal 3:28. It is Paul's more fundamental announcement in Galatians that guides wider moral reflection. We see this ambiguity regarding circumcision, in that Paul can endorse it for Timothy (Acts 16:3) while also leveling sharp criticisms against those who wish to impose it on the church – so too with slavery. Paul's cardinal rule – his pivotal idea – points to a shift in how Christians ought to view the enslaved person, and its implementation is something for which he is willing to be patient. This is his "struggle," and it is fair to recognize his impatience as he sees the church realize his greater ideals.[43]

But perhaps with Moo it is important to recognize what Philemon is and is not. This letter is not attempting to address a major social evil in the Roman world. And, certainly, we must say clearly that slavery in the Roman era – or any era – was and is evil. Paul is writing about reconciliation and fellowship and how the realities of the gospel should affect how people participate in the communities to which they belong.[44]

---

[42] So P. Head, "Onesimus the Letter Carrier and the Initial Reception of Paul's Letter to Philemon," *JTS* 71.2 (2020) 628–656; C. Green, "Paul's Letter to Philemon: Manumission or What?" *JGRChJ* 19 (2022) 96–112.

[43] Barclay, "Paul, Philemon," 185.

[44] Moo, *Colossians*, 378; Wright, *Colossians*, 170; N. Gupta, "Cruciform Onesimus? Considering How a Slave Would Respond to Paul's Cross-Shaped Lifestyle," *ExpT* 133.8 (2022) 325–333.

Bringing together a slave and his master undoubtedly tested those realities to their utmost and brought the gospel itself up against some of the strongest legal and cultural norms in Rome.

But perhaps we need to take this one step further. In this letter, Paul is not simply thinking about two men – one free and one enslaved – who can discover reconciliation. Paul is imagining – and this is true in all of his letters – a new kingdom reality that will shift everything about how we view ourselves in relation to God and how we live together as a community. There is an incendiary thought in this letter that echoes the same challenge we found in Colossians: *In Christ, something new has emerged in the world.* And proof of our attachment to Christ will be shown in how we live into difficult decisions not unlike that of Philemon and Onesimus. Philemon is now to view Onesimus *as a brother* (Phlm 16), just as Paul views Philemon as a brother (Phlm 20). And it is left for them to work out this new reality in their own setting.

OUTLINE

There is minimal disagreement on Philemon's outline.[45] The letter is simple and follows a format that is paralleled in other persuasive letters from the period. The body of the letter is in vv.8–20 (or v.21). As we have seen, the letter is likely Paul's appeal on behalf of the slave Onesimus, who may have come to Paul looking for an advocate who was a friend of his master (*amicus domini*). Such letters of mediation were well-known in Roman society, and parallels exist. If this is true for Philemon, its entire focus is on its fourteen or fifteen verses making an argument for Onesimus' return.

- A Preliminary Greeting, 1–3
- Thanksgiving and Prayers, 4–7

---

[45] See F. F. Church, "Rhetorical Structure and Design in Paul's Letter to Philemon," *HTR* 71 (1978) 17–33; G. J. Steyn, "Some Figures of Style in the Epistle of Philemon: Their Contribution towards the Persuasive Nature of the Epistle," *EkkPhar* 77 (1995) 64–80; Barth and Blanke, *Philemon*, 119–121; Witherington, *Philemon, Colossians, and Ephesians*, 51–97; and J. Weima, "Paul's Persuasive Prose: An Epistolary Analysis of the Letter to Philemon," in D. F. Tolmie, ed., *Philemon in Perspective: Interpreting a Pauline Letter* (Berlin: DeGruyter, 2010), 29–60.

- Paul's Request on Behalf of Onesimus, 8–20
- Personal Request along with Closing Greetings, 21–25[46]

Witherington prefers the formal rhetorical structures of Roman letters and gives us the following organization:[47]

- Prescript and Greeting, 1–3
- *Exordium:* Opening Thanksgiving Prayer, 4–7
- *Propositio:* An Appeal in and on the Basis of Love, 8–11
- *Probatio:* The Rationale for the Return, 12–16
- *Peroratio*, Personal Appeals, 17–21
  ○ Welcome and Repayment, 17–19
  ○ Final Plea for Benefit, Refreshment, Obedience, 20–21
- Travel Plans, 22
- Final Greetings, Benediction, 23–25

There seems little doubt that the letter is "cleverly crafted,"[48] but this should mean that it has a rhetorical strategy. It is persuasive. But it is also assuming cultural leverage in a manner that would be typical of a shame/honor society. Paul uses honoring speech for Philemon and presents his request as an opportunity for honor-gaining generosity. Onesimus is Paul's fictive "son" (v.10) who has been a burden-relieving help to Paul, and to deny Paul this request would be to make Paul's imprisonment that much harder. Still, Philemon is in control – he can grant this or not – but one wonders how much genuine agency he actually has. Once this letter is known in the church, Philemon – whom Paul describes as partner, debtor, and brother – would feel the weight of Paul's persuasive pressure. Paul has opened a door for Philemon to walk through, and on the other side of it Philemon would be honored and celebrated as contributing to Paul's mission by sending his "brother/slave" back to Paul.

A recent suggestion offers that Philemon is not just persuasive rhetoric but that it shares features with a "promissory note" (or cheirograph, *cheirographon*).[49] Elder has provided numerous examples of these and

---

[46] Weima, "Paul's Persuasive Prose," uses a different organization: 1–3, 4–7, 8–18, 19–25.
[47] Witherington, *Philemon, Colossians, and Ephesians*, 19, and throughout his commentary.
[48] Ibid., 29.
[49] N. A. Elder, "This Hand Is Validation: Philemon as a Pauline Holograph," *NTS* 70 (2024) 324–339.

has located a model that a scribe could complete like a template.[50] These cheirographs often point to the illiteracy of the scribe's client, but, even more, they included some original handwriting (*cheir* means hand) from the client to validate the document. This functioned as a signature. P.Oxy. 49.3487 shows the scribal lines clearly interrupted by an awkward line handwritten by the client.[51]

However, even if Philemon is not a proper cheirograph, still it offers suggestive parallels. Paul may not refer to an autograph (*idiographos*, cf. Col 4:18) as was common, but still in v.19 he comes close: *I Paul wrote this with my own hand: I will repay it.* To write "with my own hand" (*cheir*) means that Paul is inserting a personal pledge, holding the pen now, promising reimbursement. That Paul is aware of promissory notes is evident from Col 2:14: *God canceled the cheirograph and its demands that stood against us.* And Paul's use of debt in Phlm 19 suggests that a debt is what Philemon holds over Onesimus and that Paul will take it up.

In these writings about debit and promise, some handwriting was expected. But, in addition, we have numerous examples in which handwriting was the preferred mode of correspondence between persons. Evidence shows that first drafts were generally handwritten, but, even more, when the communication was private or personal, more handwriting was desired. People wanted to see this personal handwriting not only as validating but as a personal connection with the author. We might compare this to a modern email versus a personally written card. Cicero, for instance, wrote hundreds of letters *in his own hand* to Atticus and never dictated a letter until he was fifty.[52]

All of which leads to an interesting suggestion. All of Philemon may have been written in Paul's own hand, which is why he does not refer to his

---

[50] From P.Oxy. 33.3677 (Elder, "This Hand Is Validation," 326):
      Someone, son of someone (*tis tinos, tous tinos*), son of someone whose mother is someone from somewhere. To someone, son of someone, son of someone whose mother is someone from somewhere, greetings! (*tini tinos tou tinos mētros tinos pothen, chairein!*) I admit to having received from you through a hand in the registry such-and-such money which totals such-and-such amount which I shall repay to you as soon as you should make a request. ... The hand, which is mine – the autograph (*idiographos*) of so-and-so – written twice over is a validation of receipt in whatever place it might be brought and to anyone you might bring it.
[51] Ibid., 330.
[52] Ibid., 335.

autograph: The *entire letter* is in his hand. If Paul is alluding to cheirographs and their genre, "then writing the entire letter to Philemon in Paul's
own hand would have afforded the maximum rhetorical impact."[53] This
means that Philemon would not be surprised by receiving a handwritten
letter, and it would set apart this letter as unique in the Pauline canon.

---

[53] Ibid., 339.

IV Commentary on Philemon

1 Paul, a prisoner of Christ Jesus, and Timothy our brother. To our beloved coworker Philemon,

2 to our sister Apphia, to our fellow soldier Archippus, and to the church in your house:

3 Grace to you and peace from God our Father and the Lord Jesus Christ.

There are differences between the opening of Philemon and Paul's other letters. As was customary, Paul provides his own name as the sender (on *Paulos*, see Col 1:1), but in his other, more formal letters he describes himself authoritatively as Paul *an apostle*. The absence of his usual title here perhaps signals the informality or intimacy that he is using, since he is writing to an old acquaintance.[1] Paul is not writing to Philemon leveraging his apostolic influence, at least not overtly; he is sharing with him a concern, about which Paul is offering a solution.

When Paul describes himself as a prisoner (1) he is not speaking at first as if this were a metaphor for discipleship. Paul was actually imprisoned, awaiting trial, following his two-year captivity in Caesarea (see Col 4:3–4, 10, 18). But there is also a sense that this means more than merely a man in jail. He is a prisoner "of Christ Jesus" (Eph 3:1; 4:1; Phlm 1, 9, 23). During a later imprisonment he can say, "Do not be ashamed, then, of the testimony about our Lord or of me his prisoner" (2Tim 1:8). In what sense is Paul "his" (Jesus') prisoner? Paul was a prisoner of Rome, and yet he sees

---

[1] In 1 Timothy and 2 Timothy, letters that a partially personal, Paul uses his title. In Titus 1:1, Paul writes, "Paul, a servant of God, and apostle of Jesus Christ."

himself as united with Christ, who also was a prisoner, and here he shares Jesus' prisoner status while he sits in Rome. Both Aristarchus (Col 4:10) and Epaphras (Phlm 23) are named prisoners, but while they are not formally incarcerated like Paul, still they share in this identity-jeopardy by standing with Paul (and Jesus) in close proximity to imprisonment.

But arrest and imprisonment were not uncommon in Paul's life. Paul routinely met hostility during his first tour (Acts 13:50; 14:19), his second (Acts 16:22–24), his third (Acts 20:3), and his final trip to Jerusalem (Acts 23:12). In some cases it resulted in imprisonment. In Philippi he was imprisoned after being beaten (Acts 16:22), and after a riot in Jerusalem he spent two years in the Roman military prison at Caesarea (Acts 23:23–35). There is also the likelihood that his lengthy stay in Ephesus was an imprisonment (1Cor 15:32; Acts 18:11). In Ephesus Paul tells the Corinthians about his many imprisonments (2Cor 11:23), and this may explain the "fighting wild beasts in Ephesus" (1Cor 15:32; 2Cor 1:8).

Box 4.1 A Closer Look: Paul's Accommodations in Rome

In Chapter I and at Col 4:3–4 we surveyed the possibilities for Paul's imprisonment and his experiences in Rome.[2] The fact that he was under "free custody" and likely had rented an apartment in Rome gives us some hint as to the Roman confidence in his prospects for release and how little threat he posed. Not unlike major modern cities, Rome was extremely expensive. Only the wealthy few could rent a private house, while the majority of Rome's residents lived in multistory apartment blocks (*insulae*) throughout the city.[3] Ancient sources from fourth-century Rome indicate that there were about 45,000–46,000 *insulae* in the city. These were multiunit residential buildings often four stories high. Rome's port of Ostia has provided many examples of what these looked like, and they may have been built using Rome as its model.[4] These buildings imitated the Roman atrium and provided an open courtyard at the center as a public space. Still, many of these buildings in poorer areas were small, dark, cheaply built, and subject to fire.[5] Nevertheless, Paul was helped by fellow believers in Rome (Acts 28:17, 23, 30), who no doubt found a safer, more accommodating setting. That he was receiving visitors in Rome also indicates

---

[2] For a full survey, sce B. Rapske, *Paul in Roman Custody*, volume 3 in the series The Book of Acts in Its First Century Setting, ed. B. Winter (Grand Rapids: Eerdmans, 1994).
[3] J. E. Packer, "Housing and Population in Imperial Ostia and Rome," *JRS* 57 (1967) 83.
[4] Ibid., 83–84.
[5] See Rapske, *Paul in Roman Custody*, 228–236 for a discussion of apartment life in Rome in the first century CE.

the quality of his rooms. Like many such *insulae*, the courtyard may well have supplied him with water, a public bath, and places for cooking. Much of life was lived outdoors, as Packer writes: "The typical Roman citizen of Rome must have lived almost entirely outside his apartment, in the streets, shops arcades, arenas, and baths of the city. The average Roman domicile must have served only as a place to sleep and store possessions."[6]

We also have to keep in mind that Paul was under guard. In severe conditions this could have meant he was chained or manacled. But this seems unlikely given the low threat of his case. Still, we have to imagine a Roman soldier at the premises at all times. Paul does say to his readers to "remember my chains" (*desmos*), but this was frequently used as a metaphor for imprisonment (Col 1:24; Eph 3:1; Phlm 9).

Timothy had become one of Paul's closest companions, and even now, in this major imprisonment, he is with him in Rome (on Timothy, see Col 1:1). In this personal letter Timothy is included no doubt because he was known to the Ephesians thanks to Paul's tours. And just as he did in Colossians, Paul describes Timothy as "our brother." The pronoun "our" implies that Paul is drawing a familial circle that Philemon should recognize. Not only is Timothy a part of it, but Philemon is too (vv.7, 20). Apphia is a sister (v.2), and here will be the surprise: Onesimus is a brother as well (v.16). Paul somewhat surprisingly names himself a "father" (v.10). This is one of Paul's most endearing titles for his coworkers. Therefore, Paul has set a rhetorical stage: Onesimus is not a problem about whom Philemon must be confronted. These followers of Jesus belong to the same family of Christ, and something must be sorted among them.

It is hard to match the honoring titles given to Philemon, the letter's recipient. He is a coworker (*synergos*), which was a common name Paul used for his colleagues: Prisca, Aquila, Urbanus, Apollos, Timothy, Silvanus, Titus, Epaphroditus, Euodia, Syntyche, Clement, Aristarchus, Mark, Jesus Justus, Demas, and Luke. This is an esteemed group, and Paul is listing Philemon among them. But, even more, Philemon is a *beloved* coworker (*agapētos*), elevating him above many. Paul uses *beloved* frequently (twenty-seven times) to describes churches he admires (Rom

---

[6]   Packer, "Housing and Population in Imperial Ostia and Rome," 87.

1:7), friends (like the "beloved Persis," Rom 16:12), or groups generally (Phil 2:12). Timothy is his beloved and trustworthy child (1Cor 14:7). Therefore, Philemon has been placed within Paul's innermost circle, not merely as a coworker but as someone valued and ranked alongside his dearest friends. It is not wrong to imagine that Paul is already beginning to use persuasive language in the letter. When a request comes from someone who has given this level of honor, it is difficult to say no.

Apphia (v.2) is likewise honored (our "sister"). Apphia (also spelled Aphphia or Aphia in other Greek writing) was an extremely common Roman name for a woman,[7] appearing in numerous inscriptions in Phrygia, suggesting that it may have been uniquely Phrygian. A common inference is that she is the wife of Philemon, which means she would have known Onesimus well, particularly if he was a domestic slave. But we know little of her outside of what we read here in Philemon.

Archippus has been sometimes deemed the son of Philemon and Apphia, but this is only legendary. An enigma appears in Col 4:17, where Paul writes, "And say to Archippus, 'See that you complete the task (*diakonia*) that you have received in the Lord.'" The use of *diakonia* could simply be general, but to some it implies a formal ministry he held. Once Colossians was circulated in the house church of the city, we can imagine enormous public curiosity helped Archippus complete this task (whatever it was). Before Paul mentions Archiuppus' task in Col 4:17, he greets the church in Laodicea, which was near Colossae. This leads to a natural question about his location. Was Archippus located in Laodicea or Colossae? But we cannot be certain.

Archippus is honored as a "fellow soldier" (*systratiōtēs*). This title is unusual for Paul and only occurs elsewhere in Phil 2:25 for Epaphroditus, "my brother and coworker, and fellow soldier." That he is not named a coworker likely indicates he was not in Paul's innermost circle but nevertheless possessed a voice and presence that contributed to the advance of the gospel in the Lycus Valley. Tales abound about his relationship to Apphia and Philemon, his martyrdom, and his role as bishop of Colossae, but these are legendary.[8]

---

[7] See Lightfoot, *Colossians*, 306–308, for references. The corresponding male name is Apphianos.

[8] Ibid., 308–310, lists them all and provides sources.

We can list the addressees by the dative nouns in vv.1–2: Philemon, Apphia, and Archippus. The fourth and final is the church itself, "to the church in your house." Here the possessive pronoun *his* does not refer to Archippus, whose name is adjacent grammatically, but back to Philemon, who heads the list. Some translators clarify this using a parenthetical phrase: *To Philemon and the church in your home – as well as to our sister Apphia and our fellow soldier Archippus.*

The church (*ekklēsia*) refers to the gathering of Christ's followers and takes its name from the Greek assemblies in cities known throughout the Hellenistic world. But as an assembly gathered in the name of Christ (and usually in a home) it was the unique platform in which the new reality of this Messianic kingdom would be realized. No doubt the early Christians found in their Jewish neighbors a form they could imitate: a place of scripture study, preaching, worship with song, and fellowship. But it was this latter reality that set it apart. These communities enacted revolutionary values that courageously disregarded the commonplace divisions in Roman society. They were inclusive, which meant that social class, gender, and ethnicity could not be leveraged for status.

Box 4.2 A Closer Look: Excavating the Earliest Known House Church

The NT frequently refers to Christian gatherings in homes, as we see here in Phlm 2. In Acts 12:12 Mary's home (mother of John Mark) is such a gathering place in Jerusalem. In Acts 21:7 Philip in Caesarea offers the same meeting place, as well as Mnason from Cyprus (Acts 21:15). Prisca and Aquila were house church hosts in Ephesus (1Cor 16:19), as well as in Rome (Rom 16:5). In Col 4:15 we meet Nympha, who used her house as a church. Chloe in Corinth (1Cor 1:11), Lydia in Philippi (Acts 16:14–15, 40), and Phoebe in Cenchreae do this as well (Rom 16:1–2). In Roman society such domestic gatherings we generally hosted by women, as we see here (see Col 4:15).

Visitors to Capernaum today will see a basalt residential area just south of the fourth-century synagogue. The ruins at the site had been known for a century, but a full archaeological study began in the mid-twentieth century with an Italian excavation that uncovered a first-century CE basalt residential area. In these remains one house had been altered, and its main public room had been plastered not long after Jesus' death. The excavation debris no longer consisted of domestic artifacts (cups, bowls) but instead of large storage jars and lamps. These were signs of a communal gathering site that was sustained for 300 years. Later plastering revealed graffiti that was explicitly Christian. And on its topmost layer sat the remains of an octagonal church. Today some speculate that this may have been Peter's home in Galilee, which, thanks to his standing in the early church, became a gathering place.[9]

Recently, another even more compelling discovery has been found in Syria. Dura-Europos was an ancient border town built in about 300 BCE on an elevated plateau over the upper Euphrates River. Today it is in northern Syria. In antiquity it was often compared with Palmyra as a vital waystation for those traversing the desert from Mesopotamia to all points west. It was abandoned in about 255 CE following a Persian siege, and nothing was ever built over it – which is fortune for us, since today it is relatively undisturbed.

In the first century CE the city was a fortified outpost held by Roman soldiers watching the eastern borders. In addition to numerous Roman temples, a synagogue has been found, complete with a Torah shrine. The synagogue was on the city's perimeter and was backfilled with soil to strengthen the city's walls during the Persian siege. Beneath this soil archaeologists discovered the earliest Jewish frescos depicting Jewish life, which are unparalleled anywhere else in the world. Today these frescoes have been moved to the National Museum of Damascus and are available for the public to view.

But recently an excavated residence in the city has revealed an ancient house church. Here too the building had been infilled with soil to strengthen the city's walls during the Persian siege, and this is to our good fortune because so much has been preserved. A hall in the building was a residence until it was replastered and used as a worship space. A nearby room held a baptistry. Its frescoes are likely the earliest Christian drawings in existence. Paintings of Jesus as the good shepherd and Peter walking on water are the earliest pictures of Jesus ever discovered.[10]

---

[9] For an early excavation summary of Capernaum, see R. North, "Discoveries at Capernaum," *Biblica* 58.3 (1977) 424–431; a current summary is at: "The House of Peter: The Home of Jesus in Capernaum?" *Biblical Archaeology Society*, October 10, 2024, www.biblicalarchaeology.org. Today the Catholic church has built a large sanctuary directly over this residential quarter, and at its center a glass window in the floor provides views of the house and octagonal church below.

[10] An excellent summary, complete with photos and a layout of the building, is a www .earlychurchhistory.org. See also N. Steinmeyer, "Is This the World's Oldest House Church in Dura Europas?" *Biblical Archaeology Society*, August 16, 2024, www .biblicalarchaeology.org. David Pettegrew provided a summary of research at the Society of Biblical Literature annual meeting in 2024, "Reimagining the Roman Empire's Earliest Christian Buildings: The Case of the Domestic Church at Dura-Europas."

Here we see Paul's strategy for resolving this matter on behalf of Onesimus. He could have made it a purely personal matter between him and Philemon, in which case the letter may have never survived and Philemon could have tucked it away in private. But Paul has enlisted other mature Christ-followers (coworkers, fellow soldiers), who could offer wisdom for this delicate problem and, if needed, provide accountability should Philemon chose to ignore Paul's request. Timothy, Apphia, and Archippus were each now a part of this story, and we can imagine – how we covet such a report! – that Apphia or Philemon wrote back to Paul describing the outcome.

Paul's formal greeting (v.3) is typical of his letters. In Col 1:2 it is abbreviated, but here he includes "and our Lord Jesus Christ." As we saw in Colossians, a common greeting among Greek speakers used some form of *chairein*, which meant "Rejoice!" or "Hail!" or "Welcome!"[11] Here Paul is adapting this greeting with a related noun *charis*, which meant "grace" and was foremost in Paul's theological vocabulary. The usual Jewish greeting was "peace" (Hebrew *shalom*). Paul then is using a hybrid greeting that recognized a feature from both cultures, and this would become his signature greeting whenever he wrote. See further on this in Col 1:2.

Is Paul setting the stage for what is to come? This letter is an overture to Philemon, seeking a revitalized understanding of the slave Onesimus. Therefore, Paul is placing this letter in a theologically significant context. His subject will not be something secular and transactional; nor will it cover the legal ramifications of Onesimus' departure. Instead, he wants this conversation – and almost all of his conversations – to be shaped by a setting infused with something unique: grace and peace. Grace points to the generous forgiveness – the gift of grace – demonstrated to us in Christ. Peace points to the result of that grace: reconciliation, goodwill, and generosity that comes only from God (Rom 5:1).

This greeting and this blessing of peace come from not only *God our Father* but equally from *the Lord Jesus Christ*. It would be easy to read this quickly and not pause to note how Paul is aligning Jesus Christ with God himself as the twin sources of the grace and peace he describes. This is a Christological affirmation casually included in the letter. Clearly by this

---

[11] Greek writers could also use *aspazomai*, which meant "Greeting!" as well. Paul uses this in Col 4:10, 12, 14, 15.

time Christians had developed a robust understanding of Jesus' place with God as *the Lord* – a title usually reserved for God. While no ontological union is implied, still we are here on the threshold of theological conclusions that will later take form in major church councils.

THANKSGIVING AND PRAYERS, 4–7

4 I thank my God always when I mention you in my prayers,
5 because I hear of your love for all the saints and your faith toward the Lord Jesus.
6 I pray that the partnership of your faith may become effective as you comprehend all the good that we share in Christ.
7 I have indeed received much joy and encouragement from your love, because the hearts of the saints have been refreshed through you, my brother.

Opening a letter with a prayer of gratitude and blessing was not only an expected courtesy in Roman letter-writing, but Paul crafted his own distinctive style in doing this. He likes to give thanks to God, to refer to his own prayers on the recipient's behalf, and to commend them for their expressions of faith and love (see Rom 1:8–9; 1Cor 1:4; Phil 1:3–4; Col 1:3–4; 1Thess 1:2–3; 2Thess 1:3).[12] If we compare this prayer to Colossians we can see that it is very similar, but this is not surprising when we remember that the letters were penned at the same time.

Paul describes how his prayers (v.4) are filled with thanksgiving. This opening is the same as that we find in other letters: Romans, Colossians, Philippians, and Ephesians. Here he refers to "my God," but this does not imply that his God is one apart from anyone else; this simply heightens the personal character of his expression. Note also that the verb (*eucharisteō*, give thanks) is singular. This indicates that while Timothy is together with Paul, still it is Paul primarily who is writing this to Philemon, and Timothy's role is secondary. The setting of this thanksgiving is whenever Paul prays, because he mentions Philemon by name when he prays. This signals at the beginning that Philemon is not a

---

[12]   However, note the striking absence of this prayer and blessing in Galatians, a letter filled with contention and concern.

remote name or casual acquaintance that Onesimus has now brought back to Paul's mind. Paul is aware of Philemon, he thinks about him, and he cares enough that, separately from Onesimus, Philemon holds a place in Paul's prayers.

Paul is keenly aware of those who are within his circle of concern and who are allies in the cause of his mission. His greetings that both begin and particularly end his letters indicate that he is intentional about knowing the names of his community. Perhaps he made lists, but at least it means that he knows who is working for Christ with him, he knows their context, and daily in his prayers he names them. The effect of this on Paul must have been significant. He is not alone despite the dangers surrounding him. He belongs to a community of faithful who are (we can infer) praying for Paul with equal fervor.

The twin virtues of love and faith (v.5) echo what Paul wrote in Colossians (1:4) about the larger church, but here Paul describes how these belong particularly to Philemon. Paul writes in the present tense (*hearing about your love* ...), and this should remind us that he is in active communication with the Christian communities he had planted during his journeys. They are writing to each other; their leaders know each other; they share news through correspondence.[13] But in this case news of Philemon and his role in the church likely came from Epaphras, the Colossian who is with Paul (Col 4:12), or Onesimus himself.

The love and faith Paul is hearing about are the basis of Paul's thanksgiving.[14] The sentence in Greek can be read as a chiasm thus:[15]

> (a) hearing about your love
>> (b) and faith,
>> (b') that is, (your faith) in the Lord Jesus Christ
> (a') and (your love) for all the saints.

---

[13]   Dunn, *Colossians*, 317, citing O'Brien, *Colossians*, 277.
[14]   The verb is found in v.4 and in v.5 we find two participles that complete his thought.
[15]   Harris, *Colossians*, 215, shows three ways that the syntax can be construed but supports the chiastic reading along with the NRSV, TNIV, and an array of scholars. The alternative is to see love and faith directed to *both* Jesus Christ and the saints: *for your love and faith which you hold for both the Lord Jesus Christ and the saints.* So NJB, NAB², Dunn, *Colossians*, 317–318. Or faith alone finds a double object: *for your love and for your faith which you have toward the Lord Jesus Christ and all the saints.* So RSV, NASB².

These ideas find more expression in the verses that follow. Faith does not simply mean that Philemon has saving trust in Jesus; faith (*pistis*) can also be a universal noun referring to "*the* faith," or perhaps "faithfulness" or "loyalty" – that is, fidelity to the apostolic teaching that had been given through Paul.[16] This is the basis of Paul's celebration: He knows that Philemon has not lost what has been given to him, that the grounding he was taught – expressed again in his letter to the Colossians – still belonged to Philemon. This man and the church that he hosts have not abandoned the *ekklēsia* of Christ, as some have done when they listened to the false teachers in Colossae.

Love is likewise prominent for Paul. A great deal should not be made of Paul's use of *agapē* in v.5 as if it bore some distinctive theological meaning. *Agapē* and *philia* shared similar meanings in the Hellenistic period, and we only have warrant to distinguish them when an author expressly does so.[17] But we can certainly affirm that love is central to how Christians conduct themselves both in the world and among themselves. This is central to Jesus' teaching (Mark 12:28–33; John 13:34–35), as well as to that of Paul (Gal 5:6; Rom 13:10; 1Cor 13; Eph 5:2, etc.).

But faith and love are clearly the twin virtues of the Christian life. Faith and love are often connected in Paul. In Gal 5:6 Paul demotes theological orthodoxy that is void of love: "For in Christ Jesus neither circumcision nor uncircumcision counts for anything; the only thing that counts is faith working through love." The ideal synthesis-of-the-heart is the union of stable faith focused on Christ and a love for Christ's people (*the saints*, see Col 1:4). Together these balance the affections of the heart with the theological convictions of the mind, which, when unbalanced, lead to a disordered spiritual life.

Box 4.3 Bridging the Divide: Loving the Saints

Two ideas in v.5 should make us pause. First, Paul has this remarkable expectation that followers of Christ should simply love *other Christians*. More generally, they should love the church. In this letter he is giving thanks to God because he sees this

---

[16]   Bruce, *Colossians*, 209. Paul is unusual in using *pros* in relation to faith when we might expect *eis*. Both can carry similar meanings of *for* or *to*, and since Paul uses *eis* for "the saints," this may simply be a case of stylistic variation.

[17]   McKnight, *Philemon*, 67; TDNT 1:37–38.

love (along with faith in Christ) in the life of Philemon (see similarly Col 1:4). This slave owner had not lost the capacity to love others who lie beyond the usual circle of those whom Philemon would naturally love. And this reflex – this capacity to love – should include Onesimus.

Such love seems foreign in our time. When we navigate the world and its many differences and tensions, imagine if we were committed to loving fellow believers wherever we found them. Would this include Russia? China? Palestine? Would this love cross internal political divides in our own communities? When we visit countries that are majority Muslim, Jewish, or Hindu, finding brothers and sisters who celebrate Jesus should be cause for celebration. I have two pastor/theologian friends, one of whom is Ukrainian and the other is Russian. Our conversations transcend the politics of their countries' war. If they could only travel between Kyiv and Saint Petersburg, I know they would find immediate friendship.

Second, Paul makes use of an unusual term for the object of this love: *He rejoices because Philemon loves "the saints."* The term here is *hagios* (plural *hagioi*). This is a noble word in Greek that we often translate as "saints," but it does not refer to perfection. From its Hebrew use it refers to separation – but not an elitist detachment. It could easily mean dedication.[18] That is, it refers to "separation from" but also "attachment to" or "dedicated for." "The saint is someone dedicated to God and, because of that dedication and consequent proximity to God's presence, separated from common (worldly) usage."[19]

This is a remarkable and difficult idea. And if loving our enemies seems a stretch, simply loving our churches and the people who worship and serve in them may be a place to start. Loving our pastors should also fall under this expectation. This year (2025) I was asked to speak via Zoom to a church in Pakistan. And as I met them I thought: How miraculous is this? Our lives could not be more different: I live in the affluent West; they live in a poor neighborhood of Lahore. And yet we share something in common: our faith in Jesus – and our commitment to love one another.

Paul's commendation of Philemon here is likely setting the stage for Paul's request. If Philemon loves *all (pantas) the saints* as Paul affirms, then this means that whoever belongs to Christ – whoever is living within the church – should be the object of this love. We have already seen in Col 3:11 how Paul imagines the church to be a Messianic community with no boundaries that separate those with privilege from those without.

---

[18] McKnight, *Philemon*, 67.
[19] Ibid., 68.

Onesimus, as a believer, is thus one of those whom Philemon ought to love. Philemon's grounding in the gospel and his generous love for those who share his faith now present him with a remarkable conundrum. Philemon is bound to an ethic of love if he is one with Christ and faithful to his teaching. *He loves all the saints.* And Onesimus is a saint (on *hagios* see Col 1:2, 4).

Partnership (*koinōnia*) in faith (v.**6**) is what Paul and Philemon share. They are not simply two people who have discovered they share the same convictions. There is a relationship between the two men that has been formed by that faith. They have a unity, yes, but they also share a mission – partners in a task – which is how they should view each other. The meaning of the sentence can be difficult in Greek because it is actually a clause looking for a verb.[20] This is not an error on Paul's part. Greek can suspend such clauses, and the reader is expected to reach back and know how it is connected to the main thread in the sentence. Most translations supply this verb from v.4, which the NRSV does (*I pray that . . .*) and starts a new sentence.[21] This is helpful and appropriate. The clause in v.6 then provides an explanation for the deeper purposes of Paul's prayer. His prayers are celebratory, to be sure (v.4, *I thank my God always . . .*), and v.5 provides the basis of this celebration (*because I hear . . .*). But his prayers also are purposeful. And this presents another hurdle when we read "*partnership (koinōnia) of your faith*": What does Paul mean?

Most readers are familiar with *koinonia*, but it has a range of meanings: fellowship, community, something shared, partnership, or something in common. The common thread in each of these is that Paul and Philemon have a shared, unifying experience in their commitment to the gospel and that shared experience is a partnership: Theirs is a joint effort in their mutual service to Christ. We might say that there is reciprocity or harmony between their interests because they both are devoted to "the faith" – that is, to Christ.

But Paul looks to this partnership to mature and become "effective" (*energēs*, also 1Cor 6:9; Heb 4:12). This can just as easily refer to something

---

[20] Wilson, *Colossians*, 338, cites Moule (*Philemon*, 142) that this is "notoriously the most obscure verse in the letter."

[21] The sentence beings with a conjunction (*hopōs*), which indicates purpose when followed by the subjunctive that we have (*genētai*). But the entire clause depends on a verb that needs to be supplied, likely from v.4.

active or potent (from *ergon*, work) – that this partnership they share will comprehend not simply the truth of the gospel (*in Christ*) but will also comprehend all of the good that springs from what we find in that gospel. Here is where things begin to become clear. Paul's prayer is not just a celebration but also a desire to see in their partnership the knowledge of goodness arise: all goodness, goodness that is beyond our human imaginations – goodness that alone belongs to Christ. We can see this line of thought most clearly in outline:

(1) I thank God whenever I pray (v.4).
   o *Why?* Because I hear about your love and faith.
   o *Love* for the saints; *faith* toward the Lord Jesus (v.5).
(2) I am praying.
   o *Purpose: So that* our partnership in the faith together will become effective
   o as you comprehend all good things that come to us[22] in Christ (v.6).

Paul is praying so that Philemon's comprehension of all that is good – all that Christ provides to us in our communities – will be transformative and that he will seek the good as he seeks Christ. Of course, we can see in this Paul's desire to prepare Philemon for what is to come. Not only will Onesimus be listed among the saints (v.5), whom Philemon loves, but now Paul asks what goodness can flow from the gospel. News about Onesimus is actually *good news* to be celebrated, not news that inspires anger and frustration. The question is simply: *How will Philemon welcome Onesimus?* Does Philemon understand what it means to live in a Christ-centered fellowship that brings to life all the goodness that it can? At the end of the letter, Paul taps into this fellowship-with-obligations by asking Philemon to prepare a room for him (i.e., Paul). This would be a natural welcome for the apostle. Can Philemon do the same for this slave when he arrives?

Love and faith (v.7) have been constant themes in these opening verses. For Paul they are undoubtedly the hallmarks of what it means to be a follower of Christ. They are foundational: Faith in Christ means knowing who he is and what he has done. This is the gospel. And love is the

---

[22]   A variant at the end of v.6 reads "in you" rather than "in us." See Wilson, *Colossians*, 338–339. Most follow Lightfoot and Metzger in retaining the first-person plural.

fundamental posture we have as we live in the world and in the church. These are echoes of Jesus' answer to a man who wants to distill his religious life down to principles. Jesus answers with a theological affirmation that encompasses more than the words represent ("You are to love God fully"). And he follows it with an ethical affirmation ("And love your neighbor as yourself"). These twin commitments represent "all the law and the prophets" (Deut 6:5; Lev 19:18; Mark 12:28–34; Luke 10:25–37; Matt 22:38).

However, in devoted religious communities orthodox belief is sometimes less difficult than love. The lawyer who questions Jesus in Luke 10:25–37 presses just this point. *How comprehensive is this demand to love?* Jesus' Parable of the Good Samaritan is his answer. Paul knows this difficulty and that the call to love *for Philemon* may reach beyond what he imagines. He knows that Onesimus is the Samaritan who also qualifies as a neighbor, which puts him in focus as one worthy of love.

Paul comes at this indirectly. He writes, "I have indeed received much joy and encouragement from your love." "The hearts of the saints have been refreshed through you." Paul uses the aorist tense (and the perfect), suggesting that he has in mind one gift of generosity from Philemon and that this is the source of this praise.[23] In other words, Philemon has a history of liberality when it comes to giving. And here we might easily conclude that it implies a monetary gift. These words also suggest that Philemon not only hosts the church of Colossae (v.2) but also has contributed generously to ministries beyond Colossae. He is a person of means.[24] But Paul is both reciting Philemon's generosity and indirectly implying what may still come. Paul is offering praise *in anticipation* of what he hopes to see. "You have brought me joy," which implies, "And now I hope to feel that joy again." He recites how the saints have been refreshed (v.7), and in v.20 he will ask the same refreshment for himself (*anapauō* in each case).

Joy (*chara*) and encouragement (*paraklēsis*) are the two emotions Paul connects with his memory of Philemon. Joy is linguistically related to grace (*charis*), and it "speaks of God's grace at work in believers who play their

---

[23] Caird, *Colossians*, 220.
[24] Bruce, *Colossians*, 210.

part in the story of God."[25] But it is striking that a man in prison – someone who has had a life of suffering for the gospel – could have this response in spite of his difficulties. This is because from Philemon he has also experienced *paraklēsis*. Encouragement describes the support someone gives that elevates someone in a difficult situation. Literally it refers to someone who comes alongside another or a summons to assist, particularly in a judicial setting. A *parakletos* is an advocate (Latin *advocatus*) in court or, informally, a helper. In the NT God is the source of this encouragement (2Thess 2:16; 2Cor 1:3–7; Rom 15:5), and so here in this letter Paul is acknowledging that, even now, Philemon's love has changed his life in his circumstances.

This is persuasive rhetoric that heaps obligation on Philemon because it celebrates who he has been and implies what he can still be: the source of joy and refreshment again for not only Paul but all believers ("saints"). Philemon is a brother, and Paul repeats this twice in the letter (vv.7, 20) to make it clear. But also he will say that Onesimus is a brother (v.16), and these ideas together will set up the major request Paul is holding for Philemon in vv.8–16.

PAUL'S REQUEST ON BEHALF OF ONESIMUS, 8–20

8 For this reason, though I am more than bold enough in Christ to command you to do the right thing,

9 yet I would rather appeal to you on the basis of love – and I, Paul, do this as an old man and now also as a prisoner of Christ Jesus.

10 I am appealing to you for my child, Onesimus, whose father I have become during my imprisonment.

11 Formerly he was useless to you, but now he is indeed useful to you and to me.

12 I am sending him, that is, my own heart, back to you.

13 I wanted to keep him with me so that he might minister to me in your place during my imprisonment for the gospel,

14 but I preferred to do nothing without your consent in order that your good deed might be voluntary and not something forced.

---

[25]   McKnight, *Philemon*, 73.

15 Perhaps this is the reason he was separated from you for a while, so that you might have him back for the long term,

16 no longer as a slave but more than a slave, a beloved brother – especially to me but how much more to you, both in the flesh and in the Lord.

17 So if you consider me your partner, welcome him as you would welcome me.

18 If he has wronged you in any way or owes you anything, charge that to me.

19 I, Paul, am writing this with my own hand: I will repay it. I say nothing about your owing me even your own self.

20 Yes, brother, let me have this benefit from you in the Lord! Refresh my heart in Christ.

When we read Phlm 7 we are at a transition that moves from Paul's formal prelude to the substance of his request (vv.**8–20**). But note initially Paul's approach. He acknowledges that, given his stature as an apostle, he could (theoretically) command Philemon's obedience (v.**8**). He has this sort of "boldness" that he possesses in Christ. He is a leader – an apostle, no less. And it might be true that he had a commanding personality. But this is exactly what he does not do. As Bruce notes, "This is not how one friend approaches another."[26] But we also have to imagine the undeclared (but very real) social position of Paul. He is poor and in prison (vv.**9**, **10**, **13**). Philemon is likely successful, wealthy, and hosting a church (v.**1**). Therefore, Paul's approach requires the utmost persuasive delicacy if he is to help Philemon do "what is required" (*anēkō*) at this moment. Paul wants Philemon to weigh this request and, using his own initiative, choose to complete it with honor (v.**14**).[27] But as Paul warms to his subject, he eventually reclaims his voice and speaks with increased boldness (vv.**20–21**).

Therefore, with rhetorical skill, in these verses Paul presents his request to Philemon, basing it not on his authority but on something more basic: love (v.**9**). He offers a summary of all the many ways Onesimus' story is

---

[26] Ibid., 211.

[27] For some scholars Paul's refusal to use boldness and to say that he is denying this approach is itself a means of gaining power, such as, "I could do *x* if I wanted to, but I won't in this case."

filled with the goodness he mentions in v.7: his conversion, his life with
Paul, his enormous service to him, and, as an aging man, how they have
become father and son (10). He builds this profile but leaves the more
negative features – the slave's escape, his debt – until later (vv.17–21).

Paul begins with "therefore" or "for this reason," a Greek conjunction
(*dio*) that not only marks off a new section in the letter but also is a signal
that the argument to follow is based on what went before. Given everything
Paul has said about the centrality of love and faith, given their mutual
pursuit of the goodness that can emerge from their partnered life under
Christ, and given how Philemon has a history of richly blessing the
believers both in Colossae and beyond, Paul now asks that this love be of
use again. Paul underscores his weaknesses: He is old now, and he is a
prisoner. He is powerless in more respects than Philemon may understand.
He cannot accomplish this one task that is dear to him, and so he can only
appeal to someone like Philemon who can lift a burden he cannot.
If Philemon is a man who understands and respects power, then Paul is
here declaring himself as a man on the margins of such things – which is
exactly where Onesimus is located. This slave is in jeopardy and powerless,
which parallels Paul's own position.

Paul is not trying to evoke pity nor is he being manipulative or coercive.
He is living out this combination of powerlessness and love that lives so
closely to the heart of the gospel. And perhaps this is the most meaningful
dimension of this part of Paul's letter. This is close to the meaning of a
cross-formed life ("cruciformity"). The life and death of Jesus drove home
to his followers an attitude toward power that was as countercultural then
as it is now. We have to imagine that the Jesus tradition preserved texts
such as Mark 8:31–38 because they were so arresting. Following Peter's bid
urging Jesus to forego the cross and retain the power belonging to the
Christ (8:29), Jesus' stern reply sets all traditional values on their head: "If
any wish to come after me, let them deny themselves and take up their
cross and follow me" (Mark 8:34; Matt 10:39; Luke 14:27; 17:33). He was
offering a cross-formed life that Paul was now living in prison in Rome.

Paul's direct appeal to Philemon now follows (v.10). Here for the first
time Paul spells out the name of the person in question – Onesimus. But he
does not lead with this name. His opening appeal refers to the slave as a
child (*teknon*) – a child with a father – and his name *as Philemon knew him*
only appears last. This placement arranges things in their order of

importance. Paul is subtly rearranging how Onesimus should be viewed. A literal Greek translation is: *I appeal to you concerning my child, whom I fathered in prison, Onesimus.*

That the appeal was for Onesimus hardly took Philemon by surprise. Onesimus helped deliver this letter and had presented himself to his former master![28] The name Onesimus was well-known in antiquity, particularly for slaves or freemen thanks to its meaning ("useful"; see the play on words in v.11).[29] When Paul deliberately uses child (*teknon*) rather than "son" (*huios*) he heightens the endearing quality of their relationship. Paul commonly refers to converts through his ministry as "my own child" (*tou emou teknou*), which also underscores the responsibility and devotion he feels as their spiritual father. He refers to Timothy as his *beloved child* (1Cor 4:14; cf. Phil 2:22; 1Tim 1:2, 18; 2Tim 1:2; 2:1) and the church of Galatia *my children* (Gal 4:19; also 1Thess 2:11).

But in this verse Paul does not refer to himself as Onesimus' father (*patēr*). Instead he uses a verb that means "begetting" (*gennaō*) when used by men, but when spoken by women it refers to giving birth. Therefore, Paul understands that he has indeed "birthed" Onesimus spiritually, which makes him more than a pastor/mentor – he became a father who felt love and protectiveness as any father would. Thus, Paul is less a *father with a son* (though he means this too) than one who brought to life a child who is now a child of God. And a feature of this story from Paul's perspective is that Onesimus' conversion transpired despite Paul's imprisonment in Rome (see Col 4:3–4 and Phlm 1).

The meaning of Onesimus' name ("useful") now is used in a clever pun (vv.11–12). *He was useless to you* (achrēstos*), now he is indeed useful* (euchrēstos) to both of us.*[30] The two adjectives are opposites, both using *chrēstos* (beneficial, helpful): one negating it (prefix: *a*-), giving us "useless"

---

[28] Dunn, *Colossians*, 328.
[29] Lightfoot, *Colossians*, 310, also shows how it appears in numerous inscriptions, and if a family once had a slave background, the name might be continued due to this legacy, especially in Asia Minor. In early Christian history a man named Onesimus was the bishop of Ephesus and is named by Ignatius in his letter to that city, *I.Ephesians*, 1:3; 2:1; 6:2. It is unlikely that our Onesimus and the one in this letter are the same man. Thanks to the letter to Philemon, the name must have been favored in families in the following century. Also BDAG 711.
[30] The article at the start of the sentence serves as a relative pronoun but modifies both adjectives.

or "unhelpful," and the second adding the prefix for "good" (*eu-*), giving us "very useful" or "serviceable." And here is the pun: Onesimus' name means "useful" or "profitable" (from *onēsis*). This useful slave who was once useless now is useful.

However, through his new life in Christ, Onesimus' value has broadened: He is not simply valuable because he is returning to his previous station serving Philemon's household. His value is wider. He now will be of good service to *both* Philemon and Paul. His value now is to the entire church, whose ministry Paul and Philemon both serve. This is the partnership of faith Paul mentioned in v.1. In other words, Philemon has shown his commitment to the church through hosting a congregation and supplying Paul with gifts (v.7). Philemon's community even sent an emissary and support named Epaphras (Col 1:8). Now Philemon can show his remarkable, celebrated generosity again. In an honor-centered culture, this is an ideal opportunity to gain honor.

But Onesimus' value goes beyond service (v.12). Writing about Onesimus and continuing from v.10, Paul continues: *whom I have sent back to you, him (emphatic), that is, my own heart.*[31] Dunn notes how Paul is showing that his reason for returning the slave was not about legal requirements. He is not performing his duties as a Roman citizen, nor is he reporting this slave to the authorities, which would have led to Onesimus' punishment. He is writing to a beloved Christian brother (vv.1, 7) about another believer, and he is convinced that this matter should be internal to the church. "Wrongs done among fellow believers had to be sorted out as among fellow believers (v.16; cf. 1Cor 6:1–8)."[32]

Paul's description of Onesimus' importance to him increases in intensity when he refers to the man as "my own heart." The noun here is *splagchna* (see v.7), which literally refers to "bowels or entrails" or, perhaps more closely, the abdomen, which Paul's world understood to be the seat of emotion and feeling. English correctly changes this to "heart," which conveys the same idea to us. But Philemon would recognize that Paul

---

[31]   Though the verse begins with a relative pronoun (antecedent, Onesimus), the relative clause is converted into a complete sentence by the NRSV. Scribes added to the verse to increase its clarity: *that is, my own heart whom you received* (proslabou). This phrase occurs in a variety of places. B. Metzger, *A Textual Commentary on the Greek New Testament* (New York: United Bible Society, 1971), 657–658.

[32]   Dunn, *Colossians*, 329.

has not said that Onesimus is essential to his work or vital to the church (though this may be true) – this is a highly personal, vulnerable reference to his personal feelings. Onesimus has won a place in Paul's heart. Genuine affection is involved. If Philemon loves Paul (v.5), he would hardly harm him by damaging someone whom Paul loves. But we also should imagine what this meant to Onesimus to hear such language from a man whom he likely admired deeply. Paul wrote this knowing Onesimus would hear it (or possibly would read it aloud). It is an admirable public display of love that we rarely see in Paul's formal letters. This language also contributes to the emotional context within which Philemon must make a decision. Already the outcome is weighted in favor of charity and compassion.

Box 4.4 Bridging the Divide: Men and the Language of Love

When we read Paul's letters, he is often engaged in a polemic contending with false teachers, drawing out important theological positions, or exhorting against the divisive behavior of church members. However, Philemon suggests that Paul had another side that we rarely discuss. He was not afraid to use the language of emotion. In 2 Corinthians he speaks openly about his pain and despair (1:1–2:13; 7:5–16).[33] And of course in 1Cor 13 he speaks eloquently about love in the abstract. A close reading of Philemon shows us something else.

Paul can speak openly about Philemon's love both for the church (v.5) and for him (v.7). But with Onesimus we see something more. He refers to Onesimus as his "child" (*teknon*) – not "son" – and this places a far more intimate frame around this relationship. Then he refers to himself as Onesimus' "father." Onesimus was not important to Paul because of his usefulness (v.11) but because a bond of affection had grown between them. He was sending his "own heart" (vv.7, 12) back to Philemon as he let go of Onesimus. The word "heart" here is *splagchna* (not *kardia*), and it refers to the seat of emotions or feelings in Hellenistic Greek. In the LXX it might be taken literally for the entrails of a sacrifice (2Macc 6:8 LXX), but chiefly it reflected the center of a person's emotional life (Prov 6:22; Sir 36:7 LXX). Onesimus is not just a brother; he is a beloved brother (*adelphon agapēton*, v.16).

This capacity to access emotion is not the usual profile we have for Paul. He was the debater, the scholar, the fighter for what was true and right. Above all he was the defender of the gospel. But this other dimension – this emotive feature of his life – should give us pause.

---

[33] L. L. Welborn, "Paul and Pain: Paul's Emotional Therapy in 2 Corinthians 1.1–2.13; 7.5–16 in the Context of Ancient Psychagogic Literature," *NTS* 57.4 (2011) 547–570.

I was socialized into a world where few emotions (other than anger) were permissible among boys and men. Psychologists will show – and I have seen it as well – that at young ages boys will demonstrate the same range of emotion as girls. For example, they will cry. But as we age, something happens: Emotions become unacceptable and unreachable. There is a potent socializing power that limits us. Paul can say that he and Philemon love each other. He loves Onesimus as well and holds him in a deep emotional place of affection.

Paul is comfortable with the language of love. This may have something to do with his culture. People from Middle Eastern cultures (both Jewish and Arab) are far more emotionally expressive than those from the West. And I find this enviable. Perhaps the highly rational Paul – the debater extraordinaire – has become a convenient fiction for us who elevate this one virtue over all the rest.

After introducing Onesimus at the end of v.10, Paul provides four relative pronouns that each describe this slave. Onesimus is someone (a) who has become like a child with Paul as his father (v.10); (b) who has now become deeply useful (v.11); (c) who is dear to Paul's own heart (v.12); (d) and now, is someone who could become a minister (*diakonos*) to Paul (v.13), someone who could stand in for Philemon during Paul's imprisonment for the gospel. This is the sum of Paul's argument. Onesimus is precious in so many ways that it would be unbearable to think of him returning to his life as a slave. Of course, this is also a strategy – usefulness and value – but in the end, this is Paul realizing his own commitment to seeing the gospel undermine slavery itself (Col 3:11). This approach by Paul has always been difficult for interpreters. Why does he not simply speak his mind about slavery, saying that it is wrong and it contradicts the deeper values of the kingdom? This is his dilemma. Paul avoided the danger of communicating that when a slave became a believer his owners – if they were Christians – were obligated to set slaves free. What would this mean on a larger social scale? How would the Roman authorities react? And if this mandate accompanied the gospel, how would it impede Romans coming to Christ? Instead, Paul chooses to erode slavery from the inside.

Some have wondered if the return of Onesimus spoke to other questions on Paul's mind. Was he thinking that he was vulnerable and in potential legal jeopardy? He has explicitly said that in his care Onesimus was converted to his religion and that now he would like to keep the slave "in his service." Roman law was clear that a person could be culpable of corrupting a slave, and particularly so if he encouraged him to remain as a runaway. In the sixth century, a compendium of Roman laws called the *Digesta* was published under Justinian I, who ruled as emperor from 527 to 565. Of course, this is centuries after Paul, but it may nevertheless reflect very old Roman legal beliefs. In one of its fifty volumes, the *Digesta* records rules regarding the corruption of a slave:

> But is the person liable only if he has driven an honest slave to wrong-doing, or is he also liable if he has given a bad slave encouragement or shown him how he could commit an offense? The better view is that he is also liable if he has shown a bad slave how he could commit an offense. Indeed, even if the slave would have run away of committed the theft anyway, if the person gave his approval to the slave's intention, he is liable; for wickedness ought not to be increased by the approval of others. So whether one makes a good slave bad or a bad slave more so, one is held to have made him worse.[34]

The decision to return Onesimus to his master might well have covered Paul's liability. He would then let the later decision unfold at Philemon's discretion. But we have to be clear: Paul's motives should not be reduced to self-protection. Paul is sending Onesimus back not due to legal issues but because of Onesimus' new status as a follower of Christ who now belongs to the church.[35]

If Onesimus returns to Paul and serves as a *diakonos* (NRSV: minister), it is unclear what service he would provide. For most interpreters this is service of a more personal nature ("ministry *to me*"), which reminds us that the word's most common use was for waiting on tables (Acts 6:2) or deeds of private care (Mark 1:31; 1Cor 16:5). Possibly a parallel here is Epaphroditus, whom the Philippians had sent to Rome with a gift, and he remained to minister to Paul's needs (Phil 2:25–30). Others wonder if Paul means more than this.[36] *Diakonos* can also refer to *serving the gospel* as well (Col 1:7; 4:7; 2Cor 11:23), and if so this means that Onesimus is needed in the work of advancing the gospel itself.[37] This would put him in

---

[34] Cited in McKnight, *Philemon*, 91; translation from A. Watson, *The Digest of Justinian*, 4 vols. (Philadelphia: University of Pennsylvania Press, 1985); Garland, *Colossians*, 332.
[35] Dunn, *Colossians*, 329.
[36] Moo, *Colossians*, 414; Beale, *Colossians*, thinks the meaning is ambiguous.
[37] McKnight, *Philemon*, 92.

league with Paul's many other fellow workers, among whom Philemon was listed (v.1).

When Paul reminds Philemon that he is in "chains" (*desmos*) or imprisoned, he is leveraging even more persuasion. Paul's circumstances were more compromised than Philemon's. If having Onesimus was about meeting needs, it would be hard to miss who needs this help more. By this point Philemon's decision about the slave seems to be determined. With the Colossian church knowing these things about Onesimus, Philemon's decision now seems like a foregone conclusion. How could Philemon decide otherwise without breaking all relationship with Paul?

But while Paul has expressed his desires for Onesimus (vv.11–13), he nevertheless defers to Philemon's decision in the matter (v.14): *But without your consent, I desired to do nothing.* Here the noun consent (*gnōmē*) stems from *to know* (*ginōskō*) and describes something one knows with conviction, something held firm and, thus, an opinion. In classical Greek it could be a resolution, even a vote. We might paraphrase: *But without your full support ...* And this is the basis of Paul's unwillingness to act independently. Paul confirms explicitly that he was firm from the beginning that he was never tempted to keep Onesimus unilaterally; he was resolved in this from the outset and now awaits Philemon's judgment. The past tense of the verb (or aorist, *thelō*) is closer to "I resolved" than "I preferred" (NRSV), and it conveyed a settled desire.[38] Paul was not in two minds about this.

But what Paul gives with one hand, he gently retrieves with the other. This is the rhetorical dance that we are observing. It is a delicate negotiation, and he doesn't want simply to say to Philemon, "Have it your way." Paul knows what he desires; he was unwilling to act in a heavy-handed manner, but now he explains (again) why this presents an opportunity for Philemon. "So that (*hina*) ..." (v.15b) provides the purpose for Paul's self-restraint. He wants Philemon to act *not* according to compulsion (*anagkē*), as if he were compelled and without agency. But rather he desires that this decision be completely voluntary (*hekousios* as willingly, intentionally). This decision finds its motivation in Philemon discovering an opportunity to do what is good (*ho agathos*). Recall that in v.6 it was this "good" (*agathos*) that made up Paul and Philemon's shared efforts – their

---

[38]   BDAG 447–448, *thelō* (2); this use conveys a confirmed decision rather than something hopeful. Harris, *Colossians*, 228.

partnership – in the gospel. Now that good thing has been defined. Here is how Philemon can participate in producing goodness, and this is an opportunity not only for a returned slave but for Philemon himself, demonstrating his honor as a good-bearing member of Colossae.

Box 4.5 A Closer Look: The Dance of Honor and Shame in Philemon

Readers often misunderstand Paul's approach in Philemon and imply (with frustration) that he seems to be equivocating in this letter. Is he concealing his intentions? Is he manipulating Philemon? Is he dishonest about what he wants? When he says that he doesn't want Philemon's decision to be forced (v.14), isn't this exactly what he is doing by heaping up so many reasons why Philemon must agree with him?

What we are watching in these verses is the careful reciprocity typical of honor/shame cultures. Paul knows exactly what he wants, but he lives in an ancient eastern Mediterranean culture that regards the preservation of honor and the avoidance of shame to be some of its pivotal values. Western cultures prefer directness; eastern Mediterranean cultures prefer indirectness so that a person is never dishonored but always has a way out. Few have made this clearer than Bruce Malina in his widely read *The New Testament World: Insights from Cultural Anthropology*, now in its third edition.[39] Like many things in this culture, honor is a limited good, and so its acquisition, preservation, and distribution are all carefully watched. Honor is the value someone has in both their own eyes and the eyes of their social group. It is a claim to worth that must be acknowledged by that social group or else the claim dies immediately. An athlete may claim that he or she is great, but the true and socially compelling assessment of this can only come from others.

In this short letter we are watching a challenge/response encounter linked to honor and shame. Both Philemon and Paul are bound by rules: Paul cannot say he wants to keep Onesimus – the slave is not his property, despite Onesimus' desire to remain in Rome. Paul cannot override Philemon's status as an elder, esteemed Colossian, and as the slave owner. This would be the act of a fool, and the price for this would be Paul's loss of honor in Colossae and beyond. Throughout the letter Paul *attributes* honor to Philemon not to flatter him but to acknowledge his public honor and the important role he can play. His requests, however, must be indirect, reiterated with nuance, and above all provide for an honorable way out if Philemon disagrees with him. This is the purpose of vv.15–16. If Paul does not get his wishes, then at least Philemon can celebrate Onesimus' return *not as a slave but as a beloved brother*. In this case Paul would have won too – this culture always has wins, ties,

---

[39] B. Malina, *The New Testament World: Insights from Cultural Anthropology*, 3rd edition (Philadelphia: Westminster/John Knox, 2001).

and losses. In this case, Paul has brought the slave into a new life of goodness as a beloved brother, and this is a high honor.

Upon receiving this letter Philemon must choose how to provide a publicly honoring response without shaming Paul. A blunt refusal that proclaims Paul's presumption would be risky. If word of this response circulated publicly, even in Colossae Philemon would risk shame, since Paul was a highly honored man. All matters would be indirectly conveyed, but each person knows exactly what they want or need. This is a dance, a delicately orchestrated set of movements that protects every party. The wise do it well; fools (this is what they are called) do it poorly. Philemon could write back to the apostle:

> Paul, I would give you my son if you needed him because to serve you would be his highest honor. But if you will allow me, but only if you can, let Onesimus remain here for now since this city is his home where we can welcome our new brother, and we can talk and celebrate him and your work when you visit.

This is a way to say "no" while attributing honor generously.

Paul has now made his request known with sincere deference. But now (vv.15–16) he not only explores an explanation for how this situation arose but also anticipates what might happen if things fall apart for Onesimus. Ideally (from Paul's view), on his return Onesimus would be blessed by Philemon, his faith celebrated, and he would be honored in the church before he returned to Paul, no doubt with Tychicus (Col 4:7). Onesimus' association with the highly esteemed apostle Paul would elevate the importance and honor of Onesimus in the community. Onesimus who stands among them is a close friend of Paul, even his spiritual child, and a brother to all in the congregation.

But this might not be the final outcome.

Thus far Paul has not acknowledged how Philemon might feel about these developments with Onesimus. He has not explicitly referred to Onesimus' flight, and here he treats it for the first time.[40] This slave's departure was a crime, and v.18 suggests he stole something, probably to finance his escape. Paul so far has only been able to appeal to Philemon's higher sense of love: The slave is a believer now, he is Paul's spiritual child, and he has been of utmost value to Paul – but nevertheless there is a very human possibility of

---

[40]   Moo, *Colossians*, 419.

Philemon's anger and refusal. Paul offers a suggestion, a possible way to interpret that day when Onesimus left. His opening word "perhaps" translates *tacha* and is rare in the NT (also Rom 5:7). It adds something cautious and tentative to Paul's unfolding idea.[41] If turned into a question, it might be: *What if perhaps* . . . this *is the reason?* Paul refers to Onesimus' departure using *chōrizō* in the passive voice. Literally, he *was separated*, and this is likely a "divine passive" – which suggests that God had a hand in what transpired. As Lightfoot explains, Paul does not say "he parted himself, but he was parted," not unlike the story of Joseph, whose tragedy unfolded into a redemptive plan for all Israel: "'God sent me here' (Gen 45:5) could have been Onesimus' words."[42]

Philemon needs then to look beneath the events in front of him, interpret them, and see God's working despite the frustration-inducing departure of the slave. Paul further minimizes the drama of the slave's absence by saying that he was gone "for an hour" (*pros hōran*), which is an idiomatic way of saying "for a moment" or, with the NRSV, "for a while."[43] Similarly in Gal 2:5 Paul writes about the Judaizers using the same word: "We did not submit to them *even for a moment*" (*pros hōran*, also John 3:5; 2Cor 7:8).

In contrast to Onesimus' "brief" absence, Paul now says that he has returned for the long term (*aiōnon*). This word can have a number of nuances. *Aiōnon* can be any age, epoch, or era, past or present (Luke 1:7; Acts 3:21; 15:18). But it can also refer to eternity or a time to come without end (John 6:51, 58; 14:16).[44] This aligns the phrase with Onesimus' new faith. In other words, while having a slave is temporary in this world, now both Philemon and Onesimus will have a relationship that stretches into eternity in heaven. This continues Paul's understating of the crisis: God's plan, as mysterious as it is, now is coming to something good. A slave has become a brother, a man who left has returned, and a short absence now can become an eternity with a new man whom Philemon barely knows.

---

[41]   Wilson, *Colossians*, 355.
[42]   Lightfoot, *Colossians*, 342; also Beale, *Colossians*, 421; Dunn, *Colossians*, 333; Barth and Blanke, *Colossians*, 402; Harris, *Colossians*, 230. Paul employs another divine passive in v.22.
[43]   BDAG 1102–1103. Even *hōra* alone is used idiomatically like this: Rev 18:10, 17, 19.
[44]   BDAG 32–33 with many references. John 5:58 is typical: "But the one who eats this bread will live forever."

This is a profound benefit to Philemon, but also, Paul exclaims, this is a blessing especially (*malista*, a superlative) *to him*. To see the successes of this conversion result in a new life for Onesimus in Colossae would be sufficient for Paul if that is what must be done.

When we come to v.16 we have reached the climax of Paul's appeal. He is asking that Onesimus return *no longer as a slave – but rather as a beloved brother* or *as a brother who is loved*. This is the only time in Paul's writing in which he refers to a slave as a brother, and it underscores how Paul is imagining a change in Onesimus' status. "Beloved" is what Paul calls those who belong to Christ universally (1Cor 4:14; 15:58), and it puts Onesimus among the esteemed beloved coworkers of Paul such as Timothy (1Cor 4:17), Epaphras (Col 1:7), Tychicus (Col 4:17; Eph 6:21), and the woman Persis (Rom 6:12). Even Philemon himself wears this title (Phlm 1).[45] This redefining of the slave would lead to Philemon's and Onesimus' reconciliation and an undermining of everything they knew before.

What is Paul asking here when he describes Onesimus as "more than" a slave?[46] For some interpreters Paul is hinting at manumission,[47] while others disagree.[48] We cannot be certain, since Paul does not directly say this, but the suggestion seems inevitable.[49] But we can be certain that Paul is expecting a complete shift in how Onesimus should be viewed by Philemon: no longer as property but now as a beloved brother. Paul is not working out the social or ethical tensions between slave and free in his context – he is reimagining the relationship altogether, and "brother" is his vocabulary for how this should change.

Onesimus' new dual identity – as slave of Philemon and as Christian brother – is certainly perplexing. Can Onesimus abandon one while he embraces the other? Can he hold both simultaneously? Paul is aware of this, and his final phrase is used as a reminder: *in the flesh and in the Lord*.

---

45 McKnight, *Philemon*, 97.
46 BDAG 1031(B), *hyper* with the accusative refers to excelling, surpassing, or more than. Eph 1:22: *Christ is head "over" (hyper) all things for the church.*
47 Harris, *Colossians*, 231; Martin, *Colossians* (1982), 166; Bruce, *Colossians*, 217; J. Barclay, "Paul, Philemon and the Dilemma of Christian Ownership," *NTS* 37 (1991) 161–186.
48 Garland, *Colossians*, 335; McKnight, *Philemon*, 97; Beale, *Colossians*, 424; Wilson, *Colossians*, 96.
49 Lightfoot (*Colossians*, 343), Dunn (*Colossians*, 335), and Moo (*Colossians*, 425) point to intentional ambiguity, coming close to a request for manumission but avoiding it.

In the "flesh" (*en sarki*) is an example of Paul's regular use of the phrase to describe the common affairs of human life. Thus in Rom 1:3–4 Paul defines Christ both *in the flesh*, as seen in his human descent from David, and also as Son of God, thanks to the power of his resurrection (cf. Rom 7:5; 11:4; 2Cor 4:11; Phil 1:22).[50] Jesus wears identities that now belong both to the world and to heaven. Here Onesimus is still a slave in the flesh (*en sarki*), and this has not changed. But in the "Lord" (*en kuriō*) Onesimus has a second identity. In the Lord is his new identity now binding him to Christ; with it he bears another name, another role, and another set of relationships. He belongs to the Lord and he belongs to Philemon at the same time. Paul does not want that dual identity to be forgotten.

Box 4.6 Bridging Horizons: Prisoners of Christ in Prison

For many years I have taught basic NT introduction courses in a local prison. This is a part of a degree program sponsored by Calvin University and endorsed by the Michigan Department of Corrections. Every year a cohort of twenty-five carefully selected men from throughout the state enter the program, are transferred to our local prison (Richard A. Handlon Correctional Facility), study full time, and eventually complete an undergraduate degree in about five years. The program is rigorous and holds the same academic standards as the university that accredits it. Our faculty enter the prison regularly to teach in an academic building on the prison grounds.

The correction officers want to remind us that these men are *prisoners* – and truly they are when I think of them (as Paul says) *in the flesh*. That is, their identity is clear: They have criminal records, sentences, and uniforms that set them apart. But there is another reality that lives alongside this. Most of my students are also Christians, and they share a second identity *in the Lord*. This is a dual identity that I think about every time I enter Handlon Prison.

When my classroom door closes and the correction officers are outside, we create a new reality inside. Their second identity now steps forward: They are persons (not numbers), and in that setting they are brothers in Christ. I call them by their first names (no officer does this), and together we share a sense of unity and respect prisons never achieve. I once discussed this with a class, and a brilliant fifty-something man said, "I am not defined by my past." Another chimed in, "I am

---

defined by the gospel." This is a remarkable thing to hear from a group of men of whom many are serving life sentences.

    Onesimus bore a dual identity as well. And whatever Philemon decides, when "the door closes" Philemon will need to choose whether he has the courage to accept this slave's identity *in the Lord*. I deeply admire many of the men whom I have taught in prison. A man who committed a crime at seventeen and now is fifty might be a new man when I meet him *in the Lord*. This creates complex relationships, but I am always surprised and delighted when I meet these people whom I can call my brothers.

    The reality is that the escape and return of Onesimus had financial implications (vv.**17–18**). In Roman culture the slave was property, was purchased and owned, and thus had genuine commercial value. We would be naive if we didn't think that this never occurred to Philemon. Paul is inevitably aware of it as well. Despite the man's conversion, Philemon nevertheless had the weight of law on his side. The Colossian church was filled with people who had never known a world without slaves. Slavery was a cultural assumption for them that barely arose in their thinking. To be sure, *in the flesh* Onesimus belonged to Philemon, and this was the reality that might control the conversation. Philemon may have thought, "In heaven, things may be different, but now, a slave is a slave." Paul's own realized eschatology was certainly challenging this view. The future had now arrived in the present, and it would upend the categories everyone took for granted. *In Christ there is no slave nor free.* What did that mean?

    The meaning of v.17 turns on the title Paul offers to Philemon: *If, therefore, you hold me as your* koinōnos ... The word stems from *koinos* (common), and it appears in the well-known English–Greek term *koinonia* or fellowship. *Koinōnoi* are people who share things in common, and so it can mean partner, comrade, colleague, coworker, or work companion, particularly in a trade or business. Its focus is not on friendship as much as it refers to commonality in purpose and hints at collegiality. Thus in Luke 5:10 James and John were *koinōnoi* with Peter in a fishing business. They had shared business efforts.

    This verse also begins with a conditional phrase (using "if"), but in Greek it is a form that is used not for uncertain things but for certain realities (a condition assumed to be a reality) and so can be translated "since" (Matt 4:3; Col 2:20). Paul is not saying, "If you are – and I am not certain . . ." Instead, he is saying, "Since you are my partner." In English we carry both meanings in the same word "if," but we lose this nuance if we don't employ the syntax of the sentence.[51]

Therefore, Paul's appeal to Philemon presumes *the reality* of their shared endeavors. Already Paul has named Philemon as his coworker (v.1), one of the esteemed titles held by all of Paul's most valued colleagues. Now Paul is saying that this matter of Onesimus is a feature of their shared work. Paul does the same thing in his reference to Titus in 2Cor 8:23, who is "my partner and coworker." The force of this first phrase impacts the second. *Since you are my colleague (and I know you would welcome me), so likewise welcome Onesimus.* The implication is that courtesies that would naturally be extended to Paul ought likewise to be extended to Onesimus. This request is a further implication of the request in v.16: As Paul and Philemon are brothers in Christ, and this would determine their mutual welcome, so too Onesimus belongs in the same circle. "Welcome" should be his as well.

References to "welcome" were central to life in Mediterranean societies. They meant more than a mere greeting. They were a social embrace and an invitation to a place of safety and social safekeeping with many needs met: food, housing, and perhaps introductions. But phrases like this were unknown in Roman society with reference to masters and slaves. Such generous welcome belonged to peers, as Paul is to Philemon. Here Paul is amplifying what he has said multiple times: Onesimus' return does not mean the simple return of a slave. It means the return of someone or the revisiting of something else: Onesimus-the-slave *in the flesh* is a person in every respect of the word. He is a child not only of Paul, but of God. Moreover, he is a person who is directly associated with Paul and who lives under the presumed privileges of the apostle.

If *koinōnos* implies partners in business, now (v.**18**) Paul uses the metaphor with reference to money. He acknowledges that Onesimus has brought Philemon harm (*adikeō*, meaning "has been unjust," see Col 3:25; 2Cor 7:2), and he shows that he is not minimizing the slave's behavior. Then Paul delicately skirts the issue of financial loss (he never refers to theft) but says that *since Onesimus harmed Philemon or owes him, Paul will*

---

[51] BDAG 277–278; D. M. Harris, An *Introduction to Biblical Greek Grammar* (Grand Rapids: Zondervan, 2020), 218–220.

absorb the costs. There is no doubt about this ("if" here leaves no doubt, see v.17). Theft is our conjecture, but since Onesimus was a fugitive this may be a fair assumption. Certainly Philemon was reading between the lines, and surely Paul had heard Onesimus' full confession. The language is intentionally indirect and does not say more than anyone needs to hear. But the resolution of the debt belongs to Paul. "Charge that to me" is the NRSV rendering of a Greek commercial phrase for absorbed expenses or debts (*moi ellogeō*, elsewhere only Rom 5:13). But one wonders how Paul could say this as a man in prison and, we assume, without funds.[52] We might speculate about the many gifts that had been sent to Paul and assume he perhaps had funds at the end of his life. But this is unclear. However, this promise of repayment anticipates what Paul will say in v.19. If there is a ledger of debt and repayment, Philemon has his name on it as well.

In case there is any confusion about these financial matters, Paul reinforces his pledge (**v.19**). When Paul here takes the pen and inserts his own personal, unprofessional script – he is writing "with his own hand" – he is of course heightening the intensity of his appeal. Usually Paul uses his own "signature" (writing in *his hand*) at the end of a letter to validate that a letter is his, as he does in Col 4:18 (also Gal 6:11). But something more is happening here. Paul is using the language of debt relief common in commercial contracts (a *cheirograph*, see Chapter I). Such a personal handwritten line by the payer was always expected in these contracts. Paul has now made a personal declaration directly echoing common business debts: He has made a legal promise of repayment that is binding because he now has "signed" the promise himself.

But this promise is not enough. Paul anticipates the possibility that Philemon may not acknowledge his promise of payment nor advance him the credit he needs to eventually pay this debt. In vv.19b–20 Paul elevates his appeal to its highest and most stringent level. And it is surprising. In a shame/honor society, many things need to be left unnamed (or only faintly implied). But Paul's next words could convey shame, especially if this letter circulated or was read aloud. Paul asks, "Philemon, but don't you owe me?" This is an excellent example of how grace

---

[52]　Observed by Wilson, *Colossians*, 358, and Dunn, *Colossians*, 339.

engenders reciprocity in Paul's culture. When we receive richly, we are to give similarly (Luke 12:48). Philemon had been a recipient; now he is asked to be a giver.

If this is a question about ledgers and indebtedness, Paul reminds Philemon that his name also appears in a similar (metaphorical) contract. We generally see this as Paul's own contribution to Philemon's spiritual well-being. *Paul was instrumental in Philemon's own life as a believer in Christ.* That is no insignificant debt. Therefore, if Paul will underwrite Onesimus' debt, Paul is wondering about the resolution of Philemon's own debt. How will this be resolved? "Very simply," Bruce writes, "if one reads between the lines: by sending Onesimus back to continue his usefulness to Paul in the service of the gospel."[53]

Paul has just taken a rhetorical risk. He has been direct, even bold. And in the following verse he recalibrates his approach to something more fitting his pastoral instincts (v.**20**). Addressing Philemon as "brother" immediately softens his approach. Paul has already used this title for Philemon (v.7), just as he did for Timothy (v.1). This is not to be an adversarial legal discussion but rather an appeal based on the heart. These are two brothers talking together about a third brother. But then Paul asks for two things: for some benefit from Philemon and for personal refreshment. The two terms here are suggestive. "Having benefit" is in the rare optative verbal mood (suggesting a wish) and translates *oninēmi* (see benefit or profit, *onēsis*). This is a clear echo of Onesimus' name (*Onēsimos*, see v.10), and Philemon may have noted the pun.[54] We need to see this as a colloquial expression, which the dynamic translations convey well. With Phillips: "Now do grant me this favour, my brother – such an act of love will do my old heart good." And with the NLT: "Yes, my brother, please do me this favor for the Lord's sake."

This benefit or blessing is "in the Lord," which leads to the second expression. This is refreshment that comes "in Christ." Philemon's gesture

---

53 Bruce, *Colossians*, 220. Dunn (*Colossians*, 340–341) points out Paul's social dilemma here. Paul sees Philemon as a peer ("brother," v.20), but if Paul was the source of Philemon's faith – if Paul was his patron – then Paul might call him "son." But he does not. This may indicate the level of Philemon's social standing and power in the Colossian community. Paul must both describe Philemon's debt while elevating his place of honor.

54 Harris, *Colossians*, 238; Lightfoot, *Colossians*, 345.

of generosity will become a refreshing balm for Paul, who no doubt has been living under the weight of Onesimus' dilemma for some time. Paul does not refer to "heart" (*kardia*) but instead uses *splagchna*, which was the abdomen (or intestines) and thought to be the seat of emotions (see Col 3:12; Phlm 7). In English we use the metaphor of "heart" for this, which makes contemporary translations accurate. We can infer that Paul is worried about this outcome for Onesimus. And he hopes that Philemon's response will alleviate his anxiety.

Box 4.7 Bridging the Horizons: Modern Slavery

The deeper problem presented by Philemon is what we do with slavery today and whether *in our churches* we have grown to tolerate it. The Global Slavery Index (www.walkfree.org) estimates that there are today 49.6 million people living in slavery around the world. This slavery is "hidden in plain sight" and affects the economies of almost every nation. The Index defines slavery thus: Slavery refers to "situations of exploitation that a person cannot refuse or leave because of threats, violence, coercion, or deception."[55] Males make up about 46 percent of slaves and females 54 percent. Almost 25 percent of slaves are forced into commercial sex services.

The distribution of the problem is global. While the USA scores high in actively enforcing laws criminalizing slavery, the Index estimates that there are about 1 million slaves in the USA. Europe has 6 million slaves. The UK has 122,000. Russia has a remarkable 1.9 million. But the greatest offenders are in Asia, where in total there are 29 million slaves. North Korea is unsurpassed, with 2.9 million slaves alone.

Therefore, as McKnight writes, "What can Philemon say to the modern versions of slavery? What would Paul say in our world to our churches?"[56] If the kingdom realities envisioned by Paul were to come alive in families, churches, and communities, what would that look like?

A few years ago I was speaking at one of the largest churches in Chicago, Illinois (USA), and I used these statistics as illustrative material in a sermon. But in my thinking I believed that slavery was "over there" and not "here" – until, following the service, I met my first rescued sex-slave victim. She told me that her "owner" kept her near Chicago O'Hare International Airport twenty minutes away, and she and her fellow slaves were forced "to service" an enormous number of male travelers who flew through the airport. Today she leads a ministry rescuing women from

---

[55] www.walkfree.org/global-slavery-index, accessed November 2024.
[56] McKnight, *Philemon*, 36.

American airports, and this one church backed her and invested in her, and together they help a community of women to escape such slavery. It was one of those after-the-sermon conversations one never forgets.

But then it happened again. I was in Uruguay mentoring a student serving a Christian nonprofit, and one of their ministries was distributing literature to young girls at the capital Montevideo's Carrasco International Airport. Montevideo, I learned, is one of the leading trafficking centers where young women are kidnapped and transported to Europe. But here the churches had banded together, created strategies to confront the problem, and, at considerable risk to themselves, condemned publicly what had become a nationwide problem that politicians were willing to ignore.

PERSONAL REQUEST ALONG WITH CLOSING GREETINGS, 21–25

21 Confident of your obedience, I am writing to you, knowing that you will do even more than I ask.

22 One thing more: prepare a guest room for me, for I am hoping through your prayers to be restored to you.

23 Epaphras, my fellow prisoner in Christ Jesus, sends greetings to you,

24 and so do Mark, Aristarchus, Demas, and Luke, my coworkers.

25 The grace of the Lord Jesus Christ be with your spirit.

We have learned that the Pauline letter closings were a significant part of Paul's correspondence.[57] This was true throughout the Hellenistic world.[58] Letters had an expected epistolary form, and the closing and many other such patterns appear in Paul. Personal Hellenistic letters similar to Philemon usually ended with farewell wishes such as a wish for good health or a greeting. The "confidence closing" that we see here in v.21 was also common after some request had been made.

Paul's own style differed from some of these when he developed his own Christian vocabulary. *Grace* and *peace* were commonly used in his closing. Sometimes they could be together, sometimes apart. Paul concludes with

---

[57] J. Weima, *Neglected Endings: The Significance of Pauline Letter Closings*. JSNTSup 101 (Sheffield: JSOT Press, 1994).

[58] Ibid., 12–23 provides the history of research on these closings (to 1994), and 28–56 provides a summary of typical letters from this period.

peace in Romans, 2 Corinthians, Philippians, 1–2 Thessalonians, and Galatians. Every Pauline letter closes with a *grace blessing* (including Heb 13:25 and Rev 22:21), which is what we see here in Philemon (v.25). In eight of these, Paul refers to "the grace *of the Lord*," and this is followed by either "the Lord Jesus" (Romans, 1 Corinthians) or "the Lord Jesus Christ" (2 Corinthians, Galatians, Philippians, 1–2 Thessalonians, Philemon). Galatians and Philippians use the same language as Philemon: *The grace of (our) Lord Jesus Christ be with be with your spirit.* The parallels have suggested to some that we are seeing here echoes of liturgical language that must have taken form within the early church. In other words, this is how Christians communicated with each other, signaling their identity and deepest values.

We possess thousands of nonliterary letters from this period, most having been found buried in the arid deserts of Egypt. Here we note another pattern. Letters often were written by a scribe when the letter's author was incapable or illiterate. In cases of illiteracy the scribe would often append a note at the bottom, as we see in Egyptian letters such as P.Oxy. 267: "Theon Paaetos wrote for him because he did not know how to write."[59] Or P.Ryl. 73: "Didymos, the public scribe, wrote for them because they did not know how to write."[60] But even where an author's handwriting was inadequate, we still see that the closing was written in the awkward hand of the owner. This gesture no doubt provided a personal connection and presence in the letter. This pattern arises in Philemon because in v.19 Paul indicates that he now is using his own hand, and this has led some to conclude that all of vv.19–25 were written by Paul himself as the formal conclusion.[61] This may be true. Others have suggested that v.19 instead is a personal legal note within a contractual promise (cheirograph), thus leaving Paul's conclusion to vv.21–25. This is the view taken here.[62]

---

[59] Ibid., 50.
[60] Ibid.
[61] Ibid., 232–233.
[62] So Dunn, *Colossians*, 343; Bruce (*Colossians*, 222) who suggest that it would make more sense to see v.19 as a promissory note and then have Paul dictate the balance of the letter to Timothy. Recall that some scholars (going back to Lightfoot, *Colossians*, 344) have argued that the entire letter was written in Paul's own hand and that no scribe was employed.

Paul's confidence in Philemon's obedience (v.21) might refer to Paul's sense of authority as an apostle. But this is not the approach Paul has used in this letter.[63] He is trying to persuade Philemon, and he uses every honoring tactic at his disposal to move Philemon toward generosity. The NRSV's "confident" may be too brusque or terse. The verb (*peithomai/peithō*) implies less bold confidence than it does a secure sense of conviction. It moves into the realm of trust, as if someone had been convinced of something and now they are persuaded. Paul uses a perfect participle (*pepoithōs*) for himself, leaning into what he has known about Philemon in the past. He has a history with Philemon that he is relying on, and so "he believes" that a good outcome is forthcoming. Perhaps "I have every assurance" may get at it best. So does "Depending on you entirely ..." Paul's faith in Philemon being able to see what is right at this moment is based on his experience of this man's character.

Paul's confidence is in Philemon's *obedience*. This too can take on an unnecessarily firm tone. Paul refers to obedience (*hypakoē*) not infrequently (Rom 15:18; 2Cor 7:15) when he expresses his apostolic authority. Or it may be used for a slave with his master (Rom 1:16). But in Philemon this too seems off the mark. The noun (*hypakoē*) was rarely used outside Christian writing (once in the LXX), but we know that it originated with the verb *hypakouō*.[64] Here we, of course, find the root for hearing (*akouō*), and in Greek *obedience* is connected to hearing rightly, hearing responsively, or "heedful hearing."[65] Some have suggested that "compliance" is best. Or perhaps this obedience does not refer to obedience *to Paul* but to Philemon's "obedience of faith," his ordering of his life beneath the gospel.

We must not then see Paul's words as egocentric or indulgent, consumed, perhaps, by his own power. This would be a grave misunderstanding of his purposes. Paul is confident in the gospel, and he believes that kingdom values will convincingly shape the nature of Christian communities. To this gospel Philemon has been devoted for some time. Paul says that, knowing this, and knowing Philemon as he does, he is persuaded that Philemon will be convicted by the Spirit and, in this

---

[63] Wilson, *Colossians*, 362.
[64] TDNT 1:224.
[65] Dunn, *Colossians*, 345.

conviction, realize that he must come under Christ's command. Wilson explains this well:

He [Paul] is convinced that Philemon will recognize what is his duty as a Christian in these circumstances, the more particularly since Onesimus also is now a Christian, and therefore a brother in the faith. The obedience of which Paul speaks must be obedience to Christ's command.[66]

This view of v.21 is confirmed by what follows. It is Paul's knowledge of Philemon – Paul's history with him and his knowledge of this man's character – that explains why Philemon was likely hosting the entire Colossian church at his home. Paul's persuasion leads to one more thought: Philemon will do even more than Paul requests. We do not know what this is, and most speculate that Philemon might not only welcome Onesimus home but free him altogether. But this is a request that Paul never makes in the letter. It can only be suggested; it is not something Paul could ask for overtly.[67] The resolution of this matter is now entirely in Philemon's hands. He can simply welcome back his slave and embrace him as a brother in Christ, he can commission him to return to Paul to serve the apostle on his behalf, or he can give Onesimus his full freedom.

What remains are some practical issues that are on Paul's mind (v.22). He is optimistic at this point, thinking that he will be released and that he will come to visit Colossae. Proponents of a Pauline imprisonment in Ephesus often point to this verse as evidence that Paul is nearby and that, despite his aim being to go to Spain (Rom 15:23–24), he could travel to Colossae. But we do not know about Paul's itinerary, and, in truth, his plans regarding Spain may have changed as each year of imprisonment proceeded.

In this visit he is asking not that he be shown general hospitality in Colossae but that Philemon himself be his host. *Prepare* is a second-person imperative to Philemon. Paul is presuming that, despite his earlier request, his friendship with Philemon will be intact. This is not an effort to pressure or persuade; nor is it a threat that Paul will follow up. Paul is presupposing what he believes is true. Philemon is a good man, a welcoming host, a

---

[66] Wilson, *Colossians*, 364.
[67] Scholars who believe that Colossians was written decades after Philemon see in Col 4:7–9 evidence that Philemon did set Onesimus free and that he became a coworker with Paul.

colleague, and a close friend, and together both will celebrate a reunion some day when the apostle sleeps under Philemon's roof.[68]

Paul also assumes that the Colossians are praying for him. And the outcome of this prayer is that "I will be given" (*charisthēsomai*, passive) to "you" (plural). This giving is not a gesture of Rome but instead, because it is related to prayer, this will be God himself opening doors into Paul's future and bringing Paul to Philemon personally.

Greetings (v.23) were common in almost every Hellenistic letter intended for a person or indirectly for a community. These are the names of Paul's friends and supporters during his imprisonment. Epaphras is mentioned first and provided his own greeting (*he greets you*), and this makes sense since he was from Colossae (Col 1:7; 4:12) and no doubt had many friends among the Christians there. In Colossians Paul describes him expansively as a dear fellow servant (1:7), a faithful minister (1:7), and a man devoted to prayer (4:12). And as we have seen, he is likely the founding pastor of the church of Colossae itself. Here he is described as a "fellow prisoner" (*sunaichmalōtos*),[69] a title shared with others such as Andronicus, Junia ("outstanding among the apostles," Rom 16:7), and Aristarchus (Col 4:10). But what does this mean? He may have been voluntarily sharing this imprisonment with Paul or even been taken captive as Paul's close associate. But among Christians like Paul such an imprisonment meant more: Both he and Epaphras were prisoners *in Christ Jesus.* That is, they viewed this imprisonment as a feature of their life in Christ. As Jesus told his disciples, "Remember the word that I said to you, 'Slaves are not greater than their master.' If they persecuted me, they will persecute you; if they kept my word, they will keep yours also" (John 15:20). To Timothy Paul wrote, "All who want to live a godly life in Christ Jesus will be persecuted" (2Tim 3:12). These were not casual ideas to men like these. These were lived realities. The narrative in Acts illustrates how imprisonment was common in the earliest Jesus communities.

The verb in v.23 is assumed into the next verse (v.24). Here we find Mark (see Col 4:10), Aristarchus (Col 4:10), Demas, and Luke (Col 4:14).

---

[68]   The word for "guestroom" here is *xenia*, from *xenos* (foreigner). This is a room for a guest. Thus, in the NT *philoxenos* is the term for "hospitality."

[69]   *Aichma* is a spear in Greek, which becomes a metaphor in the adjective *aichmalōtos* – taken by spear, and hence a prisoner.

These are called "fellow workers" (*sunergoi*), which is used frequently by Paul to describe his closest companions (twelve times; see Col 4:11; Phlm 1). At the beginning of this letter Philemon is listed as one of these as well. This honoring title thus puts Philemon in the same circle as Paul's most valued co-laborers. The similarities in the lists of greetings in Col 4:10–14 and Phlm 23–24 suggest that these two letters were written together.[70]

A common ending in letters of this period was *errpōso!* (singular) or *errōsthe!* (plural) for "Farewell!" – literally "Good health!" Paul never uses this (it is used in Acts 15:29). Paul ends the letter with a blessing of grace (v.**25**), as he does in each of his other letters except Romans (1Cor 16:23–24; 2Cor 13:13; Gal 6:18; Eph 6:23–24; Phil 4:23; Col 4:18; 1Thess 5:28; 2Thess 3:18; 1Tim 6:21; 2Tim 4:22; Titus 3:15). This was not only an ordinary greeting in Paul's world, but it also carried the essence of his message. If everything Paul taught were to be summed up in one word, "grace" would be sufficient. It is not a generic grace but one that Paul preached with the gospel stemming from *the Lord Jesus Christ*. It is grace that Paul discovered in his conversion and that sustained him throughout his life.[71] Paul directs this blessing of grace to "be with your (plural) spirit" (also in Phil 4:23 and Gal 6:18). The phrase "with your spirit" is a Hebrew idiom simply meaning "with you."[72] The noun *spirit* is singular but its sense is distributive – that is, may grace bless each one who is at the Colossian church. Harris paraphrases this well: "May the grace given by the Lord Jesus Christ be with you, Philemon, your household, and the whole church, sanctifying the spirit of each of you."[73]

THE OUTCOME

There are many questions about this letter that we cannot entirely resolve. Very few doubt its authenticity or its origin during Paul's imprisonment.

---

[70]   From these lists, Colossians and Philemon are identical except that Colossians adds Jesus Justus. The other names are parallel: Aristarchus, Epaphras, Mark, Demas, and Luke. See F. F. Bruce, *The Pauline Circle* (Grand Rapids: Eerdmans, 1985) and E. Ellis, "Paul and His Co-Workers," *NTS* 17 (1970–1971) 437–452.

[71]   See J. Barclay, *Paul and the Gift* (Grand Rapids: Eerdmans, 2015), 183–188, which summarizes the major themes of grace in Paul.

[72]   Wilson, *Colossians*, 368.

[73]   Harris, *Colossians*, 244.

But then questions emerge immediately such as: What was the location of Paul's imprisonment (Rome or Ephesus)? The reason for Onesimus' flight from Colossae is also unclear. In fear, did he come to Paul hoping for an advocate? Did he first find Epaphras, who brought him to Paul? Did he happen on Paul in Rome when he was a fugitive and this led to his conversion? We cannot even be sure about the relationship between Onesimus and Philemon. Since this was a slave/master arrangement, it is fair for us to presume some things with confidence, but not everything. Perhaps it is not necessary to have every answer.

What can we know? Paul and Philemon were friends (Paul refers to him as a fellow worker), and Epaphras was the emissary sent by the Colossians to support Paul. We know that Philemon had a very influential role in this church, and therefore Paul's approach with him was a matter of utmost delicacy. We also know that Paul had chosen to be an open advocate for this slave, and as he writes to persuade Philemon he is using every tactic at his disposal to make his case (without alienating his reader). We know that Paul was up against an enormous cultural obstacle – slavery – and for him (Col 3:11) this institution should break under the weight of the gospel. We can also presume that those who read Philemon also held Colossians in their other hand. Surely the themes found in one flowed to the other.

Perhaps we should view Philemon as a case study. In this sense I wonder if it has more in common with letters such as 1 Corinthians than we think. Paul must think through how his kingdom values will be lived practically in the church. Does this affect marriages and law courts? Does it affect gender roles in the Christian community? Does it affect slavery? If it is a case study, it is the most personal of any in Paul's writings.

Paul has laid out clearly his vision for this kingdom reality in Colossians and Ephesians. Portions of his other letters do the same. Romans 12–16 comes to mind, as do 1 Corinthians 12, 2 Corinthians 1–9, and Philippians (which is a pastoral encouragement and exhortation). Together these present a unified picture of life together: Christian faith was not a private experience such as that offered in a Roman mystery religion. It was a corporate life, a corporate identity – the Body of Christ – and with this new identity there were realities that directly affected "life together." Christian life brought kingdom ethics to bear on those who belonged to that kingdom. Where does Paul gain this corporate model? It is in the life of OT

Israel.[74] This is why Paul provokes his readers again and again by adopting the language of Israel for the community of Christ.

I imagine that Paul had a variety of choices before him when he met Onesimus. He might have been tempted to let Onesimus remain in Rome as a Christian or even to look away as the slave departed as a fugitive. But he doesn't do either of these. Of course, Paul knew the laws that applied to those harboring fugitives. But I like to imagine something else. Paul's decision to send Onesimus east to Colossae was primarily pastoral. Onesimus had not only committed a crime; he had severely broken a relationship with his Christian master. There was a problem in his past that he needed to address, and reconciliation was its only solution. As the old sermon puts it: *There was no going forward until Onesimus had gone back.* This is a universal truth, as important to us today as it was then. Paul's letter undermined the conditions of Onesimus' return – he was now a brother – and his larger letter to Colossae undermined the status quo of how Roman society was organized.

We cannot know what happened next. What happened when Onesimus returned? If only we had one more letter, this time from Philemon! Paul's hope is that *at least* Onesimus might return to him, and, as Philemon's representative, Onesimus could help Paul as a fellow worker. The survival of this letter suggests something important. Philemon could have destroyed the letter and regressed into a rigid Roman slave owner's mentality. Did Philemon keep the letter and permit it to be circulated? That it was attached eventually to the Pauline canon suggests good things resulted. And if this is true, we can imagine the church rethinking slavery entirely, with Onesimus as an example of what living out a kingdom life looked like. I also like to imagine Philemon as one more example. He might have become an exemplar of courage and transformation that affected him and his church directly. I also like to imagine Onesimus as free, fully manumitted by his master, celebrated by his church, and returning to Paul on a Roman ship holding a ticket from the port of Ephesus or Miletus, imagining the new, "useful" (*onēsimos*) life he had found in Christ.

Thinking about the value of the letter for the church today, Luther ended his comments on Philemon with these insights:

---

[74]   Dunn, *The Theology of Paul the Apostle,* 533–564.

Thus, we have a private epistle from which much should be learned how brethren are to be commended, that is, that an example might be provided to the church how we ought to take of those who fall and restore those who err: for the kingdom of Christ is a kingdom of mercy and grace, while the kingdom of Satan is a kingdom of murder, error, darkness and lies.[75]

There is one more curious turn of events. According to Origen, the second bishop of Antioch was Ignatius, who followed Peter.[76] We know little about Ignatius except that he traveled under guard to Rome to face martyrdom. As he traveled, he wrote a number of letters that were carefully preserved (we have seven authentic letters). In one letter Ignatius writes to the church of Ephesus and names Onesimus as their bishop.

Since therefore I have received in God's name your whole congregation in the person of Onesimus, a man of inexpressible love who is also your earthly bishop, I pray that you will love him in accordance with the standard set by Jesus Christ and that all of you will be like him. For blessed is the one who has graciously allowed you, worthy as you are, to have such a bishop.[77]

We would like to imagine that this bishop is one and the same with our Onesimus of Colossae. This idea has been nurtured among interpreters and preachers for centuries. But it is only speculation. Onesimus would have been quite old, and his was a well-known name in the era. Nevertheless, it was a common slave's name, and one wonders that a Christian bishop would bear such a name. Was this a Christian leader who was once a slave?[78]

---

[75]   M. Luther, *Luther's Works: Lectures Philemon, Titus and Hebrews* (St. Louis: Concordia, 2007), 29:105, cited in Fitzmyer, *Philemon*, 126.

[76]   Eusebius makes Ignatius the third bishop of Antioch, preceded by Euodias, who followed Peter.

[77]   M. Holmes, *The Apostolic Fathers: Greek Texts and English Translation*, 3rd edition (Grand Rapids: Baker Academic, 2007), 183–185. This is a revision of the 1891 edition written by J. B. Lightfoot and completed by J. R. Harmer.

[78]   According to tradition, Onesimus and Philemon were both martyred (Philemon in Colossae). Both received feast days in the liturgy. For Onesimus, the West celebrated him on February 16; in the East, he was celebrated on February 15. Philemon was celebrated on November 22.

Select Bibliography

Unless otherwise indicated, major commentaries will be referred to simply by the author's name followed by *Colossians* or *Philemon*. As in the present work, commentaries on Colossians generally include studies on Philemon since both letters share the same setting.

Commentaries

Abbott, T. K., *A Critical and Exegetical Commentary on the Epistles to the Ephesians and to the Colossians*. ICC (Edinburgh: T&T Clark, 1897)

Barclay, J. M. G., *Colossians and Ephesians* (Edinburgh: T&T Clark, 1997)

Barth, M., and Blanke, H., *Colossians: A New Translation with Introduction and Commentary*. AB (New York: Doubleday, 1994)
  The Letter to Philemon (Grand Rapids: Eerdmans, 2000)

Beale, G. K., *Colossians and Ephesians*. BECNT (Grand Rapids: Baker Academic, 2019)

Bruce, F. F., *The Epistle to the Colossians, to Philemon, and to the Ephesians*, 2nd edition. NICNT (Grand Rapids: Eerdmans, 1957; 1984)

Caird, G. B., *Paul's Letters from Prison* (Oxford: Oxford University Press, 1976)

Calvin, J., *Commentaries on the Epistles of Paul the Apostle to the Philippians, Colossians, and Thessalonians* (Grand Rapids: Baker Academic, 1999)

Campbell, C., *Colossians and Ephesians: A Handbook on the Greek Text* (Waco: Baylor University Press, 2013)

Dunn, J. D. G., *The Epistles to the Colossians and to Philemon* (Carlisle/Grand Rapids: Paternoster/Eerdmans, 1996)

Fitzmyer, J. A., *The Letter to Philemon: A New Translation with Introduction and Commentary*. AB (New York: Doubleday, 2000)

Garland, D. E., *The NIV Application Commentary: Colossians and Philemon* (Grand Rapids: Zondervan Academic, 1998)

Harris, M. J., *Exegetical Guide to the Greek Text: Colossians and Philemon* (Nashville: B&H, 2010)

Lightfoot, J. B., *St. Paul's Epistles to the Colossians and to Philemon*, 3rd edition (New York: Macmillan, 1879)

Lohmeyer, E., *Die Briefe an die Philipper, an die Kolosser und an Philemon*, Meyer Kommentar 9 (with additional notes by W. Schmauch, 1964) (Göttingen: Vandenhoeck & Ruprecht, 1953)

Lohse, E., *Colossians and Philemon*. Translated by W. R. Poehlmann and R. J. Harris (Philadelphia: Fortress, 1971)

Martin, R. P., *Colossians and Philemon*. NCB (Grand Rapids: Eerdmans, 1982)
  Colossians: The Church's Lord and the Christian's Liberty (Grand Rapids: Zondervan, 1972)

McKnight, S., *The Letter to Philemon*. NICNT (Grand Rapids: Eerdmans, 2017)
  The Letter to the Colossians. NICNT (Grand Rapids: Eerdmans, 2018)

Moo, D., *The Letters to the Colossians and to Philemon* (Grand Rapids: Eerdmans, 2008)

Moule, C. F. D., *The Epistles of Paul the Apostle to the Colossians and to Philemon* (Cambridge: Cambridge University Press, 1957)

O'Brien, P. T., *Colossians, Philemon* (Waco: Word, 1982)

Pao, D., *Colossians and Philemon*. ZECNT (Grand Rapids: Zondervan, 2012)

Sumney, J. L., *Colossians: A Commentary* (Louisville: Westminster, 2008)

Thompson, G. H. P., *The Letters of Paul to the Ephesians to the Colossians and to Philemon*. CBC (Cambridge: Cambridge University Press, 1967)

Thompson, M. M., *Colossians and Philemon* (Grand Rapids: Eerdmans, 2005)

Wilson, R. M., *Colossians and Philemon* (London: T&T Clark, 2005)

Witherington, B., *The Letters to Philemon, the Colossians, and the Ephesians: A Socio-Rhetorical Commentary on the Captivity Epistles* (Grand Rapids: Eerdmans, 2007)

Wright, N. T., *Colossians and Philemon*. TNTC (Downers Grove: InterVarsity Press, 1996)

Other Studies

Arnold, C. E., *The Colossian Syncretism: The Interface between Christianity and Folk Belief at Colossae* (Grand Rapids: Baker, 1996)

Ephesians: Power and Magic: The Concept of Power in Ephesians in Light of Its Historical Setting (Grand Rapids: Baker, 1992)

"Jesus Christ: 'Head' of the Church (Colossians and Ephesians)," in Green, J. B. and Turner, M., eds., *Jesus of Nazareth: Lord and Christ: Essays on the Historical Jesus and New Testament Christology* (Grand Rapids: Eerdmans, 1994), 346–366

Balchin, J. F., "Colossians 1:15–20: An Early Christian Hymn? The Arguments from Style," *VE* 15 (1985) 65–94

Balla, P., *The Child–Parent Relationship in the New Testament and Its Environment*. WUNT 155 (Tübingen: Mohr Siebeck, 2003)

Bevere, A. R., *Sharing in the Inheritance: Identity and Moral Life in Colossians*. JSNTSup 226 (Sheffield: Sheffield Academic Press, 2003)

Cadwallader, A. H., *Colossae, Colossians, Philemon: The Interface*. Novum Testamentum et Orbis Antiquus/Studien zur Umwelt des Neuen Testaments, Band 127 (Göttingen: Vandenhoeck & Ruprecht, 2023)

Cadwallader, A. H., and Trainor, M., eds., *Colossae in Space and Time: Linking to an Ancient City*. NTOA 94 (Göttingen: Vandenhoeck & Ruprecht, 2011)

Carr, W., *Angels and Principalities*. SNTSMS 42 (Cambridge: Cambridge University Press, 1981)

Copenhaver, A., *Reconstructing the Historical Background of Paul's Rhetoric in the Letter to the Colossians*. LNTS 585 (London: Bloomsbury, 2018)

Crook, A., *Law and Life of Rome, 90BC–AD212* (Ithaca: Cornell University Press, 1967)

DeMaris, R., *The Colossian Controversy*. SNTSS 96 (Sheffield: JSOT Press, 1994)

Elder, N., "This Hand Is Validation: Philemon as a Pauline Holograph," *NTS* 70 (2024) 324–339

Francis, F. O., and Meeks, W. A., *Conflict at Colossae*, 2nd edition (Missoula: Scholars Press, 1975)

Frey, P. J.-P., *Corpus of Jewish Inscriptions. Jewish Inscriptions from the Third Century B.C. to the Seventh Century A.D.* Volume 1: Europe (New York: KTAV, 1975)

Gunther, J. J., *St. Paul's Opponents and Their Background*. NovTSup 35 (Leiden: Brill, 1973)

Horsley, R. A., *Paul and Empire, Religion and Power in Roman Imperial Society* (Harrisburg: Trinity, 1997)

Huttner, U., *Ancient Judaism and Early Christianity in the Lycus Valley* [trans. D. Green]. Ancient Judaism and Early Christianity 85 (Leiden: Brill, 2013)

Lincoln, A., and Wedderburn, A. J. M., *The Theology of the Later Pauline Letters* (Cambridge: Cambridge University Press, 1993)

Lohse, L., "Pauline Theology and the Letter to the Colossians," *NTS* 15 (1968–1969) 211–220

Mitchell, S., *Anatolia: Land, Men, and Gods in Asia Minor*, vol. 1 (Oxford: Clarendon Press, 1993)

Moir, I. A., "Some Thoughts on Col. 2:17–18," *TZ* 35 (1979) 363–365

Ramsay, W. M., *Cities and Bishoprics of Phrygia* (Oxford: Oxford University Press, 1897)

Sappington, T. J., *Revelation and Redemption at Colossae*. JSNT 53 (Sheffield: Sheffield Academic Press, 1991)

Smith, I., *Heavenly Perspective. A Study of the Apostle Paul's Response to a Jewish Mystical Movement at Colossae*. LNTS 326 (London: T&T Clark, 2006)

Souards, M. L., "Some Neglected Theological Dimensions of Paul's Letter to Philemon," *PRSt* 17 (1990) 209–219

Still, T., "Philemon among the Letters of Paul: Theological and Canonical Considerations," *ResQ* 47 (2005) 133–142

Tolmie, D. F., ed., *Philemon in Perspective. Interpreting a Pauline Letter* (Berlin: DeGruyter, 2010)

Weima, J. A. D., "Onesimus: Still a Runaway Slave," in Still, T. and Myers, J., eds., *Rhetoric, History and Theology. Interpreting the New Testament* (Lanham: Lexington/Fortress, 2022), 201–230

Wengst, K., *Pax Romana and the Peace of Jesus Christ* [trans. J. Bowden] (London: SCM, 1987)

Wink, W., *Naming the Powers* (Philadelphia: Fortress, 1984)

Yamauchi, E., *The Archaeology of the New Testament Cities in Western Asia Minor* (Grand Rapids: Baker, 1980)

Zanker, P., *The Power of Images in the Age of Augustus* (Ann Arbor: University of Michigan Press, 1990)

Subject Index

Scripture Index

Index of Ancient Texts

For EU product safety concerns, contact us at Calle de José Abascal, 56–1°, 28003 Madrid, Spain or eugpsr@cambridge.org.

www.ingramcontent.com/pod-product-compliance
Ingram Content Group UK Ltd.
Pitfield, Milton Keynes, MK11 3LW, UK
UKHW022135120526
471007UK00012B/1059